4-19-99

MALES, FEMALES,
AND BEHAVIOR

MALES, FEMALES, AND BEHAVIOR

Toward Biological Understanding

Edited by
Lee Ellis and Linda Ebertz

Foreword by Milton Diamond

Westport, Connecticut
London

Library of Congress Cataloging-in-Publication Data

Males, females, and behavior : toward biological understanding /
   edited by Lee Ellis and Linda Ebertz ; foreword by Milton Diamond.
      p.   cm.
   This book is part of a culmination of a meeting held in Minot,
N.D., under the auspices of Lee Ellis and Minot State University.
   Includes bibliographical references and indexes.
   ISBN 0–275–95941–4 (alk. paper)
      1. Psychophysiology.   2. Sex differences (Psychology)   3. Sex
differences.   4. Sex differentiation.   I. Ellis, Lee, 1942–   .
II. Ebertz, Linda.
QP360.M335   1998
612.6—dc21   97–32949

British Library Cataloguing in Publication Data is available.

Library of Congress Catalog Card Number: 97–32949
ISBN: 0–275–95941–4

First published in 1998

Praeger Publishers, 88 Post Road West, Westport, CT 06881
An imprint of Greenwood Publishing Group, Inc.

Printed in the United States of America

The paper used in this book complies with the
Permanent Paper Standard issued by the National
Information Standards Organization (Z39.48–1984).

10   9   8   7   6   5   4   3   2   1

Copyright Acknowledgments

The editors and publisher gratefully acknowledge permission for use of the following material:

Figures 1.1, 1.2, 1.3, 1.4, and 1.5. Reprinted from D. E. Comings. *Search for the Tourette Syndrome and Human Behavior Genes*. (1996). Reprinted with permission from Hope Press.

Figure 3.1. Reprinted from *Personality and Individual Differences* 17, by E. M. Miller. Prenatal sex hormone transfer: A reason to study opposite-sex twins, pp. 511–529. Copyright 1994, with kind permission from Elsevier Science Ltd, The Boulevard, Langford Lane, Kidlington OX5 1GB, UK.

Figure 3.2. Reprinted from *Acta Geneticae Medicae et Gemellologiae* 44, by E. M. Miller and N. G. Martin. (1995). Analysis of the effects of hormones on opposite-sex twin attitudes, pp. 41–52. Reprinted with permission.

Figure 4.3. Reprinted from *Acta Physiologica Hungarica* 67, by G. Csaba, Á. Inczefi-Gonda, and O. Dobozy. (1986). Hormonal imprinting by steroids: A single neonatal treatment with diethylstilbestrol or allylestrenol gives rise to a lasting decrease in the number of rat uterine receptors, pp. 207–212. Reprinted with permission.

Figure 4.4. Reprinted from *Acta Physiologica Hungarica* 67, by Á. Inczefi-Gonda, G. Csaba, and O. Dobozy. (1986). Reduced thymic glycocorticoid reception in adult male rats prenatally treated with allylestrenol, pp. 27–29. Reprinted with permission.

Figure 4.11. Reprinted from *Human & Experimental Toxicology* 15, by S. Mirzahosseini, Cs. Karabélyos, O. Dobozy, and G. Csaba. (1996). Changes in sexual behaviour of adult male and female rat neonatally treated with vitamin D_3, pp. 573–576. Reprinted with permission of Macmillan Press Limited and the authors.

Figures 4.12, 4.13, and 4.14. Reprinted from G. Csaba and Cs. Karabélyos, Pubertal benzpyrene exposition decreases durably the sexual activity of the adult male and female rats, *Hormone and Metabolic Research* 27 (1995): 279–282, Georg Thieme Verlag, Stuttgart.

Figure 5.5. Reprinted from *Brain Research Bulletin* 44 (no. 4), by E. M. Hull, J. Du, D. S. Lorrain, and L. Matuszewich. (1997). Testosterone, preoptic dopamine and copulation in male rats, pp. 327–333. Copyright 1997 by Elsevier Science Inc. Reproduced with permission from Elsevier Science Inc.

Figures 5.9 and 5.10. Reprinted from *Journal of Neuroscience* 15, by E. M. Hull, J. Du, D. S. Lorrain, and L. Matuszewich. (1995). Extracellular dopamine in the medial preoptic area: Implications for sexual motivation and hormonal control of copulation, pp. 7465–7471. Reproduced with permission.

Figure 9.1. Reprinted from *Aggressive Behaviour* 13, by S. M. Pellis and V. C. Pellis. Play-fighting differs from serious attack in both target of attack and tactics of fighting in the laboratory rat *Rattus norvegicus*, pp. 227–242. Copyright © 1987, John Wiley & Sons, Inc.

Figure 9.2. Reprinted from *Neuroscience & Biobehavioral Reviews* 21, by S. M. Pellis, E. F. Field, L. K. Smith, and V. C. Pellis. Multiple differences in the play fighting of male and female rats: Implications for the causes and functions of play, pp. 105–120. Copyright 1997, with kind permission from Elsevier Science Ltd, The Boulevard, Langford Lane, Kidlington OX5 1GB, UK.

Figure 9.3. Reprinted from *Journal of Comparative Psychology* 110, by E. F. Field, I. Q. Whishaw, and S. M. Pellis. A kinematic analysis of evasive dodging movements used during food protection in the rat: Evidence for sex differences in movement, pp. 298–306. Copyright © 1996 by the American Psychological Association. Reprinted with permission.

Every reasonable effort has been made to trace the owners of copyright materials in this book, but in some instances this has proven impossible. The editors and publisher will be glad to receive information leading to more complete acknowledgments in subsequent printings of the book and in the meantime extend their apologies for any omissions.

Contents

Illustrations

TABLES

FIGURES

Foreword: Sexual Development—
Nature's Substrate for Nurture's Influence

Milton Diamond

WHY THIS BOOK?

Some might think it presumptuous in today's scientific and political climate to produce a book called *Males, Females, and Behavior: Toward Biological Understanding*. The reasons are apparent enough. Scientifically, there is such a wealth of materials that warrant inclusion—from pregnancy and health considerations to intellectual abilities and sports—that a series of volumes would seem more appropriate and the selection process horrendous. On the other hand, the political climate makes any inclusion in such a publication subject to criticism, justified or not.

The selection process was not so difficult. The choice of material was narrowed by this book being part of the culmination of a meeting held in Minot, North Dakota, under the auspices of Lee Ellis and Minot State University. It was made possible by a generous grant from the Eugene Garfield Foundation. The name of the meeting was the "International Behavioral Development Symposium: Biological Basis of Sexual Orientation and Sex-Typical Behavior." Among its more notable features, the meeting was truly international—contributors attended from Australia to the United Kingdom—and the invitees were of stellar caliber. All had earned their way by publication and reputation. The presentations were first rate, and this volume contains expanded versions of many of them.

Presumption aside, it may be that such a book is not only needed but also potentially required reading for many. Consider this statement from a recent position paper of the American Academy of Pediatrics (1996). "Research on children with ambiguous genitalia has shown that a person's sexual body image is largely a function of socialization, and children whose genetic sexes are not clearly reflected in external genitalia can be raised successfully as members of either sex if the process begins before 2½ years." The assumption this august group seems to make is that the only biology that counts is that of the genitals; other sex differences are a function of socialization. This group is not alone.

The sociologist John Gagnon (1977) has written, "At the present time the belief in powerful [biological] sex drives seems quite implausible. Most psychologists . . . prefer to argue that human beings are active and energetic organisms that are capable of learning how to be sexual in the same ways that they learn everything else. What we need to do is begin to look at how the environment promotes or does not promote various kinds of sexual activity" (p. 11). Many sociologists are more accepting than Gagnon of a biological influence to male and female sex differences and similarities, but it is probably safe to say that by the nature of their profession most attend to those factors of behavior influenced by social conditions (see Sanderson & Ellis, 1992).

There is no argument by those associated with this book that socialization and learning processes are involved in how one behaves sexually. They would, nevertheless, argue that the body and mind individuals bring to the society, culture, and schools are not neutral. From the moment of birth, people typically come to the scene ready to interact with the world as either males or females (Diamond, 1965).

The political climate I referred to is the criticism on the part of feminists, many professionals of the humanities and social sciences, and others suspicious of a biological framework for the understanding of behavior (see, e.g., Ellis, 1996a). These critiques typically question why some studies are included and not others. More often, they argue that claims of sex differences, which seem invariably to come from studying men and women in the context of biology, are either unimportant or neglectful of social factors and are usually used to the detriment of women and other minorities. Certainly it is true that biologically oriented proclamations in science have not always proved kind to these groups.

Those that critique biologically related studies come in all stripes but often divide into two camps in regard to the studies themselves. Meredith Kimball (1995) described these two as the "similarities tradition" and the "differences tradition." Both traditions challenge biological findings with the goal of improving the lot of women and eliminating what they see as their subordination. Those in the similarities school basically ignore erotic and reproductive behaviors and concentrate their attention on behaviors related to intellectual and social competency (see, e.g., Unger, 1989; 1992). Within these areas they believe differences either do not exist or are too small to be meaningful to explain existing gender differences in public and private life. Whether males are better at math than females is a common battleground here (see, e.g., Benbow & Lubinski, 1993; Hyde, Fennema, & Lamon, 1990).

Those in the differences school accept a bimodal skewing of behavioral characteristics among men and women but contend that the positive behaviors or characteristics of women have been undervalued or unappreciated in favor of those more often demonstrated by men. Nancy Chodorow (1978), for instance, uses psychoanalytic reasoning and Freudian theory to make this point; but more often it is argued with references to everyday experiences. For instance, J. C. Tronto (1987; 1993) considers "care-giving" as a behavior with notable sex differences. She argues that little attention is given to women's greater involvement in nurturing and care giving since such behavior is taken for granted and does not garner high status. In any case, professional and lay interest does indeed focus on studies related to sex differences and similarities between males and females in regard to their behaviors.

WHERE DO WE COME FROM?

Traditionally, from Biblical days until relatively modern times, the sexes were thought different and similar in ways to complement God's plan or "nature's way." Serious questioning of these features did not come to the fore until the work of Charles Darwin (1871) who saw sex differences as crucial for his theory of evolution. It was Sigmund Freud, however, who focused his, and the Western world's, attention on sex differences among humans.

Freud proposed a relationship between an individual's genital anatomy and his or her psychosexual development (Freud, 1925; 1953). Terms like the Oedipal and Electra Complex, incest taboo, and penis envy came to represent theoretical frames within which behavioral differences between the sexes could be accounted for. Freud contended that males and females were biologically different but that their intellectual and behavioral development was parallel until awareness of the phallus. The boy becomes aware that the female does not have a penis and worries that his too might be removed (castration anxiety). The female realizes she doesn't have a penis and wishes she did.

Female analysts challenged Freud. For example, Melanie Klein (1975) saw male and female behavioral differences stemming from conflicts between the girl and her mother not the presence or absence of a penis. Karen Horney's (1926) work in particular emphasized attitudinal differences between the sexes. She attributed them to distinct developmental paths for women, which emphasized their feminine traits of cooperation and altruism. As remains true of psychoanalysis today, no experimentation was involved. In-depth case studies were the window to understanding.

While the analysts argued within the purview of medicine, first anthropologists and then sociologists were arguing the role of culture and society in structuring sex differences or similarities. Every new culture found was probed for similarities and differences between the sexes. The cultures were coded for their sex roles; work, marriage, and sexual patterns; and so on. For these early anthropologists, male–female biological differences were accepted as given; and they took as their duty to see how each society accommodated to them (Lee, 1976). It was the accommodations which took center stage.

Behavior patterns of males and females were studied to see how they were adaptive, learned, used, misused, similar or different cross-culturally, and so forth. In her classical study of three societies, for instance, Margaret Mead (1935) emphasized cultural determination of and differences in what she termed sex temperament. Barry, Bacon, and Child (1957), on the other hand, studying achievement and self-reliance, emphasized the similarities among societies. The question quickly developed whether those patterns of behavior seen as cross-culturally nearly universal are genetic (biological) givens or a function of nearly universal cultural practices. When many exceptions to a practice were found, the practices were termed cultural or learned traits; and when few exceptions could be found, they were considered innate and biological.

Much of the work of animal behaviorists in the United States and ethologists in Europe and the United Kingdom was directed to understanding sex differences. With Darwin as a stepping stone, animals were studied, not only to better understand them but also for what they could tell us about humans. The work of ethologists Konrad Lorenz and Niko Tinbergen (see, e.g., Tinbergen, 1951) and animal behaviorists such as Frank Beach, Dan Lehrman, Harry Harlow (see, e.g., Harlow, 1965), and others became known for this work. This area of research, unlike that of the analysts or anthropologists, depended heavily on experimentation along with observation.

The ethologists put their findings of sex differences and similarities in the context of evolutionary adaptation and ecology. Behaviors are seen to evolve just as structures do; those that are advantageous tend to be perpetuated while those that are disadvantageous die off. The animal behaviorists concerned themselves less with the evolutionary nature of the behaviors they studied but directly asked how certain behaviors came about or could be modified. Perhaps most important in the study of sex differences and similarities, both these scientific groups directly studied and experimented with animal reproductive behaviors such as courtship, mating, and parenting. The zoologist Jean Piaget (see, e.g., 1952; 1972) followed in the ethological mode but with an interest in human adaptation. He directly observed developing children in controlled circumstances. He considered the individual's cognitive and intellectual development the key to adaptation. In so doing, he attended primarily to commonalties but also noted sex differences.

The work of psychologists like Louis Terman and Catharine Miles, L. B. Ames and L. Francis, Arnold Gesell, and later Eleanor Maccoby might be said to have ushered in the early psychologist's exploration of human sex differences and similarities. At first a great deal of attention was focused on gender stereotypes and childhood development. For instance, from their research Terman and Miles (1936) constructed so-called male–female scales where male and female were seen as polar opposites; the more male one was, the less female, and vice versa. Later Terman (1946) expanded on this work in a major review entitled: "Psychological Sex Differences." Gesell and colleagues (1940), in their classic work, extrapolated scales of development in which boys and girls were measured in characters ranging from block-building to walking to drawing. Increasingly the focus was on the development of intellectual performance and cognitive skills, personality traits, and attitudes and social behaviors. Psychologists like Lawrence Kohlberg (1966) and C. Gilligan (1982) even probed how the sexes compared in moral development. It was rare that sexual behaviors per se were investigated.[1]

Indeed, the older psychological studies mentioned, as well as most others (see, e.g., Maccoby, 1966; Maccoby & Jacklin, 1974) might better be termed gender rather than sex studies. The questions basically asked: How did boys and men differ or agree with girls and women on various characteristics—in their attitudes, modes of thinking, behaviors, and traits in nonerotic or noncopulation-related matters? Also, more often than not, the psychological research tended to focus on differences more than similarities. Differences were intuitively expected. In reviewing studies of sex and gender, Kay Deaux has written: "The accepted terminology itself suggests a belief in the existence of such differences, and failures to find difference are less often regarded as evidence of sex similarities than as a state of confusion or uncertainty" (1985, p. 54).

Research, particularly over the last two decades, on how biology affects the sexes seemed to multiply and diverge into several directions. Investigations, particularly by those using newly developed sophisticated techniques, have probed deeper into questions of male–female similarities and differences in actions, roles, attitudes, capacities, thinking, and more. Male and female characteristics and behaviors and masculinity and femininity traits are no longer seen as polar opposites but as overlapping and multidimensional (see, e.g., Constantinople, 1973; Bem, 1974; 1995). It is now widely accepted that one can have simultaneously male and female or masculine and feminine features.

WHAT SORTS OF HIGHLIGHTS CAN YOU EXPECT IN THE FOLLOWING PAGES?

David E. Comings has demonstrated that many syndromes that might be considered unrelated to sexual behavior may have genetic links to such behavior. For instance, the neuropsychiatric conditions known as Tourette syndrome and attention deficit hyperactivity disorder are both associated with genetic loading so that sex drive, sexual orientation, exhibitionism, and other behaviors are displayed proportionate to the number of related genes for these conditions seen in probands, relatives, or nonrelated controls. The implications of this are great. Physicians and lay persons alike typically overlook sexual signs of disease progression or remission in syndromes not obviously or intuitively related to sex. A wider view to disease with concern for the erotic is obviously called for.

Robert H. Lustig describes distinct male and female paths of brain cell development dependent upon the hormonal stimulus of androgen or estrogen stimulation; androgens promote axon development while estrogens promote dendritic development. Lustig's work augments research of others like Juraska (1990), who found that the type of environment in which animals spent their early life shaped the length and branching of their cortical nerve cells, and did so differently for males and females. Lustig extrapolates that these differences can affect typical male and female development. It makes me wonder if such factors can account for the behavior of androgenized women with congenital adrenal hyperplasia or men feminized by hypogonadism or DES exposure.

Alan F. Dixson, Gillian R. Brown, and Claire M. Nevison investigate the postnatal surge of testosterone seen in human and nonhuman primates. Their findings that penile growth is promoted by this postnatal androgen is clear. However, contribution of this surge to sex differences in behavior was not seen. The full effect of this surge and its relevance to behavior—to humans in particular—thus remains open. With such a dramatic physiological phenomenon, I suspect this area of research will have more to tell us in the future.

Geoff Sanders and Deborah Wenmoth find a complicated relationship between hormonal effects on verbal and visual tasks measured over the menstrual cycle and linked to hemispheric laterality. They further show that these relationships are not unlike those seen in men if estrogen titers are taken into account.

If you are an environmentalist, you will appreciate the work of György Csaba. His experiments demonstrate that sex behavior can be critically affected by different medicinals and environmental pollutants. While these effects in humans have not yet been demonstrated, their clear-cut effects on animal models is cause for concern. Csaba uses the term "hormonal imprinting" to describe a one-time influence that has continual and long-term consequences. One can compare it to the genetic process known as "genomic or parental imprinting" (see, e.g., Surani, 1991). One is again struck by the crucial influence of early biological events in organizing later behaviors (see, e.g., Diamond, Binstock, & Kohl, 1996).

The area of neurotransmitters and its analogs was reported on by Elaine M. Hull and her colleagues, Catherine A. Wilson and her coworkers, and Ilona Vathy. The Hull group demonstrated the influence of paranatal dopamine agonists or inhibitors, the Wilson group did similarly with serotonin, and Vathy showed the effects of morphine. All these scientists show that these drugs have the capacity to differentially organize the brains of males and females and thereby affect their later sexual behaviors. Of added significance is that nonsexual behaviors (e.g., exploration and agonistic behaviors) were also differentially organized.

Katharine Blick Hoyenga and her colleagues report on their use of drugs that manipulate brain serotonergic activity and look for association between gender, narcissism, and other personality traits and tendencies. In doing so, they also attempt to integrate competing theories of personality and evolution.

Studies of twins seem always to have their own fascination. Edward M. Miller uses twin sets to fathom the transplacental influences of a shared hormonal uterine environment. His analysis indicates that women who shared their mother's womb with a brother have more masculine attitudes, abilities, and behaviors than those who shared the pregnancy with a sister.

Nancy L. Segal uses twins in a quite different way. She analyzes sex differences in the ways brothers and sisters experience grief and confirms suspicions that surviving females have significantly higher levels of grief than males.

Richard Lippa used a new analysis technique he developed to study intellectual giftedness as manifest by National Merit Test scores. His findings indicate that sex nonconformity, rather than conformity, seems associated with academic achievement. This nonconforming seems to be stronger among girls than among boys. Parents might now worry less when seeing their children following a different drummer.

It had been widely held that many sexually dimorphic behaviors are distinct between the sexes, not in kind or motive but in the sense that one sex demonstrates the behavior more often than the other. Some attributed this to differences in threshold for the release of the behavior. In a new approach to this area, Evelyn F. Field and Sergio M. Pellis demonstrate that there is much more to this subject. In analyzing play fight behavior in rats, they find only the gross manifestation of the behavior can be said to be similar between the sexes. They report at least five kinds of sex-specific mechanisms that interact to produce the observed sex differences in play fighting.

RELEVANCE

The studies presented in this book are bound to be relevant to the real world as science continues to probe the complex mysteries of sex differences and similarities in behavior. They are also relevant in ways different from those that would follow from the pronouncement of the American Association of Pediatricians. A case study I coauthored with H. Keith Sigmundson (1997) seems to encapsulate aspects of male and female biology, psychosexuality, the role of the social environment, and human behavior. The case is that of a boy who, following an accident that removed his penis, had his scrotum and testes surgically removed and was then raised as a girl. This management was predicated on the theory that all significant gender features of importance could be imparted by socialization and, in the absence of a penis—with its relevance to social status—make impossible development as a male.

Despite the best of efforts by family and therapists to induce this XY individual to accept life as a girl, the experiment failed. At puberty, the individual reassigned himself to live as a boy. We interpret this as evidence of innate biological forces in sexual identity development sufficient to overcome the extensively imposed environmental influences. The role of the environment, especially of his peers, was significant, however. They provided standards of behavior patterns and other comparisons from which John (pseudonym) could see that he fits in better as a boy than as a girl. I believe everyone evaluates similarities and differences to gauge his or her own place in the sexual and gendered world (Diamond, 1997).

Let us hope that the present volume will add to the ease with which we all come to manifest and understand both our gender and our sexual identities.

NOTE

1. Ounsted and Taylor (1972) offer an update on some human biological differences of interest up to the 1970s; and Lee and Stewart (1976) provide an excellent anthology of writings on the early study of sex differences and similarities from Freud to Maccoby. Lately, many psychologists study evolutionary theory, as had the biologists earlier, in attempts to understand sex differences and similarities (see, e.g., Allgeier & Wiederman, 1994; Buss, 1994).

Preface

It is discouraging to note that as the twentieth century draws to a close, social scientists are still wrangling over the nature–nurture controversy, especially when it comes to gender differences in human behavior. Many social scientists are still going to considerable lengths to deny that biological factors make significant contributions to average differences in the way men and women behave (e.g., Fausto-Sterling, 1985; O'Kelly & Carney, 1986; Eagly, 1987; Eagly & Johnson, 1990; Nielson, 1990; Walton, Fineman, & Walton, 1996).

Consider the views offered by three social scientists who have written textbooks dealing with gender differences in human behavior. All three used a similar two-step process to counter assertions that biological influences are important. First, they exaggerate the view of those of us who believe that biological influences are important by implying that we are complete biological determinists. Second, they argue that environmental determinism is a more reasonable alternative than biological determinism.

The first example appears in a gender-studies text written by Charlotte G. O'Kelly and Larry S. Carney (1986). After providing lengthy criticisms of those who believe that "gender roles and gender stratification are biologically determined" (p. 286), these authors suggest that "only within the limits imposed by the conditions of their time and place" are the causes of human behavior to be found (p. 314). No mention is made of any biological causes.

Another example comes from an introductory anthropology text written by Richley H. Crapo (1990). He contends that "the personalities of men and women are not unambiguous manifestations of inherent characteristics that are fixed by nature." Instead, they are "manifestations of each society's culturally patterned role expectations" (p. 245). Like O'Kelly and Carney, he characterizes the views of those who believe biology is important as meaning that nothing else needs to be considered, a view that no one defends. Of course, he cites no one who takes such an extreme position (because no one does).

A third social science text that dismisses any role for biology is *Sex and Gender and Society*, written by Joyce M. Nielson (1990). She states that "evidence for the notion that much social behavior is determined by hormones is simply nonexistent," and then goes on to present what she considers much more reasonable arguments for strictly social environmental causes of social behavior (p. 164). Nielson also cites no one who asserts that hormones determine social behavior (because no one does).

Again, notice that all three of these cited sources dismiss biological influences by arguing against the view that biological factors are the sole determinant of human behavior. Without giving any recognition to a middle ground—that is, the view that *both* biological and social learning factors are important—they then assert that an exclusive social environmental perspective is more reasonable. The nature of these arguments is detrimental to progress in the study of human behavior, not only because they misrepresent the view of those who believe that biology is important for understanding gender differences in behavior, but because most students who read these textbooks are not in a position to critically assess the erroneous nature of the arguments.

The focus of this book is on how biological factors influence gender differences in behavior. We wish to emphasize that this focus is not in any way to deny the importance of learning and social environmental variables. There is no question that these variables are important. Rather, the objective common to all who have contributed chapters to this book has been to elucidate the complex role played by biological factors, not to the exclusion of social learning, but in interaction with it. Readers will see that many of the issues are as complex as they are fascinating. Most of them will ultimately take many more decades to gradually untangle.

We wish to thank those who served as reviewers of various chapters either included or considered for inclusion in this book. They include Drs. Heino Meyer-Bahlburg, György Csaba, David Holtzen, Katharine Hoyenga, Elaine Hull, Craig Kinsley, Robert Lustig, Sergio Pellis, and Nancy Segal. Our appreciation is also extended to those who participated in the International Behavior Development Symposium upon which this book was based and to David Biglione who carefully assisted in assembling the subject index. Finally, we thank Dr. Eugene Garfield for helping to finance the Symposium.

PART I

GENETIC AND PERINATAL INFLUENCES ON MALE/ FEMALE DIFFERENCES IN BEHAVIOR

Chapter 1

Some Genetic Aspects
of Human Sexual Behavior

David E. Comings

Variations in human sexual behavior are assumed by many people to be a matter of personal choice driven largely by environmental factors. This is especially true of sexual behavior. In addition to the recent study of Hamer and colleagues (Hamer, Hu, Magnuson, Hu, & Pattatucci, 1993), suggesting the presence of an X-linked gene contributing to homosexuality in males, there are a few less publicized reports in the literature suggesting that genetic factors play a significant role in the etiology of variants of human sexual behavior. These include the following: Tsur, Borenstein, and Seidman (1991) reported a concordant pair of monozygotic transsexual male twins and noted the presence of transsexualism in all ethnic groups despite wide cultural diversity. Other identical twins (McKee, Roback, & Hollender, 1976; Hyde & Kenna, 1977) and siblings (Sabalis, Frances, Appenzeller, & Moseley, 1974; Joyce & Ding, 1985) concordant for transsexualism have been reported, consistent with a role of familial–biological factors (Dörner, Poppe, Stahl, Kolzsch, & Uebelhack, 1991; James, Orwin, & Davies, 1972; Rainer, 1971; Wagner, 1974; Spoljar, Eicher, Eiermann, & Cleve, 1981; Engel, Pfafflin, & Wiedeking, 1980). Buhrich (1977) reported a family of transvestitism in a father and son, where the son was unaware of the father's behaviors. It was suggested that constitutional factors played a role in transvestitism. Other familial cases have been reported (Liakos, 1967). Gaffney, Lurie, and Berlin (1984) reported that 18.5 percent of pedophiles have another pedophile in the family, compared to 3 percent of a psychiatric control group. In 1977, Eldridge, Sweet, Lake,

Ziegler, and Shapiro, and in 1980, Nee, Caine, Polinsky, Eldridge, and Ebert, described a high frequency of exhibitionism and other inappropriate sexual activities in selected sets of Tourette Syndrome (TS) patients. In the first report these were present in 48 percent of twenty-one patients, and in the second report they were present in 32 percent of fifty patients. In 1982 we reported a case of TS with severe compulsive exhibitionism that was extinguished following treatment with haloperidol (Comings & Comings, 1982). A nephew had a milder symptom of exhibitionism.

It was my sixteen years of treating over 3,000 TS patients that stimulated an interest in the role of genes in human sexual behaviors. In this chapter I will develop two lines of evidence to support this concept. First, since TS is a genetic disorder, if TS patients show a significant increase in the frequency of a variety of sexual behaviors this would imply that genetic factors were contributing to the associated sexual behaviors. Second, if one or more of the specific genes associated with TS were identified, the same genes might play a role in the associated sexual behaviors.

SEXUAL BEHAVIOR IN TOURETTE SYNDROME

Though diagnosed on the basis of the presence of motor and vocal tics (American Psychiatric Association, 1994), TS patients present with a wide range of comorbid behaviors, including attention deficit hyperactivity, obsessive–compulsive, conduct, oppositional–defiant, anxiety, schizoid, sleep, and sexual disorders, depression, and mania (Comings, 1990; 1995; Comings & Comings, 1987a). While often thought to be due to a single abnormal gene (autosomal dominant), after studying many hundreds of TS families I have become convinced TS is a polygenic disorder; that is, due to the presence of a number of abnormal genes (Comings et al., 1996).

The sexual behavior commonly associated with TS is coprolalia, the involuntary yelling of sexual obscenities. Though often incorrectly assumed to be necessary to make a diagnosis of TS, it is actually present in fewer than 20 percent of cases. The presence of this behavior led to the question of whether other sexual behaviors were also more common in TS. Because there is universal agreement that TS is a genetic disorder, if a variety of variant forms of sexual behavior could be shown to be significantly associated with the presence of TS genes, it would provide strong evidence that these genes were playing a role in those sexual behaviors. To examine this, I used our TS database, which contains the results of an extensive thirty-two-page structured questionnaire based on the Diagnostic Interview Schedule (Robins, Helzer, Croughan, & Ratclif, 1981) and DSM-III-R (American Psychiatric Association, 1987) criteria for many different behavioral disorders. Since 1987 this questionnaire was given to all TS probands (the first member of the family to seek medical help), many of their relatives, and controls. It included eighteen questions about a wide range of sexual behaviors, including hypersexuality, sexual orientation, fetishism, masochism, sadism, pedophilia, and others (Comings, 1994b).

The frequency of these different sexual behaviors was examined in the following five different groups of subjects with progressively less loading for TS genes:

1. *TS probands + Attention Deficit Hyperactivity Disorder (ADHD)*—ADHD is present in 50 to 80 percent of TS probands (Comings & Comings, 1984) and such individuals have the most severe interference with their lives (Comings & Comings, 1984; 1985; 1987b). We have proposed that TS and ADHD are genetically re-lated entities (Comings & Comings, 1984; 1993) and assume that this group has inherited the greatest number of TS genes.

2. *Non-proband TS*—These were relatives of TS probands who also had TS. Since they were not the first to seek medical care we assume they have inherited some-what fewer TS genes than *TS + ADHD* probands.

3. *TS probands – ADHD*—These were TS probands that did not have comorbid ADHD. Since their course is clinically milder than probands who have ADHD, they are assumed to have inherited fewer TS genes that the first two groups.

4. *Non-TS relatives*—These were the relatives of TS probands who did not have TS. Since they did not have TS we assumed they inherited the fewest TS genes of family members.

5. *Controls*—Since these subjects did not have TS and were not related to TS probands, we assume they inherited the fewest number of TS genes (Comings, 1994b).

The working hypothesis was that if a given sexual behavior was strongly influenced by TS genes, there should be a significant increase in the frequency of that behavior across the five groups with progressively greater genetic loading for the TS genes. Since the relationship was assumed to approach a linear increase from controls to TS probands + ADHD, the statistical test was the Cochran–Armitage Exact Trends Test (Cochran, 1954; Armitage, 1955), using the statistical program Statt Xact (Cytel Software Corp., Cambridge, MA). The results are shown in Table 1.1.

All variables except *having been molested* showed a significant association with loading for TS genes. *Having been molested* was *a priori* expected to show the least association, because molestation is something done to the subject by someone else (a relative or an unrelated person) and thus should show a minimal correlation with the genetic makeup of the individual (except when the molestation was done by a first degree relative, who would share half of his or her genes).

The figures present some of these results diagrammatically for *recurrent thoughts about sex* (Figure 1.1), *exhibitionism* (Figure 1.2), and *a preference for the same or both sexes* (Figure 1.3). Though the numbers for *homosexuality, preference for the same sex*, or both, were small, it was approximately four times greater in the TS + ADHD group than in the other groups.

Table 1.1
Results, in Percent, of Sexual Behavior Variables on Subjects with Varying Degrees of Loading for the Tourette Syndrome Gene (n = 891)

		TS Prob +ADHD	Non-Prob TS	TS Prob ADHD	Non-TS Relat.	Cont.	p
N		217	101	141	359	73	
Sex Drive							
Sex Drive: Much greater than average		19.5	10.5	11.0	2.0	0.0	<.00000001
Recurrent thoughts about sex		32.3	27.6	25.6	7.1	7.0	<.00000001
Precocious interest in sex		33.8	27.7	12.7	8.8	11.0	<.00000001
Sex Orientation							
Sex orientation:	Same sex	4.8	1.0	0.8	0.9	1.4	.0029
Sex orientation:	Both sexes	4.8	3.0	2.3	0.3	0.0	.00001
Sex preference:	Same sex or Both sexes	9.6	4.0	3.1	1.1	1.4	.0000016
Exhibitionism							
Exhibitionism:	2-5 times or more	17.3	8.9	7.4	3.1	4.1	<.00000001
Urge to Exhibit:	2-5 times or more	18.8	13.1	8.1	3.9	2.7	<.00000001
Transvestism-Transsexualism							
Dress as the opposite sex		9.2	5.9	5.8	2.5	2.7	.00033
Born to the wrong sex		8.2	3.7	2.9	2.0	3.4	.0032
Sadism-Masochism							
Sadistic		9.1	4.0	4.5	2.0	0.0	.00000014
Masochistic		9.7	6.1	4.5	2.0	0.0	.0000044
Pedophilia							
Sexually aroused by children		7.4	1.0	2.3	0.6	0.0	.0000024
Fetishism							
Sexually aroused by objects		19.1	13.1	10.5	4.5	1.4	<.00000001
Other							
Drew dirty pictures as a child		16.5	4.1	2.9	1.1	0.0	<.00000001
Aversion to Sex							
Aversion to being touched		33.5	21.0	16.3	8.5	9.7	<.00000001
Aversion to sex		27.3	14.1	15.2	8.6	10.0	<.00000001
Having been Molested							
Molested		25.7	29.3	20.2	21.4	18.1	.NS

Note: p values calculated by Cochran–Armitage Exact Trends Test (Cochran, 1954; Armitage, 1955).

Two representative family genograms or pedigrees are presented to illustrate the presence of TS in some members and homosexuality in close relatives. In Figure 1.4 the female proband (arrow) had TS (denoted as a black half). She had a son with drug (D) and alcohol (A) dependence, homosexuality, and AIDS, and her daughter's five-year-old son had chronic motor tics.

Figure 1.1
Excessively Recurrent Thoughts about Sex

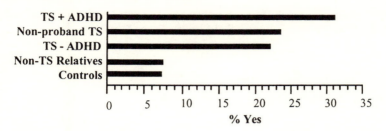

Source: Reprinted from D. E. Comings. *Search for the Tourette Syndrome and Human Behavior Genes*. (1996). Reprinted with permission from Hope Press.

Percentage of subjects responding yes to the question about recurrent thoughts of sex, in five groups of subjects ranging from having many TS genes (TS + ADHD) to few TS genes (controls).

Figure 1.2
Exhibitionism

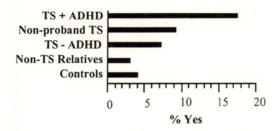

Source: Reprinted from D. E. Comings. *Search for the Tourette Syndrome and Human Behavior Genes*. (1996). Reprinted with permission from Hope Press.

Percentage of subjects responding yes to the question about exhibitionism, in five groups of subjects ranging from having many TS genes (TS + ADHD) to few TS genes (controls).

Figure 1.3
Preference for Same or Both Sexes

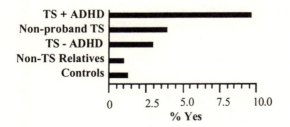

Source: Reprinted from D. E. Comings. *Search for the Tourette Syndrome and Human Behavior Genes*. (1996). Reprinted with permission from Hope Press.

Percentage of subjects responding yes to the question about sexual preference, in five groups of subjects ranging from having many TS genes (TS + ADHD) to few TS genes (controls).

Figure 1.4
Family Pedigree Showing Homosexuality and Tourette Syndrome (Half Solid)
or Chronic Motor Tics (Quarter Solid) in the Same Family

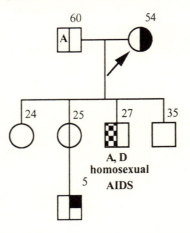

Source: Reprinted from D. E. Comings. *Search for the Tourette Syndrome and Human Behavior Genes*. (1996). Reprinted with permission from Hope Press.

Key: A = alcoholism, D = drug abuse, Numbers = ages.

In Figure 1.5, the proband (arrow) had three brothers with chronic motor tics and one homosexual brother. His wife's sister was a homosexual. One of their children had TS, and the other had chronic motor tics and autism. This pedigree illustrates well the concept of TS as a polygenic spectrum disorder with genes being contributed by both parents.

This concept that homosexuality is polygenic explains one of the presumed paradoxes of the genetic theory of homosexuality. If genes are involved in homosexuality, why do the genes not die out as a result of the much lower fertility rates in homosexuals? If multiple genes are involved and if they are the same genes that play a role in a range of disorders, including impulsive, compulsive, and addictive behaviors, then in some combinations these genes could lead to behaviors (hypersexuality, having children earlier, having more children) that would produce selection for the genes. The resulting selection for some of these genes could balance the loss of similar genes occurring when other combinations of the genes produced homosexuality.

SOME OF THE GENES CONTRIBUTING
TO TS HAVE BEEN IDENTIFIED

One of the major theories concerning the cause of TS is that of a genetic defect in the dopaminergic neurons (Comings, 1987; 1990; Chase, Geoffrey, Gillespie, & Burrows, 1986; Devinsky, 1983). This is because dopaminergic

Figure 1.5
Family Pedigree Showing Homosexuality and Tourette Syndrome (Half Solid),
Chronic Motor Tics (Quarter Solid), ADHD, and Other Disorders, Behaviors,
and Occupations in the Same Family

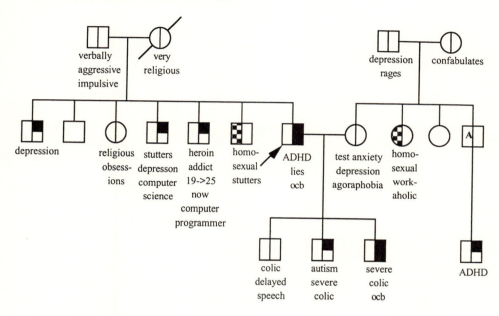

Source: Reprinted from D. E. Comings. *Search for the Tourette Syndrome and Human Behavior Genes*. (1996). Reprinted with permission from Hope Press.

Key: OCB = obsessive–compulsive behaviors.

agonists such as methylphenidate or dexedrine often make the tics worse, and dopamine D_2 receptor antagonists, such as haloperidol and pimozide, are among the drugs of choice for the treatment of the tics. My colleagues and I were thus quite intrigued when Blum et al. (1990) reported a significant increase in frequency of the A1 gene marker of the dopamine D_2 receptor *(DRD2)* gene in subjects with severe alcoholism. We noticed a significant increase in the frequency of alcoholism in TS probands and non-proband TS relatives and other relatives in TS families (Comings, 1989; 1990; 1994a). Because these family studies suggested a commonality between the genes for alcoholism and for TS, we wondered if there might also be an association between the D_2A1 allele and TS. This proved to be the case. In our initial study (Comings et al., 1991), the D_2A1 allele was present in 44.9 percent of 147 TS probands versus 24.5 percent of 314 controls ($p < 0.0001$). The D_2A1 allele was also significantly increased in subjects with ADHD, autism, and polysubstance abuse. In a subsequent study (Comings, 1992) we found a progressive increase in the prevalence of the D_2A1 allele passing from mild (35.0%, n =

20), to moderate (40.4%, n = 146), to severe (55.5%, n = 54) TS (p < 0.0001). Others have also examined TS subjects; 432 non-Hispanic white TS probands have been examined by additional different groups (Devor, 1992; Gelernter, Pauls, Leckman, & Kurlan, 1992; Gelernter, Pauls, Leckman, Kidd, & Kurtan, 1994; Nöthen et al., 1994). Of these, 40.7 percent carried the D_2A1 allele versus a prevalence of 25.9 percent in 714 non-Hispanic whites (p = 0.00000016). We also examined the prevalence of the D_2A1 allele for various behaviors across three groups: controls without the behavior, TS probands and relatives without the behavior, and TS probands and relatives with the behavior. There was a significant (p < 0.005) increase in prevalence of the D_2A1 allele across these three groups for the following behaviors: sexual, stuttering, obsessive–compulsive, schizoid, manic, ADHD, tics, conduct disorder, oppositional defiant disorder, alcohol abuse, learning problems, and sleep disorders. The most significant association (p = 0.0007) was with sexual behaviors. The sexual behavior score consisted of a summation in each individual of a response of 0 (absent) or 1 (present) for each of eighteen sexual-behavior variables (Comings et al., 1996). These results were consistent with the dopamine D_2 receptor gene being one of a polygenic set of genes involved in a range of impulsive, compulsive, and addictive behaviors.

We then examined a second dopamine gene, dopamine β-hydroxylase (DβH) (Comings et al., 1996). The DβH enzyme converts dopamine to norepinephrine. As such, it plays a major role in the regulation of dopamine levels. Studies of serum levels have implicated a role of low DβH levels in conduct disorder and ADHD. Using the same technique, we observed a significant progressive increase in the prevalence of the *Taq* I B1/B1 genetic marker (d'Amato et al., 1989) of DßH across the same three groups of subjects for the following behaviors: ADHD, learning problems, academic problems in grade school, oppositional defiant disorder, tics, mania, alcohol abuse, reading problems, drug abuse, sleep disorders, stuttering, and obsessive–compulsive behaviors. Here the most significant results were for ADHD (p = 0.0001), learning problems, and oppositional–defiant disorder. These results were consistent with the DßH gene also being one of a polygenic set of dopaminerigic genes involved in these behaviors.

A third locus we examined was the dopamine transporter *(DAT1)* gene (Comings et al., 1996). The dopamine transporter protein directs the reuptake of dopamine from the synapse back into the cytoplasm from which it was released. Cocaine and methylphenidate produce part of their effect on dopaminergic neurons by inhibiting the function of the dopamine transporter. We examined the 40 base pair repeat in the *DAT1* gene (Vandenbergh, Persico, & Uhl, 1992). Again, using the same technique, we found a significant increase in the prevalence of the 10/10 genotype (containing 10, 40 base pair repeats on both chromosomes) for the following behaviors: somatization, alcohol abuse, ADHD, major depression, panic attacks, obsessive–compulsive behaviors, general anxiety, mania, oppositional–defiant disorder, sexual behaviors, and reading problems. Somatization disorder was most significant at p = 0.0009. Sexual behaviors were significant at p = 0.013. Cook et al. (1995) also reported an association between genetic variants at the *DAT1* locus and ADHD.

These studies provided us with evidence that three of the major dopaminergic genes played a role in a spectrum of interrelated behaviors (Comings et al., 1996). Our next question was whether the effect of these genes was additive, as expected in polygenic inheritance. This was examined by performing the genetic tests for all three genes on the same subjects. We then examined the means for a number of continuous behavioral variables across four groups, those positive for 3 of 3, 2 or 3, 1 of 3, and 0 of 3 of the gene markers. If the alleles were additive, the means of one or more scores should show a progressive decrease across these four groups. This progression was significant for the following behaviors: ADHD, stuttering, oppositional–defiant disorder, tics, conduct disorder, obsessive–compulsive behaviors, mania, alcohol abuse, and general anxiety (Comings et al., 1996). The sexual behavior score also showed a progressive decrease across these four groups (1.12, 0.62, 0.58, and 0.53, respectively), but the ANOVA F-ratio was not significant. Other genes that have shown a correlation with various behaviors in TS patients are the tryptophan 2,3-dioxygenase and dopamine D1 receptor gene (Comings, 1996). These studies were consistent with the hypothesis that a number of behavioral disorders are inherited in a polygenic fashion, a number of dopamine genes are involved, and the effect of the genes transcend several different behavioral disorders.

Some of our ongoing, still to be published research has shown a significant correlation between markers of dopamine receptor genes *(DRD1, DRD2, DRD4)* and the age of initiation of sexual intercourse (Miller et al., 1996), and between dopamine receptor gene *(DRD4)* and *GABA* receptor gene *(GABA$_A$ B3)* and the number of children (MacMurray et al., 1996). We anticipate that these and similar studies with additional genes will continue to provide evidence at a molecular level of the role of genes in many aspects of human sexual behavior.

SUMMARY

This chapter suggests that first, some aspects of human sexual behavior are genetically influenced, and second, some of the individual genes involved have been identified. Studies of a hereditary neuropsychiatric disorder, Tourette syndrome, provide evidence for the first. Here, 891 subjects consisting of TS probands, their relatives, and controls were given a structured questionnaire based on the NIMH Diagnostic Interview Schedule. The responses to the eighteen questions relating to a range of sexual behaviors were examined to determine if the number of positive responses was significantly greater in groups of individuals assumed to have the greatest number of TS genes, compared to groups of individuals assumed to have few TS genes (genetic loading). This was true

Sex Hormonal Modulation of Neural Development *in Vitro*: Implications for Brain Sex Differentiation

Robert H. Lustig

Most animal species which undergo sexual reproduction, whether invertebrate or vertebrate, have evolved such that the two sexes of the species are easily discernable. This is true for general appearance, external and internal sexual organs, and how the two sexes behave, both in general (cognitive behavior), and toward each other (reproductive behavior). Much study on sex differences in behavior has taken place over the past century, in particular in the past twenty-five years. Recently, specific sex differences in brain structure have been elucidated. However, the biologic causes of these sex differences remain elusive. It appears that factors such as genes, hormones, and environmental cues all play roles in brain sex dimorphisms. This chapter will focus on the role of sex hormones in brain development, and their implications for brain sex differentiation.

Studies on neuroanatomic sex differentiation thus far have been descriptive and inferring causation based on *in vivo* sex differences. Our lab has instead attempted to define specific cellular effects of sex hormones on neurons to directly examine causation. Though the details of this chapter focus on *in vitro* models of sex hormones on neurons rather than whole animal phenomena, and though these models come from rodent cells, it is this author's belief that these phenomena are likely transferable to other species, including humans. In this chapter, a molecular/cellular hypothesis of neuroanatomic brain sex differentiation is offered, and the reader is invited to compare these principles to their own models or paradigms to determine the universality of this hypothesis.

FUNCTIONAL SEX DIFFERENCES IN HUMAN
PERCEPTION, COGNITION, AND BEHAVIOR

In the human, various parameters of cognition, perception, and behavior diverge between the two sexes (Money & Ehrhardt, 1972; Wittig & Petersen, 1979; Halpern, 1992), suggesting that brain organization is sex-dependent. Many studies have suggested sex differences in various cognitive parameters, including mathematical (Benbow & Stanley, 1983) and spatial abilities (Gaulin & FitzGerald, 1986), and handedness (Oldfield, 1971). In addition, several developmental disorders demonstrate a sex difference, such as dyslexia (Galaburda, 1992), attention deficit disorder (Whalen & Henker, 1984), and autism (Taylor, 1974). Other chapters in this volume summarize many of the advances that have been made in the scientific study of sex differences. It is now thought that sex hormonal influences during central nervous system development *in utero* may account for some of these sex-specific cognitive differences, though the mechanisms remain unclear.

In the human, it is difficult to evaluate the effects of antenatal estrogen exposure on CNS organization or function, since all fetuses are exposed to high levels of placental estrogen throughout gestation. Meyer-Bahlburg (1997) addresses the possible prenatal effects of estrogen on brain function. The effects of antenatal androgen exposure in the human brain *in utero* are much better studied, especially in girls with virilizing congenital adrenal hyperplasia (CAH) (Nass & Baker, 1991), who have a higher incidence of left-handedness (Nass et al., 1987), and higher scores on spatial tasks (Resnick, Gottesman, Berenbaum, & Bouchard, 1986) than do females generally.

NEUROANATOMIC SEX DIFFERENCES
IN THE HUMAN BRAIN

Neuroanatomic studies of the human brain have suggested that sex dimorphisms may exist in specific brain areas, which could underlie some of these sex-dependent cognitive and behavioral differences. For instance, the suprachiasmatic nucleus (Swaab & Hofman, 1990), interstitial nucleus of anterior hypothalamus-3 (Allen, Hines, Shryne, & Gorski, 1989; LeVay, 1991), bed nucleus of the stria terminalis (Zhou, Hofman, Gooren, & Swaab, 1995), anterior commissure (Allen & Gorski, 1992), and corpus callosum (Witelson, 1989) have all been shown to exhibit various sex differences, and suggest that factors early in development (possibly sex hormones) may influence the differentiation and development of these structures.

FUNCTIONAL AND NEUROANATOMIC
SEX DIMORPHISMS IN THE RAT BRAIN

Adult male and female rat brains also differ in several cognitive, behavioral, and biochemical parameters (McEwen, Lieberburg, Chaptal, & Krey,

1977; Gorski, Harlan, Jacobson, Shryne, & Southam, 1980; Williams, Barnett, & Meck, 1990). This is best illustrated by the sex difference in response to estrogen administration (McEwen, 1983). Behaviorally, females respond to estrogen with a response known as lordosis, while males respond to a much diminished extent (Sodersten & Larsson, 1974; Larsson, Sodersten, Beyer, Morali, & Perez-Palacios, 1976). Similarly, females respond to estrogen by hypersecretion of gonadotropin-releasing hormone leading to a luteinizing hormone (LH) surge and ovulation, while males do not (McEwen et al., 1984). Biochemically, females respond to estradiol by induction of progestin receptors, upregulation of muscarinic and serotonergic receptors, cholinergic enzymes, and endogenous opioid peptides in various areas of the hypothalamus (Rainbow, Parsons, & McEwen, 1982; Fischette, Bigeon, & McEwen, 1983; Luine & McEwen, 1983; Romano, Mobbs, Lauber, Howells, & Pfaff, 1990), while males demonstrate little effect of estrogen on these parameters.

These functional dimorphisms also may have neuroanatomic correlates. In the male rat, the gray matter of the left hemisphere is grossly thinner than on the right and than that noted in the female (Diamond, Dowling, & Johnson, 1981); this is possibly related to a hormonal inhibition of neuronal migration within the cortices during development. There is a sex dimorphism in the extent of axonal growth in the rat hippocampus (Loy & Milner, 1980). On a synaptic level, sex differences have been noted in the pattern of neuronal connectivity in various parts of the limbic system, such as the preoptic area (Raisman & Field, 1973), arcuate nucleus (Matsumoto & Arai, 1980), and amygdala (Nishizuka & Arai, 1981a). Most notable is the sex difference in the "sexually dimorphic nucleus" (SDN), a region of the preoptic area which is several times larger in males due to increased neuron number (Arnold & Gorski, 1984) and also exhibits greater neuritic growth and extent (Hammer & Jacobson, 1984; Kolb & Stewart, 1991). These sex-dependent alterations in neural migration, outgrowth, and synaptogenesis are thought to be secondary to effects of antenatal or perinatal androgen and estrogen in neurons possessing estrogen receptors (ER) and androgen receptors (AR).

ROLE OF NEONATAL SEX STEROIDS IN ONTOGENIC SEX DIMORPHISMS IN THE RAT BRAIN

Interneuronal connections occur via specialized contacts between their neuritic processes, and consist primarily of synapses and gap junctions. Synapses occur between axons and dendrites, and gap junctions occur between dendrites. Therefore any process which can alter either dendrite or axon development, morphology, or outgrowth is likely to alter the pattern of interneuronal connectivity. Sex hormones are potent influences on these processes.

The rat brain undergoes sex-specific neural organization in two hormonally dependent patterns: androgen-induced "masculinization," and estrogen-induced "defeminization" (formed *in situ* by aromatization of testicularly derived androgens) (McEwen et al., 1977; McEwen et al., 1984; Vreeburg, Van Der Vaart,

& Van Der Schoot, 1977; Luttge & Whalen, 1970; MacLusky, Clark, Naftolin, & Goldman-Rakic, 1987). These phenomena are presumed to account for the sex differences in the activation of biochemical and behavioral responses in the adult; males undergo both processes in the perinatal period, while females undergo neither process (though the neonatal ovary produces estrogen, the presence of plasma α-fetoprotein, which binds estrogens avidly in the perinatal period, prevents its crossing the blood–brain barrier, thus preventing defeminization) (Toran-Allerand, 1984; Adkins-Regan, 1981).

Many of these brain sex dimorphisms are responsive to neonatal hormonal manipulation. Neonatal castration of male rat pups results in a symmetrical cortical mantle (Diamond, 1984). Similarly, either castration or administration of an aromatase inhibitor (to block estrogen synthesis) to neonatal male rats results in a decrease in the size of the adult SDN (both neuron number and synaptic density) (Gorski, 1984), while perinatal androgen or estrogen exposure to neonatal females will increase adult SDN size (Jacobson, Csernus, Shryne, & Gorski, 1981). Also, neonatal male castration or aromatase inhibition facilitates adult lordotic behavior and the genesis of estradiol-induced LH surges in adulthood (Luttge & Whalen, 1970; Corbier, 1985). Conversely, administration of testosterone to neonatal female rat pups alters brain sex differentiation leading to the obviation of the adult lordosis reflex (Whalen & Rezek, 1974), and the facilitation of mounting behavior in the adult (Luttge & Whalen, 1970; Sodersten & Hansen, 1978). Similarly, testosterone administration to neonatal females results in an increase in the size and density of the adult SDN similar to that seen in males (Jacobson et al., 1981). In the spinal cord, neurons in the spinal nucleus of the bulbocavernosus (which innervate muscles involved in sexual function) normally exhibit cell death in neonatal females, but testosterone or dihydrotestosterone (DHT) administration to neonatal females leads to preservation and growth of these neurons and development of dendritic architecture (some of this androgenic effect may actually be on the effector muscles with indirect anterograde sparing of the neurons) (Goldstein, Kurz, & Sengelaub, 1990; Breedlove, Jacobson, Gorski, & Arnold, 1982; Sasaki & Arnold, 1991; Matsumoto, Micevych, & Arnold, 1988).

Estrogen Effects on Neurite Outgrowth, Spines, and Synaptogenesis *in Vivo*

Sex differences in brain structure are a consequence of developmental changes in neuritic outgrowth and synaptogenesis. The axon grows using an organelle called a growth cone; these are varicosities at the tips of axons. The growth cone is able to forge a path to an appropriate target area and recognize target dendrites for synapse formation. Thus, the growth cone plays a primary role in synapse formation (Landis, 1983). In addition, dendritic spines also play a role in synaptogenesis. Spines are ports for synaptogenesis on dendrites (Steward, 1983; Steward & Reeves, 1988; Rao & Steward, 1991;

Kleiman, Banker, & Steward, 1990). An axonal growth cone makes contact with a dendritic spine, and this complex forms into a synapse (Steward et al., 1988). Sex hormones affect both of these organelles directly.

Estrogen increases neuritic outgrowth in the developing rat brain. Toran-Allerand originally showed that the addition of estradiol to the medium of fetal male or female mouse hypothalamic explants (tissue removed and placed in culture) increased neurite outgrowth (Toran-Allerand, Gerlach, & McEwen, 1980; Toran-Allerand, Hashimoto, Greenough, & Saltarelli, 1983), while addition of antiestrogen antibodies negated this effect (Toran-Allerand, 1980). These data suggest that estrogen promotes neuritic outgrowth in various estrogen-sensitive brain areas of the neonate (Gorski, 1985; Toran-Allerand, 1984). Caceres, using dissociated fetal hypothalamic cultures, demonstrated the estrogenic induction axon-specific proteins, along with stabilization of microtubules, leading to axonal elongation (Ferreira & Caceres, 1991; Diaz, Lorenzo, Carrer, & Caceres, 1992). Conversely, in fetal amygdala, he found an estrogenic augmentation of dendritic outgrowth and arborization (Lorenzo, Diaz, Carrer, & Caceres, 1992). Thus, estrogen may affect axons and dendrites of neurons in different brain areas and in different ways.

Estrogen also leads to increased synapse formation in the developing rat brain. Matsumoto (1991) noted that the number of synapses in the hypothalamus were similar at birth between the sexes, but by adulthood there was a clear increase in synaptic number in males. Castration of neonatal males reduced the number of adult synapses to the female level, while testosterone treatment of neonatal females increased the adult synaptic number to that of males.

Last, estrogen also alters neuronal organization in ER-positive areas of the adult rat brain. Several reports have documented increased numbers of synaptic terminals and dendritic spines in the hypothalamus (Gorski, 1985; Carrer & Aoki, 1982; Clough & Rodriguez-Sierra, 1983; Matsumoto & Arai, 1979; Pozzo Miller & Aoki, 1991; Frankfurt, Gould, Woolley, & McEwen, 1990; Segarra & McEwen, 1991), brainstem (Chung, Pfaff, & Cohen, 1988), and hippocampus (Gould, Woolley, Frankfurt, & McEwen, 1990) in adult ovariectomized rats after estrogen administration. In addition, the number of dendritic spines in the hypothalamus (Frankfurt, Gould, Woolley, & McEwen, 1990) and hippocampus vary with the estrous cycle (Woolley & McEwen, 1992), suggesting that the neural circuitry in these areas are inherently plastic and constantly remodeled by the cyclic fluctuations of peripheral plasma estradiol.

Androgen Effects on Neurite Outgrowth and Branching *in Vivo*

The role of testosterone on neural morphology and axonal regeneration has been investigated in the adult rodent nervous system. In the adult ferret SDN, testosterone administration to castrated males increased soma size and promoted dendritic branching and arborizaton (Cherry, Tobet, DeVoogd, & Baum, 1992). In the adult rat spinal cord, castration decreased the number of synaptic contacts on proximal dendrites, while testosterone replacement prevented this decrease (Matsumoto, 1992). Testosterone has been shown to regulate both the somatic and dendritic size of motoneurons (Matsumoto, Micevych, & Arnold, 1988) and the appearance of gap junctions between neurons in the spinal cord (Matsumoto, Arnold, Zampighi, & Micevych, 1988). In the axotomized hamster facial nerve (Kujawa & Jones, 1990) and rat hypoglossal nerve (Yu & Yu, 1983), testosterone accelerated axon regeneration rates. However, since testosterone can be aromatized to estradiol within certain neurons, it is often difficult to sort out which effects of testosterone are androgenic and which are estrogenic.

SEX HORMONE EFFECTS ON NEURONS *IN VITRO*

Unfortunately, the cellular and molecular mechanisms of sex hormone-induced neuromorphologic alterations and their relation to synaptogenesis cannot easily be determined *in vivo*. The reasons are legion, including (1) the heterogeneity of brain areas, especially in the limbic system; (2) the technical difficulties of working with fetal tissue; (3) the difficulties of examining the same neuron at two points in time; (4) the complex interconnectivity of the brain; (5) the inability of investogators to completely control the local hormonal environment; (6) the inability to control for the vast number of local growth factors; (7) the ability of certain neurons to convert testosterone to estradiol through aromatization; (8) the ability of other neurons to reduce testosterone to dihydrotestosterone (DHT), a pure androgen; (9) the inability to make neuromorphometric measurements with ease; and (10) the inability to count new synapse or gap junction formation. To do away with some of these obstacles, we can directly study sex hormone effects on single mammalian neurons *in vitro*. Unfortunately, studies examining hormonal effects on neurons *in vitro* also suffer from some disadvantages, such as (1) dissociating neurons from their neighbors, which normally supply electrical signaling and/ or growth factors; (2) the artificial media in which neurons are grown, which may suppress some growth characteristics; (3) the inability to passage (resume growth once removed from a culture surface) primary neurons in culture; (4) the heterogeneity of primary neurons in culture; and (5) the hormone nonresponsiveness of the various self-propagating neural tumor lines thus far characterized. Clearly, what is needed is a consistent and homogeneous cell system in which to study these effects. The following sections describe two *in vitro* systems which appear to recapitulate sex hormonal effects *in vivo* and the implications of such results on the study of brain sex differentiation.

SEX HORMONE RECEPTOR-TRANSFECTED PC12 CELLS

Over the past decade, several neural cell lines have been isolated, immortalized, or constructed in attempts to study the responses of neurons during the growth and maturation of the nervous system. Of these, the PC12 rat pheochromocytoma (adrenal tumor) cell line (Greene, Aletta, Rukenstein, & Green, 1987) has several inherent advantages, including (1) ease of growth and maintenance, (2) ability to extend neurites in response to low doses of Nerve Growth Factor (NGF), (3) no appreciable morphologic or biochemical response to either androgen or estrogen, and (4) easy and persistent transfectability with various eukaryotic DNA expression vectors (a method for inserting new genes into cells to code for new proteins) (Donis, Ventosa-Michelman, & Neve, 1993). However, this cell line also has the inherent disadvantages of expressing neurites that are axonal (not dendritic) in nature (Jacobs & Stevens, 1986) and lacking homologous synaptogenesis in culture. Thus, these cells have limited usefulness in studying the entire neuronal repetoire. Nonetheless, they serve as a useful parent cell line for studying some morphologic aspects of hormone–neuron interaction (Lustig, Hua, Yu, Ahmad, & Baas, 1994; Lustig, Hua, Smith, Wang, & Chang, 1994).

Wild-type PC12 cells contain little AR or ER, and are thus not hormone-responsive. We stably transfected (permanently inserted a gene into) these cells with one of two expression vectors: pCMV-ERα-neo, a vector which codes for the full-length human ER complementary DNA (hER cDNA) (Jiang & Jordan, 1992); or pCMV-AR-neo, which codes for the human AR complementary DNA (hAR cDNA) (Mowszowicz et al., 1993). These vectors consist of a constitutive (always turned on) promoter, spliced to a piece of DNA coding for either the hER or hAR, then spliced to the cDNA for neomycin phosphoribosyl transferase *(neo)*, an enzyme which inactivates neomycin, which is toxic to eukaryotic cells. Thus, cells not expressing a vector will die in the presence of neomycin, while cells expressing a vector will grow in its presence. Wild-type PC12 cells were also transfected with the control vector pCMV-neo, without any hormone receptor-coding region. Clones of transfected cells containing hER, hAR, and the control vector were selected by chronic neomycin exposure, and expanded. The hER-transfected cells are known as SER8, the hAR-transfected cells are called AR8, and the control vector-transfected cells are NEO9. Preliminary studies using Northern blotting (for messenger RNA expression) and Scatchard analysis (for steroid binding) demonstrated an ER mRNA species and specific estrogen protein binding in SER8 cells only, an AR mRNA species and specific androgen protein binding in AR8 cells only, and no sex hormone receptor mRNA species or hormone binding in wild-type PC12 or NEO9 cells.

Estrogen Effects

Morphometric analyses were performed on each of these cell lines in response to increasing concentrations of estradiol (Lustig, Hua, Yu et al., 1994). In SER8 cells (ER-positive), estradiol was able to induce short neurite outgrowth in the absence of NGF exposure and augment NGF-induced long neurite outgrowth. However, the number of neurites produced by each cell did not change. These results suggest that estradiol is able to act as an adjunct to increase NGF effectiveness in this line only. Furthermore, estradiol was able to augment the otherwise infrequent production of neuritic spines and gap junctions. Both of these membrane specializations are involved in interneuritic structural contact, and their induction suggests that one of estrogen's chief roles is the promotion of interneuronal communication. Thus, PC12 cells respond to estrogen by stereotypic morphologic changes which promote interneuronal communication.

Androgen Effects

Effects of the nonaromatizeable androgen DHT on AR8 cells were quite different (Lustig, Hua, Smith et al., 1994). In the absence of NGF, DHT had no effect on morphology in any of the transfected PC12 cell lines. However, in conjunction with NGF, DHT administration led to a dose-dependent increase in total neurite length in AR8 cells only. Statistically, increases in neurite length can be achieved either by increasing the number of neurites (i.e., those emanating from the cell body), increasing the length of these neurites, or increasing the amount of neuritic branching or arborization. In a computerized evaluation of DHT-treated AR8 cells, both the number and length of neurites were unaffected, but the branch order (a measure of neuritic arborization) increased with DHT dose. DHT treatment increased the frequency of secondary, tertiary, and further neurite formation. A correlate of such an increase in branch order is a concomitant increase in the neuritic field area (defined as the polygon obtained when the outermost tips of the branches of one primary neurite are connected) of the cell. Thus, though DHT treatment did not increase direct communication between AR8 cells, it did increase the receptive field for each AR8 cell, and thus the chance that any two nearby AR8 cells would contact each other.

Interpretation

We hypothesize that androgen and estrogen exert different yet complementary effects on AR- and ER-transfected PC12 cells *in vitro*. By increasing the number and arborization of neurites, androgen acts to increase the target area of individual neurons, thereby increasing the chances of interneural communication. Conversely, by increasing the formation of spines and gap junctions, estrogen acts to increase the contact potential of nearby cells, thus actually altering interneural communication. It would appear that the ultimate goal of both sex hormones is the alteration of neural organization in such a way as to promote interneural communication.

Interestingly, within verebrate neurons both spines and gap junctions tend to be dendritic (rather than axonal) in location. PC12 cells do not normally make structural dendrites (Jacobs & Stevens, 1986), yet SER8 cells made spines and gap junctions. Though no objective criteria consistent with dendritogenesis has been noted in SER8 cells (e.g., development of synapto-genesis, expression of the adult form of the dendritic protein microtubule-associated protein 2 (MAP2), or bipolarity of neuritic microtubules), the estrogenic regulation of dendritic specializations in an otherwise axonal environment has enormous potential implication for the role of estrogen in neural development *in vivo*. Second, while branching and arborization occurs in dendrites to a minor extent, it is predominantly an axonal phenomenon. Thus, the effects of DHT on the neuritic arborization in AR8 cells suggest an androgenic regulation of axonal development and growth. The possibility that the effects of androgen and estrogen on neurons might be morphologically compartmentalized into effects on axons and dendrites, respectively, is an intriguing one, and will be explored in the next cellular model.

DISSOCIATED PRIMARY RAT HIPPOCAMPAL NEURONS IN CULTURE

The advent of primary (direct, nonrenewable) rat hippocampal neuronal culture has provided the cell biologist with a tool for the morphologic characterization of process outgrowth and synaptogenesis in developing neurons (Bartlett & Banker, 1984a; 1984b; Baas, Dietch, Black, & Banker, 1988). The rat hippocampus appears to be a primary target for sex hormone action. This area is sexually dimorphic with respect to axonal growth (Loy & Milner, 1980), suggesting that sex hormones in the prenatal period may play a role in hippocampal function. A relative abundance of AR mRNA and protein is noted in the CA1 region (a region of the hippocampus) in the adult (Simerly, Chang, Muramatsu, & Swanson, 1990; Kerr, Allore, Beck, & Handa, 1995). Conversely, the ontogeny of ER within the hippocampus demonstrates a peak in ER concentration during the perinatal and postnatal period (Shughrue, Stumpf, MacLusky, Zielinski, & Hochberg, 1990; Toran-Allerand, Miranda, Hochberg, & MacLusky, 1992; O'Keefe & Handa, 1990), with a falloff to low levels by adulthood (Bettini, Pollio, Santagati, & Maggi, 1992; Maggi, Susanna, Bettini, Mantero, & Zucchi, 1989). Thus, fetal hippocampal cells seemed to be a suitable primary culture system for examining sex hormone action on neurons because of (1) their ease of culture; (2) a large literature on their properties; (3) their abilty to grow in hormonally defined media; (4) the expression of ER and AR during development suggests that they are hormone-responsive; (5) their ability to form spines, synapses, and possibly gap junctions *in vitro* (Kosaka & Hama, 1985; Andrew, Taylor, Snow, & Dudek, 1982; Bartlett & Banker, 1984b); and (6) the ease of differentiating dendrites from axons both by light microscopic morphology and by protein immunofluorescence (IF). However, this culture system also suffers from some disadvantages: its regional and cellular heterogeneity (i.e., different areas and cell types may expressing different hormone receptors and at different times), and the effects of estrogen or androgen on hippocampal neurons in culture were previously unknown. Nonetheless, we have now validated the use of this system for the effects of sex hormones on neurons (Lustig, Sharp, & Baas, 1995).

AR and ER Expression

To examine AR and ER positivity in fetal hippocampal neurons, rat fetuses were sacrificed at Day E18 (three days before birth), their hippocampi dissected out and macerated, and neurons were trypsinized and plated on polylysine-coated glass coverslips suspended above an already growing rat glial feeder monolayer (Baas et al., 1988; Yu & Baas, 1994). Cells were treated briefly with DHT or estradiol to localize receptors within the cell nucleus, and then fixed and incubated with primary antibodies against the AR or ER and stained with secondary antibodies coupled to fluorescein or rhodamine for IF. These studies documented that approximately 95 percent of the neurons visualized were stained for both AR and ER, suggesting that these neurons contained both receptors, and would likely respond to both hormones.

Sex Hormone Effects on Neurite Morphometry and Morphology

To assess the effects of sex hormones on neuronal development, hippocampal neurons were plated on Day 0 in media containing DHT or estradiol, and examined serially for neurite elongation and arborization by light microscopy on Days 1, 3, and 5. Videoprints of each cell were traced into a computer digitizing system. Quantitation of the outgrowth of neuritic processes demonstrated that neither DHT nor estradiol exerted significant effects on total cell neurite length at each time point. However, the frequency of primary neurites per cell decreased significantly with DHT, even on Day 1, when neurons were just beginning to extend processes. Standardization of the total cell neurite length relative to the number of primary neurites revealed a marked induction by DHT. Thus, androgen induced these cells to produce fewer and longer neurites. Last, branch order level was increased by DHT. Estradiol had no effect on any of these quantitative parameters.

Morphometry of these neurons also documented effects of androgen. Hippocampal neurons normally grow in a stereotyped pattern: (1) The cell initially grows by extending 5 or 6 minor processes from its perikaryon; (2) one of the minor processes become the axon, which maintains its thin and cylindrical shape and extends rapidly and branches frequently; and finally (3) the remaining minor processes mature into long, tapering dendrites with frequent interdendritic connections. DHT exposure disrupted the normal morphogenetic pattern of these neurons. Even by Day 1, DHT-stimulated cells had fewer and longer primary neurites than those cells treated with vehicle or estradiol. Many DHT-treated neurons produced multiple long neurites, which remained thin and cylindrical during extension and were more likely to branch.

These neurites were most consistent with axons. Conversely, DHT-treated dendrites were less frequent, shorter, and more rudimentary than in cells treated with vehicle or estradiol.

MAP2 (Dendrite) versus Tau (Axon) Expression

To examine the identity of these neurites, neurons were fixed and simultaneously coincubated with mouse monoclonal antibody to the predominantly dendritic protein MAP2, and with rabbit polyclonal antibody to the predominantly axonal protein tau. These cells were counterstained with anti-mouse and anti-rabbit IgGs conjugated to fluorescent dyes. Neurons treated with estradiol demonstrated intense MAP2-IF throughout extensive and well-developed dendritic networks, which tapered from their origins at the perikaryon down to the tips of the dendrites. Many nearby neurons appeared to interact with each other through interdendritic communications. In addition, a few long, thin, tau-IF neurites corresponding to axons were also noted throughout. However, DHT treatment altered both neurite morphology and IF pattern. Though the DHT-treated dendrites contained some MAP2-IF, these neurites were few in number, short, rudimentary, and poorly developed. Nearby neurons, even when in close proximity, did not develop interdendritic communications. Often, DHT-treated cells had more than one tau-IF axon, and these axons were longer and branched more frequently than in vehicle or estradiol-treated cells.

Interpretation

The results of these studies demonstrate the importance of dissociated rat hippocampal neurons in culture as a model system for the study of hormone–neuron interactions. Estradiol did not alter these neurons' normal stereotypic development of one axon and several dendrites per neuron, and these neurons frequently engaged in interneural communication through their dendrites. Conversely, DHT was able to significantly alter neuritic development by inducing more than one axon per cell, which branched frequently and did not participate in interneural communication. Androgen was seemingly able to activate an inherent neural morphogenetic program which promoted axonal development at the expense of dendrite development in this *in vitro* model.

SUMMARY AND IMPLICATIONS

This chapter describes two *in vitro* models for the effects of sex hormones on neurons. In sex hormone receptor-transfected PC12 cells, estrogen promoted neurite outgrowth and spine and gap junction formation, resulting in altered intercellular communication, while androgen promoted neuritic branching which increased the statistical likelihood of interneural contact. In primary hippocampal neurons, estrogen promoted dendritic outgrowth and interneural communication, while androgen promoted axonal outgrowth and branching but did not increase interneural communication.

The results of these two *in vitro* models recapitulate in part some of the effects of estrogen and androgen on neurons *in vivo*. Both systems share striking similarities. In both, estrogen was able to induce or promote the formation of either dendrites or dendritic specializations, and these specializations were then able to induce interneural communication. In both, androgen was able to promote the development of axons that branched frequently while not directly promoting interneuronal contact. In these ways, it seems likely that both sex hormones are acting as neurotropic factors in neurons that express the appropriate receptor, leading to specific changes in neurite outgrowth and pattern formation. A schema of these hormonal effects on neurons is depicted in Figure 2.1, which demonstrates the dichotomous but complementary effects of estrogen and androgen on neural development. It also suggests that local changes in the hormonal milieu can lead to large changes in brain development and structure, which would of necessity have some impact on brain function (e.g., behavior).

This hypothesis of hormonal control of neural development is consistent with the generally recognized concept of masculinization/defeminization as the basis of brain sex dimorphisms discussed earlier. For instance, one can imagine that the high levels of antenatal androgen present in girls with congenital adrenal hyperplasia would lead to an increase in neuritic arborization, which might lead to alterations of interneural connectivity in specific brain areas, thus leading to structural and functional brain changes in adulthood. Alternatively, decreases in androgen levels, as in male hypogonadism or DES exposure *in utero*, may alter neuritic organization and interneuronal connections prior to birth, leading to changes in cognitive abilities in adulthood (Hier & Crowley, 1982; Reinisch, Ziemba-Davis, & Sanders, 1991). Though purely speculative, the alterations in hypothalamic structure in homosexual and transsexual men (LeVay, 1991; Zhou et al., 1995) may have occurred as a result of local changes in sex hormonal concentration or effect.

As the chapters in this book attest, it is now generally accepted that genetic influences, hormonal cues, and environmental stimuli (e.g., stress, drugs) all play a role in the development of sex-specific cognition, behavior, and, possibly, sexual orientation. The contribution of the hormonal milieu to this process is undeniable, and underscores the biological nature of sex-specific cognition, behavior, and likely sexual orientation. Still missing from our evidence of hormonal control of brain development are quantitative analyses of brain morphology in autopsies of patients with antenatal hormonal disturbances, and analyses of which developmental genes are important for brain sex differentiation. As these studies continue, we yet shed further light on the cellular and molecular processes that underlie the basic fabric of who we are and how we came to be that way.

Figure 2.1
Scheme of Androgen and Estrogen Effects on Neurons

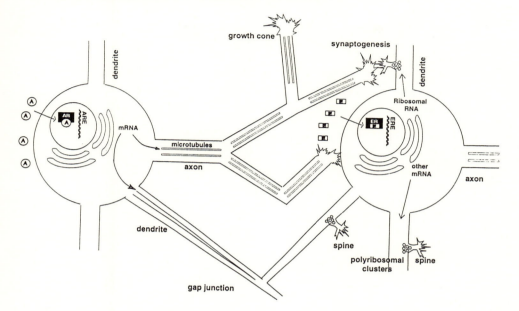

Androgen acts by diffusing into AR-containing neurons and forming a ligand-receptor complex with the AR in the cell nucleus. The androgen–AR complex localizes to specific androgen response elements (ARE) in the promoter region of androgen-dependent genes. This leads to the transcription of specific mRNAs and the production of androgen-dependent proteins, which somehow lead to the promotion of axonal development and arborization. By doing so, androgen increases the likelihood that any neuron will come into contact with other neurons. Similarly, estrogen acts by diffusing into ER-containing neurons and forming a complex with the ER in the nucleus. The estrogen–ER complex localizes to specific estrogen response elements (ERE) in the promoter region of estrogen-dependent genes. This leads to the transcription of specific mRNAs and the production of estrogen-dependent proteins, which leads to the promotion of dendritic development and dendritic specialization such as spines and gap junctions. By doing so, estrogen actually induces interneural communication. Thus, though androgen and estrogen act through diverse and separate mechanisms, the goal of both hormones is to foster interneural communication.

ACKNOWLEDGMENTS

The author wishes to note the collaborative efforts of Dr. Peter Baas and Dr. Chawnshang Chang of the University of Wisconsin, Madison, of Dr. Craig Jordan of Northwestern University, and of Dr. Howard Federoff of the University of Rochester. He would also like to thank Ping Hua, David Sharp, Wenqian Yu, Fridoon Ahmad, Lincoln Smith, and Kathleen Spencer for their technical expertise in the enactment of this work.

Chapter 3

Evidence from Opposite-Sex Twins for the Effects of Prenatal Sex Hormones

Edward M. Miller

The animal literature reports that females that are adjacent to males in the uterus develop more masculine morphological and behavioral traits than do females adjacent only to other females. This can be attributed to hormones transferring between the fetuses and in turn altering the developing brain.

   If the effect occurs in humans, twins whose womb mates were of the opposite sex (OS) would be morphologically or behaviorally less sex typical than twins whose womb mates were of the same sex (SS). This chapter will start by reviewing the animal literature. It will then discuss various morphological effects in humans that might be explained by hormone transfer, notably some otherwise inexplicable dental data. Various human behavior and cognitive ability data relating to opposite-sex twins are then presented; opposite-sex twins seem less sex typical in their abilities and emotions. This is followed by research done by the present author, using British and Australian data sets, showing that the sex of the co-twin affects the attitudes of female twins, such that females who shared the womb with males have more masculine attitudes than those who shared the womb with females. The results are interpreted as support for the joint hypotheses that hormones transfer and prenatal hormones affect the extent to which the brain exhibits masculine and feminine typical behaviors and abilities. In closing, a plea is made for more opposite-sex twin research.

THE EFFECT OF UTERINE POSITION
IN LABORATORY ANIMALS

Vom Saal (1989) has provided a good survey of the uterine position literature; and Gandelman (1992, Ch. 3) has summarized the uterine position literature, as well as the evidence for effects of fetal androgens on animal and human behavior. Clemens (1974) was the first to report a uterine position effect. He found that female mice adjacent to male mice in the uterus had larger ano-genital distances and later exhibited more masculine behavior than females adjacent to females. This was attributed to testosterone from the male fetuses somehow affecting the female fetuses, since the effect on ano-genital distance did not appear when the mothers were treated with antiandrogens. A possible mechanism was suggested when Fels and Bosch (1971) showed that testosterone could diffuse across amniotic membranes in rats. Gandelman, vom Saal, and Reinisch (1977) showed that the position of female mice in the uterus affected the potential for female aggressive behavior. After the mice were injected with testosterone, females that had been between two male mice showed more aggressive behavior than those that had been between females. These female mice more closely resembled male mice in aggressiveness than they did female mice that had been between two females.

The weight of both male and female mice from soon after birth until weaning depends on intrauterine position (Kinsley, Miele, Wagner et al., 1986). Males are the heavier sex in mice. Within each sex, those mice who were between two males (hence exposed to some of the testosterone from them) were heavier than those who were between two females (significantly so for females, and almost so for males). The effect was large enough so those females between two males (high testosterone exposure) had body weights that were in the male range. These masculinized females actually weighed more than the feminized males who had been between two females.

In the same experiments, female mice located between two males (higher testosterone levels) displayed less locomotor activity (measured by interruptions of infrared photobeams) than females between females (Kinsley, Miele, Konen et al., 1986). Female mice generally display more locomotor activity than male mice do. The effect was large enough so that the females who had been affected by testosterone from male fetuses actually resembled male mice more in activity than did the unexposed female mice (due to being between females *in utero*). This shows not only that hormones can transfer, but also that sufficiently large amounts can transfer to have effects comparable in magnitude to the normal male–female differences.

Aggression was twice as common for females between two males during pregnancy and over twice as great during lactation in the same sample of mice (Kinsley, Konen, Miele, Ghiraldi, & Svare, 1986). There was also a statistically significant uterine position effect for the size of litter females produced.

Clark, Galef, and associates (Clark & Galef, 1988; 1989; Clark et al., 1988; Clark et al., 1990; Clark, Tucker, & Galef, 1992; "Big and Smelly," 1992) found that numerous aspects of gerbil morphology and behavior depended on the adjacent fetuses' sex. Males between females weighed more, had larger scent glands, sired larger litters, and were more attractive to females. Conversely, females between two females matured faster and gave birth to more litters than those between two males. Male gerbils adjacent to two males had higher blood testosterone than males between two females (Clark, vom Saal, & Galef, 1992).

Vom Saal and Bronson (1980) showed that blood serum and amnonitic fluid concentrations of testosterone for female mice depended on uterine position, as did the sexual attraction of female mice to males. Other traits found in mice that depended on uterine position include ano-genital distance in males (Lephart, Fleming, & Rhees, 1989), ano-genital distance and time of vaginal opening in females (McDermott, Gandelman, and Reinisch, 1978), and infanticide and parental behavior in males (vom Saal, 1983). In mice, these effects are attributed to hormones diffusing across amniotic membranes.

The conditioned taste aversion reaction (in which rats learn to avoid a substance that has made them ill) following testosterone treatment depends on uterine position in female rats (Babine & Smotherman, 1984). This taste reaction is sexually dimorphic in rats, so that this finding suggests that testosterone transferring from male fetuses caused female rats to develop a more masculine brain. Also, in female rats, Glick and Shapiro (1988) showed that the preferred body rotation direction depends on the number of males in the litter, a result they interpreted as being due to testosterone transfer from the male fetuses (p. 153). Mankes, Glick, Van der Hoeven, and LeFevre (1991) found that the alcohol consumption and hepatic alcohol dehydrogenase activity of male rats between two males was significantly less than that of males between two females. The effect was strong enough so that the males between two females were shifted to the female range with regard to alcohol consumption and hepatic alcohol dehydrogenase activity. As shown by this discussion, in rats and gerbils adult testosterone levels are influenced by fetal position. If similar effects occur in humans, adult behavior may be influenced by prenatal hormones.

Though Fels and Bosch (1971) had shown that testosterone could diffuse across rat amniotic membranes, Meisel and Ward (1981) presented evidence that masculinizing effects on female rats of womb position were probably due to transfer of testosterone through maternal blood circulation. These effects were observed in female fetuses downstream from males, but not in those upstream. Richmond and Sachs (1984) found supporting evidence by showing that the presence of a male on the caudal side of the uterine horn had more influence than contiguity per se. Gandelman (1986) found that, in the guinea pig, both contiguity to males and positioning of the male fetus were necessary conditions for females treated with testosterone to exhibit male-type copulatory behavior.

Pigs are the only nonrodents for which a clear effect of uterine position has been observed. In pigs, Rohde Parfet et al. (1990) found no difference with uterine position in ano-genital distance or body weight at birth or after 120 days of *ad libitum* access to food. However, there was a statistically significant tendency for males between two males *in utero* to gain more weight from 175 to 270 days of age. During this period, the pigs were under restricted feeding conditions in which they had to compete with each other for food. The higher weight gain under these conditions was interpreted as being due to greater aggressiveness, and confirmed by observations that indicated such males tended to dominate in competitive encounters.

In cows, there is the well-known freemartin effect. Freemartins are bovine OS females with ovotestes. They are frequently sterile. This is apparently due to the sharing of placental circulation and hormone transfer. However, the substance producing the effect does not appear to be testosterone, since injecting testosterone into pregnant cows does not produce the same effects. Thus, the mechanism causing the freemartin effect differs from that found in rodents, where the effects have been shown to be due to transfer of testosterone or estradiol (vom Saal, 1989, p. 1827).

An obvious question is whether similar effects occur in humans. The human equivalent of a uterine position effect would appear in OS twins. Several authors have speculated that one twin fetus could affect the other. Vom Saal, Grant, McMullen, Kurt, and Laves (1983) documented that behavior of male mice not only depends on their uterine position, but that the prenatal hormone concentrations of estradiol vary with the sex of the adjacent fetuses. They then noted that in humans much of the estrogen in the maternal circulation is of fetal origin. The prominent neurologists Geschwind and Galburda (1987) speculated from the animal studies that "Since male twins both produce testosterone, each will conceivably be exposed to higher levels than he would be if he were a singleton. By this hypothesis, the females of opposite-sex pairs should have a high rate of left-handedness, because of exposure to testosterone produced by the male co-twins" (p. 141). Apparently, no effort was made to search the literature for such an effect. Evidence supporting this hypothesis will be presented later in discussing Koch's work.

IS THERE INTRAUTERINE MOBILITY OF HUMAN HORMONES?

Phoenix (1974) and Phoenix, Goy, and Resko (1968) showed that injecting testosterone propionate into the mothers could masculinize Rhesus monkeys both morphologically and behaviorally. This experiment was inspired by the observation that testosterone propionate injected into female guinea pigs masculinized their female offspring (Phoenix et al., 1968, p. 34), as it did in rats (p. 38). Later, eight such artificially masculinized monkeys were shown to display more masculine play behavior than control monkeys at twelve months of age (Goy & Resko, 1972, p. 720). The importance of the latter experiment is not just that behavior is affected by prenatal testosterone, but that testosterone (injected into the mother in the experiment) can pass through the placenta from the mother to the fetus in primates, and plausibly can do the same in humans.

Meulenberg and Hofman (1990) have shown that maternal blood testosterone levels depend on the sex of the fetus being carried. They conclude, "As a consequence of a maternal–fetal gradient, unbound testosterone crosses the placenta from the male fetus toward the maternal circulation, whereas the opposite direction applies to a female fetus" (p. 53). This observation makes very plausible an effect of a male twin on the female co-twin's testosterone level, since testosterone appears able to pass from fetus to mother (human), and from mother to fetus (at least in monkeys, guinea pigs, and rats).

There is strong evidence that estrogen concentrations in blood and in urine during human pregnancy correlate positively with birth weight (Ekbom, Trichopoulos, Adami, Hsieh, & Lan, 1992, p. 1017). While it could be that estrogen somehow promotes fetal growth (or is correlated with a factor that promotes it), the simplest explanation is that estrogen produced by the fetus enters the maternal circulation. Since large fetuses presumably produce more estrogen, the observed estrogen–birth weight correlation is easily explained.

When hormones in the amniotic fluid of human fetuses were measured (Carson et al., 1982), two male hormones, testosterone and androstenedione, were found to be significantly higher in male fetuses than in female fetuses at mid-term (15 to 21 weeks). In a sample of twenty, there was only one fetus from each sex whose testosterone fell in the range of the other sex. The average male value was 0.30 ng/mL in males, versus 0.08 ng/mL in females. Thus, transfer of one-third of the testosterone would more than double the typical female concentration. For androstenedione, the concentrations were 0.96 ng/mL in the male and 0.56 ng/mL in the female, a much smaller difference. Near birth, the males still had higher levels, but the differences were no longer statistically significant. Other measured hormones, including progesterone, did not display statistically significant differences between the sexes, with males actually showing the higher concentrations of progesterone in late gestation. Thus, in humans, a male fetus might appreciably raise the level of testosterone, or of another male hormone, in an adjacent female fetus. While female hormones probably also transfer, the absence of large sex differences suggests that a male's level would not vary with the co-twin's sex.

Individuals with inadequate levels of sex hormones might develop to be neither fully male nor fully female, and leave no descendants. Hence, natural selection would be expected to provide for a large safety margin in fetal sex hormone levels. Thus, even under adverse conditions, fetuses would develop morphologically and behaviorally into reproducing adults. Human twins are rare (and OS twins even rarer). Thus, if genes for high male hormone levels reduce the risk of inadequate hormones reaching male singleton fetuses, a

small effect (even if adverse) on co-twins would not have appreciably retarded the evolution of such high fetal sex hormone levels. If even a small
part of these hormones reaches the other fetus, the quantity could be large
relative to what is required for observable behavior changes.

Prenatal female hormones do not appear necessary for genital feminization in
mammals, while male hormones are necessary for genital masculinization
(Gandelman, 1992). Thus, an effect of male hormones diffusing into females
may be more likely than an effect of female hormones diffusing into males.

The human hormonal system is very complex, even more complex than
this discussion suggests. Much of the estrogen in the blood is combined with
a substance, alpha-fetoprotein, which increases the molecular size and prevents the combined form from crossing the blood–brain barrier. However,
testosterone does not combine with alpha-fetoprotein. It thus can cross the
blood–brain barrier from the blood to the brain. Inside the brain, testosterone
is believed to be converted by aromatase into estrogen, the so-called female
hormone. This is believed to be the substance that actually masculinizes the
male brain (Ellis, 1996b, p. 40).

If most estrogen is bound and cannot reach the brain, an effect of one fetus
on the blood estrogen levels of another human fetus may not imply any effect
on the level of estrogen in the brain of the latter fetus. This makes it plausible
that testosterone transfer effects would be more important than estrogen transfer
effects. However, prenatal exposure to female hormones does affect the brain
(Halpern, 1992, pp. 111–112). Neonatal ovariectomy defeminizes behavior
and alters the rat's corpus callosum in a male direction at a development stage
corresponding to when the human is prenatal (Fitch, Cowell, Schrott, &
Denenberg, 1991). This suggests the possibility that human development may
be affected by prenatal exposure to female hormones.

There is a large and complex literature on maternal and fetal hormones.
This literature's underlying assumption is that maternal, fetal, and placental
hormonal states affect each other, either by direct transfer of the hormones
from one compartment to the other, or through transfer of precursors (see
Tulchinsky & Ryan, 1980; Schindler, 1982). Solomon (1988) states that "steroids readily cross the placenta" (p. 2085). Though the author has not found
direct discussion of the possibility of one fetus directly affecting another,
nothing has been found that would preclude such effects. Evidence that the
fetus affects its mother's hormones, and that the mother affects its fetuses'
hormones, makes an effect of one fetus on another quite plausible. Even more
complex interactions may occur.

It should be noted that the sex-related hormones are chemically quite similar to each other, all consisting of three six-membered carbon rings and one
five-membered ring joined to each other by common sides (Schulster et al.,
1976, pp. 4–5). This makes it plausible (but far from certain) that if one steroid hormone diffuses, the others can also. In particular, cortisol, which is
structurally similar to testosterone (p. 5), is believed to transfer from the mother

to the fetus. The maternal contribution to fetal cortisol is calculated at 25 to 50 percent, and to fetal cortisone at nearly 100 percent (Gibson & Tulchinsky, 1980, p. 134). By injecting radioactive forms into the mother and observing radioactivity in the fetus, cortisol and dehydroepiandrosterone have been shown to transfer from the maternal circulation to the fetal circulation (Schindler, 1982, p. 91). If steroids can transfer between maternal and fetal circulation, it is very likely that they can also transfer between two fetuses.

There is some evidence that handedness (Ellis & Peckham, 1991) and human sexual orientation is affected by maternal stress (Ellis, Ames, Peckham, & Burke, 1988). The effects are argued to occur through the stress affecting the levels of maternal stress hormones (adrenaline, cortisol, and corticosterone). These then reach the fetus through the placenta in humans. If these effects are real, it would provide human evidence that hormones structurally similar to sex hormones can pass from the mother to the fetus. As noted, cortisol has a structure very similar to testosterone.

TambyRaja and Ratnam (1981) have reported higher levels of plasma estrogen in mothers of twins than were found in mothers of singletons. They speculate that "The high oestrogen levels in twin pregnancy may have been as a result of the four fetal adrenal glands producing an excess of precursor DHEAS and two fetal livers producing enough 16-hydoxylase for formation of these steroids" (p. 193). Trapp et al. (1986) report 40-percent higher estradiol levels in mothers of twins than in mothers of singletons. If these female hormones transfer between the maternal and the fetal circulations, it makes it more plausible that the structurally similar male hormones could transfer from one fetus to the other.

Having shown plausibility of hormone transferal between fetuses, let us turn to reports in human twins that OS and SS twins differ in a way that could be explained by hormonal transfer.

MORPHOLOGICAL EFFECTS HORMONE TRANSFER MIGHT EXPLAIN

Dental Asymmetry

Boklage (1985) examined the asymmetry in dental diameters in human twins. He found that males generally had larger teeth in the right jaw (which is consistent with the larger sizes for the right hemisphere of their brains), and that it was rather easy to separate males from females. He went on to say the following (SS refers to same sex, OS to opposite sex, and DZ to dizygotic): "A linear discriminant function sex-classification rule correctly classified 42 of the 44 SS-DZ in our sample, but misclassified 12 of our 20 OS-DZ twins ($X21 = 21.6$, exact $p = 3 /X 10^{-7}$), eight of the 10 females, and four of the 10 males. . . . A quadratic discriminant function sex-classification rule that correctly classified 123 out of 128 SS twins of both zygosities misclassified

16 of the 20 OS-DZ twins ($X21 = 72.1$), seven of the 10 males, and nine of the 10 females" (p. 601). The most plausible interpretation of these results is that something is transferring from the co-twin (presumably testosterone, estradiol, or another hormone) that causes OS females to become more masculine and/or male fetuses to become more feminine.

Fetal Death Rates

Boklage (1987) has also reported, from an analysis of another database, that fetal death rates (i.e., deaths before birth) in OS males are lower than for other (SS) male twins (Table 3, p. 282). A plausible explanation would be a hormonal effect, with transfer of a female hormone being most plausible, though elevation of testosterone in SS twin males could play a role. No similar effect is found in females, whose fetal death rates do not depend on their twin's sex. For neonatal deaths, there is a tendency for death rates in both sexes to be greater in SS DZ twins than in OS twins. Combined fetal and neonatal deaths show lower rates for OS twins (Table 2, p. 281). Again, a possible explanation is hormonal transfer.

Resemblance to Father or Mother

Zazzo (1960) has found an interesting effect regarding whether twins were reported to more closely resemble their mothers or fathers in appearance (p. 698). Not surprising, twins normally more closely resembled the parent of their sex. However, this effect was weaker (to a statistically significant degree) in OS twins. In particular, the OS females more closely resembled their fathers (56.4%) than their mothers (43.6%), while the SS DZ females more often resembled their mothers (57.1%). While this effect was statistically significant, OS males had only a slightly greater tendency to resemble their mothers (47.2%) than did DZ SS males (44.4%). However, they greatly (significantly at the 0.001 level) exceeded the maternal resemblance shown by the monozygotic (MZ) males (31.9%). While OS males differed from SS males, OS females differed little from SS females.

A plausible interpretation is that the OS twins were less sex typical due to hormone transfer. They were thus perceived as having less resemblance to their same-sex parents. Presumably, since sex differences are very obvious, the resemblance to a particular parent is reported after mentally adjusting for the expected sex difference. When the expected sex differences are lacking, an adjustment for the expected sex difference is then made and the twin is then seen as less likely to resemble the parent. Thus, a relatively nonmasculine-looking male twin is less likely to be reported as resembling his father. Likewise, a relatively masculine female would be reported as more closely resembling her father than her mother. The greater paternal resemblance of OS female twins could be explained if transfer of male hormones contributed to a more masculine appearance. In a corresponding table for psychological resemblance, no significant differences were reported among twin types.

A puzzling result (Zazzo, 1960) is that for many characteristics, the OS twins were less alike than MZ twins, but more alike than SS DZ twins (p. 642). While the former is expected, the latter is unexpected. One would normally expect OS twins to be even more different than SS DZ twins, rather than more similar, since they have sex differences in addition to genetic differences. A possible hormonal explanation is that the sex differences are less than normally expected, making it easier for OS twins to resemble each other as much as SS twins.

Swedish Body Dimensions

Before leaving morphology, one negative result should be reported. It was hypothesized that if hormones transfer some of the sexually dimorphic body dimensions might differ depending on the co-twin's sex. This was thought to be especially likely for the ratio of the shoulder to hip. Tanner (1989) states that "Cartilage cells in the hip joint are specialized to respond to female sex hormone (oestrogen) and cartilage cells in the shoulder region are specialized to respond to male sex hormones (androgens, primarily testosterone)" (p. 68). He also states that "The shoulder–hip dimorphism has long been used as a measure of bodily androgyny, i.e., the degree to which a male resembles a female, or vice versa." Dahlberg (1926), in a classic book, provided an appendix giving anthropomorphic dimensions for 486 Swedish twins, many of whom were OS. These data were entered and analyzed. No statistically significant effects for the co-twin's sex were found for the ratio of shoulder to hip widths.

PSYCHOLOGICAL EFFECTS HORMONAL TRANSFER MIGHT EXPLAIN

Spontaneous Otoacoustic Emissions

Spontaneous otoacoustic emissions are continuous sounds that are produced in the cochlea and propagate into the external ear canal, where they can be recorded. It is not known exactly how these are produced or why they are more common in females, but McFadden (1993a) believes that they may be due to differences in the strength of efferent inhibition delivered to the cochleas. McFadden (1993b) has reported that the number of spontaneous otoacoustic emissions in human female OS twins is in the male range. SS females show appreciably higher rates than OS females and higher rates than males, as do female nontwins. If he is right, the reported opposite-sex twin effect in females may be evidence that hormonal effects on these neurons differ between SS and OS females twins.

Motor Coordination

Whitfield and Martin (1992) have examined the reactions in human twins to a variety of variables considered relevant to alcohol consumption. Female behavior did not depend on whether the co-twin was male or female. For males, a significant effect existed for only one of fourteen variables. However, for six out of seven tests, the OS males had more feminine reactions. Of course, these results could have occurred by chance. The one statistically significant result in males was related to the number of incorrect responses to the motor coordination task. Here the score dropped from 17.7 (standard error = 1.2) for SS DZ males to 12.5 (standard error = 1.6) for OS DZ males. The SS female values were 12.8 (standard error = 1.2), versus 9.9 (standard error = 1.2) for OS females. Thus, the OS males have values in the female range. While this result could be due to chance, since the possible effect is of large size and in the direction predicted, further research is called for.

Sensation Seeking

Resnick, Gottesman, and McGue (1993) have examined sensation seeking in a sample of 422 British adult twin pairs including 51 OS pairs. Age-adjusted measures of sensation-seeking behavior showed a statistically significant increase in OS females as compared with SS females. The increase was statistically significant for an overall measure, as well as for subscales apparently measuring disinhibition (interpreted as tapping interest in socially and sexually disinhibited activities), and experience seeking (interpreted as seeking of new experiences in a nonconformist way through travel, new aesthetic interests, or consciousness-altering drugs). OS females had elevated scores for thrill and adventure seeking and for boredom susceptibility. For all scales, there was a statistically significant tendency for males to score higher. Thus, the OS females' attitudes were consistently more masculine than those of the SS females. No consistent pattern was found in comparing the SS males to the OS males.

Spatial Performance

Cole-Harding, Morstad, and Wilson (1988) reported that OS DZ females had significantly higher baseline spatial scores on the Vandenberg modification of the Shepard–Metzler Mental Rotations test than SS females. The OS females over three trials showed greater improvement than did the SS females. "By the third trial, the scores of these OS/DZ females were not significantly different from those of their twin brothers," though sex differences were otherwise found. Notice that the effect was large enough to eliminate the sex differences. This was interpreted as follows: "These results suggest the possibility that exposure to testosterone in utero improves spatial ability in females, thus supporting the theory that differences in prenatal exposure to testosterone are at least partially responsible for the gender differences in spatial ability."

Effects on Intelligence and Ability

Studies of cognitive abilities and school performance have been examined to see if the performance of OS twins shifted in the direction of their co-twins. Such an effect would be expected only where performance showed an appreciable sex difference. Record, McKeown, and Edwards (1970) reported verbal ability scores derived from the British 11 Plus Examination (which they interpreted as a test of verbal intelligence) for 2,164 twins born between 1950 and 1957 in Birmingham, England. The females had the higher scores. OS males did not differ appreciably in scores from SS males. However, females were different. The scores of 342 OS females averaged 96.15, which was below the 97.6 average of 478 SS females. Having a twin brother appeared to lower the female score 43 percent of the way toward the male average. While the published data do not give standard deviations for the different groups, given the large sample size, this effect is probably not due to chance. The direction of the effect is consistent with testosterone transfer from the male fetus to the female fetus, with a resultant brain masculinization lowering verbal abilities. Of course, an alternative is that having a brother provides less verbal stimulation, thus producing the effect, or possibly makes studying harder, and this lowers the female scores.

Fischbein (1978) has reported a twin study of Swedish students' aptitude and school achievement that included fifty-three to seventy (number depending on the exact data reported) OS pairs. The results were reanalyzed (with the aid of some additional data kindly provided by Professor Fischbein) with the sex hormone transfer hypothesis in mind. For Swedish third-grade children, there were no significant sex differences in performance, or any evidence that performance depended on the co-twin's sex.

However, for sixth-grade mathematics, when puberty is beginning to occur and many hormonally driven sex differences appear, there is evidence consistent with a possible hormonal effect. In this sample, as in other studies, males do better at mathematics than females. The seventy OS twin girls average scores were 38.5, versus an average of 34.65 (a weighted average of Fischbein's MZ and DZ data) for SS twin girls. A male co-twin appears to have a significant positive effect on female mathematics performance. This is consistent with the joint hypothesis that hormones transfer, and that prenatal testosterone exposure sensitizes the brain in such a way that with the puberty hormonal change a sex difference appears in the ability to learn mathematics.

Fischbein kindly provided data from the intelligence tests taken by these children. The only large sex difference was in perceptual speed, for which females were superior. A comparison of the SS females with the OS females

showed that having a brother (rather than a sister) made a statistically significant difference. Having a twin brother appeared to shift the female score over
halfway toward the male value.

Though a social explanation is possible, it is not obvious what type of
socialization difference would cause females to have higher perceptual speed
differences. Even less obvious is a social mechanism that would cause perceptual speed to vary with the co-twin's sex. However, the joint hypothesis
that testosterone from a male fetus affects the female fetus and that prenatal
testosterone exposure reduces perceptual speed can explain these results.

One other peculiarity emerged from studying this set of twins. Fischbein, Frank,
and Cenner (1991) reported that OS males were most popular, and OS females
unusually unpopular. While sampling variability or social interpretations are possible (and offered in the paper), hormonal interpretations are also possible. Testosterone is believed to lead to higher levels of aggression (see Kemper, 1992, for
citations) and to a personality high in psychoticism, characteristics that would
lower popularity. The OS females, having been exposed to extra testosterone,
would be less popular, while OS males, having had their testosterone partially offset by female hormones, would be more popular than other males.

Husen (1959) reported a study of Swedish draftees (virtually all of the
male population aged about 20 years) for 1949 to 1952 which included data
on SS male twins and OS ones. In most cases the SS male twins and the OS
ones did not appear to differ in intelligence (statistical significance tests are
not supplied). This is not surprising, since sex hormones probably do not
affect intelligence. However, an interesting peculiarity is that on all four subjects for which primary school marks were available the OS males did better
than either the MZ or the DZ SS male twins. This is highly unlikely if the co-
twin's sex is unimportant.

In comparing SS to OS male twins, it is found that OS twins have a statistically significant (5% probability) advantage in reading and history, and an
almost statistically significant advantage in writing (t = 1.78). Husen (1959)
did not give standard deviations for each figure, but reported that standard
deviations had an average of about 0.45, which is the figure used in these
calculations (p. 62). These are subjects in which girls generally do better. The
better performance of OS males is consistent with female hormones passing
into male fetuses and raising performance. Husen also reported the percentages that were regarded as having had unsatisfactory school marks. OS draftees consistently had lower such percentages than SS draftees, though the
absence of standard deviations makes tests of statistical significance impossible. However, the same pattern for all four subjects would be unlikely if
there were truly no differences.

The results discussed in this section are very consistent with the joint hypothesis that hormones transfer between fetuses and that hormones (testosterone probably) change the brain's structure in such a way as to make it more
or less masculine. At the time most of these results were reported, the theory

that hormones could transfer between fetuses had not been developed and the differences between same- and opposite-sex twins was just an unexplained peculiarity in the data. Now that we have a theory able to explain these results, they are much more interesting than when they were originally published. Rather than just being odd results, casually mentioned in passing, they are important pieces of evidence for the role of prenatal hormones in creating the male–female difference in the pattern of cognitive abilities.

The High Correlation between OS Twins

Unfortunately, most studies that have utilized OS twins have been interested in estimating heritability (the percentage of the variability in a trait that is due to genetic causes) or other genetic parameters, and have reported only the correlations between the members of twin pairs, not the absolute values tabulated by zygosity (whether the twins were identical or fraternal) and sex. A finding of these studies has been that OS twins correlated about as closely, or even more closely, as did SS twins. This is surprising, because one would have expected that the sex differences would lead to an appreciably lower correlation between the twins. For instance, the average over nine studies of the correlation coefficients for the intelligence of OS twins is the same 0.53 average obtained for eleven studies of like-sex twins (Erlenmeyer-Kimling & Jarvik, 1963). If hormones do transfer, any sex-related differences within twin pairs would be attenuated, helping to explain these otherwise puzzling results.

Carter (1932) examined the extent to which twins, predominantly junior and senior high school students, were similar on the Strong Vocational Interest Inventory. His major finding was that MZ twins were more similar than SS DZ twins, indicating a substantial heritability. An unexpected finding was that OS twins correlated 0.30, which greatly exceeded the 0.20 correlation for SS males, and was approximately equal to the 0.32 correlation for SS females. This was puzzling, since male and female interests are normally quite different (probably more so in the thirties), and the sex differences would be expected to cause the OS twins to correlate much less than the SS twins. It is possible that hormonal transfer reduces the effect of sex differences.

However, Carter & Strong (1933), in a later paper on sex differences, provided scores on the Strong Vocational Interest Blank for thirty-four OS pairs, and a second sample of 100 boys and 100 girls. To test the hormone-transfer hypothesis, I compared the sex differences in the two samples. This did not support the hypothesis of OS twins affecting each other in the hypothesized direction. The differences in scores between the twins were actually a little greater than between the singletons (those borne singly rather than as part of a multiple birth). The joint hypothesis that hormones transfer and that hormones affect vocational interest scores would have predicted a somewhat smaller difference in twins, since the transfer of hormones would have reduced the sex difference.

Incidentally, Carter and Strong's (1933) rationale for studying the OS twins was that they were exactly paired for age, family environment, social and economic status, and the like, leaving only the sex-related differences (whether due to biology or socialization). If hormones transfer, this is an incorrect strategy for determining how large typical sex differences are. Of course, they could not have been aware of this potential problem.

Koch's Behavior Research

Masculinity and Femininity in OS Twins   Koch (1966) reported a very large number of measures of personality for a sample of twins and matched controls (young children cross-classified by both zygosity and sex). Unfortunately, she had only nineteen OS twin pairs. Thus, relatively few individual items show statistically significant differences. However, the effects were often in the direction hypothesized here. Her most revealing statement is that "The striking divergence noted between the sexes when two groups, uniform in sex, are compared is not apparent in the two sex groups derived from opposite-sex pairs" (p. 163). This follows on the sentence that the OS female twins "did not seem to be 'masculinized' by their brother's influence as much as the brothers were 'feminized' by theirs." Koch (writing in the environmentally oriented 1960s) interprets the results as being due to differential socialization, but the result is also consistent with this chapter's hormonal hypothesis.

The section on OS male twins states the following: "These DZOS males were described as rather sober and subdued when compared with nontwins—they were rated lower in activeness, loudness, confidence, intensity, selfishness, and inclination to project blame. There was an intimation of a tendency on their part to play more with girls. At first it was thought these DZOSm's showed their sisters' influence in being relatively feminine in behavior patterns—less selfish, more responsible, more obedient, less exhibitionist, less moody, and less active than parallel singletons" (Koch, 1966, p. 159). Thus, in comparisons with the SS matched controls, the results are consistent with the males displaying more feminine behavior patterns. However, Koch follows immediately with "The DZOSm's did not, however, differ significantly from the DZSSm's in these traits. Hence it looks as if the former were, at least in part, conforming to generally approved behavior patterns rather than merely copying the sisters' behavior pattern." The interpretation is a socialization one, which Koch consistently prefers. However, she does go on to note that "Although the DZOSm's differed insignificantly from the DZSSm's, the small differences between them were in the direction of the feminine."

Inspection of Koch's (1966) tables shows how large a difference can be and still not be statistically significant in a small sample. She constructed a "masculinity in attitude" by averaging normalized ratings by teachers for six traits (resistance, moodiness, revengefulness, tendency to project blame, tendency to tease, and social apprehensiveness) (pp. 92–93) with a mean of 4.0 and a standard deviation of 1.0. There were, after adjustment for social class (Table 72), appreciable sex differences on these for MZ twins (4.11 for males versus 3.74 for females). Almost identical averages were computed for DZ twins (4.11 versus 3.72), suggesting a difference of 0.37 to 0.39 standard deviations between the sexes. However, for OS twins the difference shrunk greatly. The averages were 3.87 for males (i.e., the males moved almost two-thirds of the way to the female value) versus 3.83 for females (the females moved over one-quarter of the way toward the male values), leaving a male–female difference of only 0.04 standard deviations. Essentially, the sex difference has been eliminated. However, this effect does not achieve statistical significance. Unfortunately, with her sample size and the small size of the male–female differences, a complete shift of the males to the female pattern would not be statistically significant. With a population whose average age is six, these differences are not as large as they become later. Often an effect that falls short of statistical significance is concluded not to exist. Here, where the effect as measured was large (an almost total disappearance of the sexual difference), a better conclusion is that there is a potentially important effect that should be studied further, but with a larger sample. Now that there is a theory that predicts such a reduction in sex differences, such a study is especially desirable.

A similar result was found for Koch's (1966) "femininity in attitude," which was based on the six traits of affectionateness, tenacity, obedience, cheerfulness, responsibleness, and friendliness to children. For MZ twins, the score were 3.73 for males versus 4.20 for females. Similar values were found for DZ SS twins, 3.77 versus 4.23. The sex effects were 0.47 and 0.46 standard deviations, respectively. However, the male OS value was 4.05 and the female value was 4.19, shrinking the sex effect to 0.14 standard deviations. About 70 percent of the sex effect has disappeared through the males moving almost two-thirds of the way toward the female values, while female values remain essentially unchanged. Again, the results were reported as not statistically significant.

Some interesting results show up in the comparisons of twins with matched singletons (Koch, 1966, Table 73). There are statistically significant (p < 0.01) tendencies for the MZ females to be less masculine (0.41 standard deviations) and more feminine (0.34 standard deviations). For DZ females, the trends are in the same direction but much weaker (0.13 and 0.15). As pointed out earlier, TambyRaja and Ratnam (1981) and Trapp et al. (1986) report higher levels of female hormones in mothers of twins. Thus, a possible hormonal explanation is that extra hormones from one female twin made the other twin even more feminine. A social explanation might involve modeling on the other twin. The size of the female twin feminization and demasculinization effect, when compared with the controls, were about the same (0.13 for masculinity and 0.10 for femininity), which was not statistically significant.

Male twins with male co-twins were more masculine in all four comparisons with singletons (MZ and DZ each for masculinity and femininity), but the effects lacked statistical significance (Koch, 1966). SS males were less masculine (by 0.23 standard deviation units) and more feminine (by 0.12 standard deviation units), but neither effect was statistically significant.

Handedness in OS Twins   One variable reported on by Koch (1966) and believed to be influenced by hormones (testosterone) is hand preference. Earlier, the Geschwind and Galaburda (1987, p. 141) hypothesis that OS twins should show more left-handedness was mentioned as an early speculation about sex-hormone transfers in humans. Koch's data (Table 29) show that the percentage of OS females that were left-handed (24% at some time before seven, and 18% at the time of the study) exceeded the corresponding percentages for OS males (18% and 12%, respectively), while in SS twins there was the usual tendency for the males to be more often left-handed. However, due to the small sample size (19 OS twins), the difference could be due to chance.

Left-handedness is often considered to be caused by testosterone. Koch's data (1966, Table 30) provides some indirect evidence for a hormonal effect. She finds a significant tendency for the more dominant twin to be left-handed (p reported as between 0.01 and 0.001), and also a tendency for the dominant twin to be more competitive (probability between 0.1 and 0.05). Both competitiveness and dominance are today believed to be related to testosterone (Kemper, 1992).

Physical Defects in OS Twins   Koch (1966) reports a tendency for physical defects of various types to be more common in OS females than in SS females. In SS twins, males had more defects than females, while in OS twins this was reversed (Table 12). In nontwin studies, males have more birth defects, an effect that is often attributed to testosterone. Thus, extra testosterone could create defects in female co-twins. The reversal of the usual effects in OS twins appears due to much higher defect rates in the OS females than in SS female twins.

Female Dominance in OS Twins   Koch reports one other interesting finding. In 80 percent of the OS twins, the dominant twin was female. This is surprising, because in most social dyads (i.e., marriage) the male is usually dominant. She attributes this striking finding to the greater verbal skills (probably due to earlier maturation) of females in early childhood (her subjects were about age six). This is plausible, but the females may have been assisted in achieving dominance by a reduction in the usual prenatal hormonal differences.

Another report of female dominance in OS twins exists. Zazzo (1960, p. 645) also reports that OS females are more commonly dominant in a sample aged from one year up. High female dominance is reported for all ages, though it is not statistically significant for those aged eleven to fifteen, or for those over twenty. It is especially striking that in the sixteen to twenty age range, where males would normally be dominant, there were fourteen female dominant pairs versus only five male dominant pairs, a statistically significant effect. Greater female prenatal testosterone exposure could be part of the explanation.

Implications of Koch's Behavior Research In Koch's (1966) study the data are tabulated in such a way as to permit comparisons by sex of OS twins on a number of variables. Unfortunately, the small size of her OS sample and the fact that the research concerned young children at an age when sex differences are small prevent saying more than that her results are consistent with hormones produced by one twin somehow reaching and affecting the OS twin. Of course, if there really is an effect by which OS twins become more like each other with regard to sex-typed behavior, it could be due to learning behavior from the OS twin, rather than to hormonal effects. If typical feminine or masculine attitudes were learned, one would expect that learning would occur in OS siblings.

Fortunately, Koch (1955) had done a very similar sibling study prior to her twin study. Children of the age used in the twin study, drawn from a similar population, and living with only one other sibling (the twins studied were selected to be without other siblings, which implied each twin had only a single sibling), were compared using the same psychological measures. Her description of this study makes no mention of a general tendency for siblings to become more like their siblings of the opposite sex. The strongest sex-specific effect found is that "Children with brothers were rated as more competitive, ambitious, enthusiastic, and less wavering in decisions than children with sisters. . . . Our results suggest that children with brothers are also less likely to build alibis and to be more tenacious of purpose than are those with sisters. In all of the traits mentioned, except ambition and tenacity, the effect of a male sibling is significantly different from that of a female only in the case of girls" (p. 47).

The author's impression, after reading both of Koch's reports (1955; 1966), is that the sibling effects and the twin effects are quite different (the reports' formats differ, making exact comparison difficult). If she had thought her twin-study results were similar to her earlier sibling study, she would have commented on the resemblance. However, she makes no such comparisons. If learning from one's sibling were the primary mechanism by which one sibling affected another in both studies, one would expect the nature and direction of the effects to be similar in both studies. Both studies used children of the same age, from the same population, and controlled to have only a single sibling (the co-twin for the twin study). Such similarity is not apparent. The most parsimonious way to account for the absence of similar effects from siblings in the two studies is that a twin's effects on its co-twin are caused by a different mechanism than the effects of a sibling on its nontwin sibling. Since hormonal effects are not found among nontwin siblings but could be among twins, hormonal effects are an obvious candidate for this mechanism.

Mitchel, Baker, and Jacklin (1989) examined masculinity and femininity in twins, but since their sample included only nine OS twin pairs, it has little power for hypothesis testing. However, on the two femininity scores reported (Table 1), there is a shift of the males toward greater femininity and of the females toward greater masculinity, such that the OS males actually have higher femininity scores than the females. No such shifts appear for the masculinity scores. Given the small sample size, it is not surprising that none of these effects even approach statistical significance. Still, it is interesting that the effect is similar to that reported by Koch, and to that predicted by theory.

Though many of the effects reported by Koch (1966) and Mitchel et al. (1989) are not statistically significant, the absence of statistical significance is consistent with a practically important effect. Given a theoretical reason for suspecting an effect, further research with larger samples would appear to be justified.

Ocular Defects

Koch (1966) discovered that significantly more opposite-sex twin children (in a sample of 172 six-year-old twins) wore glasses than did same-sex dizygotic twins (no refractions were performed). The difference between the two groups of dizygotic twins was significant at the 0.001 level. The rate was much higher among all twins than in the singleton population. The 38 percent opposite-sex twin rate (13 of 34 opposite-sex twins) far exceeded the 4.39 percent rate among 3,000 nontwin controls (kindergarten and first-grade children enrolled in similar classes). She suggested that "retrolental fibroplasia" (now referred to as retinopathy of prematurity) may have played a role, because severely premature children born in the period she studied were routinely given oxygen, which can lead to that condition. It is known that prematurity greatly increases the myopia rate, as does retinopathy of prematurity. However, prematurity seems unlikely to account for her findings, because while "prematurity" (indicated by birth weight) was more common among the opposite-sex twins, the effect was not statistically significant. Because her evidence for visual defects was the wearing of glasses, the problem could have been refractive hyperopia or astigmatism, though myopia appears more likely (merely on the statistical argument that it is the most common cause for wearing glasses among children).

Stocks and Karns (1933), as part of a twin study of a large number of variables, measured vision "by means of Snellen type tests, without glasses, at a distance of 6 meters" for 90 opposite-sex and 174 like-sex London school twins. They reported a statistically significant tendency for the vision of opposite-sex twins (in both the right and the left eyes) to be worse than in the nontwin controls. The differences were close to statistically significant for opposite-sex twins as compared to same-sex twins. Refractions or detailed visual tests were not performed, but in children myopia is the most common cause for poor visual acuity, suggesting the problem was myopia.

Stocks and Karns (1933) offered no hypothesis to explain their findings, though similar differences (opposite-sex twins less sensitive) were reported for cutaneous sensibility (as measured by the minimum distance two sharp points had to be separated before they could consistently be distinguished when applied to the anterior surface of the left forearm), and for the upper limit of hearing. It is of course possible that some type of birth complication (possibly affecting the brain) was more common in the opposite-sex twins, but examination of the IQ data reported (p. 27) showed the IQs of the opposite-sex twins to be virtually identical to those of the controls, whereas the same-sex twins had IQs below those of the controls, an observation that is opposite to what would have been predicted from a brain-damage hypothesis.

A search was made for other studies reporting on vision in opposite-sex twins, but none were found, though a study by Quinn et al. (1992) apparently contains enough multiple births to permit a separate analysis of opposite-sex twins. The author has examined the literature on myopia (see Miller, 1992) and found no discussion of hormonal effects. However, a possible hormonal mechanism can be imagined. The growth of certain brain tissues is affected by sex hormones, including estrogen. Possibly sex hormones differentially affect those tissues that become the lens and those that determine the size and shape of the rest of the eye. An eye whose axial diameter is too long or too short for the power of the lens produces an ocular defect, which is usually corrected by glasses. Natural selection should have produced a situation in which the different parts of the eye develop in the proper ratio in the typical hormonal environment for their sex. However, if the hormonal environment is unusual, and the eye's different parts are affected differentially, the result could be increased myopia.

Tanner (1989) states that "The eye probably has a slight adolescent growth spurt [and that] although myopia increases continuously from at least age 6 to maturity, a particularly rapid rate of change occurs at about 11 to 12 in girls and 13 to 14 in boys, as would be expected if there was a rather greater spurt in the axial dimension of the eye than in its vertical dimension" (p. 17). Since the puberty growth spurt is caused by sex hormones, this would suggest some sensitivity to sex hormones at this age, and possibly earlier, making this theory more plausible. He also states that "There is a clear adolescent growth spurt, coincident with the height spurt, in most facial dimensions, though not in the width of the eyes or the distances between them" (p. 67). Since the adolescent growth spurt is known to be caused by sex hormones, it is possible that some parts of the eye respond to sex hormones more than other parts.

Public Opinion Questionnaire Data

A large-scale twin study conducted in London, summarized by Eaves, Eysenck, and Martin (1989, Appendix D) provided suitable data for another test. As part of a larger study of 1,650 twins in the early 1970s, a sixty-question Public Opinion Inventory dealing with such topics as sexual behavior, religion, and politics had been administered. The author of this chapter analyzed the published data in order to test the hormone-transfer hypothesis (the results were initially reported in Miller, 1994a).

For the majority of questions there was not a statistically significant difference between the answers of those twins that shared a womb with one of the same sex and those that shared a womb with one of a different sex. For females, in only sixteen out of sixty questions was the difference statistically significant at the 5 percent level. However, only three such significant results would be expected from chance alone, thus suggesting that who one shared the womb with has important effects.

However, for fourteen of these sixteen statistically significant comparisons, the difference took the form of the female OS twins answering the questions more often as males answer them. In only two cases (question 16, dealing with the importance of family, and question 55, dealing with homosexuality) were the answers more in the feminine direction. For both of these questions the magnitude of the sex effect was small.

For males there were only five questions (3, 15, 30, 36, and 52) in which there were statistically significant effects for the sex of the wombmate. However, in all five of these cases the male twins that shared a womb with a female had more feminine opinions than those with twin brothers did.

A preliminary question was whether the standard of comparison for a twin that shared the womb should be all twins that did not share a womb with an opposite-sex twin or just the other dizygotic twin. The sex differences were quite similar, whether estimated from monozygotic or dizygotic twins (r = 0.836). Since there were appreciably more monozygotic twins (650 female twins and 240 male twins) than there were dizygotic twins (388 females and 118 males), more precise estimates of sexual differences could be obtained using all SS twins. Thus, the difference between the answers of all the male and all the female same-sex twins were taken as measuring the sex difference. The opposite-sex twins were excluded because of the possibility that they might display less sex-typical behavior because of a different hormonal environment within the womb (testing this hypothesis was the study's goal). As a measure of the sex effect, the differences between the sexes in answers to the questions were computed (the average male score minus the average female score). The term feminine or masculine here refers merely to how females or males typically answered, rather than to any a priori designation of certain answers as typical of males or females. For each item, the difference in average scores was computed between the female twins with a twin brother and the female twins with a twin sister. This series measures the effect on a female twin of her co-twin's sex. The two series (the sex series and the sex of wombmate series) had a correlation of 0.54. This is statistically significant. Figure 3.1 plots the magnitude of the sex of wombmate effect against the magnitude of the sex effect. The sex of the wombmate effect is in the same direction as the sex effect. Adult females with twin brothers answered in a more masculine way than those with sisters did.

Figure 3.1
Twin Type Difference versus Sex Difference

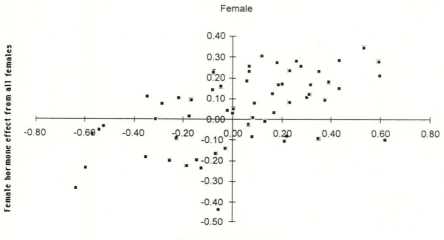

Source: Reprinted from *Personality and Individual Differences 17*, by E. M. Miller. Prenatal sex hormone transfer: A reason to study opposite-sex twins, pp. 511–529. Copyright 1994, with kind permission from Elsevier Science Ltd, The Boulevard, Langford Lane, Kidlington OX5 1GB, UK.

A similar computation for the males gave a correlation of –0.22. The negative sign means that the male's answers were shifted toward the female's answers. This is to say, their opinions became more feminine. The effect, while in the predicted direction, is not quite statistically significant (p = 0.096).

A Potential Statistical Problem

One statistical problem arises because the data on dizygotic females are used both for calculating the difference attributed to sex of wombmate and for calculating the differences between the sexes. The errors in the two variables are not independent. An error in this variable would contribute to both differences, possibly creating a spurious effect. For instance, suppose that, by luck, the female same-sex dizygotic twins happened to answer a question so as to raise their score by 0.1 over what the score would be if we sampled an infinite number of twins on a question on which males had the higher score. This would reduce the male–female difference. If female twins with male co-twins normally answered more in the male manner, this would also reduce the size of the wombmate effect. Now suppose luck (sampling variability) had the opposite effect of reducing these twins' scores by 0.1. This would raise both the sex difference and the wombmate effect. Thus, the effect of sampling variability is to increase the correlation.

While this effect is probably minor, it could produce a nonexistent correlation. To eliminate this statistical effect, the wombmate effect was also calculated in a way that would not include the same twins used to calculate the sex effect. Thus, the sex differences were determined using only monozygotic twins, and the wombmate effect using only dizygotic twins. The magnitude of the sex effect was calculated by subtracting the female monozygotic twins' average score from the male monozygotic twins' average score. This increased the error due to sampling variability in the sex effect. The wombmate effect was then calculated using only dizygotic twins (again by subtracting the scores for those females who had a female wombmate from those who had a male wombmate). This had the additional benefit of making the wombmate effect depend only on dizygotic twins, eliminating any possible error from some uncontrolled-for difference between monozygotic and dizygotic twins. The effect was to reduce the correlation coefficient for female twins from 0.54 to 0.47. The percentage adjustment in the female values towards the male values was reduced from 31 to 24 percent. Since the estimate of the coefficient was still approximately four times its standard error, the effect still existed.

The cost of eliminating this statistical problem is to reduce the size of the sample used to calculate the sex differences from 1,038 to 650 and, more seriously, to reduce the size of the sample used to calculate the differences by twin type from the same 1,038 to the 388 dizygotic female twins. This reduction in power was judged to be a greater loss than avoiding a small degree of common error variance, and emphasis is consequently placed on the equations estimated with the larger samples.

Sensitivity to Additive Genetic and Environmental Effects

It was hypothesized that if the effect were related to what was being inherited (perhaps because the inheritance was related to testosterone), the correlation coefficient would be larger for the ten items found by Eaves, Eysenck, and Martin (1989) to have the largest additive component of variability (p. 322). These are items believed to be heavily genetically influenced. For females, the correlation coefficient was 0.77 ($p < 0.01$) for these items. The high correlation suggests that the genetic influence could be primarily through the level of testosterone or another genetically influenced hormone.

For the ten items identified as having the largest between-families component of environmental variance (i.e., the variables whose variability between sets of twins for environmental reasons was greatest), the correlation coefficient was also high (0.70, $p < 0.02$). This high level could have happened if these items were also influenced by testosterone levels, but mothers differ in the testosterone levels their children are exposed to for environmental reasons (possibly related to stress or the number of previous children). The high correlations found here could also be merely because these items are those heavily influenced by personal contact with other family members, and the most influential family member for a twin would be the co-twin.

The ten items with the largest within-families component of variance had a correlation coefficient of −0.10 (which is nonsignificant). Testosterone appears to have very little to do with these items. The process was repeated for males. The correlation coefficients were 0.10, 0.25, and −0.42. None were large enough to be statistically significant, probably because each group had only ten questions.

Australian Twin Data

Given the results of this study, a replication in another sample was called for. Fortunately, a suitable data set was available. As part of another study (described in Martin, Eaves, Heath, Jardine, Lynn, Feingold, & Eysenck, 1986), a sample of Australian adult twins, including 905 opposite-sex pairs, 1,982 female pairs, and 916 male pairs had been given a fifty-item version of the Wilson–Patterson conservatism scale. This comprises a series of one-word items to which the subjects rate their agreement by circling yes, ?, or no. The data are the same data that have been previously used (Martin et al., 1986; Eaves, Eysenck, & Martin, 1989) to show that more of the family resemblance in social attitudes is caused by genetic influences than by shared environmental influences (culture). The results were originally reported in Miller and Martin (1995).

For purposes of this study, the three possible answers were converted to a numeric scale by scoring yes as 0, ? as 0.5, and no as 1. These scores were then cross-tabulated by sex and whether the twin pairs were of opposite or same sex. Professor A. C. Heath of Washington University supplied the tabulations. For most of the items, males and females differed in their responses. A measure of this sex difference was calculated by subtracting the female score from the male score for both the same-sex and opposite-sex twins. The subtraction was algebraic, retaining the sign of the differences. The magnitude and direction of the sex differences were very similar in the same-sex and in the opposite-sex pairs.

A statistically significant difference was frequently found in the attitudes of the twins, depending on the sex of the other twin. For females, the average difference in the absolute value of the opinions between members of opposite-sex and same-sex pairs was 0.024. This average difference was 0.015 for males. Some of these differences reflect only sampling variability. There were fewer male pairs than female pairs. Thus, if the differences between OS and SS twins were due only to sampling variability, it would be greater among the males. However, it is greater among the females. This suggests that there is something about females that makes their opinions more sensitive to their co-twin's sex.

Indeed, the male answers in the opposite-sex pairs showed no systematic differences from the answers of the males in the same-sex pairs. Their answers were almost as "masculine" as the same-sex males. (Because any significant sex differences were virtually always in the same direction in both the same-sex and opposite-sex twins, there is very little ambiguity in referring to a certain direction as masculine.) The correlation coefficient between the difference in male twin attitudes and the sex difference was 0.21, explaining less than 5 percent of the variance. This was not a statistically significant effect.

· The most striking finding can be seen in Figure 3.2. The horizontal axis shows the sex differences on each question, with the questions where males had the higher scores on the right. Ones where females scored higher are to the left. The vertical axis shows how big a difference (with sign retained) the sex of the female's twin made. If females with brothers scored higher, the difference is positive and above the zero axis. As can be seen, there is a strong tendency for female twins with twin brothers to give more masculine answers.

It was decided to measure the sex differences from the same-sex twin answers to avoid any attenuation from the greater similarity of the opposite-sex twins. In a regression of the difference in female attitudes between twin types on the sex difference, the coefficient for the sex difference was 0.16. The regression coefficient is interpreted as the OS female attitudes moving an average of 16 percent of the way toward the typical male's attitudes. The standard error of the regression coefficient was 0.04, making it highly unlikely that the correlation is due to chance. The regression explains 24 percent of the variance in the difference between SS and OS female twin opinions, corresponding to a correlation coefficient of 0.49.

Possible Explanations

The basic pattern of results from this large Australian sample rather closely resembles the results from the London twins. Two studies conducted at opposite ends of the world with different instruments have given similar results.

A hormonal explanation for the sex-of-twin effect requires accepting the joint hypothesis that hormones both affect opinions and transfer between twin fetuses. If OS females become more masculine in their opinions but OS males do not become more feminine, the effects are presumably caused by transfer of a male hormone, probably testosterone. The basic mammalian pattern is female. A fetus develops as a female unless exposed to testosterone from the fetal testes. It is plausible that the brain contains testosterone receptors such that after exposure to testosterone the brain can easily learn masculine beliefs and adopt masculine behavior patterns. This would explain both sex differences and (with testosterone transfer) the masculinization of the OS females' attitudes. Other evidence exists for such masculinization.

The reported observations can be explained by either prenatal or postnatal (social) effects. Either way it is necessary to explain why the females show a systematic tendency to shift their opinions in the masculine direction, while the males do not. A social explanation would have to assume a much stronger ten-

Figure 3.2
Australian Female Twin Attitudes

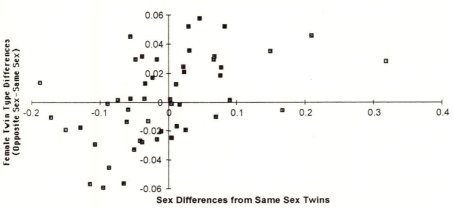

Australian Female Twin Attitudes

Source: Reprinted from *Acta Geneticae Medicae et Gemellologiae* 44, by E. M. Miller and N. G. Martin. (1995). Analysis of the effects of hormones on opposite-sex twin attitudes, pp. 41–52. Reprinted with permission.

dency for females to change their opinions to agree with those who are emotionally close to them than for males. Admittedly, such a tendency probably exists. It may even be biological. The hormonal explanation would be that testosterone affects the females greatly, but that fetal ovaries produce either little female hormones or the male is little affected by any female hormones that may reach him.

Inheritance of Hormonal Levels

There is one previous study that can help cast some light on the hypothesized plausibility of the behavioral variables in question responding to hormones that could diffuse between fetuses. Saki, Baker, Jacklin, and Shulman (1992), working with identical and fraternal same-sex twins (unfortunately, no OS twins were included), found evidence of significant genetic influences on levels of progesterone and estradiol, but not testosterone. However, evidence was found for a strong effect of shared environments on testosterone levels. If the public opinion questions that exhibit additive genetic effects and shared environmental effects are being influenced by hormones that move between fetuses, the results found would seem to be consistent with what is known about the inheritance of fetal hormones.

It should be noted that the work of Saki et al. (1992) was done with blood taken from the umbilical cord (right after birth), which reflects hormonal levels at birth. The maximum sex-related differences in fetal testosterone levels occur well before birth. At birth the sexes actually overlap in hormone levels. If levels of sex hormones produce sexual differentiation in the brain, the effect most likely occurs well before birth, when the hormonal differences are largest. Thus, this study's failure to find evidence for inheritance of testosterone levels at birth does not show that earlier levels are not genetically determined. Indeed, the strong sexual differences found earlier make it very likely that genes play a major role (since sex is a genetically determined variable).

Possible Socialization Effects

An obvious alternative to a prenatal hormonal effect is a postnatal socialization effect. Since twins spend much time with each other when young and develop a special bond, perhaps they come to think alike, and this similarity persists into adulthood even though the twins no longer live together. This could cause female twins with brothers to be more masculine in their opinions, and brothers with sisters to be more feminine. If females (at least as adults) are more affected by socialization by their twins than males are, a greater female than male shift could be explained.

The closest analogy to an opposite-sex twin relationship for intensity of feeling is marriage. Spousal opinions on public opinion questionnaires are known to be highly correlated. If spousal resemblances result primarily from living together, the opinions of married couples should resemble each other more the longer the couples had been married. However, spousal resemblance does not appear to increase with age (a good surrogate for length of marriage), suggesting that living with and having extensive contact with someone of the opposite sex does not shift one's own opinions in the direction of that person's opinions (Eaves, Eysenck, & Martin, 1989, p. 376).

Ernst and Angst (1983) reported that both imitation (when siblings resemble each other) and contrast (when siblings contrast with each other) hypotheses have been proposed for how siblings affect one another, and provided examples of studies reporting both types of effects (p. 173). They concluded that "The hypothesis that sex of sib has no general and lasting influence on personality has not been refuted" (p. 175). Leventhal (1970) reported in a study of college students that evidence (depending on the item) could be found for both contrast and imitation hypothesizes among second-born males. Using the Gough Scale of Psychological Femininity, Rosenberg and Sutton-Smith (1968) reported significant imitative effects among college females from two-sibling families. While the score of females with sisters moved from 23.61 (for females with sisters) to 22.41 (females with brothers), a statistically significant shift, this move was still small in relation to the male–female gap (their brothers averaged 15.9). While the sibling's sex had a statistically significant impact, the brother's femininity score had virtually no impact (correlation of 0.03) on his sister's femininity score, which goes against the imitative hypothesis. Landers (1970) found evidence for imitation effects in sports participation and femininity among college females.

In considering these studies using college students, it should be remembered they probably still live with, or very recently lived with, their siblings. However, the adult twins discussed here had typically lived apart from their co-twins for many years. Typically, among the adult twins, the member of the opposite sex they saw the most was a spouse rather than their co-twin. Given the amount of time spent with a spouse, having an adult opposite-sex twin probably added little to the exposure to the opposite sex's opinions.

Butcher and Case (1994) presented evidence from three large data sets that women who had brothers have more years of education (about 0.5 years more) than similarly situated women who had sisters. This argues against the belief that families would give preference to males in financing education, causing the females with brothers to obtain less education than those with sisters. The simplest explanation for this result is that brothers influence their sisters in the direction of more education, perhaps by causing them to value education more highly. This would be evidence of an imitation effect on the attitudes of sisters. Another possible explanation is that parents urge sons to obtain more education. To maintain equity among the siblings, they then also urge their daughters to obtain more education.

POSSIBLE DIRECT TESTS OF HORMONAL TRANSFER

There is considerable further research to be done. It would be very useful to directly confirm that the hormonal environment experienced by a twin does depend on the wombmate's sex. Even if there were no evidence for the joint hypothesis of hormonal transfer and hormonal effects on behavior and morphology, showing that hormones transferred would be useful. If OS twins were known to develop in an unusual hormonal environment, but a certain aspect of their behavior, morphology, or disease risk did not depend on the co-twin's sex, this would be evidence that the aspect of behavior, morphology, or disease risk was not sensitive to prenatal hormone levels. This would be very important evidence relating to the role of prenatal hormones in the origin of sex differences.

There are several possible ways to study hormone transfer. One would be to examine the hormonal content of umbilical cords and placentas at birth. Such measurements have been made in singletons (Maccoby, Doering, Jacklin, & Kraemer, 1979), and have shown that umbilical cord hormone levels correlate with childhood behavior (Jacklin, Maccoby, & Doering, 1983). Another approach might use blood samples from stillborn fetuses. The latter might provide evidence on hormonal environments experienced during earlier stages of pregnancy.

It is possible to measure amniotic fluid hormones. For instance, tables in both Schindler (1982, pp. 55–57) and Belisle and Tulchinsky (1980, p. 174) showed that testosterone levels are much higher (especially in midpregnancy) in fluid surrounding males than in the fluid surrounding a female. The various amniotic fluid measurements are usually interpreted as indicating fetal levels. Amniotic measurements might tell more about the relative levels during the critical periods for sex differentiation than umbilical cord measurements would. While the risk of taking amniotic fluid samples precludes doing so only for research purposes, amniotic fluid sampling is common enough so that studies of OS twins should be possible. The mothers of DZ twins are typically older than singletons' mothers. Valid medical reasons exist for sampling the amniotic fluid of older mothers. Thus, finding twin samples may be easier than the number of twin pregnancies would suggest.

It would also be useful to have information on physical variables, since these are unlikely to be influenced by merely interacting with an OS twin after birth. A particularly interesting variable to study might be pelvic shape, since this is reported to vary considerably between males and females. Individuals with pelvises shaped like those of the opposite sex have been reported to resemble that sex more in behavior (see Eysenck & Wilson, 1979, pp. 37–39).

USING OS TWINS TO STUDY THE EFFECTS
OF PRENATAL HORMONES

Assuming that hormones do transfer between twins, this provides a whole new reason for studying twins. Not only can twins provide unique information about heritability; they can also provide evidence about the effects of prenatal sex hormones. There is evidence for prenatal hormonal effects on human behavior (see Hines, 1982; Levin, 1987, pp. 79–88; Halpern, 1992, pp. 110–120; Kemper, 1992; or Moir & Jessel, 1992 for reviews), but the topic remains highly controversial, with some believing all gender differences in behavior are due to differential socialization.

Inability to directly manipulate prenatal exposure to sex hormones has prevented the question from being definitely resolved for humans. Effects in experimental animals are well established. Some information has been obtained by studying children whose parents were given the nonsteroid estrogen diethylstilbestrol, which has been shown to have a masculinizing effect on behavior. However, for good reasons, this drug is no longer commonly given to pregnant mothers, and new subjects are no longer becoming available. Additional information has been obtained from observing children who have unusual hormonal environments due to various disease states (such as congenital adrenal hyperplasia), unusual karotypes (XO, XYY, etc.), or prenatal exposure to adrenal androgens (for a review, see Reinisch & Sanders, 1992; Walsh, 1995, pp. 122–133). However, suitable subjects are rare, and many of these conditions are diseases with multiple effects (not all of which are sex-hormone related). Thus, such evidence has not been decisive. Fortunately, OS twins are common and easily identified from birth records. Being a twin is not considered a disease state, and twins are broadly representative of the general population. Thus, the probability that OS twins are exposed to an unusual prenatal hormonal environment could provide a valuable new research tool.

Most twin studies have collected data only on SS twins. Even most of the large Scandinavian population-based twin registers have included only SS twins. This is unfortunate, since it would have been feasible to include OS twins. The first stage in constructing such registers is to search the birth record for children with the same surnames born on the same date and at the same place. This gives a first approximation to a list of all twins, including the OS ones. Even if the ultimate goal is a register of SS twins, the list of OS twins excluded should be retained for future use. A major expense in constructing a SS twin register is determining whether the twins are DZ or MZ. This expense is avoided for OS twins. They are always DZ.

Fortunately, one population-based twin register does include OS twins. This is the Finnish twin register, which was recently expanded to include 23,000 sets of twins born between 1958 and 1986 (Kaprio, Koskenvuo, & Rose, 1990). This register includes 7,922 OS twin pairs. This large sample could provide the basis for many useful OS twin studies.

In the standard genetically oriented twin study, no useful data are obtained if only one twin responds. Fortunately, even if only one twin participates in a hormonally motivated study, useful data are still obtained. Since such studies require only comparing twins with male co-twins to twins with female co-twins, the co-twin's refusal to participate does not make the responding twin's answers useless. In questionnaire studies, data from only one member of a pair should be retained. It may be useful for studies of prenatal hormones.

If a questionnaire is returned without any identifying marks, as may be done in studies of such sensitive topics as sexual behavior, asking the co-twin's sex is important. This permits examining possible hormonal effects. For instance, this would be a very useful question if OS twins were studied to determine if differing exposures to prenatal sex hormones affected the incidence of homosexuality, as is widely suspected (see Blyne & Parsons, 1993 for a review). Though study of OS twins might cast light on the widely discussed hypothesis that lower than normal exposure to prenatal sex hormones causes or contributes to homosexuality, the major published studies to date have used only SS twins (see Bailey & Pillard, 1991; Bailey, Pillard, Neale, & Agyei, 1993, for references). Fortunately, a study has been undertaken by Martin and Bailey using Australian OS twin data. Results are not yet published.

The possibility that twins provide an opportunity to study individuals raised in an unusual hormonal environment could assist in obtaining financing for twin studies. In many studies, prenatal hormonal hypothesizes could easily be included. This might make it possible to obtain sufficient additional funding to cover at least the added cost of including OS twins (especially since there would be no expenses for determining zygosity).

Breast cancer is a medical area receiving increased funding where the study of OS twins might be useful. One hypothesis is that prenatal estrogen exposure affects breast cancer risk (Ekbom et al., 1992). Breast cancer patients exhibit reversed cerebral asymmetry (Sandson, Wen, & LeMay, 1992). The most plausible explanation for this surprising finding (who would have guessed a brain–breast linkage?) is that prenatal hormones affect both cerebral asymmetry and vulnerability to breast cancer. A small study (Hsieh et al., 1992) found data consistent with the hypothesis that breast cancer risk was higher in twins, as Holm (1988) had found earlier.

If hormones do transfer between twins, this may influence the disease risks of OS twins. Having an OS twin could prove to be a risk factor for many diseases. So far the only disease for which it has been shown to be a risk factor is myopia, but there appears to have been little investigation of this possibility for other diseases. Since there are large numbers of OS twins, and membership in such a pair is readily determined, the possibility that it is a risk factor should be studied. Doing so could provide an additional source of financial support for twin studies.

Economic Policy Implications

A case has been made that hormones transferring from one fetus to another affects fetal development. In turn, this provides evidence that much of the observed differences between males and females are due to prenatal hormone exposure, a belief that is supported by many other lines of evidence. If this is so, it does have economic implications. Much of current policy has been based on the idea that males and females are biologically identical in all aspects (except for certain anatomical differences). If they are indeed biologically different due to prenatal hormone exposure, this is useful prior information that can be used for economic decision making. When two groups differ in their averages on some trait, Bayes's Theorem suggests the appropriate estimate for an individual is a weighted average of the mean for the individual's group and the measurements made on the individual (Miller, 1994b). Thus, for the mental traits where there appear to be sex differences, the test results should be adjusted for the individual's sex. Of course, different group means need not be due to biological causes.

CONCLUSION

There is reasonably strong evidence that hormones can transfer from one fetus to another. This is made plausible both on the basis of evidence from the medical literature of hormones crossing the placenta, and from various observations that OS twins differ from SS twins, as this chapter's hypothesis predicts. While social learning effects or other theories can explain some of the behavioral observations, some cannot. It is especially hard to explain the disappearance of the sex difference in dental asymmetry in opposite-sex twins by a social learning effect. The best explanation of all of the results in the literature, including the research reported here, is that hormones do transfer from one fetus to another and that prenatal hormone exposure does affect the organization of the brain and its ability to display male or female typical abilities and behaviors. Alternatives involve a series of ad hoc explanations for each study, and are much less parsimonious.

Consider abilities. Opposite-sex females had higher spatial abilities than same-sex females, and after practice these opposite-sex females were performing at the male level. This suggests that prenatal hormone exposure contributes to the sex differences in spatial, mathematical, and verbal abilities. In another study (Fischbein, 1978), female opposite-sex twins did better in sixth-grade mathematics than same-sex females, but worse in perceptual speed. Mathematics and spatial abilities are frequently correlated and appear to be somehow related. This suggests that prenatal hormone exposure contributes to the sex differences in both spatial and mathematical abilities.

Also striking is the effect observed in a large sample taking the British 11 Plus Exam in which females generally do better (Record, McKeown, & Edwards, 1970). Here, having shared the womb lowered the female performance (i.e., moved it toward the male performance). In all these cases, the most plausible explanation is an effect of prenatal exposure to testosterone from the male fetus on the female brain.

An effect on the male brain of prenatal hormones is provided by the study (Husen, 1959) of virtually all twin Swedish draftees from 1949 to 1952, where primary school grades were higher in all four subjects for the opposite-sex twins. Again, a hormonal effect is the most plausible explanation, though it is not clear whether it is acting on abilities or personality.

Other evidence exists for effects on personality. Koch (1966) found major reductions in sex differences in the opposite-sex twin six-year-olds in her sample. Especially striking was that the female member was usually the dominant one. Zazzo (1960) also found that OS females are more commonly dominant, even in the sixteen to twenty age range. This points to a powerful effect on personality, since one would normally expect males to be dominant in dyads. Resnick et al. (1993) showed that sensation seeking (a trait males are normally stronger in) is increased in OS females. Again, the most plausible interpretation of these facts are that prenatal exposure to hormones (probably testosterone) affects these aspects of personality, and that hormones can transfer prenatally.

Especially interesting is the author's research in which the attitudes of female twins in both Britain and Australia are more masculine as adults if they shared the womb with a male than if they shared it with a female. Added to the evidence that the pattern of abilities depends on the co-twin's sex and that sensation seeking varies with the co-twin's sex, this provides evidence that at least some male–female differences are indeed the result of prenatal hormone exposure, and hence not the result only of social conditioning. This has implications for economic and social policy, implying that society may have to adjust to some differences rather than seeking to eliminate them through social policy.

Examination of how twin behavior is affected by the sex of the co-twin provides a methodology for studying the effects of prenatal hormone exposure, especially exposure to male hormones. Since ethical considerations forbid directly manipulating prenatal hormonal exposure, this may be one of the few ethical ways to study the possible hormonal basis for behavioral sex differences.

Chapter 4

Effects of Perinatal and Puberal Steroid Imprinting on Sexual Behavior of Adult Rats

György Csaba

The maturation of hormone receptors runs parallel with the differentiation of the cell (Hubbert & Miller, 1974). For instance, binding capacity of insulin receptors in rat liver is low during the fetal period and gradually increases as the fetus approaches the time of birth (Margolis, Tanner, Seminara, & Taylor, 1990). Despite existing variations, receptor maturation is usually completed by the end of the first postnatal month (Blazquez, Rubalcava, Montesano, Orci, & Unger, 1976).

The maturation process is not spontaneous, as the first encounter of the receptor with the hormone in the perinatal critical period plays a decisive role. Without the presence of the appropriate hormone, the receptor is not able to accomplish its normal maturation and the resultant unmatured receptor is unable to transmit the information and have the cell evoke its normal response (Csaba & Nagy, 1985). Subsequently, the first encounter with the hormone leads to "hormonal imprinting," after which the binding capacity of receptors—mainly their density—increases, and consequently the magnitude of the cell's reaction is enhanced (Csaba, 1980; 1981; 1984; 1986; 1994). This means that hormonal imprinting is a necessity for receptor development, as the cell is waiting for the first encounter with the hormone (see Figure 4.1). Hormonal imprinting has an evolutionary basis and its importance in the phylogeny of receptors is worth noting (Csaba, 1985; 1994). In fact, the ontogenetic development of the receptors is a repetition of this evolutionary event, with a metazoan–physiological significance.

Figure 4.1
Diagram Showing Normal and Abnormal Hormonal Imprinting

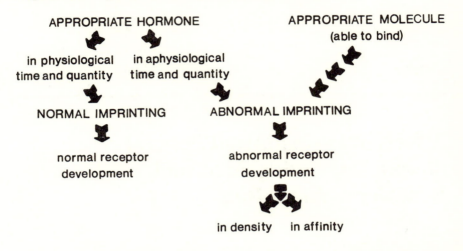

Normal imprinting develops if the appropriate hormone meets the developing receptor in
normal time and quantity. If time or quantity is not physiological, faulty imprinting develops as well, as in the case of the receptor's encounter with a molecule which is able to bind
to the receptor while its structure is different from that of the appropriate hormone.

The structure of receptors is determined at the gene level. Hormonal imprinting only fine-tunes and regulates the maximal number of receptors needed
for the perinatal adjustment of the receptor-bearing and hormone-producing
cells which contain the same genome. Once established, the effect of hormonal imprinting lasts throughout the life. This is due to the fact that the
imprinting information is transmitted to the progeny generations of the directly imprinted cell.

The perinatal period is the primary time for hormonal imprinting, though
the phenomenon may also take place later in life. In adulthood, imprinting
takes place during cell formation in mature organs or events like regeneration, which continuously produce new cells as the cells go through differentiation or dedifferentiation (Csaba, Inczefi-Gonda, & Dobozy, 1989; Csaba
& Inczefi-Gonda, 1990). Such phenomena imply that hormonal imprinting is
not an age-dependent but rather a developmental stage-dependent phenomenon (see Figure 4.2).

The development of immature receptors can be influenced during the
perinatal period. Molecules different from the appropriate hormone are able
to bind to the immature receptors and physiologically alter hormonal imprinting (see Figure 4.1), leading to unusual functional characteristics (Csaba,
1984; 1986; 1991; 1994). The misimprinting or faulty imprinting can be caused

Figure 4.2
Imprintability of Open Systems

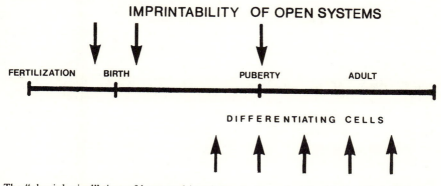

The "physiological" time of hormonal imprinting is the perinatal critical period. Nevertheless, in puberty and adulthood there are differentiating cells present which could be imprinted in a normal (by the appropriate hormone), or false (by foreign molecules) way.

by related hormones, by hormone analogues, or by molecules having a similar basic structure to that of the hormone. Faulty imprinting lasts as long as
normal physiological imprinting. In addition, the excess amount of an appropriate hormone can cause faulty imprinting during a critical period of development and differentiation.

Pituitary hormones belong to a hormone family. The alpha subunits of go-
nadotropic hormones (GTH) and thyrotropic hormone (TSH) are identical
except for a small difference in the amino acid sequence of the beta chains
accounting for their specificity (Ward, 1974). In adults, these hormones can
bind to each other's receptors without any harmful consequence (Amir,
Sullivan, & Ingbar, 1978; Azukizawa, Kutzman, Pekary, & Herschman, 1977).
However, in the perinatal critical period, a single GTH treatment dramatically decreases the binding capacity of TSH receptors for life, as a single
TSH treatment does with GTH receptors (Csaba & Nagy, 1976; 1978). Similarly, neonatal treatment with a synthetic steroid hormone (dexamethasone)
causes a lifelong decrease in thymocytic glucocorticoid binding (Inczefi-Gonda
& Csaba, 1985). There is also a cross-talk between the receptor and hormone
families. For example, neonatal sexual-steroid treatment decreases glucocorticoid receptor binding capacity (density) (Inczefi-Gonda, Csaba, & Dobozy,
1986). This means that the perinatal adjustment of receptor and hormone is a
well-balanced phenomenon, though easily disturbed and manipulated by a
single meeting with a foreign (but able to bind) molecule (Csaba, 1991), which
can cause a faulty (false) imprinting. Therefore, it seems to be very reasonable to study the effects of abnormal (faulty) imprinting in such complex
systems as the development and differentiation of sex, since in previous stud-

ies neonatal effects of sexual hormones on adult sexual behavior were observed (Barraclough, 1967; Döhler, 1978; Ellis, 1996b). Barraclough (1967) was the first to demonstrate that perinatal manipulation in the quality or quantity of sexual hormones can alter the development of sexual behavior. Since then, a mass of publications have searched to uncover the causes of this phenomenon. Many experiments have demonstrated that perinatal sexual hormone treatments have long-lasting morphological, functional, and receptorial influences on the sexual organs (Bern, Gorski, & Kawashima, 1973; Bern, Jones, Mori, & Young, 1975; Csaba, 1980; 1981; Campbell, 1983; Iguchi, 1992; Sato et al., 1994; Gibson, Roberts, & Evans, 1991; Gray Nelson, Sakai, Eitmann, Steed, & McLahlan, 1994; Arriaza, Mena, & Tchernitchin, 1989). Such observations, demonstrating the presence of imprinting-like phenomena, have called attention to the possibility of a broader scope of perinatal hormone-like factors participating in the provocation of imprinting in mammals.

This chapter will present evidence of a broad spectrum of synthetic steroids and steroid-like molecules affecting perinatal and puberal imprinting on sexual behavior in adult rats. The neonatal influence of molecules affecting the steroid receptor superfamily on the sexual parameters (hormone receptor, hormone level, and sexual behavior) will also be discussed.

EFFECT OF PERINATAL STEROID TREATMENT ON THE STEROID RECEPTOR SUPERFAMILY IN ADULTS

Diethylstilbestrol (DES), a synthetic steroid employed to preserve endangered pregnancies, can cause malignant transformations in the adolescent progeny of mothers treated with the substance during pregnancy (Herbst, Uhlfelder, & Postkanzer, 1971; Herbst, Postkanzer, Robboy, Fridlander, & Scully, 1975). In many countries the administration of this substance was forbidden for this reason. Allylestrenol (AE), a new synthetic steroid without such adverse effects, has been introduced to replace DES. However, experiments in rats demonstrated that a single neonatal treatment with either DES or allylestrenol dramatically decreases the number of uterine estrogen receptors in adults (see Figure 4.3) by as much as 66 percent or 50 percent, respectively (Csaba, Inczefi-Gonda, & Dobozy, 1986). This means that perinatal treatment with these synthetic hormones causes a faulty imprinting and this is manifested in reduced estrogen receptor numbers. Later it was clarified that even excessive amounts of naturally occurring sex steroids, such as estradiol or progesterone, can also provoke faulty imprinting with the same consequences brought about by the synthetic hormones (Csaba & Inczefi-Gonda, 1992b).

These observations are in harmony with research on the morphological and developmental effects of perinatal steroid treatments (Bern et al., 1973; Bern et al., 1975; Campbell, 1983; Iguchi, 1992; Sato et al., 1994; Gibson et al., 1991; Arriaza et al., 1989). Prenatal and neonatal sex hormone treatments influence the receptors of not only their own, but also other members of the steroid receptor superfamily (structurally similar receptors for the binding of steroid hormones,

Figure 4.3
Receptor Kinetic Analysis of the Effect of Neonatal DES or AE Treatment

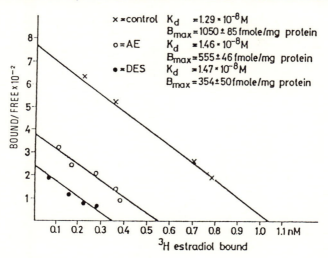

Source: Reprinted from *Acta Physiologica Hungarica* 67, by G. Csaba, Á. Inczefi-Gonda, and O. Dobozy. (1986). Hormonal imprinting by steroids: A single neonatal treatment with diethylstilbestrol or allylestrenol gives rise to a lasting decrease in the number of rat uterine receptors, pp. 207–212. Reprinted with permission.

Single neonatal diethylstilbestrol or allylestrenol treatment causes the reduction of adult's uterine estradiol receptor density to a third or a half, respectively (Scatchard plots).

thyroid hormones, vitamins A and D, and peroxisome proliferators). Allylestrenol treatment, for example, reduced the number of thymic glucocorticoid receptors (Inczefi-Gonda, Csaba, & Dobozy, 1986). This called attention to a multireceptorial effect of this substance (see Figure 4.4). As enzymes are also ligand-binding structures (like receptors), there is a possibility of enzyme imprinting. Theoretically, if molecules similar to the enzyme's substrate are given in the critical period, this could influence the enzyme function throughout life. In fact, microsomal enzymes are influenced by this imprinting for life (Bagley & Hayes, 1980; Csaba, Szeberényi, & Dobozy, 1986; Shapiro & Bitar, 1991; Karabélyos, Szeberényi, & Csaba, 1994). This appears to be a very important phenomenon, considering that these enzymes have a significant role in the metabolism and transformation of steroids (see Figure 4.5).

Aromatic hydrocarbons have a steroid-like structure. Their Ah receptor was earlier believed to belong to the steroid receptor superfamily (Gustafsson, Carlstedt-Duke, & Poellinger, 1987; Poellinger, Gottlicher, & Gustafsson, 1992). Recently it has been shown that this receptor has a helix–loop–helix structure which is different from that of the steroid receptors (Hankinson, 1994). Likewise, as a transcription factor, the Ah receptor can affect the cellular function at the gene level. The aromatic hydrocarbons with steroid structure can disturb the normal imprinting of steroid receptors. Dioxin (TCDD),

Figure 4.4
Receptor Kinetic Analysis of the Effect of Neonatal Allylestrenol Treatment

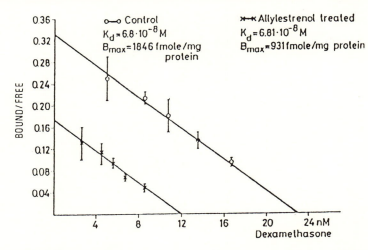

Source: Reprinted from *Acta Physiologica Hungarica* 67, by Á. Inczefi-Gonda, G. Csaba, and O. Dobozy. (1986). Reduced thymic glucocorticoid reception in adult male rats prenatally treated with allylestrenol, pp. 27–29. Reprinted with permission.

Single neonatal allylestrenol treatment causes the dramatic reduction of thymic dexamethasone receptor numbers. This means that there are overlaps on related receptors during hormonal imprinting.

after a single neonatal treatment, decreased the binding capacity of glucocorticoid receptors (Csaba, Mag, Inczefi-Gonda, & Szeberényi, 1991). Benzpyrene did the same with early or late prenatal or neonatal treatment (Csaba & Inczefi-Gonda, 1984; 1992a; Csaba et al., 1991). In addition, a neonatal treatment with benzpyrene strongly decreased the estradiol binding of uterine estrogen receptors (see Figure 4.6) (Csaba & Inczefi-Gonda, 1993b). The effect of benzpyrene is so strong that the receptor's binding capacity is even reduced in those animals whose mothers had been treated with it during lactation, thereby exposing the offspring through breast-feeding (Csaba & Inczefi-Gonda, 1994).

With regard to the effect of allylestrenol and benzpyrene on glucocorticoid or estrogen receptors, there is essentially no significant difference. However, there are molecules acting at the level of the steroid receptor superfamily which discriminate between the receptors, influencing one and not influencing others. Neonatal treatment with triiodothyronine (T_3) significantly increased (not decreased) the thymus glucocorticoid receptor's binding capacity, while there is no change in the binding capacity of thymic or uterine estrogen receptors (Csaba & Inczefi-Gonda, 1996). This is interesting. Though T_3 receptors belong to the steroid receptor superfamily (Evans, 1988), T_3 itself has no steroid structure. The difference is attributable to the acceptor also, considering recent data that there is no response to glucocorticoids in the ab-

Figure 4.5
Effect of Steroids As Ligands to Different but Correlative Systems

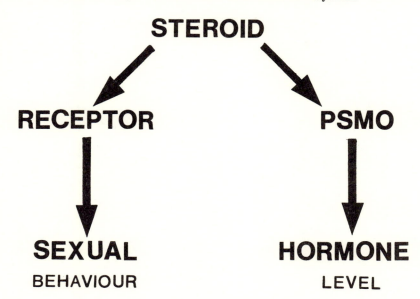

Steroids can influence the development of steroid receptors and by this the sexual behavior as well, as in the liver the microsomal enzyme systems (PSMO). This causes differences in adult sexual hormone levels.

sence of T_3 or T_3 receptor (Leers, Steiner, Rankowitz, & Muller, 1994). Conversely, though T_3 binds to the estrogen responsive element with a high affinity, it inhibits estrogen dependent activation (Glass, Holloway, Devary, & Rosenfeld, 1988).

Neonatal treatment (imprinting) with vitamin A (retinol) significantly increased the density of thymic glucocorticoid receptors and the affinity of uterine estrogen receptors measured at adult age. This means that the effect to the receptors was different in the two organs, however the binding capacity was increased alike (Gaál & Csaba, 1997).

The peroxysome proliferator activated receptor, which binds, for example, lipid level lowering drugs, herbicides, and so on, also belongs to the steroid receptor superfamily (Green, 1992; Issemann & Green, 1990); however, a molecule (clofibrate) bound to this does not significantly influence the glucocorticoid or estrogen receptors (Csaba, Inczefi-Gonda, Karabélyos, & Pap, 1995). This also seems to be interesting, as the ligands of this receptor are not steroids and are also heterogeneous (Issemann & Green, 1990). Considering the effect of aromatic hydrocarbons having a receptor structurally different from the steroid receptor superfamily, this demonstrates that the ligand's steroid structure is more important in the development of imprinting than the affiliation of the receptor.

Figure 4.6
Receptor Kinetic Analysis of the Effect of Neonatal Benzpyrene Treatment

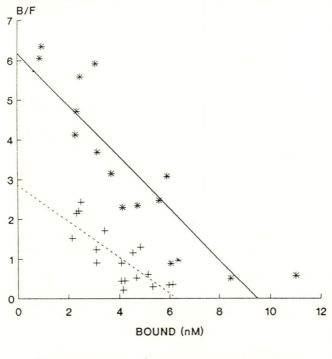

Neonatal benzpyrene treatment reduces the uterine estrogen receptor number in adult rats. This means that a steroid-like molecule with cytosol receptors of different forms can influence durably a member of the steroid receptor superfamily.

Another interesting phenomenon was produced in the case of synchronous imprinting with more than one material. Combined neonatal imprinting with allylestrenol, benzpyrene, vitamin A, and D_3 significantly increased the thymic glucocorticoid receptor density of male and female animals and decreased the receptor affinity in females (Csaba & Inczefi-Gonda, 1997). The results demonstrated the dominance of the positively influencing retinol in the case of the combined imprinting.

EFFECTS OF PERINATAL STEROID TREATMENTS ON HORMONE LEVELS OF ADULT RATS

One single neonatal allylestrenol treatment significantly increases (practically doubles) the testosterone level of adult male rats (Pap & Csaba, 1995a). At the same time, the progesterone level is decreased. Considering these facts, it is obvious that either the hormone producing cells are influencing the neonatal synthetic hormone treatment or the system which is responsible for the transformation of steroid hormones is involved. Since it is very difficult to imagine the genetic change of hormone-producing cells by a simple hormonal effect, the imprinting of the microsomal (polysubstrate monooxygenase; PSMO) system seems to be likely. The imprintability of this system by neonatal influences is well known and the effects of this imprinting last for life.

Neonatal and prenatal allylestrenol treatment can influence the adult hormone level in the same way. Treatments of female rats on Days 15, 17, and 19 of their pregnancy showed that the male offspring's testosterone level was higher and the female offspring's progesterone level was lower than those of the controls (Pap & Csaba, 1995b). This means that the imprintable microsomal system is sensitive during pregnancy; however, its degree of maturity is different from that of the neonatal one providing sexual differences (Conney, 1986). This is manifested in the differences of progesterone level after prenatal or neonatal treatments while the tendency of testosterone levels are the same.

Allylestrenol treatment in the adult rat does not influence hormone levels after one week. Repeated allylestrenol treatments of prenatally or neonatally allylestrenol treated animals in adult age abolished the early effects or at least lowered the values under their control (Pap & Csaba, 1995b). This means that the reaction of perinatally treated animals is changed relative to the untreated ones.

This changed reaction is manifested in the animals treated with allylestrenol neonatally and with benzpyrene when adult. One and three weeks after adult benzpyrene treatment in neonatally nontreated male animals there is no change in the testosterone level compared to the untreated controls. The testosterone level of neonatally allylestrenol treated males is also normal one week after benzpyrene treatment, but enormously elevated (almost threefold of the control) after three weeks (Pap & Csaba, 1994). The difference between the results at one and three weeks could be explained by the function of the microsomal enzyme system as to the time it needs for the transformation of benzpyrene (see Figure 4.6).

EFFECT OF PERINATAL TREATMENT ON THE
SEXUAL BEHAVIOR OF ADULT RATS

Prenatal treatment (i.e., days 15, 17, and 19 with the synthetic steroid hormone allylestrenol) dramatically decreases the sexual activity of adult female rats and increases the sexual activity of male rats (Csaba, Karabélyos, & Dalló, 1993). A three-time treatment from birth to day 7 decreases the sexual activity of females and males alike (see Figures 4.7, 4.8, and 4.9). Figures 4.7 and 4.8 clearly demonstrate the decreased "libido" of females as an effect of the faulty imprinting.

If the prenatally allylestrenol treated females were castrated and treated with sexual hormones in adulthood (hormone-induced sexual behavior), their

Figure 4.7
Meyerson Index of Female Rats

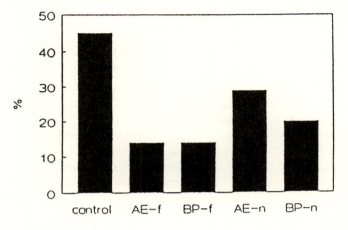

Neonatal (n) or fetal (f) allylestrenol or benzpyrene treatment (imprinting) significantly reduced the Meyerson index (the female's positive response to the first mounting).

Figure 4.8
Lordosis Quotient of Female Rats

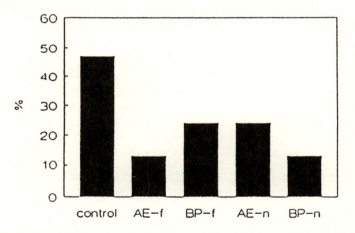

Neonatal (n) or fetal (f) allylestrenol or benzpyrene treatment significantly reduced the lordosis quotient (a female's number of positive response to ten mountings).

sexual activity would not be significantly lower relative to the allylestrenol nontreated controls (Karabélyos, Csaba, & Dalló, 1994). In the case of a similar treatment of newborns, there was no difference in hormone-induced sexual behavior. Treatment of adult female rats with contraceptive steroids signifi-

Figure 4.9
Sexual Behavior of Male Adult Animals Prenatally Treated with Allylestrenol or Benzpyrene

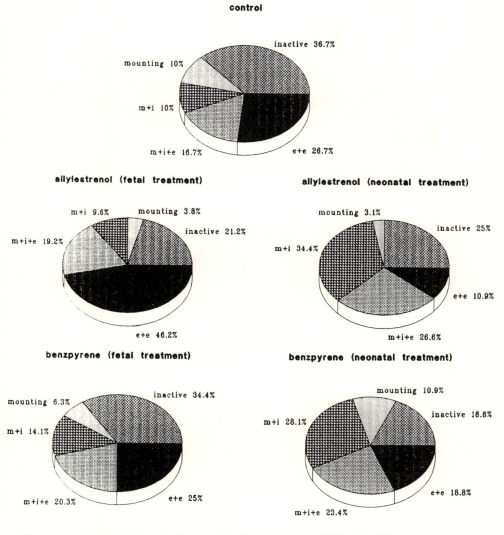

Key: m = mounting; i = intromission; e = ejaculation; e + e = multiple ejaculation.

Fetal treatment with allylestrenol caused a profound increase in sexual activity in contrast to the case of neonatal treatment, when the sexual activity decreased. Benzpyrene was ineffective in males.

cantly reduced their receptivity. This diminished receptivity was not influenced by the neonatal allylestrenol treatment (Karabélyos, Dalló, & Csaba, 1994).

Figure 4.10
Sexual Behavior of Vitamin D₃ Treated Male Rats

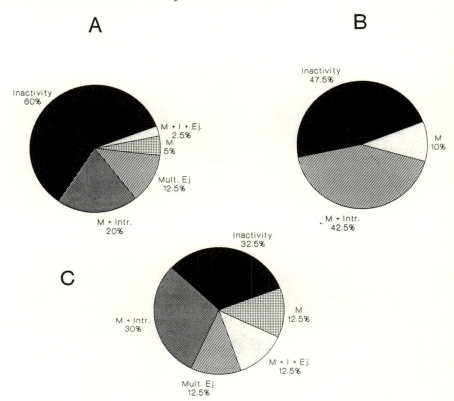

Key: m = mounting; i = intromission; e = ejaculation; e + e = multiple ejaculation.

In adult male rats neonatally treated with 2.5 µg vitamin D₃ (B), mounting and intromission is higher than control (A), however there is no ejaculation at all. In the case of 250 µg treatment (C), there is less inactivity and more ejaculations than in the control.

Prenatal or neonatal benzpyrene treatment profoundly decreased the sexual activity of female rats (see Figures 4.7 and 4.8) (Csaba et al., 1993). In the experiments studying hormone-induced sexual behavior, the prenatal benzpyrene treatment significantly decreased the receptivity of female offspring. However, significantly reduced sexual activity of contraceptive-treated adult rats is not influenced by the neonatal benzpyrene treatment. The peroxysome proliferator activated receptor bound clofibrate only moderately influenced the sexual behavior of males and females (Csaba et al., 1995).

Vitamin D₃ is an endogenous hormone with a steroid structure. Neonatal treatment with only 2.5 µg of vitamin D₃ can completely inhibit the ejaculation of males and slightly influence other sexual activities (see Figure 4.10) (Mirzahosseini, Karabélyos, Dobozy, & Csaba, 1996). A treatment of 250 µg

Figure 4.11
Meyerson Index and Lordosis Quotient of Vitamin D₃ Treated Female Rats

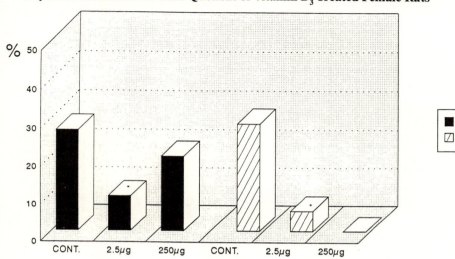

Source: Reprinted from *Human & Experimental Toxicology* 15, by S. Mirzahosseini, Cs. Karabélyos, O. Dobozy, and G. Csaba. (1996). Changes in sexual behaviour of adult male and female rat neonatally treated with vitamin D₃, pp. 573–576. Reprinted with permission of Macmillan Press Limited and the authors.

In the case of neonatal treatment with 2.5 µg vitamin D₃, both indexes decreased significantly. After 250 µg treatment, there was no response at all to the first mounting of the male.

*Significant difference at $p > 0.01$ compared to the respective control.

vitamin D₃ influenced sexual desire and ejaculation alike. In females, the sexual activity was depressed by both doses (see Figure 4.11). Comparing the results of clofibrate and vitamin D₃, the importance of steroid structure and not the affiliation of the receptor is again emphasized.

Vitamin A is a nutrient factor which has receptors among the members of the steroid receptor superfamily. Neonatal imprinting with vitamin A dramatically reduced the sexual activity of adult male rats (Csaba & Gaál, 1997). Considering also the results gained by vitamin D treatment, this means that not the structure of the vitamin but the influence on a member of the steroid receptor superfamily is responsible for the false imprinting.

EFFECT OF STEROIDS GIVEN TO ADOLESCENT RATS ON THE RECEPTORS AND BEHAVIOR

The synthetic anabolic steroid nandrolone is used as a therapeutic in medicine and as a doping substance in sports. The effect of nandrolone on thymic glucocorticoid receptors and on uterine estrogen receptors has been studied (Csaba & Inczefi-Gonda, 1993a). After a treatment at six weeks and measurement at twelve weeks, the density of both receptors decreased in females

Figure 4.12
Meyerson Index of Adult Female Rats Treated with Steroids at Puberty

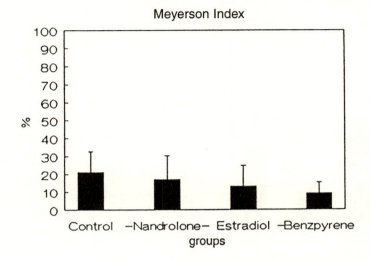

Source: Reprinted from G. Csaba and Cs. Karabélyos, Pubertal benzpyrene exposition decreases durably the sexual activity of the adult male and female rats, *Hormone and Metabolic Research* 27 (1995): 279–282, Georg Thieme Verlag, Stuttgart.

There is a nonsignificant decrease in the Meyerson index of adult rats.

with no noticeable change in the density of glucocorticoid receptors in males. A single treatment with benzpyrene of five-week-old male and female rats resulted in significantly lower sexual activity in three-month-old animals (see Figures 4.12, 4.13, and 4.14) (Csaba & Karabélyos, 1995).

Nandrolone, effective in influencing receptor density, is almost neutral in influencing sexual behavior. Benzpyrene in males completely inhibits ejaculation (see Figure 4.14). These data suggest that the imprinting for sexual indices can be fulfilled not only perinatally but even later in life.

CONCLUSIONS

Sexual development is a gradual process. Determined first by sex chromosomes, the gonads differentiate and in turn determine the development of the inner and outer sexual organs. However, sexual behavior is perinatally adjusted by steroid hormones and is under the control of continuously or cyclically produced trophic hormones. The final stage of sexual development begins at puberty.

Hormonal imprinting is the general phenomenon pointing to the significance of the first encounter of the developing receptor and a predetermined hormone. Hormonal imprinting has significance for all types of hormones (amino acid, polypeptide, and steroid), and is needed for future interactions of hormone and receptor. Since hormones travel throughout the body and receptors are

Figure 4.13
Lordosis Quotient of Adult Female Rats Treated with Steroids at Puberty

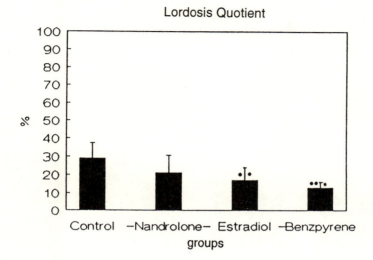

Lordosis Quotient

Source: Reprinted from G. Csaba and Cs. Karabélyos, Pubertal benzpyrene exposition decreases durably the sexual activity of the adult male and female rats, *Hormone and Metabolic Research* 27 (1995): 279–282, Georg Thieme Verlag, Stuttgart.

There is a significant decrease in the lordosis quotient (sexual activity) in the adult rats after estrogen or benzpyrene treatment at puberty.

merged in a hormone-containing fluid, hormones can influence the receptors of several organs. This is also valid in the case of receptors meeting with foreign molecules (faulty imprinting), either related hormones or environmental pollutants, which are similar to the appropriate hormone. From the point of view of sexuality, this means that not only steroid hormones but also structures similar to them, or molecules not similar to steroid hormones but able to bind to a member of the steroid receptor superfamily, can interact with different developing receptors. The effects are as obviously varied as the molecules provoking them. From this aspect, the perinatal adjustment of sexuality observed by Barraclough (1967) and studied by others is only part of the whole mechanism working for the homeostasis of the organism.

Our experiments have mentioned a broader spectrum of the steroid effects in the perinatal critical period. Either molecules of steroid type or molecules which can bind to a member of the steroid receptor superfamily were used. All these molecules have some practical significance from a medical or a public-health viewpoint. Allylestrenol (Gestanon) was and is used as a successor of diethylstilbestrol (DES) for preserving endangered pregnancies. Vitamin D_3 used to be systematically given to pregnant and lactating women as well as infants. Nandrolone is used as a health restorer, as a treatment for osteoporosis, and as a doping substance in sports (Adami et al., 1991; Kuipers,

Figure 4.14
Sexual Parameters of Male Rats Treated with Steroids at Puberty

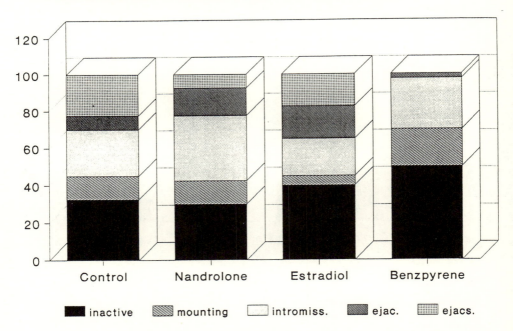

Source: Reprinted from G. Csaba and Cs. Karabélyos, Pubertal benzpyrene exposition decreases durably the sexual activity of the adult male and female rats, *Hormone and Metabolic Research* 27 (1995): 279–282, Georg Thieme Verlag, Stuttgart.

Nandrolone treatment at puberty significantly decreased multiple ejaculation, and benzpyrene treatment practically eradicated ejaculation in adults.

Wijnen, Hartgens, & Willems, 1991). Clofibrate is a representative of peroxysome proliferators; hence, it has a lipid-lowering effect. Benzpyrene, one of the aromatic hydrocarbons, is the most frequently occurring environmental pollutant. This means that the results obtained by the use of these materials can be projected to human medicine and may serve as models for the general steroid effects on sex.

It is worth mentioning that the effect of perinatal imprinting is long-lasting. This means that the change (adjustment) evoked perinatally can be observed during the entire lifespan. Whenever the manipulation of imprinting occurs, its effects and presence can be shown anytime during the lifespan of the animal. In addition, a single treatment (meeting) with the imprinter in a dose similar to that used in human therapy is enough for this lifelong effect. This unequivocally demonstrates the sensitivity of the system and the crucial requirement of the cells for appropriate imprinting.

The experiments demonstrate that the critical period is present not only perinatally but later as well. This is true whenever cells are differentiating, as continously exhibited by uterine epithelium, by lymphoid tissue, and by other haemopoietic organs. In these nonperinatal critical periods not all of the steroid-like molecules can provoke imprinting and not all the organs containing steroid receptors can react; yet many are able to respond to the imprinting provoking agent. In this case, sometimes a snippet of the human dose (e.g., in case of nandrolone, which is used for doping in a high dose) could provoke an intensive and long-lasting reaction. The experiments demonstrate that not only hypothalamic receptors are involved in a perinatal (or later) steroid effect, but the whole steroid receptor system is involved. Simultaneously, the microsomal enzyme system is imprinted, which also influences the actual effective level of the steroid. The systems reciprocally influence each other, and by this the variability of sexual behavior and its accessories become influenced.

Analyzing the medical significance of the experiments a question is raised for the possibility of faulty imprinting in human beings by the materials used in the animal experiments (or similar materials). In addition, there is also a possibility of altered reaction provoked by giving similar substances to the human adults as imprinted cases. This could happen when prenatally or perinatally steroid treated (e.g., for saving endangered pregnancy, giving steroids as surfactants, or giving vitamin D_3) persons take steroid-like substances for medical purposes (contraceptives) or as environmental pollutant (benzpyrene). In these cases, the physician has to consider the possibility of perinatal or pubertal imprinting in our rather contaminated environment.

Such effects are sometimes potentiated. For instance, an infant gets benzpyrene from the air and through breast milk, especially if the mother smokes, so it is quite probable that benzpyrene is introduced to the organism over and over. In our experiments, benzpyrene, as a steroid-like material, always affects the receptors in each period of life. This shows the outstanding importance of this pollutant and its deleterious effect on the activity of sexual and other steroid hormone receptors.

Systematic changes as a consequence of faulty imprinting on the basis of the action–reaction principle can influence sexual orientation and sex-typical behavior. The number and quantity of chemicals causing faulty imprinting shows a continuously increasing tendency, which also poses the possibility of an increase in aberrations.

ACKNOWLEDGMENT

This work was supported by the National Research Fund (OTKA, T-017775) and by the Scientific Research Council, Ministry of Welfare (T11-708), Hungary.

PART II

NEUROLOGICAL MANIFESTATIONS OF PERINATAL SEXUAL DIFFERENTIATION

Chapter 5

Organizational and Activational Effects of Dopamine on Male Sexual Behavior

Elaine M. Hull, Daniel S. Lorrain, Jianfang Du, Leslie Matuszewich, Daniel Bitran, J. Ken Nishita, and Laura L. Scaletta

This chapter will summarize evidence that the neurotransmitter dopamine can affect both the developmental organization and the adolescent/adult activation of male rat sexual behavior. Furthermore, these effects are at least partially independent of hormonal influence. Specifically, evidence will be presented that (1) dopaminergic drugs administered perinatally can affect sexual differentiation without altering fetal or adult testosterone levels; (2) dopaminergic drugs, even in the absence of testosterone, can activate male-typical behavior in adult rats; (3) dopamine is released in the medial preoptic area (MPOA) of the basal forebrain of male rats before and during copulation; and (4) MPOA dopamine release in the presence of a receptive female depends on the recent, but not concurrent, presence of testosterone.

It is a central dogma of our field that testosterone and its metabolites masculinize mammalian brains and genitals during early development and activate male-typical behavior in adulthood (e.g., Ellis, 1996b, p. 36). The sex-determining region on the Y chromosome (Sry) of male mammals encodes a transcription factor, testis-determining factor (TDF), which induces the formation of testes from the primordial gonads and stimulates the secretion of testosterone (Gubbay et al., 1990; Sinclair et al., 1990). In male rats, a surge of testosterone on embryonic Days 18 and 19 (Weisz & Ward, 1980) is thought to initiate processes of masculinization and defeminization of numerous brain structures, including those that regulate neuroendocrine control and reproductive behavior. Evidence for the central roles of gonadal hormones in these processes is extensive, and will not be reviewed here. However, the assumption that hormonal influences are necessary and sufficient to organize the substrates and to activate male-typical behavior has recently been questioned (e.g., Hull, Nishita, Bitran, & Dalterio, 1984; Pilgrim & Hutchison, 1994; Reisert & Pilgrim, 1991; Scaletta & Hull, 1990).

PERINATAL MANIPULATION OF DOPAMINE RECEPTORS

In particular, the neurotransmitter dopamine may also have both organizational and activational effects on male rat sexual behavior. Dopamine agonists have long been known to enhance sexual function of men (Barbeau, 1969; Bowers, van Woert, & Davis, 1971; Lal, 1988; Pierini & Nusimovich, 1981) and of male rats (Malmnas, 1973; reviewed in Bitran & Hull, 1987; Melis & Argiolas, 1995). Accordingly, some years ago we began to question whether perinatal treatments with dopaminergic drugs could modify the sexual differentiation of rats (Hull et al., 1984). To test this idea, we initially used a perinatal regimen that had been shown to affect dopamine receptors and behavioral sensitivity to dopaminergic drugs in adulthood. Rosengarten and Friedhoff (1979) had administered the dopamine antagonist haloperidol, a common antipsychotic drug, to mother rats during pregnancy or lactation. Haloperidol administered only during gestation decreased the numbers of dopamine receptors in the brains of the adult offspring and also decreased their behavioral sensitivity to dopamine agonists. On the other hand, postnatal treatment with haloperidol, via lactation, resulted in increased numbers of dopamine receptors and in supersensitivity of behavioral responses to dopamine agonists. Because dopamine antagonists had been reported to impair the sexual behavior of male rats (Malmnas, 1973), we hypothesized that decreased numbers of dopamine receptors in adulthood, due to prenatal haloperidol, would also impair sexual behavior. Furthermore, since dopamine agonists had increased copulatory behaviors in male rats (Malmnas, 1973), we also hypothesized that increased dopamine receptors, due to postnatal haloperidol, would enhance sexual behavior.

We treated mother rats with either haloperidol or saline from Day 7 of gestation until postnatal Day 21 (Hull et al., 1984). Half the pups from each litter were cross-fostered to a mother given the opposite treatment, thereby forming four groups: those receiving haloperidol only prenatally, only postnatally, both prenatally and postnatally, or neither. Weekly copulation tests began on postnatal Day 65. As we expected, males treated prenatally with haloperidol showed fewer ejaculations than did saline/saline controls (Figure 5.1). Unexpectedly, the postnatally treated animals also showed impairments on the first test; however, on Tests 2 and 3 the postnatally treated animals were not different from controls.

The decrease in ejaculations reflected primarily a decrease in the number of males that were able to ejaculate within thirty minutes after the first intromission;

Figure 5.1
Effects of Pre- and/or Postnatal Haloperidol on Number of Ejaculations per Test

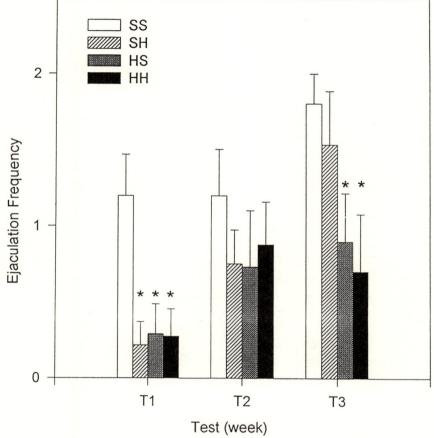

Source: From data presented in Hull, Nishita, Bitran, & Dalterio (1984).

there was no difference in the number of tests on which an intromission occurred. Prenatal haloperidol-treated males ejaculated on only about 50 percent of all tests in which an intromission occurred, whereas postnatal haloperidol-treated males ejaculated on about 70 percent of such tests and control males ejaculated on almost 90 percent of those tests. Therefore, the primary deficit was in the ability to elicit an ejaculation, rather than in sexual arousal. There were no differences in female-typical behavior of the female littermates, or in body weights or maturational milestones of any animals. Furthermore, maternal behavior could not have been a factor in the demasculinization, since males treated both prenatally and postnatally with haloperidol showed deficits similar to those of males treated prenatally with haloperidol but cross-fostered to saline treated mothers at birth. There were also no differences in testosterone levels of male fetuses at Day 18 of gestation, the day of the major testosterone surge. Therefore, (1) blocking dopamine receptors at any time during early development demasculinized male sexual behavior, and (2) this demasculinization did not result from decreases in testosterone levels or body weight, or from retarded development or poor maternal behavior.

Since blocking dopamine receptors either pre- or postnatally had demasculinized sexual behavior, we next tested whether perinatal stimulation of dopamine receptors with the dopamine agonist apomorphine might enhance adult male sexual behavior (Hull et al., 1984). For contrast, we administered the dopamine synthesis blocker alpha-methyl tyrosine to a second group of dams. A third group received the combination of apomorphine and alpha-methyl tyrosine; control rats received saline. We predicted that stimulation of dopamine receptors with apomorphine would enhance masculine development, and that blocking dopamine synthesis would impair it. The effects of the combined agonist and synthesis inhibitor were expected to cancel out and have little effect on adult sexual behavior. In order to test whether improvement across tests was due to experience or to time since drug treatment, half the males in each group began weekly tests on Day 60, and the other half began on Day 90. There were no differences between the two series, and they were combined for statistical analysis. As in the perinatal haloperidol experiment, all drug treatments impaired ejaculatory ability on at least one test. There was a decrease in the number of ejaculations by all drug-treated males on the second and third tests (Figure 5.2). As in the haloperidol experiment, this decrease reflected fewer tests on which ejaculation occurred within thirty minutes after the first intromission (saline, 93%; apomorphine, 67%; alpha-methyl tyrosine, 55%; combination, 67%). In addition, those drug-treated animals that did ejaculate on Test 3 had longer latencies than controls. Again, there were no differences in body weights, developmental milestones, or female-typical behavior among groups.

We also measured adult testosterone levels in separate groups of animals that were given prenatal and postnatal treatments with haloperidol, apomorphine, or alpha-methyl tyrosine that were identical to those that produced behavioral deficits, to test whether the behavioral impairment of drug-treated males might be related to low levels of the hormone at the time of testing. However, no drug treatment produced significant alterations compared to controls at sixty days of age. In fact, the perinatal haloperidol-treated group had slightly (nonsignificantly) higher levels of testosterone than did saline-treated controls. Therefore, it is likely that these dopaminergic drugs produced a direct change in neural development, rather than acting simply by altering hormone levels.

A subsequent study of dopaminergic influence on sex differentiation reported somewhat similar results (Gonzalez & Leret, 1992). In that experiment, a relatively large dose of dopamine (2 mg/kg in 1 µl, or about 10 to 15 µg per pup) was

Figure 5.2
Effects of Dopaminergic Drugs, Administered both Pre- and Postnatally, on Number of Ejaculations per Test

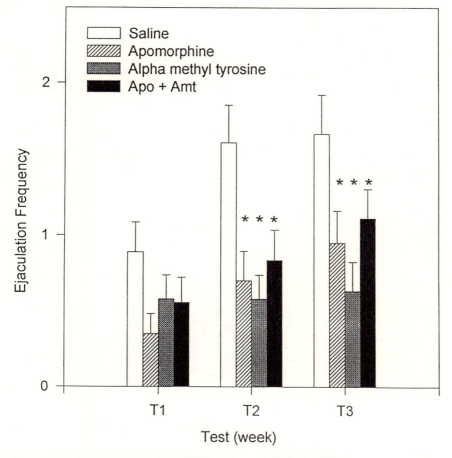

Source: From data presented in Hull, Nishita, Bitran, & Dalterio (1984).

administered intraventricularly on postnatal Day 1. Dopamine-treated males, tested in adulthood, showed fewer mounts and intromissions in a ten-minute test, compared to saline-treated animals. On the other hand, adult testosterone levels were actually higher in the dopamine-treated males than in controls. Therefore, the impairment of sexual behavior could not be attributed to a decrease in testosterone levels in adulthood. An injection of norepinephrine in a dose even higher than the dose of dopamine (20 mg/kg in 1 μl on postnatal Day 1) also increased testosterone levels in adulthood, but failed to affect sexual behavior. Therefore, the behavioral impairment produced by dopamine administration probably did not result from osmotic or other nonspecific effects of the injection, or from a decrease in adult testosterone levels.

SEX DIFFERENCES IN DOPAMINE NEURONS

These studies suggest that perinatal manipulation of dopaminergic systems can exert nonhormonal organizational effects on neurons that are destined to control male sexual behavior. There have also been reports that embryonic dopaminergic neurons can develop sex-differentiated morphology and function in the absence of sex steroids (Reisert & Pilgrim, 1991). *In vitro* cultures of midbrain or diencephalic (posterior part of forebrain) dopaminergic neurons, taken from Day 14 fetuses, were maintained for up to thirteen days. Because these cultures were obtained before gonadal differentiation and the resultant testosterone surge, hormones could not have mediated any differences that might be observed. Diencephalic neurons from female fetuses were smaller, but had greater activity of tyrosine hydroxylase, the rate-limiting enzyme in dopamine synthesis, than did similar neurons from their male littermates. Female diencephalic neurons also had higher levels of dopamine and greater dopamine uptake than did comparable neurons from males. On the other hand, midbrain neurons from female fetuses had lower dopamine uptake but were more numerous than neurons from male fetuses. Therefore, there were region-specific and sex-specific differences in dopaminergic neurons *in vitro* in the absence of any hormonal treatment. The study found that addition of either estradiol or testosterone to the culture medium decreased dopamine levels and tyrosine hydroxylase activity in diencephalic cultures from both male and female fetuses, whereas estradiol, but not testosterone, increased dopamine uptake in midbrain cultures from female, but not male, fetuses. The authors suggested that sexual dimorphisms of some neural structures may develop under direct genetic control, not mediated by hormonal influences. Perhaps it is these dopaminergic neurons and/or their postsynaptic partners that are affected by perinatal dopaminergic drugs.

GENE INFLUENCES ON SEX DIFFERENTIATION

A gene on the Y chromosome induces the masculinization of XY individuals. This gene, termed the sex-determining region of the Y chromosome, encodes a protein, the testis-determining factor, which affects the transcription of other genes. TDF has been thought to affect only the primitive gonads, which then, via testosterone and its metabolites, masculinize the brain and external genitals. However, there are recent reports that Sry may be expressed as early as the two-cell stage of the mouse embryo (Zwingman, Erickson, Boyer, & Ao, 1993), long before the formation of testes. This early expression suggests that TDF may affect sex differentiation directly, rather than acting only through testosterone produced by the testes. One gene whose transcription may be affected directly by TDF is the gene coding for the aromatase enzyme, which converts testosterone to estrogen (Haqq, King, Donahue, & Weiss, 1993). There are sex differences in the expression of this enzyme in cultures of embryonic mouse brains, obtained before differentiation of the testes and the subsequent testosterone surge (Beyer, Wozniak, & Hutchison, 1993).

There are additional genes on the short arm of the Y chromosome that may encode sex-specific transcription factors (reviewed in Graves, 1995; Pilgrim & Hutchison, 1994). Therefore, both Sry and other genes may contribute to sex differentiation in both hormone-dependent and hormone-independent ways. Figure 5.3 contrasts the classic view of sex differentiation, according to which masculinization and defeminization of neurons are mediated entirely by hormones, with a more complex, partially hormone-independent model.

DOPAMINERGIC INFLUENCES ON SEX DIFFERENTIATION OF THE BRAIN

One particularly interesting possibility is that dopamine neurons may not only exhibit sex differences themselves, but may lead to sex differentiation of other neurons that possess dopamine receptors (reviewed in Lauder, 1993). For example, dopamine may suppress neurite outgrowth, acting through the

Figure 5.3
Alternative Pathways of Masculine Differentiation

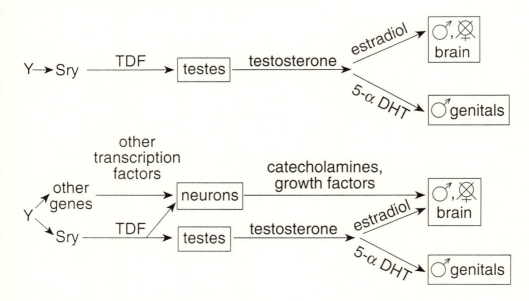

The top pathway represents the common view that the Sry gene causes the primordial gonads to become testes; testosterone and its metabolites masculinize and defeminize the brain and genitals. The second pathway includes direct effects of neurotransmitters and other factors.

D_1 family of dopamine receptors (Lankford, DeMello, & Klein, 1988), or may enhance neurite outgrowth by stimulating the D_2 family of receptors (Todd, 1992). (Five subtypes of dopamine receptors have been cloned; however, they fall into two families, D_1-like and D_2-like, based on structural, pharmacological, and physiological criteria [Civelli et al., 1993].) Even within the D_2 family, there may be subtle differences. Stimulation of D_2 receptors increased the number and branching of neurites, but not neurite extension; stimulation of D_3 or D_4 receptors promoted both branching and extension of neurites (Swarzenski, Tang, Oh, O'Malley, & Todd, 1994). Therefore, cells with different distributions of subtypes of dopamine receptors may respond to the same neurotransmitter with a variety of responses. The effects of D_1-like receptor stimulation may be mediated in part by the activation of genes that code for transcription factors that in turn promote the expression of yet other genes (Liu, Takahashi, McKay, & Graybiel, 1995). Thus, increases or decreases in the amount of dopamine available to bind to D_1- or D_2-like receptors may have far-reaching repercussions. Both the physical growth of neurons and their expression of other regulatory factors may be affected. In summary, dopamine neurons show hormone-independent sexually dimorphic patterns of development, and they can, in turn, influence the development of other sexually dimorphic neural systems, through actions on D_1- or D_2-like receptors and regulatory genes.

ACTIVATIONAL EFFECTS OF DOPAMINE
ON MALE SEXUAL BEHAVIOR

Dopamine also exerts activational effects on male sexual behavior (reviewed in Bitran & Hull, 1987; Melis & Argiolas, 1995). In some ways, dopamine's effects parallel those of steroid hormones. Steroids enhance intracellular biochemical processes that increase the responsiveness of neurons to sexually relevant stimuli (Figure 5.4). This long-term enhancement is referred to as *priming*.

However, even with steroid priming, neurons may not be fully responsive to sexual stimuli. They are subject to ongoing inhibition by GABAergic neurons. (GABA, gamma amino butyric acid, is a common inhibitory neurotransmitter which dampens the responsiveness of other neurons.) Dopamine may be released over a period of minutes, or in some cases, an hour or more. It may diffuse some distance from sites of release, though levels outside the synaptic cleft may be markedly reduced compared to that inside the cleft (Gonon, Suaud-Chagny, Mermet, & Buda, 1991). Dopamine acts, in part, by inhibiting those GABAergic interneurons, resulting in the disinhibition of the output neurons (Chevalier & Deniau, 1990). In this way, sensorimotor integration is enhanced and relevant stimuli can elicit a sexual response (Figure 5.5). Dopamine does not directly elicit behavior, but rather makes it easier for a stimulus to evoke a response.

Figure 5.4
Activational Effects of Steroid Hormones on Neurons That Control
Sexual Behavior

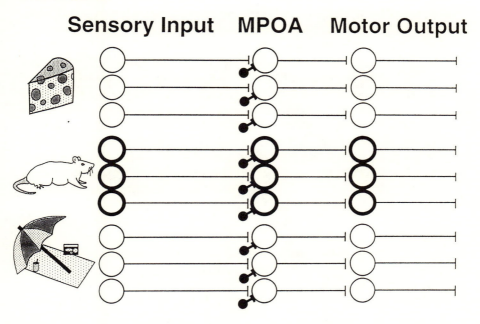

Sensory Input MPOA Motor Output

Gonadal steroids upregulate the responsiveness of neurons that process sexually relevant stimuli and responses; however, inhibitory GABAergic neurons prevent their full responsiveness.

INFLUENCES OF THREE DOPAMINERGIC
BRAIN SYSTEMS

There are three main dopamine systems that influence male sexual behavior. Stimuli from the estrous female or from copulation increase the release of dopamine in each of three integrative hubs, brain areas that receive sensory input and elicit relevant motor output (Figure 5.6). The nigrostriatal dopamine tract, degeneration of which causes Parkinson's disease, prepares for the motor components of copulation (Robbins & Everitt, 1992).

The mesolimbic tract increases responsiveness to a variety of motivational stimuli (reviewed in Kiyatkin, 1995). The medial preoptic area (MPOA) is essential for male copulatory behavior of all vertebrate species that have been studied, from fish to primates (reviewed in Meisel & Sachs, 1994). Dopamine in the MPOA helps to orchestrate genital reflexes (Hull et al., 1992), and also contributes to specifically sexual motivation (Moses, Loucks, Watson, Matuszewich, & Hull, 1995; Pfaus & Phillips, 1991; Warner et al., 1991) and

Figure 5.5
Activational Effects of Dopamine on Neurons That Control Sexual Behavior

Sensory Input   MPOA   Motor Output

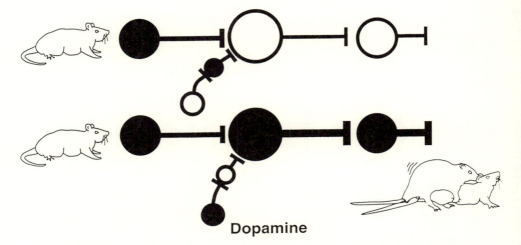

Dopamine

Dopamine neurons inhibit the GABAergic neurons, thereby disinhibiting the processing of sexual information; this increases the likelihood that a sexually relevant stimulus will evoke a sexual response.

probably also to stereotyped mounting and thrusting patterns (reviewed in Meisel & Sachs, 1994).

We have been especially interested in the MPOA, which receives dopamine innervation primarily from the A14 periventricular system (Simerly et al., 1986; reviewed in Moore & Lookingland, 1995). Briefly, certain levels of dopamine are necessary for normal sexual behavior. Stimulation of MPOA dopamine receptors, using the classic D_1/D_2 agonist apomorphine, facilitated copulation (Hull et al., 1986) and ex copula genital reflexes, measured in male rats restrained on their backs with the sheath surrounding the penis retracted (Pehek, Thompson, & Hull, 1989). Stimulation of D_1-family receptors within the MPOA facilitated the early stages of copulation (Markowski, Eaton, Lumley, Moses, & Hull, 1994) and increased the number of ex copula penile erections and anteroflexions (penile movements sometimes referred to as "flips") (Hull et al., 1992). On the other hand, high doses of apomorphine or a D_2-family agonist facilitated ejaculation (Hull et al., 1989) and increased the number of ex copula seminal emissions (Bazzett et al., 1991; Hull et al., 1992). Ejaculation and seminal emission are elicited by the sympathetic nervous system. Therefore, stimulation of low-threshold D_1-family receptors in the MPOA may promote parasympathetically mediated erections, whereas

Figure 5.6
Effects of Dopamine in Three Intregrative Hubs That Regulate Male Sexual Behavior

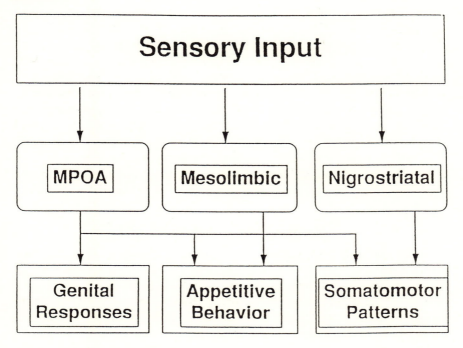

Source: Modified from Hull (1995).

Stimuli from an estrous female elicits dopamine release in each hub. Dopamine in the nigrostriatal tract promotes the initiation of somatomotor patterns of copulation. Dopamine in the mesolimbic tract enhances general appetitive behavior. Dopamine in the medial preoptic area facilitates genital reflexes, enhances specifically sexual motivation, and promotes copulatory motor patterns.

stimulating high-threshold D_2-family receptors in the MPOA may shift autonomic balance to favor ejaculation as opposed to erection.

Consonant with the facilitative effects of dopamine agonists on male sexual behavior, dopamine antagonists microinjected into the MPOA impair those same functions. Blocking dopamine receptors in the MPOA using the classic D_1/D_2 antagonist cis-flupenthixol decreased the number of males that copulated and slowed the rate of those that did (Pehek et al., 1988). Cis-flupenthixol also decreased ex copula erections and anteroflexions and decreased sexual motivation, measured as the percent of trials on which the male chose the female's goal box in an X-maze (Warner et al., 1991). Cis-flupenthixol did not affect measures of motor activity in the X-maze (Warner et al., 1991) or eating or locomotion in the home cage (Pehek et al., 1988); therefore, the effect on sexual behavior was relatively specific. Both D_1 and D_2 families of receptors contributed to sexual motivation, since both types of antagonist mimicked the effects of cis-flupenthixol in the X-maze (Moses et al., 1995). On the other hand, decreasing activity of the mesolimbic dopamine tract, extending from the ventral tegmental area (VTA) to the nucleus accumbens (NAcc) and several other sites, decreased motor activation but did not affect specifically sexual motivation (Hull, Bazzett, Warner, Eaton, & Thompson, 1990; Hull et al., 1991; Moses et al., 1995).

These data suggest that dopamine has an important facilitative influence in the MPOA, which is a major integrative hub for the activation of male sexual behavior. Furthermore, MPOA dopamine appears to influence several aspects of sexual behavior, including sexual motivation, genital reflexes, and the rate and efficiency of copulation. On the other hand, dopamine in the mesolimbic tract appears to facilitate the appetitive aspects of numerous motivated behaviors and to promote general sensorimotor activation (reviewed in Kiyatkin, 1995).

DOPAMINERGIC INFLUENCES IN CASTRATES

Dopaminergic drugs can also partially restore copulatory behavior in castrated male rats. The classic D_1/D_2 dopamine agonist apomorphine was administered systemically, either 56 days after castration, at which time about a third of vehicle-treated animals were able to copulate (Malmnas, 1977), or after suboptimal testosterone replacement (Malmnas, 1973). Apomorphine increased the numbers of animals mounting, intromitting, and ejaculating in both experiments. We tested whether apomorphine could facilitate sexual behavior even in long-term castrates that had not mounted on two successive weekly tests (Scaletta & Hull, 1990). (Because a behavioral criterion was used to begin the counterbalanced drug tests, the actual number of days postcastration varied considerably; the numbers given here represent the mean days for all animals.) Systemically administered apomorphine dose-dependently increased the numbers of mounts and intromissions in animals tested between 80 and 108 days postcastration (Figure 5.7A). They were then given five weekly subthreshold testosterone injections (20 µg each) three days before weekly behavioral tests, which occurred on days 115 to 143 postcastration. Again, the number of mounts was increased by apomorphine; however, the testosterone alone slightly increased the number of intromissions, so that the comparison with the apomorphine and testosterone treatment was not statistically significant (Figure 5.7B). In order to test whether repeated hormone injections had an additive effect on behavior, mounts and intromissions within each test day were summed across treatments and compared statistically. However, there was no improvement in responsiveness to apomorphine over the four weeks of subthreshold testosterone tests and no decrease in responsiveness over the four weeks of steroid-free tests.

Those same animals were then surgically implanted with cannulae aimed at the MPOA and received apomorphine microinjections on tests between

Figure 5.7
**Effects of Systemically Administered Apomorphine on Sexual Behavior of
Long-Term Castrates**

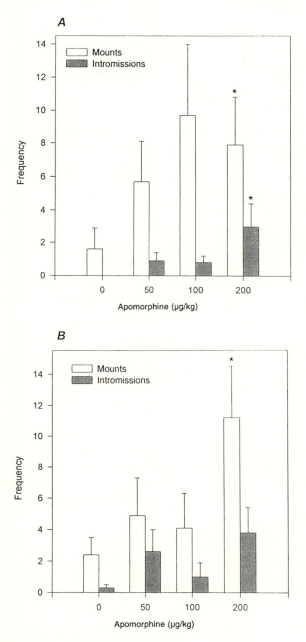

Source: From data presented in Scaletta & Hull (1990).

A. Apomorphine increased the number of mounts and intromissions per thirty-minute test. **B.** Apomorphine administered during a subthreshold testosterone regiment (20 μg/week, injected three days before testing) increased the number of mounts per thirty-minute test.

179 and 200 days postcastration. Apomorphine resulted in a significant dose-dependent increase in the numbers of mounts (Figure 5.8A), but no animal intromitted. An additional regimen of subthreshold testosterone revealed a nonsignificant apomorphine-related increase in mounts on days 207 to 228 postcastration (Figure 5.8B); two animals intromitted after apomorphine micro-injections. These data show that even in very long-term castrates, stimulation of dopamine receptors, either systemically or in the MPOA, could partially restore copulatory behavior. The lack of effectiveness of MPOA injections compared with systemic injections in restoring intromissions may have been related either to the greater length of time after castration that the animals were tested or to the requirement for stimulation in other brain areas in addition to the MPOA. In light of the lack of change in responsiveness to apomorphine across weeks of each experiment, it seems likely that the greater effectiveness of systemic apomorphine injections resulted from stimulation of dopamine receptors in multiple areas. In summary, a dopamine agonist, administered either systemically or into the MPOA, partially restored copulatory behavior in males tested approximately three to eight months after castration.

DOPAMINE RELEASE IN THE MPOA BEFORE
AND DURING COPULATION

We have recently developed a very sensitive assay for dopamine in the MPOA, using microdialysis and high-performance liquid chromatography with electrochemical detection. In sexually experienced, gonadally intact males, dopamine levels increased in the first six-minute sample after an estrous female was placed across a perforated barrier from the male (Figure 5.9) (Hull, Du, Lorrain, & Matuszewich, 1995). Dopamine increased further when the barrier was removed and the animals were allowed to copulate. If the precopulatory period was lengthened to one hour, dopamine rose in the first two samples and then fell back toward baseline as the male lost interest in the female (Figure 5.10). When the barrier was finally removed, the animals immediately began to copulate and dopamine rose as before. Therefore, the level of extracellular dopamine in the MPOA may be a sensitive indicator of the male's interest in the female.

If another male was placed across the barrier, instead of the estrous female, dopamine levels rose only slightly (nonsignificantly). Therefore, there is something special about the stimuli from the estrous female. We also tested whether the motor components of copulation could account for the dopamine increase. Animals received five weeks of daily access to an activity wheel; controls were allowed to explore a locked wheel but could not run until the test day. Voluntary running in a running wheel increased dopamine levels only slightly, and previous running experience did not affect the dopamine response to running on the test day. The motor activity exhibited by these males was greater than that required for copulation. Therefore, the motor components of copu-

Figure 5.8
Effects of Apomorphine Microinjected into the Medial Preoptic Area on Sexual Behavior of Long-Term Castrates

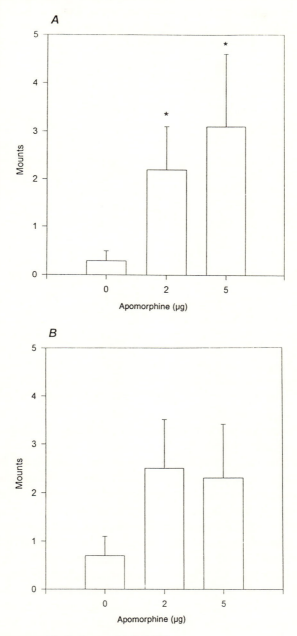

Source: From data presented in Scaletta & Hull (1990).

A. Apomorphine increased the number of mounts per thirty-minute test in animals tested without subthreshold testosterone. **B.** Apomorphine produced a nonsignificant increase in mounts when administered with subthreshold testosterone.

Figure 5.9
Extracellular Dopamine in the Medial Preoptic Area of Male Rats
(during a precopulatory period, with an estrous female across a perforated
barrier, and during three six-minute periods after the barrier was removed
and the animals were free to copulate)

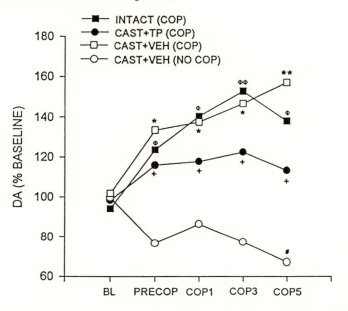

Source: Reprinted from *Journal of Neuroscience* 15, by E. M. Hull, J. Du, D. S. Lorrain, and L.
Matuszewich. (1995). Extracellular dopamine in the medial preoptic area: Implications for sexual
motivation and hormonal control of copulation, pp. 7465–7471. Reproduced with permission.

lation cannot account for the increase in extracellular dopamine that we normally see during copulation.

We are currently investigating some of the biochemical factors that promote the dopamine response to the female. The first factor that we have studied is the recent or concurrent presence of testosterone (Hull et al., 1995).
Castrates received either one or two weeks of testosterone propionate (TP) or
oil injections. All TP-treated animals showed the precopulatory dopamine
response, and all copulated after the barrier was removed (Figure 5.9). Nine
of fourteen oil-treated one-week castrates also showed the precopulatory
dopamine response, and all of these copulated after the barrier was removed.
The remaining five of the oil-treated one-week castrates, and all of the oil-
treated two-week castrates, failed to show the precopulatory dopamine response, and also failed to copulate when the barrier was removed. In every
animal, the male's precopulatory dopamine response predicted his subsequent
copulatory behavior. Two conclusions can be drawn from this experiment:
(1) The precopulatory MPOA dopamine response to the estrous female is a

Figure 5.10
Extracellular Dopamine in the Medial Preoptic Area during a Prolonged Precopulatory Period Followed by Copulation

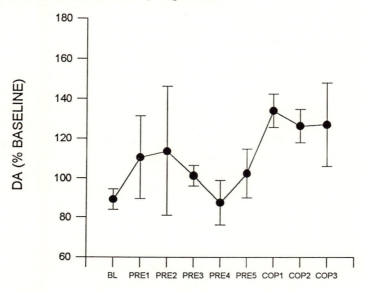

Source: Reprinted from *Journal of Neuroscience* 15, by E. M. Hull, J. Du, D. S. Lorrain, and L. Matuszewich. (1995). Extracellular dopamine in the medial preoptic area: Implications for sexual motivation and hormonal control of copulation, pp. 7465–7471. Reproduced with permission.

very consistent predictor of the ability and/or inclination of a male rat to copulate, and (2) the recent but not concurrent presence of testosterone may be necessary for both the dopamine response and copulation.

CONCLUSION

Stimuli from an estrous female elicit dopamine release in three integrative hubs in intact male rats. Dopamine in the nigrostriatal tract prepares the male for the motor components of copulation. Dopamine in the mesolimbic system increases responsiveness to a variety of environmental stimuli that have motivational significance. And dopamine in the MPOA increases responsiveness to sexual stimuli. This latter effect results in an increase in specific sexual motivation, a facilitation of genital reflexes, and coordination of stereotyped motor patterns of copulation. It may also be related to partner preference. Recent exposure to testosterone facilitates dopamine release in the MPOA and may thereby contribute to copulation.

Finally, it is important to emphasize the parallel effects of gonadal steroids and dopamine in the organization and activation of male sexual behavior. Undoubtedly, the steroid effects are more powerful and far reaching, while dopamine's effects are more subtle and may serve to fine tune or amplify integrative mechanisms of the sexual system. The organizational effects of dopamine appear to be at least partially independent of steroidal influence. Sex differences have been reported in cultures of dopamine neurons obtained before the gonads differentiated and began to secrete hormones. These sex differences may derive from transcription factors coded by the Sry gene or other genes on the Y chromosome. Dopamine neurons may in turn influence the development of other neurons, either alone or in combination with other growth factors. In adulthood, dopamine agonists can facilitate several measures of sexual behavior in intact males and can partially restore copulatory behavior in long-term castrates. Furthermore, testosterone may facilitate the activation of male-typical sexual behavior, in part by promoting the release of dopamine in several integrative hubs, including the MPOA. Possible mechanisms of steroidal influence on dopamine release are currently under investigation.

ACKNOWLEDGMENTS

This research was supported by NIMH grants MH40826 and MH35939 to EMH. We express thanks to Dr. Susan Dalterio for conducting the testosterone assays for the perinatal experiments; those assays were supported by NIH grant HD16329 to Dr. Dalterio. We also gratefully acknowledge the extensive work of Dr. Elizabeth A. Pehek, especially in developing the tests of ex copula genital reflexes cited here. We also appreciate the contributions of former students Dr. Terence J. Bazzett, Dr. Vincent Markowski, and Dr. Jason Moses, whose work is cited here, and Dr. Lucille Lumley, who assisted in these experiments and developed additional contributions of her own. The data concerning apomorphine's effects on long-term castrates were from the master's thesis of Laura L. Scaletta, presented in partial fulfillment of requirements for the MA from SUNY at Buffalo.

Chapter *6*

Gender-Specific Alterations in Adult Sexual Behavior and Brain Neurotransmitters Following Prenatal Morphine Exposure

Ilona Vathy

Studies of the consequences of fetal exposure to opiates demonstrate that prenatally morphine- and methadone-treated animals exhibit considerable developmental lags, altered motor activities, and impaired learning behavior (Hutchings, 1993; Hutchings, Zmitrovitch, Brake, Malowany, Church, & Nero, 1992; Hutchings, Zmitrovitch, Brake, Church, & Malowany, 1993; Zagon, MacLaughlin, & Thompson, 1979a; 1979b). These developmental and behavioral effects appear to result from delays in brain DNA synthesis, cell proliferation, and synaptogenesis in exposed rat pups (Ricalde & Hammer, 1991; Hammer, 1993; Seatriz & Hammer, 1993; Slotkin, Whitmore, Salvaggio, & Seidler, 1979). It has been thought for some time that drugs exert their effects on organisms through interaction with specific receptors (Langley, 1906). The influence of a specific drug on the developing brain is thus dependent on the presence of specific cellular recognition sites for the drug, the maturational state of the receptive sites, and the maturational state of neural circuitry. In rats, receptors for gonadal steroids, catecholamines, and endogenous opioids, all of which regulate the expression of adult sexual behaviors, begin to appear in the central nervous system (CNS) during the second half of gestation (Antelman & Caggiula, 1977; Clendenin, Petriats, & Simon, 1976; Coyle & Pert, 1976; McEwen, 1978; Vito, Bates, & Fox, 1979). Thus, mid- to late gestational morphine exposure could potentially influence the development of those systems that have important roles in the display of adult sexual behavior.

GENDER AND BRAIN DEVELOPMENT

It is generally accepted that, in mammals, sex chromosomes determine the genetic sex of the individual. This genetic sex then sets the environment for gender-specific development of anatomy, physiology, and behavior. The rate and timing of brain development as well as hormonal background are different in the two sexes (Beyer & Feder, 1987); such differences could subsequently produce differential responses of developing males and females to prenatal drug exposure. The existence of sexual dimorphism in the adult CNS of rodents is well established, and these dimorphisms result largely from sex differences in the hormonal environment during early development (Beyer & Feder, 1987). Sex-specific patterns of morphology and neurochemistry in brain regions such as the hypothalamus and limbic system are thought to underlie sex differences in reproductive behavior and adult responses to gonadal hormones (Gorski, Harlan, Jacobson, Shryne, & Southam, 1980; Hammer & Jacobson, 1984; Matsumoto & Arai, 1980; Nishizuka & Arai, 1981b; Perez, Naftolin, & Garcia Segura, 1990; Siddiqui & Gillmore, 1988; Teyler, Vardaris, Lewis, & Rawitch, 1980).

Catecholamines are known to be involved in the control of the hypothalamus–pituitary–gonadal axis (Weiner & Gagnong, 1978). Dopaminergic (DA) and noradrenergic (NE) systems have been implicated in sexual differentiation of the brain (Agarwal, Glisson, & Himwich, 1966; Gonzalez & Leret, 1992; Hruska & Silbergeld, 1980; Leret, Gonzalez, Tranque, & Fraile, 1987; Matsumoto & Arai, 1986; McEwen, Pfaff, & Zigmond, 1970). Tissue culture studies provided evidence that in male and female rats DA and NE neurons have different patterns of developmental maturation (Ahnert-Hilger, Engele, Reisert, & Pilgrim, 1986; Reisert & Pilgrim, 1991), and that DA and NE neurons develop morphological and functional sex differences in the absence of sex steroids (Engele & Pilgrim, 1987; 1989; Engele, Pilgrim, Kirsch, & Reisert, 1989; Engele, Pilgrim, & Reisert, 1989).

There are also sex differences in the maturation of rat brain catecholamine systems in some brain regions *in vivo* (Vathy, Rimanóczy, Eaton, & Kátay, 1995). The NE system matures in the hypothalamus and preoptic area (POA) of male rats prior to puberty, but in female rats not until after puberty. A similar sexually dimorphic maturational pattern of DA systems in the hypothalamus and POA was also observed (Vathy et al., 1995). Our data are in agreement with others demonstrating that the development of NE and DA neurotransmitter systems is gender specific, with maturation occurring in different brain regions at different developmental ages in the two sexes (Agarwal et al., 1966; Coyle, 1973; Coyle & Axelrod, 1971; Hamdi, Boutroy, & Nehlig, 1991; Loizou, 1972). Thus, male and female brains develop differently. Therefore, one might expect to find sexually dimorphic changes in brain and behavior development following prenatal exposure to morphine or other psychoactive drugs.

In this chapter, we will discuss long-term, possibly permanent alterations in adult sexual behavior and brain neurochemistry in gestationally morphine-exposed rats. We will demonstrate that prenatal morphine exposure alters (1) adult male and female sexual behavior, (2) genital reflexes, (3) hypothalamic NE content and turnover, and (4) hypothalamic μ opioid receptor density. We will also provide evidence that these alterations are gender specific in exposed adult progeny. Thus, the data described here demonstrate that exposure of the developing brain to morphine during mid- to late gestation induces permanent alterations in the CNS and in behavior, and that the nature of these changes is gender specific.

GENDER-SPECIFIC EFFECTS OF
PRENATAL MORPHINE

For the past several years we have been examining possible mechanisms by which mid- to late gestational exposure to morphine permanently alters neural development such that adult sexual behavior is modified in rats. In all of our studies animals are injected with morphine (10 mg/kg) or saline, two times a day during gestation Days 11 to 18 (for details, see Vathy, Etgen, & Barfield, 1985; Vathy, 1995). To reduce interference with parturition and maternal behavior due to withdrawal effects following chronic exposure to morphine, we stop the drug administration four days prior to parturition. However, it is likely that morphine is still present in the fetal circulation during the early period of brain sexual differentiation, which in rats occurs between the last few days of gestation and the first week after parturition (MacLusky & Naftolin, 1981; McEwen, 1978; Toran-Allerand, 1984).

Effects of Prenatal Morphine Exposure on Adult
Male and Female Sexual Behavior

In our early work we demonstrated that female rats exposed to morphine prenatally entered puberty earlier than controls (Vathy et al., 1985). Vaginal opening occurred in 40 percent of the morphine-exposed female rats before it was detected in control females. Despite the somewhat precocious vaginal opening in morphine-exposed females, they had normal four to five day estrous cycles. When we tested these females for estrous behavior in adulthood, they exhibited greatly reduced receptive and proceptive behaviors in response to appropriate ovarian steroid treatment. Thus, mid- to late gestational morphine inhibited adult estrous behavior without altering estrous cyclicity in young adult female rats. In contrast, morphine-exposed male rats displayed normal or somewhat enhanced copulatory behavior in adulthood. They had significantly shorter postejaculatory intromission latencies (PEI) than controls. This reduction in the PEI may reflect an increase in sexual motivation (Vathy et al., 1985).

To determine whether the behavioral deficit in morphine-exposed females was due to a loss of brain estrogen receptor function, we examined the depletion and replenishment of hypothalamic cytosol estrogen receptors in females (Vathy et al., 1985). There was slightly less depletion in morphine- than in saline-exposed females at each time after a single injection of 8 μg of estradiol benzoate (EB), but the pattern of depletion and replenishment of estrogen receptor was essentially identical in both groups. Moreover, the induction of hypothalamic cytosol progestin receptors forty-eight hours after the EB injection was identical in both groups of females. Thus, estrogen indeed was transported into brain cell nuclei, and some physiological responses (i.e., progesterone receptor induction) were triggered.

We recently replicated our earlier findings that female rats exposed to morphine display significantly reduced lordosis behavior in response to ovarian hormones administered in adulthood and that male rats show increased copulatory activities (Vathy & Kátay, 1992, Tables 6.1 and 6.2). As before, drug-exposed male rats had shorter PEIs. They also demonstrated more frequent mounting and intromitting behaviors, and had shorter latencies to initiate such activities after their first test. However, drug-exposed males required more time to achieve an ejaculation than controls (Table 6.2). More frequent mounting and shorter PEIs may be regarded as indicative of increased sexual motivation, but the increased latency to achieve an ejaculation suggests that morphine-exposed males are not more efficient copulators. In fact, the longer latency to ejaculate could suggest that the sensory stimulation coming from mounting and intromitting are reduced at the periphery, perhaps at the level of the penis. A reduction in sensory stimulation could also suggest alterations in nociceptive sensory transmission in the spinal cord.

Effects of Prenatal Morphine Exposure on Genital Reflexes of Adult Male and Female Rats

We tested the hypothesis that the sensitivity of genital sensory neurons in the spinal cord was altered by gestational morphine exposure in both male and female rats (Vathy & Marson, 1998). The sensory and hormonal inputs leading to sexual arousal initiate a cascade of reflexive or motor behaviors, including erection and lordosis (Hart, 1967; Meisel & Sachs, 1994; Schwartz-Giblin & Pfaff, 1990). The neural mechanisms that control these reflexive responses involve both spinal and supraspinal mechanisms. One spinal reflex is the urethrogenital (UG) reflex. The UG reflex is elicited by urethral stimulation in anesthetized, spinally transected male and female rats, and this reflex is independent of gonadal steroids in both sexes (Chung, McVary, & McKenna, 1988; McKenna, Chung, & McVary, 1991).

The UG reflex consists of coordinated sympathetic, parasympathetic, and somatic rhythmic nerve activity. In the male, it comprises penile erection, ejaculation, and rhythmic contraction of the perineal muscles. In the female,

Table 6.1

Effects of Prenatal Morphine on Sexual Behavior of Adult Male Rats

Week of Test	Prenatal Treatment (n)	Behavioral Measures		
		MF	IF	PEI (sec)
1	Saline (13)	11.3 ± 2.3	10.7 ± 2.3	382 ± 1
	Morphine (14)	14.7 ± 2.7	13.1 ± 2.4	198 ± 6**
2	Saline (13)	9.1 ± 2.2	9.9 ± 2.2	398 ± 6
	Morphine (14)	22.4 ± 3.3*	22.9 ± 2.9*	147 ± 6**
3	Saline (13)	7.7 ± 2.0	10.2 ± 2.4	420 ± 7
	Morphine (14)	21.6 ± 3.0**	25.0 ± 3.9**	142 ± 5**

Source: Modified from Vathy and Kátay (1992).

Note: Values are expressed as means ± SEM.

Key: MF = mount frequency; IF = intromission frequency; PEI = postejaculatory intromission latency.

* $p < 0.05$ vs. saline; ** $p < 0.01$ vs. saline.

it comprises vaginal and uterine contractions and rhythmic contractions of the perineal muscles. The UG reflex cannot be elicited by urethral stimulation in the intact preparation, as it is tonically inhibited by neurons in the ventral medulla (Marson & McKenna, 1990; 1994; Marson, List, & McKenna, 1992; McKenna, Chung, & McVary, 1991). However, in both males and females the UG reflex can be elicited by urethral stimulation in the spinally transected preparation (Chung, McVary, & McKenna, 1988; Marson & McKenna, 1990; 1992; 1994; McKenna, Chung, & McVary, 1991). Thus, we measured the threshold pressure, latency, number of bursts, and duration of the UG reflex in both intact and spinally transected male and female rats following prenatal exposure to morphine.

In utero morphine exposure did not influence the supraspinal inhibition of the UG reflex in either sex, as evidenced by an inability to induce the reflex in the spinally intact preparation. In spinally transected rats, the UG reflex was qualitatively similar in all groups. However, morphine-exposed male rats required twofold greater pressure to elicit the UG reflex and had a shorter latency to onset than controls. Thus, the normal inhibitory control of the UG reflex is increased by prenatal morphine in exposed males. The reduced latency to onset of the UG reflex in prenatally morphine-exposed male rats may be related to the shorter PEIs found in morphine-exposed male rats (Vathy & Kátay,

Table 6.2
Effects of Prenatal Morphine on Sexual Behavior of Adult Female Rats

Week of Test	Prenatal Treatment (n)	Behavioral Measures	
		LQ	QL
1	Saline (15)	70 ± 2	1.3 ± 0.3
	Morphine (14)	10 ± 1*	0.1 ± 0.1
2	Saline (15)	90 ± 1	2.2 ± 0.2
	Morphine (14)	13 ± 1*	0.2 ± 0.1

Source: Modified from Vathy and Kátay (1992).

Note: Values are expressed as means ± SEM.

Key: LQ = lordosis quotient; QL = quality of lordosis

* p < 0.05 vs. saline.

1992). Thus, if the UG reflex is purely a motor and autonomic sexual reflex, the present findings of shorter latency and higher threshold to onset of the UG reflex in morphine-exposed males supports the hypothesis that drug-exposed males require a stronger stimulation to achieve an ejaculation.

In contrast with the results in male rats, prenatal morphine did not alter the UG reflex in exposed female rats. Neither the threshold, latency, number of bursts, nor burst duration were affected by prenatal drug treatment. Thus, the spinal mechanisms governing the UG reflex are less sensitive to gestational morphine exposure in females than in males. The differential alterations in the UG reflex of male and female rats parallel our previous observations that prenatal morphine exposure has gender-specific effects on adult sexual behavior (Vathy & Kátay, 1992). It is interesting that both the gonadal hormone-dependent and gonadal hormone-independent components of sexual behavior are affected in a gender-specific manner by gestational morphine exposure.

Effects of Prenatal Morphine on Brain Catecholamine Systems

Because brain catecholamines have been shown to be involved in both male and female sexual behavior (Meyerson & Malmnas, 1978; Mitchell, Beauvillian, Poulain, & Mazzuka, 1977; 1988; Vathy, van der Plas, Vincent, & Etgen, 1991; Wilson, 1993), we examined whether early exposure to morphine affects the synthesis and utilization of NE and DA in the adult brain of exposed animals. We measured NE and DA content and turnover in several brain regions, including the hypothalamus, POA, cortex, and cerebellum (Vathy & Kátay, 1992; Vathy, Rimanóczy, Eaton, & Kátay, 1994). Prenatal morphine-induced sexually dimorphic alterations in hypothalamic NE content and turnover (Table 6.3). Prenatally morphine-exposed female rats, which showed reduced lordosis behavior in adulthood, had reduced content and turnover of NE in the hypothalamus relative to controls. Prenatally morphine-exposed male rats, whose copulatory behaviors were enhanced, had elevated NE content and turnover in the hypothalamus. No alterations in NE systems in other brain regions, or in DA systems in any brain region, were observed. Thus, prenatal morphine exposure, which differentially affects adult male and female sexual behaviors, also alters hypothalamic NE content and turnover in a sexually dimorphic manner. It is interesting that the differences in NE content and turnover were localized to the hypothalamus of prenatally morphine-exposed animals, as was reported following prenatal benzodiazepine and cocaine treatment (Kellogg & Rettel, 1986; Vathy, Kátay, & Mini, 1993). It seems then that the hypothalamus is particularly sensitive to gestational drug exposure.

Effects of Prenatal Morphine on Brain Opioid Systems

There is also evidence for interactions between endogenous opioid peptides and catecholamine neurotransmission. Behaviors which are stimulated by catecholamines, including sexual behaviors, are often inhibited by endogenous and exogenous opiates (Meyerson & Malmnas, 1978; Mitchell, Beauvillian, Poulain, & Mazzuka, 1977; Pfaus & Gorzalka, 1987; Vathy & Etgen, 1989; Vathy, van der Plas, Vincent, & Etgen, 1991). These inhibitory

Table 6.3
Effects of Prenatal Morphine on Hypothalamic NE Content and Turnover

Sex	Prenatal Treatment (n)	NE Content pg/mg protein	NE Turnover pg/mg/h protein
Male	Saline (5)	4679 ± 558	187 ± 22
	Morphine (5)	7895 ± 930	$473 \pm 55 *$
Female	Saline (5)	5768 ± 631	808 ± 88
	Morphine (5)	4007 ± 152	$361 \pm 14 **$

Source: Modified from Vathy, Rimanóczy, Eaton, & Kátay (1994).

Note: Values are expressed as means ± SEM.

* $p < 0.05$ vs. saline male; ** $p < 0.01$ vs. saline female.

actions of opiates are generally thought to result from tonically active, endogenous μ opioid inputs to NE terminals (Kalra & Kalra, 1984; Mitchell, Beauvillian, Poulain, & Mazzuka, 1977). We have also shown that an acute morphine injection inhibits both sexual behavior and hypothalamic NE release in normal adult female rats (Vathy, van der Plas, Vincent, & Etgen, 1991). Therefore, we tested the hypothesis that exposure to morphine during mid- to late gestation alters the development of endogenous opioid systems in the hypothalamus of exposed animals (Rimanóczy & Vathy, 1995). Because of their inhibitory effects on sexual behavior and NE neurotransmission, we measured the binding capacity and affinity of μ opioid receptors in several brain regions, including the hypothalamus, POA, striatum, ventral tegmental area, frontal cortex, and cerebellum.

There were no alterations in μ opioid receptor binding affinity in either male or female rats exposed prenatally to morphine (Rimanóczy & Vathy, 1995). The density of μ receptors was not affected in intact male rats; however, it was decreased in the hypothalamus of morphine-exposed female rats relative to controls. Thus, prenatal morphine-induced alterations in hypothalamic μ opioid receptor density are sexually dimorphic. In addition, morphine influenced the response of hypothalamic μ opioid receptors to estrogen in adult, ovariectomized females. Estrogen increased μ opioid receptor density in morphine-exposed females but not in saline-treated controls. An estrogen-induced increase in hypothalamic μ opioid tone might contribute to the reduced hypothalamic NE content and turnover and the decreased estrous behavior that characterize prenatally morphine-exposed females (Vathy, Etgen, Rabii, & Barfield, 1983; Vathy, Etgen, & Barfield, 1985; Vathy & Kátay, 1992; Vathy, Rimanóczy, Eaton, & Kátay, 1994). We are presently conducting experiments to assess the effects of prenatal morphine on delta and kappa opioid receptor binding characteristics to examine the impact of gestational morphine exposure on other opioid systems.

The distribution of the endogenous μ opioid peptide β-endorphin coincides with NE projections in many brain regions, including the hypothalamus (Khachaturian & Watson, 1982; Mitchell et al., 1988). Endogenous opioids inhibit NE neurotransmission in both the hypothalamus and extrahypothalamic brain areas (Abercrombie, Levin, & Jacobs, 1988; Kalra, 1981; Sharma, Chan, & Gintzler, 1988; Tanaka, Ida, & Tsuda, 1988). It is, therefore, possible that μ opioid receptors may exert inhibitory effects on NE release (Arakawa, De Jong, Mulder, & Versteed, 1991; Diez-Guerra, Augood, Emson, & Duer, 1987; Jackisch, Gepper, & Illes, 1986; Mulder, Hogenboom, Wardeh, & Schoffelmer, 1987; Mulder, Wardeh, Hogenboom, & Frankhuyzen, 1989; Mulder, Burger, Wardeh, Hogenboom, & Frankhuyzen, 1991; Werling, Brown, & Cox, 1987). We used an *in vitro* brain slice preparation to test the hypothesis that prenatal morphine alters μ opioid inhibition of NE release in the adult hypothalamus, augmenting it in females and reducing it in males (Vathy & Etgen, 1996).

In contrast with our prediction, neither basal nor KCl-stimulated release of NE from hypothalamic slices of adult offspring was affected by prenatal exposure to morphine. In addition, prenatal morphine had no effect on the response of slices to opioid drugs or on estrogen modulation of opioid effects in females (Vathy & Etgen, 1996). The release of NE from nerve terminals in the CNS, however, is under a variety of control mechanisms, such as calcium influx and negative feedback mediated by autoreceptors (Langer, 1977). Thus, we may find alterations in hypothalamic NE release in the presence of intact NE afferents measured using *in vivo* microdialysis rather than an *in vitro* slice preparation (Vathy & Etgen, 1996).

SUMMARY AND DISCUSSION

Our work demonstrates that exposure to morphine on gestation Days 11 to 18 alters adult sexual behavior in male and female rats differently. Morphine-exposed adult male rats displayed significantly greater mounting and intromitting frequencies and shorter PEIs than saline-treated controls. These behavioral alterations demonstrate that under our experimental conditions prenatal morphine exposure does not demasculinize male reproductive behavior. This contrasts with data from other laboratories following gestational opiate exposure in rats (Ward, Orth, & Weisz, 1983) and in hamsters (Johnston, Payne, & Gillmore, 1992; 1994). Ward and colleagues (1983) reported decreased male copulatory behavior and increased female sexual (lordosis) behavior in adult male rats exposed to morphine during the second half of gestation. Johnston and coworkers (1992; 1994) demonstrated that exposure to morphine throughout gestation increased the capacity for lordosis behavior but did not change masculine sexual behavior in male hamsters.

Our results then appear to differ from the findings of demasculinized behavioral tendencies by Ward and colleagues (1983). In the latter study, morphine was administered on Days 15 to 22 of gestation; therefore, the morphine injections corresponded in time with the prenatal testosterone surge believed to be necessary for behavioral masculinization (Ward & Weisz, 1980; 1984; Weisz & Ward, 1980). In addition, Ward and colleagues (1983) used a higher dose of morphine and administered it every eight hours rather than every twelve hours. These procedural differences may account for the apparent discrepancy between the two laboratories.

We have also collected some preliminary data to assess whether gestational morphine feminize adult males, as was shown by Ward and colleagues (1983) and Johnston et al. (1992; 1994). We gonadectomized morphine- and saline-exposed males in adulthood, and three weeks later primed them on week one with an injection of 30 µg EB. On the following week they received 30 µg of EB and forty-eight hours later an injection of 1,000 µg of progesterone. They were tested for female sexual behavior four hours after progesterone. Neither saline- nor morphine-exposed males exhibited female sexual behavior when tested with stimulus males. A week later we repeated the testing after 60 μg of EB and 1,000 μg of progesterone. The experimental males still did not assume the lordosis posture in response to the mounting attempts of the stimulus males; rather, they mounted the stimulus males. Thus, our preliminary work shows that exposure to morphine on gestation Days 11 to 18 does not demasculinize or feminize adult male sexual behavior.

It is possible that we have interfered with the natural prenatal surge of endogenous testosterone by discontinuing morphine administration at the time of this critical event. In normal adult male rats, chronic opiate exposure reduces testicular testosterone secretion (Azizi & Apostolos, 1974; Cicero, Meyer, Bell, & Koch, 1976; Cicero, O'Connor, & Bell, 1976; Meyerson & Terenius, 1977). Methadone administration during the last week of gestation also reduces plasma testosterone levels in fetuses (Singh, Purohit, & Ahluwalia, 1980). It is possible that morphine administration during mid- to late gestation reduced plasma testosterone levels in male fetuses, and the withdrawal of the drug on gestational Day 18 exaggerated the naturally occurring testosterone surge. An increase in the levels of prenatal testosterone might be responsible for the enhanced male sexual behavior of prenatally morphine-exposed adult males.

If elevated levels of circulating gonadal androgens also affected neighboring fetuses, one would predict partial defeminization in morphine-exposed females. This could perhaps explain reduced estrous responsiveness in adult females exposed prenatally to morphine. However, this interpretation is unlikely. If circulating androgens were elevated by morphine during the prenatal period, morphine-exposed females should have been masculinized perinatally. This would be reflected in longer anogenital distances in drug-exposed than in control females. However, no masculinization of anogenital distance is evident in morphine-exposed females (Vathy, Etgen, Rabii, & Barfield, 1983). Another possible interpretation is that morphine-exposed females displayed aversive responses to the mounting attempts of males. In fact, drug-exposed females reacted very aggressively toward stimulus males after receiving a mount, with or without an intromission, indicating possible deficits in sexual motivation. To get a better indication of female sexual motivation, we plan to test females with tethered stimulus males, permitting them to pace copulation (Erskine, 1989).

Our work further suggests that the developing hypothalamic, catecholaminergic, and endogenous opioidergic systems are sensitive to mid- to late gestational morphine exposure. Interestingly, gestational morphine exposure differentially alters hypothalamic NE content and turnover and hypothalamic opioid receptor density in male and female offspring. There may be several mechanisms by which morphine exposure altered brain and behavioral development. It is possible that the differences in hypothalamic NE content and turnover rate in morphine-exposed animals result from alterations in the density of NE innervation of the hypothalamus. To assess NE innervation of the hypothalamus of morphine-treated offspring, the distribution of tyrosine hydroxylase and dopamine beta-hydroxylase immunoreactive fibers is currently being evaluated using immunocytochemical staining techniques.

Why might one expect that prenatal exposure to psychoactive drugs would differentially influence the development of catecholamine neurons in males and females? Currently it is believed that brain sexual differentiation is dependent on the action of gonadal steroids during a critical period of development (MacLusky & Naftolin, 1981; McEwen, 1978; Toran-Allerand, 1984). However, there is evidence that catecholamine neurons differ in male and female fetuses beginning as early as gestation Days 14 to 16 (Reisert & Pilgrim, 1991; Eusterschulte, Reisert, & Pilgrim, 1991). Morphometric measures show no differences in size of the Wolffian duct of rat embryos prior to gestation Day 16, indicating that testosterone is not secreted into the circulation prior to that day (Eusterschulte, Reisert, & Pilgrim, 1991). Thus, gender-linked differentiation of catecholamine neurons is initiated independent of the presence of gonadal testosterone. Sex differences in catecholaminergic systems begin to develop considerably earlier than gonadal steroid-dependent brain sexual differentiation (Reisert, Engele, & Pilgrim, 1989; Reisert & Pilgrim, 1991).

Our biochemical studies suggest that the most sensitive site for mid- to late gestational morphine exposure is the hypothalamus. It is, however, not the only site at which morphine induces alterations. Prenatal morphine administration has widespread effects on the CNS because it also modifies hormone-independent UG reflexes. Prenatal exposure to morphine increases the threshold of the UG reflex in exposed males, suggesting the presence of alterations in the spinal cord. Therefore, to understand the impact of prenatal morphine exposure on adult brain and behaviors, a thorough examination of underlying mechanisms is essential. Moreover, to fully understand the long-term consequences of prenatal morphine exposure on adult neurobehavioral development, lifespan studies which include gender as an essential variable must be conducted.

Chapter 7

The Involvement of Neonatal 5HT Receptor-Mediated Effects on Sexual Dimorphism of Adult Behavior in the Rat

Catherine A. Wilson, M. Isabel Gonzalez,
M. Emmanuella Albonetti, and Francesca Farabollini

The brain is sexually dimorphic and this leads to the sexual differences in centrally controlled physiological functions and behaviors (MacLusky & Naftolin, 1981). This differentiation of the brain is under the control of testosterone secreted by the fetal/neonatal testicles over a critical period which, in the rat, extends over the last days *in utero* and the first two weeks postpartum (MacLusky & Naftolin, 1981; Wilson, George, & Griffin, 1981). In the presence of androgens, the brain is masculinized and, compared to the female, some brain areas develop differently in size, neuronal population, synaptic connections, and neurotransmitter concentrations and activity (Breedlove, 1994; de Vries, 1990). It seems likely that the steroid-induced differences in neurotransmitter activity occurring early in life are the links between the neonatal hormone and the sex differences in adulthood.

Among the various transmitters, 5-hydroxytryptamine (serotonin; 5HT) is an important candidate for causing sexual differences in brain functioning and behavior (Jacobs & Azmitia, 1992). 5HT, like the androgens, has organizational effects over the neonatal period and can promote the development of its own system (Whitaker-Azmitia & Azmitia, 1986) as well as stimulate the growth and differentiation of other neuronal systems (Lauder, 1990; Whitaker-Azmitia, 1992). The actions of 5HT are mediated by at least seven receptor subtypes (5HT-1, 5HT-2, etc.), with further divisions within each subtype; so far, for instance, 5HT-1 receptors are further classified as 5HT-1A, -1B, up to -1F (Watson & Girdlestone, 1995). Both 5HT-1A and 5HT-2 receptors increase over the neonatal period and then density is above that seen in adulthood over the second and third week of life with a regression to adult levels over the fourth week (Pranzatelli, 1994). The 5HT-2 receptor mediates the effects of 5HT in promoting cell proliferation, growth, and differentiation (Morilak, Somogyi, Lujan-Miras, & Ciaranello, 1994), and the excess of 5HT receptors in the second week of life may therefore be of organizational importance since proliferation and maturation of 5HT nerve terminals occurs over this period (Loizou, 1972; Tissari, 1975).

In rats, sex differences in brain levels of 5HT occur over the second week after birth for a transient period of about twenty-four hours (either on Day 12 or 14), which is under the control of the previous androgen environment. Thus, levels of 5HT and its chief metabolite, 5-hydroxyindole acetic acid (5HIAA), are higher in the whole hypothalamus and the preoptic area of the female compared to the male. Perinatal androgenization of the female reduces levels of 5HT to similar concentrations seen in the male over the second week postpartum (Ladosky & Gaziri, 1970; Giulian, Pohorecky, & McEwen, 1973; Gladue, Humphreys, De Bold, & Clemens, 1977; Simerly, Swanson, & Gorski, 1985).

Figure 7.1 illustrates our own findings on hypothalamic 5HT and 5HIAA levels over the neonatal period (Wilson, Pearson, Hunter, Tuohy, & Payne, 1986). One can see that on Day 14, 5HT and 5HIAA levels are higher in female than male hypothalami. On closer inspection, however, the difference in 5HIAA levels on Day 14 is due to a reduction in concentration in the male rather than an increase in the female. Some authorities suggest that concentrations of 5HIAA are a marker of 5HT release from nerve terminals (Johnson & Crowley, 1982; Moore & Johnston, 1982). Perhaps, therefore, the reduced male 5HIAA levels indicate an androgen-induced inhibition of 5HT release.

In this chapter we describe experiments investigating the interaction of 5HT and neonatal androgens in the control of sexual differentiation of the CNS with resulting behavioral sexual dimorphism. Our results suggest that 5HT acts to antagonize the effects of neonatal testosterone, possibly preventing masculinization that might occur in the female neonate that is exposed to unusually high levels of androgen. In the male, the reduction of endogenous 5HT activity allows testicular androgens to exert their effects on sexual differentiation (i.e., their masculinizing effects) unhindered.

TYPICAL EXPERIMENTAL DESIGN

We have designed experiments in which testosterone levels were manipulated on the day of birth in males and females and their brain 5HT concentrations were manipulated over the second week of life (to cover the transient dimorphism in 5HT levels). The animals were left until they reached adulthood (around Day 90 postpartum) and then subjected to a number of tests for behavior known to be sexually dimorphic, such as exploration (Russell, 1977; Beatty, 1979), anxiety (Archer, 1975; Gray, 1979; Stevens & Goldstein, 1981),

Figure 7.1
**Concentrations of 5HT and 5HIAA in the Hypothalami of Males and Females
on Days 10 to 16 of Life**

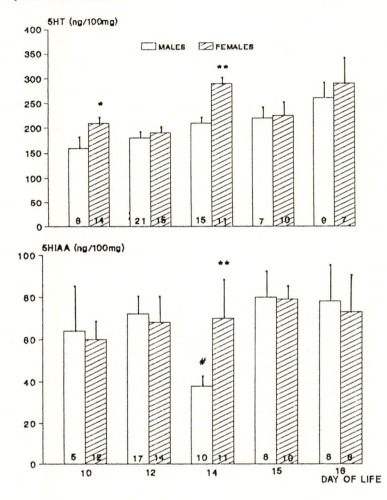

Source: Adapted from Wilson, Pearson, Hunter, Tuohy, & Payne (1986).

Note: * $p < 0.05$; ** $p < 0.01$ significance of difference between males and females; # $p < 0.05$
significance of difference between males values on Days 12 and 14; number of samples are
given within each histogram and vertical lines indicate standard errors.

sexual activity (Pfaff & Zigmond, 1971; de Jonge, Muntje Werff, Loumerse,
& van de Poll, 1988), and agonistic activity (Scholtens et al., 1986; Blanchard,
Shepherd, Carobrez, & Blanchard, 1991). Using this design, it was hoped
that any interaction between neonatal testosterone, neonatal 5HT, and genetic sex would be revealed.

Four groups of rats were used: normal males, normal females, females neonatally androgenized by treatment with testosterone proprionate (0.25 mg/pup S/C on day of birth), and, in one experiment, males in which neonatal androgens were absent due to castration on the day of birth. Each group of rats was treated daily over Days 8 to 16 with either saline, agents that increase 5HT activity, or agents that decrease 5HT activity. In earlier experiments, such treatments were also given to groups of rats over Days 1 to 7 postpartum, but were ineffective in all cases and so the results are not reported here.

Table 7.1 shows the drugs used in the experiments and their mode of action, and Table 7.2 shows that treatment with the 5HT synthesis inhibitor p-chlorophenylalanine (PCPA) significantly reduced hypothalamic levels of 5HT and 5HIAA while 5-hydroxytryptophan (5HTP; the precursor of 5HT) raises 5HT levels (Wilson et al., 1986).

The other agents employed were agonists and antagonists (selective to 5HT receptor subtypes). (Agonists mimic 5HT activity and antagonists inhibit it. As mentioned in the introduction, there are a number of different receptors that 5HT binds to and which mediate its effects, often a specific receptor stimulating a specific effect; these receptors are designated as subtypes.) A large number of 5HT receptor subtypes have been cloned (Watson & Girdlestone, 1995), some of which have no known function as yet. We have confined our experiments to employ drugs selective for the 5HT-1A and 5HT-2 receptors, as in the adult animal both these receptor subtypes are known to mediate a number of physiological functions, in particular social and nonsocial behavior.

All the animals were kept in reversed lighting (lights off 7:00–19:00h) and were weaned on Day 21 and housed in cages of five of the same model and treatment. In adulthood, around Day 90 of life, behavioral tests commenced. Vaginal smears were taken from the normal females so that the stage of their oestrous cycle could be identified, and they were tested on the day of proestrus. Androgenized females were not smeared, as their vaginae remained closed. The order of the behavioral tests was the same for all the rats, with the test for anxiety (elevated plus maze) and for exploration (head-dipping test) carried out on the first afternoon. The test for agonistic behavior (neutral environment with an unknown conspecific) took place a few days later and tests for sexual orientation followed immediately by sexual activity, approximately two weeks after that. All tests were carried out between 13:00h and 18:00h in dim red light. Details of these tests have been reported in full elsewhere (Gonzalez, Albonetti, Siddiqui, Farabollini, & Wilson, 1996; Albonetti, Gonzalez, Siddiqui, Wilson, & Farabollini, 1996).

RESULTS

Sexual Activity

To assess sexual orientation, the test rat was placed in a familiar open field and had the choice of investigating a male or a female rat (incentives) placed

Table 7.1

Drug Treatments over Days 8 to 16 Postpartum

DRUG	ABBREVIATION	DOSE	MODE OF ACTION
5-hydroxytryptamine (serotonin)	5HT	-	Endogenous neurotransmitter released from nerve terminals in the CNS
5-hydroxyindole acetic acid	5HIAA	-	Chief metabolite of 5HT and thought to only be formed after release of 5HT from its nerve terminals
5-hydroxytryptophan	5HTP	20mg/kg S/C	Precursor of 5HT and so raises its brain levels
p-chlorophenylalanine	PCPA	100mg/kg S/C	Inhibitor of 5HT synthesis
1-(2,5-dimethoxy-4-iodphenyl)-2-aminopropane-HCL	DOI	0.25mg/kg S/C	5HT-2 agonist
Ritanserin		0.25mg/kg S/C	5HT-2 antagonist
8-hydroxy-2-(di-n-propylamino)tetralin	8OHDPAT	0.25mg/kg S/C	5HT-1A agonist
WAY 100135 (N-tert-butyl-3-(4-methoxyphenyl)piperazin-1-yl)	WAY	0.25mg/kg S/C	5HT-1A antagonist

Source: Adapted from Wilson, Pearson, Hunter, Tuohy, & Payne (1986).

on the periphery of the field and separated by open mesh caging so that they could be approached but no contact could be made. The time spent in front of and investigating each incentive animal was noted in a ten-minute test. Figure 7.2 shows the time spent in front of each incentive animal by males, females, and androgenized females treated with saline or PCPA (the 5HT synthesis inhibitor) over Days 8 to 16 (Farabollini, Hole, & Wilson, 1988;

Table 7.2

The Effect of 5HTP and PCPA Administered Daily over the Second Week Postpartum on Hypothalamic Indole Concentrations (Ng/100 Mg ± SE)

Treatment	MALES		FEMALES	
	5HT	5HIAA	5HT	5HIAA
Saline	(6) 192.5 ±10.9	(6) 65 ±83	(10) 181 ±14.1	(10) 64 ±5.3
20mg/kg 5HT	(8) 257 ±10.0**	(8) 78 ±8.7	(8) 259.5 ±25.3*	(8) 69 ±11.2
100mg/kg PCPA	(7) 64 ±4.1**	(7) 12 ±8.0**	·(8) 74 ±11.0**	(8) 15 ±6.7**

Source: Adapted from Wilson, Pearson, Hunter, Tuohy, & Payne (1986).

Note: * p < 0.01; ** p < 0.001 significantly different from saline control; ( ) indicates number of samples.

Wilson, Gonzalez, & Farabollini, 1991). One can see that males spent significantly more time in front of the incentive female and PCPA significantly increased this time. PCPA had a similar effect on androgenized females and no effect on normal females. When similar groups of rats were treated with selective 5HT-1A and 5HT-2 agonists and antagonists (see Table 7.1), the 5HT-1A agents and ritanserin (5HT-2 antagonist) had no effect on any of the groups. However, the 5HT-2 agonist, DOI (see Table 7.1 for full name), significantly reduced the time spent in front of the female by normal males and androgenized females. Figure 7.3 shows the effects of the 5HT-2 agents. The results are expressed as a ratio of time spent in front of females to time in front of males (Gonzalez, Albonetti, Siddiqui, Farabollini, & Wilson, 1996).

Turning to heterosexual behavior, though others have shown that reducing brain 5HT over the neonatal period with PCPA enhanced adult male sexual behavior (Hyyppa, Lampiren, & Lehtinin, 1972), we have found little or no effect with PCPA, 5HTP, the 5HT-1A agents, or ritanserin (Wilson et al., 1986; Farabollini et al., 1988). However, DOI (the 5HT-2 agonist) did show an effect in males by significantly reducing male sexual activity as indicated by the lengthening of time taken to initiate mounting and intromitting (see Table 7.3). It is difficult to say whether this reduction in sexual activity is due to a nonspecific decrease in arousal. Against this suggestion is the fact that DOI did not affect exploration in males. On the other hand, the 5HT-2 antagonist, ritanserin, seemed to increase arousal in a conflict situation, specifically in males.

Figure 7.2
Effect of Neonatal PCPA on Sexual Orientation Tests

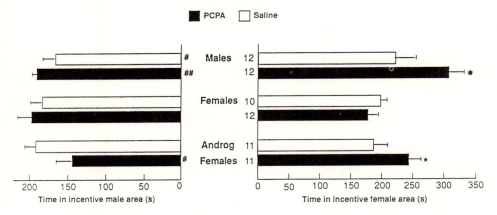

Source: Adapted from Farabollini, Hole, & Wilson (1988) and Wilson, Gonzalez, & Farabollini (1991).

Note: * p < 0.05 significantly different from saline control; # p < 0.05; ## p < 0.005 time in female area vs. male.

None of the compounds affected sexual behavior in normal females, but neonatally androgenized females manipulation of neonatal 5HT did show some effects. Figure 7.4 shows that graded doses of testosterone given on the day of birth (Day 1) to females cause a dose-dependent increase in inhibition of lordotic activity (this represents one of the defeminizing effects of neonatal androgens). Treatment with either 5HTP or PCPA over the second week of life significantly shifted the dose response curve, the 5HTP to the right indicating inhibition of the testosterone action and the PCPA treatment to the left indicating enhancement (Wilson et al., 1986).

We have suggested that a serotonergic (5HT) system in the brain may antagonize the masculinizing effect of neonatal testosterone. Focusing on sexual activity, it is well established that neonatal testosterone induces masculinization of sexual behavior with an enhanced sexual orientation toward a female and the male copulatory pattern. The neonatal testosterone also induces defeminization with a reduction in the female patterns of behavior. We have evidence that an increase in 5HT-2 activity, employing the 5HT-2 agonist DOI, decreases male sexual activity, while reducing 5HT levels enhances testosterone-induced behavior, such as orientation towards a female. In normal females, manipulation of 5HT had no effect on sexual behavior, possibly related to the absence of testosterone. However, in the presence of testosterone, as in the androgenized female, increasing 5HT antagonized the defeminizing effect of testosterone while reducing 5HT activity had an enhancing

Figure 7.3
Effect of Neonatal 5HT2 Drugs on Sexual Orientation

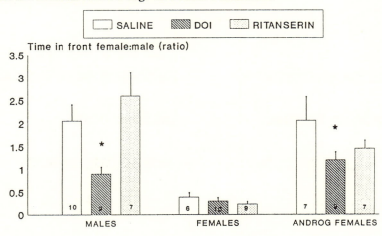

Source: Adapted from Gonzalez, Albonetti, Siddiqui, Farabollini, & Wilson (1996).

Note: * p < 0.05 significantly different from saline control; number of animals given within histogram and vertical lines indicate standard errors.

effect. The fact that the manipulation of neonatal 5HT was only effective on adult sexual behavior in males and androgenized females and not in normal females indicates that it is dependent on testosterone but independent of genetic sex.

Table 7.3
Effects of Neonatal DOI on Male Sexual Behavior

	Mount Latency(s)	Intromission Latency(s)	No. Mounts + Intromissions	Ejaculation Latency(s)
Saline (10)	35.7 ±8.1	46.9 ±10.6	24.0 ±2.2	754.7 ±184.4
DOI (9)	448.6* ±124.7	527.1* 126.0	18.6 ±2.0	1178.6 ±212.7
RIT (7)	80.5 ±22.1	92.8 ±23.8	32.3 ±7.1	943.3 ±219.3

Source: Adapted from Gonzalez, Albonetti, Siddiqui, Farabollini, & Wilson (1996).

Note: * p < 0.05 significantly different from saline control; ( ) indicates number of animals.

Figure 7.4
Effect of PCPA and 5HTP on Inhibition of Female Sexual Behavior

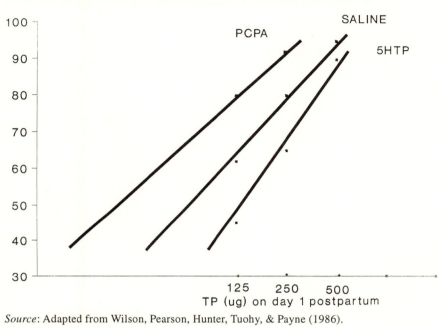

Source: Adapted from Wilson, Pearson, Hunter, Tuohy, & Payne (1986).
Note: n per group = 10 to 22.

Exploration

The level of exploratory activity is dependent on neonatal testosterone, with males showing significantly less activity than females (Blizard, Lippman, & Chen, 1975; Beatty, 1979). We have confirmed this by showing females treated neonatally with testosterone have lower levels of exploration in adulthood as compared to normal females. This was revealed in a five-minute holeboard test where the number of head dips performed by androgenized females treated with saline was significantly lower than shown by the normal females. Raising 5HT levels with 5HTP reversed the effect of the neonatal testosterone (see Figure 7.5), and had no effect on normal females (not shown). PCPA had no effect on either female group (Wilson et al., 1991).

In a later experiment, when males, females, and androgenized females were tested for exploration, the testosterone-induced dimorphism was not seen and the 5HT-1A agents and ritanserin were ineffective in all groups. DOI, on the other hand, enhanced head-dipping duration in the females compared to the saline-treated females (Table 7.4). Though this may be a specific effect of DOI, it is also possible that there is a mutual antagonism between the 5HT-2 system and testosterone, as in this experiment we saw that DOI could only exert its effect in the absence of testosterone and was ineffective in males and androgenized females.

Figure 7.5
Effect of Neonatal 5HTP and PCPA on Exploration (Holeboard Test)

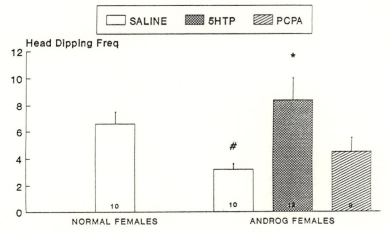

Source: Adapted from Wilson, Gonzalez, & Farabollini (1991).

Note: * $p < 0.05$ significantly different from saline control; # $p < 0.05$ significantly different from normal females; number of animals given within histogram and vertical lines indicate standard errors.

Neonatal testosterone reduces exploratory activity in males. In continuance with our hypothesis, we have shown that raising brain 5HT levels with 5HTP antagonizes the effect of neonatal testosterone on exploration and, conversely, testosterone prevented the action of a 5HT-2 agonist (DOI) on this behavior.

Table 7.4
Effect of 5HT Agents on Exploration in the Holeboard Test (Duration of Head-Dipping in Seconds)

	Saline	DOI	RIT	Saline	80HDPAT	WAY
Males	(10) 26.5 ±2.9	(9) 31.9 ±4.5	(7) 29.2 ±2.7			
Females	(6) 25.8 ±6.4	(10) 60.5 ±5.5*	(9) 41.2 ±4.5	(11) 45.0 ±5.9	(9) 37.7 ±7.3	(11) 37.7 ±3.1
And. Females	(7) 36.2 ±6.5	(9) 42.4 ±6.0	(7) 49.0 ±7.4	(10) 34.4 ±7.7	(12) 40.5 ±4.7	(12) 38.5 ±5.4

Source: Adapted from Wilson, Gonzalez, & Farabollini (1991).

Note: * $p < 0.05$ significantly different from saline control; ( ) indicates number of animals.

Anxiety

Anxiety was assessed in a five-minute test on the elevated plus maze where the proportion of time spent on the open arms is an inverse measure of anxiety (Pellow, Johnston, & File, 1987; Handley & Mithani, 1984). Anxiety is sexually dimorphic in rats, with males showing higher levels than females (Archer, 1975; Gray, 1979). Our results showed this tendency, in that saline-treated normal females spent a little longer time in the open arms than the corresponding saline-treated males and androgenized females, but the difference was not significant.(percentage time in open arms was as follows: normal females 6.3 ± 2.5 [n = 11]; androgenized females 4.0 ± 1.4 [n = 10]; males 3.5 ± 2.1 [n = 10]).

In early studies we have shown that reducing 5HT levels with PCPA has an anxiolytic effect on the three "sex" models; that is, females, males, and androgenized females (Farabollini et al., 1988; Wilson et al., 1991). This was shown by the increase in time spent on the open arms of the elevated plus maze. In later experiments this was reproduced by the 5HT-2 antagonist but only in females (see Figure 7.6). This indicates that the anxiogenic effect of 5HT is independent of sex and in females may be mediated by a 5HT-2 system, while the presence of testosterone appears to alter the receptor system involved. This is feasible, as steroids are known to induce and alter a variety

Figure 7.6
Effect of Neonatal PCPA and Ritanserin on Anxiety (Plus Maze Test)

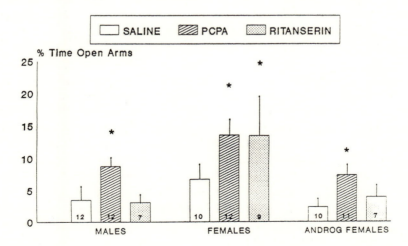

Source: Adapted from Farabollini, Hole, & Wilson (1988); Wilson, Gonzalez, & Farabollini (1991); and Gonzalez, Albonetti, Siddiqui, Farabollini, & Wilson (1996).

Note: * $p < 0.05$ significantly different from saline control; number of animals given within histogram and vertical lines indicate standard errors.

of receptor types (Wilkinson, Herdon, Pearce, & Wilson, 1979; Sumner & Fink, 1993). It is unlikely that the 5HT-1A receptors are involved since the 5HT-1A antagonist, WAY 100135 (see Table 7.1), did not mimic PCPA, and further investigations using other receptor-selective agents are required.

Any putative antagonism between neonatal testosterone and 5HT could not be shown employing anxiety as a behavioral parameter, since reducing endogenous 5HT synthesis with PCPA had an anxiolytic effect in all the animal categories tested and was independent of genetic sex and testosterone. However, testosterone may affect the receptor subtype mediating the anxiogenic effect of endogenous 5HT, with 5HT-2 receptors mediating the effect in females, while the presence of testosterone induces a switch to another receptor type yet to be elucidated.

Agonistic Behavior

Agonistic activity consists of offensive and defensive behaviors and usually males show a greater level of offensive activity (Blanchard, Shepherd, Carobrez, & Blanchard, 1991). We have studied the interaction of testosterone and 5HT on these two components of agonistic behavior in females, males, androgenized females, and, in some experiments, neonatally castrated males. The agonistic activity was assessed by placing the test animal in a "neutral" environment (i.e., not the home cage) with a sex, age, weight, and endocrine-matched conspecific. Both animals had been made familiar with the area by placing them in the observation cage at separate times for the two previous consecutive days for ten minutes each day. The test lasted twenty minutes. The expected sexual dimorphism in agonistic activity was noted, as males showed lower levels of defensive behavior compared to females. Defense in androgenized females tended to be lower as well, but did not reach significance (Figure 7.7).

In an earlier study we showed that PCPA enhanced offensive and reduced defensive behavior in normal males (i.e., enhanced the masculinizing pattern of activity) (Farabollini et al., 1988). Turning to more selective agents, we have found that, like PCPA, the 5HT-2 antagonist ritanserin enhanced offensive behavior in males and also in androgenized females, but had no effect in normal females (Figure 7.8). The 5HT-2 agonist, DOI, had no effect on offensive behavior but stimulated defensive behavior in males and androgenized females, with no effect on normal females (see Figures 7.7 and 7.8). Collectively, these data suggest that a 5HT-2 system acts in the neonatal period to antagonize the masculinizing effect of testosterone on agonistic behavior and this is dependent on the presence of testosterone and independent of genetic sex. It should be noted that ritanserin increased both offensive and defensive behavior, but only in males, which has been interpreted as a general arousal effect and responsiveness to stimuli (Albonetti, Gonzalez, Farabollini, & Wilson, 1994).

Figure 7.7
Effect of Neonatal 5HT2 Drugs on Defense

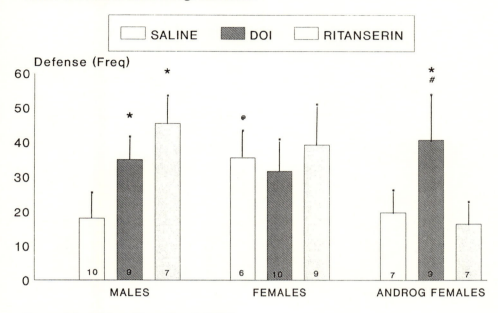

Source: Adapted from Albonetti et al. (1994).

Note: * p < 0.05 significantly different from saline control; # p < 0.05 significantly different
from ritanserin; @ p < 0.05 significantly different from saline-treated males; number of
animals given within histogram and vertical lines indicate standard errors.

The effects of 5HT-1A agents on agonistic behavior are reported in Figure
7.9. In addition to the usual three models of males, females, and androgenized
females, we were able to include neonatally castrated males. This added to
the analysis of the relative importance of genetic sex and neonatal testosterone, since there were two models which had "seen" neonatal testosterone
(intact males and androgenized females), and two that had not (intact females
and neonatally castrated males). The 5HT-1A antagonist, WAY 100135 (see
Table 7.1), increased defensive behavior in males and androgenized females
and had no effect in the absence of testosterone, as seen in normal females
and neonatally castrated males. The effect of 80HDPAT, 5HT-1A agonist (see
Table 7.1), in opposition to WAY 100135 (5HT-1A antagonist) reduced defensive behavior in males. Interestingly, in the absence of testosterone (i.e.,
the females and castrated males), 80HDPAT significantly enhanced defensive behavior. Rather in the same manner as ritanserin, WAY 100135 not only
stimulated defensive but also offensive behavior (Albonetti et al., 1996) (see
Figure 7.10). The fact that both a 5HT-2 and 5HT-1A antagonist stimulates
the two aspects of agonistic activity in males only suggests a genetic sex-

Figure 7.8
Effect of Neonatal 5HT2 Drugs on Offense

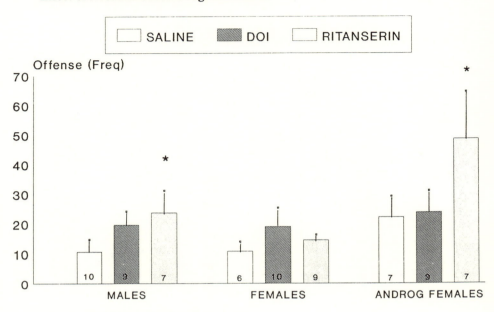

Source: Adapted from Albonetti et al. (1994).

Note: * p < 0.05 significantly different from saline control; number of animals given within histogram and vertical lines indicate standard errors.

dependent action. As mentioned, this may be a nonspecific general arousal and responsiveness to stimuli involving agonistic behavior.

In conclusion, while the 5HT-2 agonist (DOI) enhances defensive behavior in the presence of testosterone in both sexes, the 5HT-1A agonist (80HDPAT) reduced defense in the presence of testosterone in both sexes. If neonatal testosterone exerts its masculinizing effect by decreasing defensive behavior, then the 5HT-2 system appears to antagonize this while the 5HT-1A system enhances it. A rise in 5HT-1A often inhibits the release of endogenous 5HT (autoregulation) by acting on receptors sited on 5HT nerve terminals (presynaptic receptors). Thus, the effect of the 5HT-1A agonist 80HDPAT in enhancing the testosterone action may be due to a reduction in 5HT release.

When the levels of testosterone are low or nonexistent, a stimulatory effect of 80HDPAT on defensive behavior is unmasked. A possible explanation may be that testosterone alters the relative numbers or sensitivity of the presynaptic and postsynaptic 5HT receptors. (Postsynaptic receptors mediate the effect of their transmitter on another tissue or neurone. Presynaptic receptors are present on the neurone itself and, when stimulated, will inhibit release of their own transmitter from the nerve terminal; this is called *autoregulation*.)

Figure 7.9
Effect of Neonatal 5HT1A Drugs on Defense

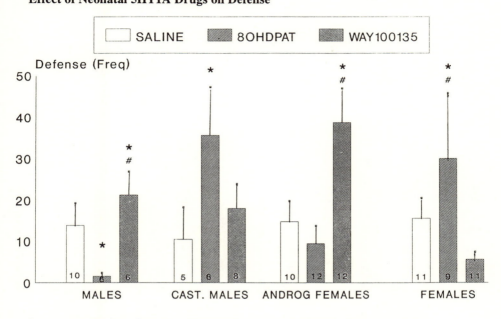

Source: Adapted from Gonzalez, Albonetti, Siddiqui, Farabollini, & Wilson (1996).

Note: * p < 0.05 significantly different from saline control; # p < 0.05 significantly different from other treatment; number of animals given within histogram and vertical lines indicate standard errors.

Thus, one can speculate that, in the absence of testosterone, endogenous 5HT stimulates defensive behavior via both 5HT-1A and 5HT-2 postsynaptic receptors, while in the presence of testosterone the presynaptic 5HT-1A receptors dominate and autoregulation is enhanced, resulting in inhibition of 5HT release and thus postsynaptic activity is reduced. It is well established that steroids can alter 5HT receptor density (Biegon & McEwen, 1982; Sumner & Fink, 1993), and in particular testosterone can alter the affinity of 5HT-1A receptors toward their agonist (80HDPAT) (Bonson, Johnson, Fiorella, Rabin, & Winter, 1994). It is possible the testosterone enhances the sensitivity of the presynaptic receptors selectively and this increases the autoregulatory effect on endogenous 5HT release.

The antagonism between 5HT and testosterone is revealed in their interaction on the control of agonistic behavior. The two components of agonistic activity are offense and defense, the latter being reduced after neonatal masculinization. In the presence of testosterone, the 5HT-2 agonist (DOI) enhanced defense, while offense was increased by the 5HT-2 antagonist (ritanserin). This indicates a 5HT-2 system antagonizes the action of neonatal testosterone. In

Figure 7.10
Effect of Neonatal 5HT1A Drugs on Offense

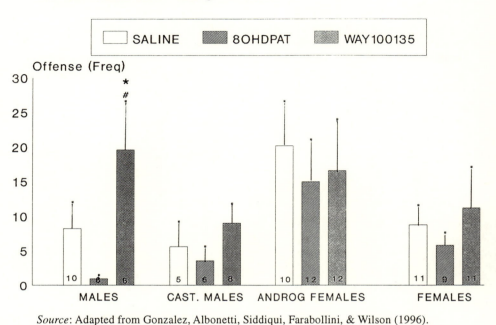

Source: Adapted from Gonzalez, Albonetti, Siddiqui, Farabollini, & Wilson (1996).

Note: * p < 0.05 significantly different from saline control; # p < 0.05 significantly different from other treatment; number of animals given within histogram and vertical lines indicate standard errors.

the presence of testosterone, the 5HT-1A agents had the opposite effects. The agonist (80HDPAT) reduced defense and the antagonist (WAY 100135) increased it. We suggest this is due to a 5HT-1A-induced inhibition of endogenous 5HT release. In the absence of testosterone, the 5HT-1A agonist mimicked the effect of the 5HT-2 agonist, perhaps because it is now acting like 5HT-2 agents via a postsynaptic rather than a presynaptic receptor. This 5HT-1A-mediated effect on defense is therefore not a simple antagonism between testosterone and 5HT, as for many of the other behaviors, but a differential effect dependent on the presence or absence of testosterone.

DISCUSSION

It is well established that, in the rodent, neonatal testosterone induces sexual dimorphism of sexual behavior (Pfaff & Zigmond, 1971), agonistic activity (Blanchard, Shepherd, Carobrez, & Blanchard, 1991), anxiety (Archer, 1975), and exploration (Beatty, 1979). Testosterone-induced CNS differentiation ultimately results in changes in neurotransmitter activity, noted in some cases almost at once during the neonatal period, as with 5HT, while sexual dimorphism of other neurotransmitters only show up in adulthood, as with the dopaminergic system (Tanila, Taira, Piepponen, & Honkanen, 1994; Morissetti & di Paolo, 1993). It is likely that the early neurotransmitter changes are markers of the systems mediating and modulating effects of the neonatal androgens. We have focused on 5HT, which is well known for having marked effects on adult behavior, but also has organizational effects on the CNS and interactions with neonatal androgens over the developmental period (Jacobs & Azmitia, 1992).

Manipulation of 5HT in the neonatal period has some immediate effects on ontogeny of certain functions. Neonatal 5HT activity reduces reactivity to novel stimuli and pain in pups (Mabry & Campbell, 1974; Spear, Enters, Aswad, & Lonzan, 1985), causes impaired locomotion and limb coordination in pups (Lucot & Seiden, 1986; Myoga, Nonaka, Matsuyama, & Mori, 1995), and eventually may be involved in the onset of puberty (Fajer, Hoffman, & Shillito, 1970; Hyyppa et al., 1972).

Turning to the effect of 5HT given over the neonatal period on organization of adult behavior, two main points emerge. First, in spite of the fact that 5HT-1A receptors are functional over the neonatal period (Pranzatelli, 1992) and do not develop tolerance when stimulated daily by a 5HT-1A agonist (Johansson-Wallsten, Berg, & Meyerson, 1993), 5HT-1A activity does not seem to be as involved as 5HT-2 in organizational effects, the only exception being agonistic behavior. Second, the main effect of neonatal 5HT is to antagonize the masculinizing and defeminizing effects of neonatal testosterone (with the exception of its effects on anxiety), and this antagonism is independent of genetic sex since it can be noted in both normal males and androgenized females. Examples of this antagonism could be noted on sexual orientation, male and female sexual behavior, exploration, and the offensive and defensive components of agonistic behavior. The data were first obtained by general manipulation of whole brain 5HT, using 5HTP and PCPA, and certain results were replicated using the selective 5HT-2 agents DOI and ritanserin. Though anxiety is sexually dimorphic in adulthood, it is not clear whether 5HT can modulate the effects of neonatal testosterone on anxiety, since manipulation of 5HT with PCPA had an effect independent of both testosterone and genetic sex. It is possible that while 5HT has a direct influence on development of the system-controlling anxiety in both sexes, 5HT can also modulate neonatal testosterone effects via a non-5HT-2 or 5HT-1A receptor.

As well as noting that 5HT modulated the effect of neonatal testosterone, we also obtained results indicating a converse relationship; that is, testosterone reduced the actions of 5HT and this was observed in both males and androgenized females. Thus, the presence of testosterone masked or inhibited the effect of DOI on exploration and of ritanserin on anxiety (which were thus only seen in females) and, most clearly, completely reversed in the actions of the 5HT-1A agonist and antagonist on defense behavior. It is suggested that these effects are a result of steroid-induced changes in receptor density and/or affinity.

Many reports show that 5HT in adulthood is involved in the control of a variety of behaviors. Thus, 5HT drugs given to adult rats have a marked sex-dependent effect on sexual behavior. 5HT-1A activity stimulates male and inhibits female sexual behavior (at postsynaptic receptors) (Mendelson & Gorzalka, 1986; Aiello-Zaldivar, Luine, & Frankfurt, 1992), while 5HT-2 activity has the opposite effects (Gorzalka, Mendelson, & Watson, 1990; Wilson & Hunter, 1985). In contrast, stimulating 5HT-1A and 5HT-2 receptors can have similar effects on agonistic behavior and anxiety. Selective agonists for both 5HT-1A and 5HT-2 receptors reduced aggressive behavior in a variety of tests (Bonson & Winter, 1992; Datla, Mitra, & Bhattacharya, 1991; Mos, Olivier, Potts, & van Aben, 1992; Sijbesma et al., 1991). On the elevated plus maze, enhancement of both 5HT-1A (acting on postsynaptic receptors) and 5HT-2 activity is anxiolytic (Critchley & Handley, 1987; Pellow et al., 1987; Inoue, 1993).

Though it is oversimplistic to expect similarities in the organizational (neonatal) and activational (adult) effects of 5HT, there are a few parallels, in that at both periods 5HT-2 activity reduces male sexual behavior and relatively reduces the aggressive (offensive) component compared to the defensive component of agonistic activity. Neonatal and adult 5HT appears to have the opposite effects on anxiety, as measured on the elevated plus maze, but anxiety is not a unitary concept (File, 1992) and there are multiple mechanisms controlling it. The other important difference in response to neonatal and adult administration of 5HT lies in the relationship of 5HT and testosterone. In the neonatal period there is a mutual antagonism which seems to be important for differentiation of the brain. In adulthood, with the exception of 5HT-2 activity and testosterone in the control of male sexual behavior, this antagonism is lost (Gonzalez, Farabollini, Albonetti, & Wilson, 1994).

SUMMARY

In the rodent, sexual differentiation of the brain is controlled by a rise in testosterone occurring over the last few days *in utero* and the first two weeks postpartum. This rise induces structural and biochemical changes in the brain, including a transient reduction in serotonin and 5-hydroxyindole acetic acid in the second week postpartum (Day 12 or 14). It is assumed that these changes cause sexual differentiation of certain behavioral parameters in adulthood. In particular, neonatal testosterone increases adult male sexual behavior, reduces exploration, and increases anxiety and aggressive behavior.

In order to investigate the relationship between testosterone and 5HT activity in the neonatal period, we have manipulated testosterone on the first day postpartum and 5HT activity over the second week. Four categories were used: males, females, androgenized females, and, in one experiment, neonatally castrated males. The serotonergic agents were given over Days 8 to 16 postpartum and comprised of 5-hydroxytryptophan (5HTP; 5HT precursor), p-chlorophenylalanine (PCPA; 5HT synthesis inhibitor), 80HDPAT (5HT-1A agonist), WAY 100135 (5HT-1A antagonist), DOI (5HT-2 agonist), and ritanserin (5HT-2 antagonist).

In males and androgenized females, PCPA increased sexual orientation toward a female conspecific. Conversely, DOI reduced heterosexual orientation in both males and androgenized females and reduced sexual activity in males. None of the treatments affected any component of female sexual activity in normal females, but in androgenized females raising 5HT antagonized the defeminizing effect of neonatal testosterone, while PCPA enhanced it. These results indicate that 5HT only affects sexual motivation and activity in the presence of testosterone (i.e., in males and androgenized females), when it acts to antagonize the masculinizing and defeminizing effects of testosterone. This action is probably mediated via 5HT-2 receptors.

5HTP antagonized the reduction in exploration produced by neonatal testosterone in androgenized females. DOI increased exploratory activity in females but had no effect in males or androgenized females (i.e., in the presence of testosterone). Thus, it seems that 5HT and testosterone are mutually antagonistic on exploration.

PCPA was anxiolytic in males, females, and androgenized females, while ritanserin was anxiolytic only in females. Thus, it seems 5HT-2 activates the anxiety system in females in the presence of testosterone; however, other receptors seem to be involved.

In both males and androgenized females, ritanserin increased aggressive behavior while DOI increased defense, so their effects depended on neonatal testosterone rather than genetic sex. 80DPAT also enhanced defense, but only in the absence of testosterone (females and neonatally castrated males) and decreased it in males. We suggest that the 5HT-2 system antagonizes masculinization of agonistic behavior in the presence of testosterone; that is, 5HT-1A activation exerts a presynaptic effect inhibiting the release of endogenous 5HT and so opposing the postsynaptic effects of 5HT. In the absence of testosterone, 5HT-1A postsynaptic activity predominates and increases defense in the same way as the 5HT-2 system.

Overall, the following generalization can be made: Neonatal testosterone effects on adult male sexual behavior, exploration, and aggression are opposed by raising 5HT activity and enhanced by 5HT inhibition, independent of genetic sex. This antagonist effect of 5HT seems to be mediated by 5HT-2 receptors for all three forms of behavior. Anxiogenic behavior is independent of testosterone and genetic sex, but the selection of the controlling 5HT receptor subsystem is affected by testosterone.

Gould, Collins, & Wallen, 1989; for marmoset, see Lunn, Recio, Morris, & Fraser, 1994). The neonatal testosterone surge may therefore play some role in maturation of the pituitary–gonadal axis during puberty. Third, there is the question of whether perinatal changes in testosterone secretion might influence sexual differentiation of the brain and behavior in primates as in many other mammals (Goy & McEwen, 1980; DeVries et al., 1984; Balthazart, 1990). Given that primates produce "precocial" offspring (i.e., the eyes are open and the nervous system relatively well developed at birth), the expectation is that any "critical periods" for effects of androgen upon brain development should occur *in utero*.

Experiments using the rhesus monkey have confirmed that prenatal androgenization has a significant impact upon behavioral development in female offspring of this primate species (Goy & Resko, 1972; Goy, Wolf, & Eisele, 1978; Goy, Bercovitch, & McBrair, 1988; Phoenix, 1974). This is also the case in human females exposed to heightened levels of androgens *in utero* as a result of congenital adrenal hyperplasia (Money & Ehrhardt, 1972; Dittman et al., 1990; Hines & Kaufman, 1994). Nonetheless, some evidence has been obtained that both prenatal and postnatal exposure to androgens are required for complete behavioral masculinization in the rhesus monkey (Pomerantz, Goy, & Roy, 1986; Eisler, Tannenbaum, Mann, & Wallen, 1993; Wallen, Maestripieri, & Mann, 1995).

This chapter reports experiments conducted on marmosets and rhesus monkeys in order to investigate the effects of neonatal castration, or testicular suppression, upon subsequent behavioral and genital development. Three main points will be made in describing these experimental studies. First, in the marmoset, neonatal castration has pronounced effects upon the development of sexual and aggressive behavior. However, such effects are largely reversible by testosterone replacement in adulthood and do not represent an irreversible deficit in organization of the brain due to removal of the testes in infancy. Second, in the rhesus monkey, suppression of testosterone secretion during the first six months has no significant effect upon the development of sexually dimorphic patterns of playful or sociosexual behavior. Third, in both these primate species, the postnatal testosterone surge affects penile growth and, in the case of the marmoset, deficits in penile growth are only partially reversible by treating neonatally castrated males with testosterone in adulthood. It appears therefore that the penis is sensitive to endogenous androgens during early infancy, indicating that testosterone must be biologically active in this context and not inextricably bound to sex-hormone binding globulin. Thus, though effects of the postnatal testosterone surge upon the development of brain and sexually dimorphic behavioral patterns are probably modest in monkeys, indirect effects involving phallic development may be significant. These findings on monkeys are also discussed in relation to the functions of the postnatal testosterone surge during development of the human male. Given that human infants are born in a less well-developed condition and that the human brain undergoes an enormous increase in size and complexity during the first year of life, it is possible that the early postnatal testosterone surge may have different consequences in man than in marmosets or rhesus monkeys.

EFFECTS OF NEONATAL CASTRATION IN THE MARMOSET

The common marmoset (*Callithrix jacchus*) offers several advantages for studies of effects of early postnatal androgen upon behavioral development. In these monkeys, oppositely sexed dizygotic twins share a placental circulation and develop as haemopoietic chimeras (Benirschke, Anderson, & Brownhill, 1962). Despite this, there is no masculinization of the female twin *in utero* (i.e., freemartinism; see Wislocki, 1939). It has been hypothesized that some aspects of neural sexual differentiation are delayed until early postnatal life in marmosets (Short, 1974), particularly during Days 1 to 90 of infancy, when plasma testosterone levels are elevated (Figure 8.1). Support for this idea derives from the observation that early postnatal exposure to testosterone masculinizes certain aspects of sexual behavior in the female marmoset (Abbott, 1984). Moreover, in the closely related saddleback tamarin (*Saguinus fuscicollis*), neonatal castration causes marked deficits in copulatory behavior (Epple et al., 1978; Epple, Alveario, & Belcher, 1990).

To examine the behavioral significance of the postnatal testosterone surge in the marmoset in more detail, experiments were conducted in order to compare the effects of castration performed during three periods of life (neonatally, prepubertally, and in adulthood) upon sexual behavior and aggression in adulthood (Dixson, 1993a; 1993b). Behavior of adult marmosets which had been castrated in infancy (between Days 1 and 7; n = 8) was compared to that shown by males castrated prepubertally (between Days 140 and 180; n = 7) or in adulthood (between 2.5 and 3.0 years of age; n = 8) as well as to eight age-matched intact adult males. All monkeys were reared in their natal family groups until two to three years of age and then housed singly prior to behavioral testing in a series of paired encounters with unfamiliar conspecifics of the same sex or the opposite sex.

Aggressive Behavior

Encounters between neonatally castrated (NC) males and females were characterized by much higher frequencies of mutual aggression than in tests with the other three male groups. It was necessary to terminate 66 percent of encounters between NC males and females to avoid possible injuries (Figure 8.2A). Both sexes initiated aggression and no clear-cut dominance relationships were established in 75 percent of tests. By contrast, no tests between females and adult castrates (AC) or adult intact (AI) males were terminated;

Figure 8.1
Changes in Plasma Testosterone in Male Marmosets

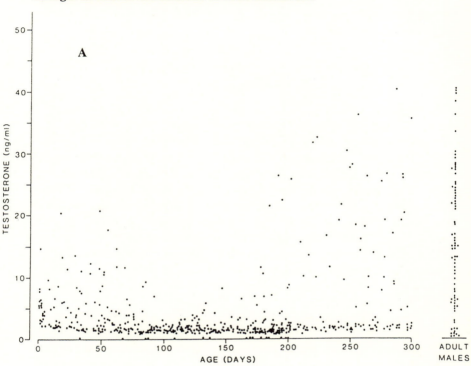

females never attacked males belonging to these experimental groups and aggression occurred at very low frequencies. Encounters between females and prepubertally castrated (PC) males did involve high frequencies of mutual aggression, but significantly less so than in the case of NC males; 32 percent of tests with PC males were terminated to avoid possible injuries. Females initiated aggression more frequently than PC males, and this often occurred in association with females' refusals and terminations of males' mounts and their repeated failures to attain intromission.

Data on aggressive interactions between males in the four experimental groups and intact adult males during paired encounters are shown in Figure 8.2B. As expected, encounters between intact adult males resulted in frequent aggression and 58 percent of tests were terminated. Tests between intact males and castrates (NC, PC, and AC males) resulted in less aggression and this effect was most pronounced in the case of encounters between intacts and NC partners. However, there were no statistically significant differences in tests between intact males and NC or PC males (Figure 8.2B), except that intacts showed higher frequencies of noncontact aggression toward PC partners than toward NC males (Dixson, 1993b).

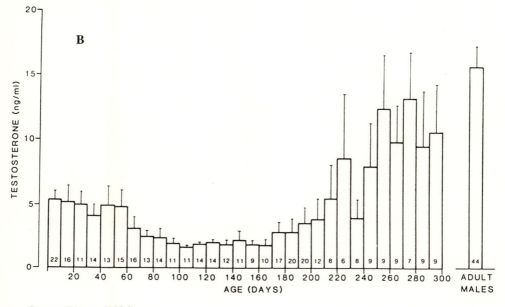

Source: Dixson (1986).

A. Postnatal changes in plasma testosterone in male marmosets during Days 1 to 300 and in adulthood. Each point represents a single testosterone determination. **B.** Mean (± SEM) plasma testosterone levels in male marmosets during consecutive ten-day periods from birth until 300 days of age. The numbers of males sampled during each period is shown at the foot of each histogram. Mean (± SEM) testosterone levels for adult males are shown on the right.

Sexual Behavior

Data on copulatory behavior for the four experimental groups are shown in Figure 8.3. NC males did not attempt to mount females during pair tests, whereas PC, AC, and AI males all mounted their female partners frequently (Figure 8.3A). None of the PC males achieved intromission; though these males achieved erection and made vigorous thrusting movements, the small size of the phallus in these subjects probably interfered with normal copulatory behavior. Adult castrates intromitted less frequently than AI males and only one AC male achieved ejaculation (Figure 8.3A). Females rarely invited copulation from NC males; frequencies of females' proceptive tongue-flicking displays were significantly lower in tests with NC partners than during encounters with PC, AC, or AI males (Figure 8.3B). Likewise, NC males invited copulation, by tongue flicking, significantly less than males in the three other experimental groups. As regards female receptivity, the major effect concerned PC males, whose mounts were refused or terminated by females 60 percent of the time (Figure 8.3B). Many of these refusals or terminations occurred in response to repeated mounts and failures to intromit by PC partners.

Figure 8.2
Aggressive Interactions between Male Marmosets in the Four
Experimental Groups

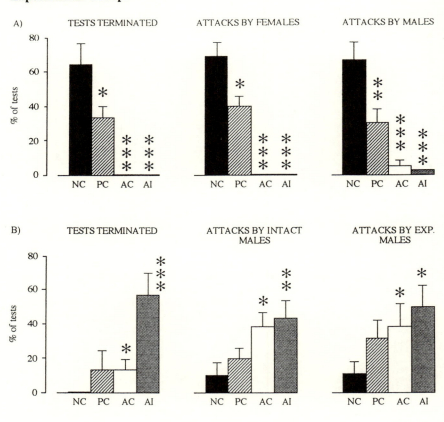

Source: Dixson (1993b).

A. With ovariectomized, oestradiol-treated female partners. **B.** With intact male partners. Data are mean (± SEM) percentages of tests.

Note: Black bars = neonatally castrated males; hatched bars = prepubertally castrated males; open bars = adult castrates; stippled bars = age-matched, intact adult males. Statistical comparisons are between NC males and those in each of the remaining groups. * = p 0.05; ** = p 0.01; *** = p 0.001 (Mann Whitney-U test: 2-tailed).

When males of the four experimental groups were pair tested with sexually experienced intact adult males, it was notable that the latter frequently attempted to mount males belonging to the three castrate groups (NC, PC, and AC groups), but only rarely behaved in this way toward AI partners. Mount frequencies were highest with NC males, but did not differ statistically from those measured with either PC or AC males. The NC males did not behave in

Figure 8.3
Sexual Behavior during Paired Encounters between Male Marmosets in the Four Experimental Groups and Ovariectomized, Oestradiol-Treated Females

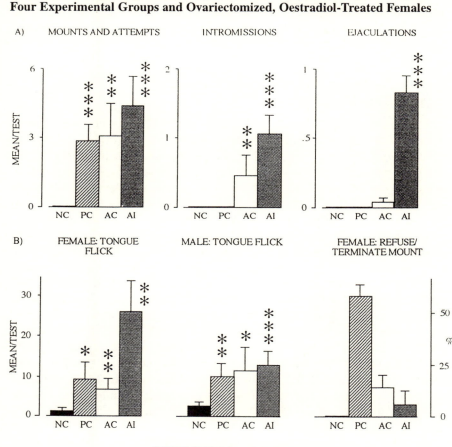

Source: Dixson (1993b).

A. Copulatory behavior by males. **B.** Precopulatory tongue-flicking displays and females' refusals or terminations of males' mounts. Data are individual means (± SEM) per test. Females' refusals and terminations are shown as mean percentages.

Note: Black bars = neonatally castrated males; hatched bars = prepubertally castrated males; open bars = adult castrates; stippled bars = age-matched, intact adult males. Statistical comparisons are between NC males and those in each of the remaining groups. * = p 0.05; ** = p 0.01; *** = p 0.001 (Mann Whitney-U test: 2-tailed).

a more "feminine" manner than males castrated later in development. Thus, NC males initiated only 4 percent of mounts received from intact adult male partners. The NC males refused or terminated 67 percent of mounts by intact partners; there was little evidence that NC males were more sexually receptive than PC or AC males during such tests. Three of the NC males behaved passively and tolerated mounts by at least one of the four intact partners they encountered during their pair tests. Only one NC male exhibited tongue flicking while mounted by an intact male partner. The behavior observed appeared to be submissive rather than sexual, and was in keeping with the virtual absence of aggression between NC and intact adult male partners.

Effects of Testosterone Propionate Administered to NC Male Marmosets

Subsequent to the experiments outlined, the eight NC males were treated with testosterone propionate (TP) (by subcutaneous injection in arachis oil, thrice weekly at a total dosage of 7 mg per week). Hormone treatment continued for eighty days prior to recommencement of behavioral testing. Pair tests consisted (as before) of a series of ten-minute encounters between NC males and unfamiliar adults of the same or the opposite sex (Dixson, 1993a). The most remarkable finding was the ability of TP treatment to reverse the previously reported effects of neonatal castration upon aggressive and sexual behavior. Thus, TP treatment activated mounting behavior in seven out of the eight subjects (Table 8.1). One male attempted to mount his female partner on only one occasion, but the remaining seven males mounted, exhibited penile erections, and made pelvic thrusting movements during the majority of tests. However, the small size of the penis in these subjects resulted in a failure to achieve intromission, except in the case of male No. 319, which intromitted and ejaculated on three occasions. A moderate degree of penile growth occurred in all males, but the penes of NC males never attained adult dimensions. Though TP resulted in some growth of the shaft, emergence of the glans from the prepuce, and growth of keratinized "penile spines" on the surface of the glans, the penis retained the overall dimensions of a PC male and was morphologically abnormal (Figure 8.4).

Females were markedly more proceptive toward NC males after the latter had received testosterone propionate. In association with this, aggression between the sexes diminished dramatically (Figure 8.5A). Conversely, aggression between intact males and NC subjects increased significantly after the latter had been treated with TP, and it was necessary to terminate 56 percent of tests to prevent possible injuries (Figure 8.5B). Intact males exhibited fewer sexual invitations toward TP-treated NC subjects; only three intact males made mount attempts, and these were refused.

Some Conclusions: Significance of Testosterone Secretion in Infant Male Marmosets

Castration during the first postnatal week in the male marmoset has measurably different effects upon sexual and aggressive behavior in adulthood than castration during the prepubertal period. Neonatally castrated male mar-

Table 8.1
Effects of Testosterone Propionate upon Sexual Behavior of Neonatally Castrated Marmosets during Paired Encounters with Ovariectomized, Oestradiol-Treated Females

Male No.	Attempts + mounts	Mounts + penile erection	Mounts + pelvic thrusting	Intromission	Ejaculation
316	1.50	0.75	0.50	0.00	0.00
317	4.25	3.75	2.25	0.00	0.00
319	6.00	4.75	3.25	0.75	0.75
320	6.00	5.00	4.25	0.00	0.00
322	4.00	2.75	2.00	0.00	0.00
323	2.00	1.5	1.50	0.00	0.00
328	2.75	2.5	1.75	0.00	0.00
335	0.25	0.00	0.00	0.00	0.00
Mean	**	**	**		
±SEM	3.3 ± 0.7	2.6 ± 0.6	1.9 ± 0.5	0.1 ± 0.1	0.1 ± 0.1

Source: Dixson (1993a).

Note: Data are mean frequencies per test for each NC male with four separate female partners; ** $p = 0.02$ by comparison with pre-TP treatment data (Wilcoxon test); only data for TP treatment are shown, as prior to hormone treatment none of the NC males had attempted to mount a female.

mosets exhibit no mounting behavior when paired with females in adulthood. However, it is probable that the high frequencies of mutual aggression between NC males and females might have masked the expression of sexual behavior during paired encounters. Treatment of NC males with testosterone in adulthood reduces aggression in oppositely sexed pair tests and activates mounting and pelvic thrusting behavior. The neural substrates serving for the expression of these copulatory patterns are presumably at least partly orga-

Figure 8.4
Perineal Views of the Penises of Adult Male Marmosets (Aged 3 to 4 years; dissected to include the ischiocavernosus muscles and bulbocavernosus muscles)

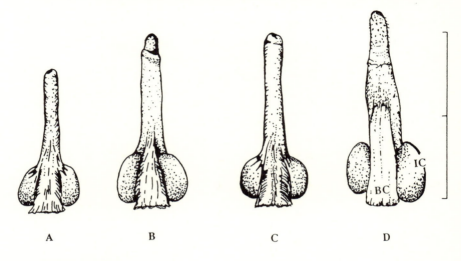

Source: Dixson (1993a).

A = A male castrated neonatally. **B** = A male castrated neonatally and treated with testoster-one propionate for 101 days in adulthood. **C** = A male castrated prepubertally, between 160 and 180 days of age. **D** = An intact adult male. The scale is in centimeter divisions. IC = ischiocavernosus muscles. BC = bulbocavernosus muscles.

nized prior to birth in the male marmoset, or do not require the postnatal testosterone surge for their organization. In this context it is notable that re-versible suppression of testosterone secretion in male marmosets by luteiniz-ing hormone releasing hormone (LHRH) antagonist treatment during the first fourteen weeks of infancy does not prevent expression of normal copulatory behavior in adulthood (Lunn, Recio, Morris, & Fraser, 1994).

Neonatal castration does not prevent masculinization of copulatory pat-terns in male marmosets; neither is it associated with feminized sexual be-havior. Though intact adult males mount NC partners and attempt copulation, the latter refuse or terminate the majority of mounts. Also, NC males do not invite copulation from intact partners; in this respect their behavior is similar to that of males castrated later in life, except that they tend to be more sub-missive toward intact partners. It appears that socially, as well as sexually, unfamiliar conspecifics react toward NC males as if they are females. These castrates were treated antagonistically by adult females and as potential sex partners by intact adult males. Neonatally castrated males also behaved in a socially "feminine" manner, threatening and attacking female strangers but reacting affiliatively toward male strangers.

Figure 8.5

Effects of Testosterone Propionate Administered to Neonatally Castrated Male Marmosets in Adulthood upon Their Aggressive Interactions during Pair Tests

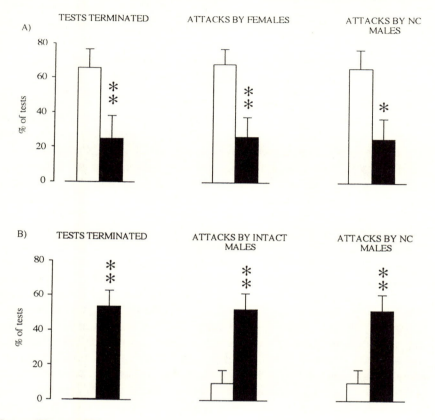

Source: Dixson (1993a).

A. With ovariectomized, oestradiol-treated female partners. **B.** With intact male partners. Data are mean (± SEM) percentages of tests.

Note: Open bars = no hormone; black bars = TP treated; * = p 0.05; ** = p 0.02 (Wilcoxon test).

It is possible that nonbehavioral cues from NC males, as well as their behavior, affected their interactions with conspecifics. Olfactory communication via cutaneous glandular secretions and urine plays a most important role in sexual recognition, individual recognition, and "dominance"-related behavior in marmosets and tamarins (Epple et al., 1993). Early castration may have affected the development of scent glands and chemical cues more profoundly than castration performed later in postnatal life. In addition, it should be noted that the external genitalia of NC males had an abnormal and infantile appearance; whether the genitalia provide visual cues affecting sexual recognition and behavioral responses by unfamiliar conspecifics is unknown. It is possible that infancy represents a critical phase for phallic growth and for "priming" the responsiveness of phallic tissues to androgens secreted later in development. This hypothesis also arises with respect to observations on penile growth in infant rhesus monkeys, as described in the following section.

EFFECTS OF POSTNATAL TESTOSTERONE IN INFANT RHESUS MONKEYS

In an attempt to explore the functions of the postnatal testosterone surge in male rhesus monkeys in a less invasive fashion, we have employed a luteinizing hormone releasing hormone agonist rather than surgical castration to block testosterone secretion during infancy in a reversible fashion. Pulsatile release of LHRH by the hypothalamus is essential for maintenance of LH secretion by the pituitary gland, and this in turn stimulates production of testosterone by the testes. However, chronic (as opposed to pulsatile) treatment with a LHRH agonist leads to down-regulation of pituitary LH receptors and hence blocks testosterone production.

Male infants born into small breeding groups of rhesus monkeys were implanted subcutaneously with a potent LHRH agonist (meterelin) during the first postnatal week and again at thirteen weeks of age. As a control procedure, some males received sham operations. Female infants in these groups were implanted subcutaneously with small silastic capsules containing testosterone to mimic the testosterone surge which occurs in males. Implants were replaced every four weeks, and a second group of females received empty silastic capsules as a control procedure. All infants in these experimental groups were observed for four thirty-minute sessions each week until six months of age. Data were collected (using a computerized system) on mother–infant interactions; sociosexual, playful, and aggressive behavior; as well as grooming and other interactions between the infant and mother or other group members. Every two weeks, each mother–infant pair was removed from its group and sedated in order to obtain body measurements and a blood sample from the offspring for testosterone radioimmunoassay. These studies are still in progress; here we present preliminary data collected on fifteen infants during their first six postnatal months.

Effects of Hormonal Treatments on Behavioral Development

Figure 8.6A shows serum testosterone levels in infant rhesus monkeys throughout the first six postnatal months, together with effects of LHRH agonist treatment in infant males and testosterone treatment in infant females. A postnatal surge of serum testosterone was measured in the four control males and especially in blood samples collected at night on Weeks 5, 11, 17, and 23, with a progressive decline in mean testosterone levels being apparent across

Figure 8.6

Serum Testosterone Levels, Frequencies of Mounting, and Frequencies of Rough and Tumble Play during the First Six Months in Infant Rhesus Monkeys

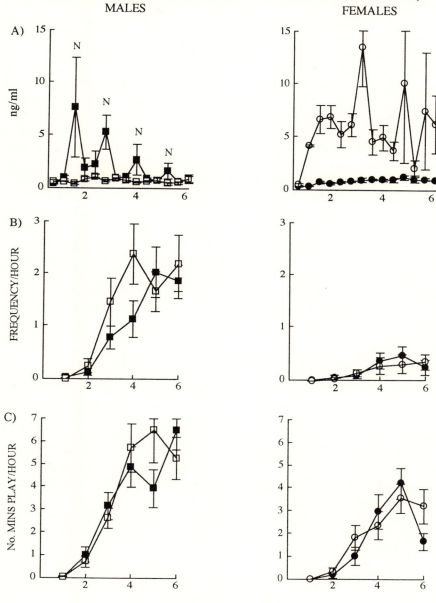

AGE OF INFANTS (MONTHS)

A. Serum testosterone levels (n = a blood sample collected at night between 20:45 and 22:00 hours). **B.** Frequencies of mounting. **C.** Frequencies of rough and tumble play during the first six months in infant rhesus monkeys.

Note: ■ = control (sham-operated) males (n = 4); □ = LHRH agonist (meterelin) implanted males (n = 4); • = control (sham-operated) females (n = 3); ○ = testosterone-implanted females (n = 4). Data are means (± SEM) at biweekly intervals (testosterone levels) and monthly intervals (behavioral data).

this time span. Implanting four males with a long-acting LHRH agonist was effective in suppressing serum testosterone to nondetectable levels. Conversely, subcutaneous implantation of silastic capsules containing testosterone into four infant females produced marked elevations of serum testosterone. The levels achieved varied considerably between subjects and were higher on average than testosterone levels in male infants.

Figures 8.6B and 8.6C show the emergence of two sexually dimorphic patterns of behavior in these infant monkeys during the first six months: rough and tumble play and mounting. Increases in mounting in male controls were apparent from three months of age onward, and frequencies were considerable higher than in female controls. Thus, at six months of age males were mounting nine times more frequently, on average, than age-matched females in these social groups. However, testosterone treatment of infant females or LHRH agonist treatment of infant males had no effect upon mount frequencies. The same picture emerges when the development of rough and tumble play is considered (Figure 8.6C). A sex difference in the behavior was apparent from three months onward, with males exhibiting consistently higher frequencies of rough and tumble play than females. As with mounting behavior, hormone treatments had no effect on the emergence of this sexually dimorphic behavior. Though only two behavioral patterns are shown in Figure 8.6, these data are representative of other sexually dimorphic patterns which we studied in these infants.

Effects of Hormonal Treatments on Genital Development

At birth the phallus is prominent in male rhesus monkeys, but the glans penis is not usually visible as it is concealed within and adheres closely to the prepuce. Progressive lengthening of the penis and separation of the glans from the prepuce (foreskin) occurred during the first six months in control males. This effect was striking in three of the subjects and they were readily distinguishable from males which had received LHRH agonist. Agonist-treated males had markedly shorter penises and the prepuce failed to separate normally in these subjects (Figure 8.7). The sensitivity of the clitoris to androgenic stimulation was also very marked in infant females. The length of the clitoris increased threefold in testosterone-treated females and the glans clitoris enlarged in all four subjects (Figure 8.7).

CONCLUSION

It has been suggested that the early postnatal period represents another critical phase during which testicular androgen effects development in male primates (Mann et al., 1989; Mann & Fraser, 1996). However, as far as behavior is concerned, evidence linking the postnatal testosterone surge to the development of sexually dimorphic patterns of behavior is not impressive.

Figure 8.7
Effects of LHRH Agonist (Meterelin) or Testosterone Treatment upon Penile or Clitoral Growth in Infant Rhesus Monkeys

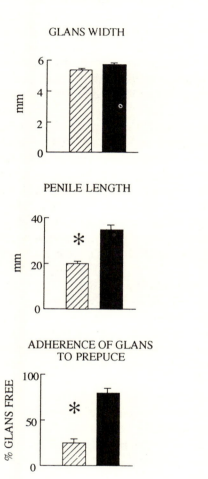
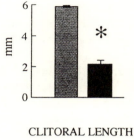
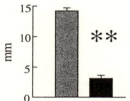

Data are means (± SEM) for infants aged between five and seven months.
Note: Black bars = control (i.e., untreated) males and females; hatched bars = male infants treated with meterelin to block testosterone secretion; stippled bars = females treated with testosterone; * p = 0.05; ** p = 0.01 (Mann Whitney-U test: 2-tailed).

The behavior of male rhesus monkeys treated with LHRH analogues to block the postnatal surge is essentially normal in adulthood (Eisler et al., 1993), as is also the case in the male marmoset (Lunn et al., 1994). Our studies indicate that neonatal castration has marked effects upon sexual and aggressive behavior in the marmoset and that these effects are significantly greater than those which occur in prepubertally castrated males. However, testosterone treatment in adulthood largely reverses such effects, and those which remain (e.g., failure to intromit and ejaculate) are mainly attributable to faulty penile development in neonatal castrates rather than to an organizing effect of testosterone upon neural substrates.

Sexually dimorphic patterns of behavior such as mounting and rough and tumble play are much more readily studied in the rhesus monkey than in the marmoset. These patterns are not affected by a reversible blockade of the pituitary–testicular axis in infant males or by treating infant female rhesus monkeys with supraphysiological doses of testosterone during the first six months.

However, subtle effects of the postnatal testosterone surge on behavioral development in the rhesus monkey cannot be dismissed. Wallen and colleagues (1995) report that affiliative behavior between infant males and their mothers or other group members is greater following suppression of the postnatal testosterone surge. This observation applied to yearling males and we are currently studying a larger cohort of infants in order to examine this question. As far as pronounced sexually dimorphic patterns are concerned (e.g., play or sociosexual behavior), it appears that prenatal androgenization, rather than early postnatal testosterone secretion, plays the major role in organizing relevant neural substrates (Goy & McEwen, 1980, pp. 50–54).

Penile growth is affected by the postnatal testosterone surge in both the rhesus monkey and the marmoset. Whatever the dynamics of sex-hormone binding globulin and levels of free testosterone may be in such infants, it is clear that testosterone is available to the penile tissues and is biologically active at this time. Priming of the genital tissues by androgen during infancy may also influence responsiveness of the penis to testosterone later in life, when males reach puberty.

The relevance of the postnatal testosterone surge in human development remains an open question. Though data obtained from monkeys do not indicate a strong case for testosterone affecting behavioral development during human infancy, the possibility cannot be dismissed. Human infants are born in a less well-developed condition than are infant monkeys and the human brain undergoes an enormous increase in size and complexity during the first year of life. Thus, the early postnatal surge of testosterone may have different consequences for brain development in man than in rhesus monkeys or marmosets. Finally, it should be noted that a sexually dimorphic nucleus (SDN–POA) occurs in the anterior hypothalamus of the human brain and that this structure only differentiates from approximately the fourth postnatal year onward (Swaab & Hofman, 1988). Whether the postnatal testosterone surge might contribute to development of a larger SDN–POA in the human male remains speculative, but it might be possible to test this hypothesis in experiments which block postnatal testosterone secretion in male rhesus monkeys, since an SDN–POA is also present in this primate species (Swaab, personal communication).

ACKNOWLEDGMENTS

We are most grateful to the British Medical Research Council and to the University of Cambridge (Sub-Department of Animal Behaviour) for financial support. Our thanks to Dr. R. Deghenghi and his colleagues at Europeptides Ltd. for meterelin implants, to Dr. Hamish Fraser (MRC, Edinburgh) for measuring testosterone levels in infant rhesus monkeys, and to Mr. David Rayment for technical assistance during studies of the rhesus monkeys.

Chapter 9

Sex Differences in the Organization of Behavior Patterns: Endpoint Measures Do Not Tell the Whole Story

Evelyn F. Field and Sergio M. Pellis

In 1959, Phoenix, Goy, Gerall, and Young demonstrated that the potential for either masculine or feminine sexual behavior in guinea pigs is dependent on early exposure to gonadal hormones. Males undergo masculinization of male-typical characteristics and defeminization of female-typical characteristics due to the action of gonadal hormones in early development. Postpubertally, hormones activate the expression of these sex differences. Since this early work, a number of studies using different species have replicated these findings (Baum, 1979; Baum, Carroll, Cherry, & Tobet, 1990), supporting the idea that gonadal hormones have an organizing effect early in development and an activating effect in adulthood. In addition, the development of sex differences between males and females has been extended beyond reproductive behavior patterns to include sexual orientation (Adkins-Regan, 1988), spatial behavior (Williams, Barnett, & Meck, 1990; Williams & Meck, 1991), spontaneous/exploratory activity (Stewart & Cygan, 1980; Mead, Hargreaves, & Galea, 1996), rotational behavior (Carlson & Glick, 1996), micturition in dogs (Beach, 1974), and play (Meaney & Stewart, 1981; Meaney, 1988; 1989; Pellis, Pellis, & McKenna, 1994).

Even though sex differences in mammals exist in both reproductive (Ward, 1992) and nonreproductive behaviors (Beatty, 1992), most sexually dimorphic behaviors are dimorphic only in the sense that one sex is more likely to perform them than the other (Aron, Chateau, Schaeffer, & Roos, 1991; Goy & Roy, 1991). Except for some behavioral patterns that are associated with parturition, most sexually dimorphic behavior patterns are described as sex-typical, not sex-exclusive. Sexually dimorphic behavior patterns may therefore occur in both sexes, but have a lower threshold for elicitation in one sex versus the other (Money, 1988). Males differ from females not in what they do, but in how likely they are to perform particular behavior patterns. Similarly, when more than one behavior pattern exists to perform the same functional outcome, the same model may apply. For example, two sex-typical behavior patterns are used for micturition by dogs after puberty; while females squat, males raise a hindleg; prior to puberty, however, males squat like females (Beach, 1974). Thus, it can be concluded that a change in threshold has occurred for the elicitation of the female-typical pattern of micturition in males. For these reasons, most studies of sex-typical behavior patterns (see Beatty, 1992, for a review) have focused on differences in the relative frequency of occurrence of a specific behavior pattern for each sex. Our studies, however, suggest that it cannot be assumed that when males and females are performing what appears to be the same behavior pattern that they are in fact using the same combination of movements.

In this chapter we show that in four different behavior patterns males and females utilize a different combination of movements. These sex differences are seen in horizontal turns occurring in exploratory movements (Pellis, Pellis, & Field, 1995), forward locomotion (Pellis, Field, & Pellis, 1995), and evasive lateral dodges which occur during both play fighting (Pellis & Pellis, 1990), and when protecting a food item (Field, Whishaw, & Pellis, 1996). Simply scoring the occurrence of specific behavior patterns by their functional outcome—that is, an endpoint measurement—is insufficient in revealing sex differences at a motoric level. We will also argue that these sex differences at the level of motor organization add a valuable new dimension for the analysis of the development of sex differences.

PLAY FIGHTING

Play fighting or rough and tumble play is an activity common to juveniles of many species of mammals and some birds (Fagen, 1981). It is commonly believed to involve species-typical behavior patterns of agonistic attack and defense used in a nonserious manner (Meaney, Stewart, & Beatty, 1985). In rats, as in most other mammals so far studied, males typically engage in play fighting more frequently than females (Beatty, 1992; Meaney, 1988; 1989). Indeed, it is commonly believed that "Sex differences in social play are quantitative and not qualitative, referring to the frequency and not the forms of behaviors" (Meaney, 1989, p. 247). This quantitative difference in play fighting has been shown to be dependent upon the action of steroid sex hormones in the perinatal period. Castration at birth reduces the frequency of play fighting to female-typical levels, whereas androgenization of females perinatally raises play fighting to near male levels (Meaney et al., 1985). The evidence strongly supports the role of gonadal hormones in the organization of male-typical levels of play fighting (Beatty, 1992; Meaney, 1988).

Whereas there are a number of quantitative differences in the play fighting of male and female rats, we have found that there are also qualitative differences (Pellis, Field, Smith, & Pellis, 1997). Play fighting in rats involves attack and defense of the nape (Pellis & Pellis, 1987), where attacks involve the initiator attempting to rub its snout into the back of the neck of the partner. About 90 percent of attempted nape contacts are resisted by the recipient, who adopts several defensive tactics so as to protect the nape from being contacted. In addition, the defender will also launch counterattacks of its own in order to contact the partner's nape. An example of this is illustrated in Figure 9.1. The attacker approaches from the rear and reaches for the nape (a, b). The defender then rotates cephalocaudally around its longitudinal axis to lie supine (c–h). From this supine position, the defender can use its paws to hold off the attacker who is standing above and making lunges at the nape. The supine defender can also launch its own attacks on its partner's nape (i); these counterattacks can often be blocked by the attacker (j, k). If the supine defender can successfully free itself, it may then initiate a new nape attack (l–o). Such interactions can proceed for several seconds before stopping and then starting again.

Males and females differ in the likelihood of using particular behavior patterns to defend their napes from playful attack (Meaney & Stewart, 1981; Pellis & Pellis, 1990). With the approach of puberty, this difference is magnified, as male rats switch to a more adult form of defense when playfully attacked (Meaney & Stewart, 1981). This change includes a switch from using evasion or rolling over to supine to only partially rotating to supine. From this partially rotated position, where at least one hindpaw remains in contact with the ground, they can either rise to an upright posture or push against their partner with their flank (Pellis, 1989; Pellis & Pellis, 1987). In contrast, females do not exhibit this age-related change in defensive tactics (Pellis & Pellis, 1990). The male-typical change in defense tactics at puberty is contingent on the identity of the partner. As adults, females use the same pattern of defense whether interacting with a male or a female. Males, however, show the age-related change in their defensive behavior when interacting with females or subordinate males, but maintain a more juvenile pattern of defense when interacting with a dominant male (Pellis & Pellis, 1990; Pellis, Pellis, & McKenna, 1993). Recent work in our laboratory has shown that this age-related change in the defensive tactic used is dependent on the presence of androgens neonatally (Smith, Forgie, & Pellis, 1998), but not on the presence of androgens at puberty (Smith, Field, Forgie, & Pellis, 1996). However, in some situations females will use the partial rotation tactic (Pellis & Pellis, 1990; Pellis, Pellis, & Whishaw, 1992; Pellis et al., 1996). Therefore, these are sex-typical changes; while both males and females are able to perform all these defensive tactics, they differ in the likelihood of their use.

In some cases, however, the difference is at the level of motor organization, not the choice of behavior pattern. Close examination of a particular defensive behavior pattern, that of swerving away laterally from an approaching

Figure 9.1
A Long Sequence of Play Fighting Depicted for a Pair of Thirty-One-Day-Old Rats

Source: Reprinted from *Aggressive Behaviour* 13, by S. M. Pellis and V. C. Pellis. Play-fighting differs from serious attack in both target of attack and tactics of fighting in the laboratory rat *Rattus norvegicus*, pp. 227–242. Copyright © 1987, John Wiley & Sons, Inc.

Repeated attempts to attack and defend the nape area are depicted. Drawn from 16-mm movie film taken at 48 frames/second.

partner, has revealed that males and females use a different composition of movements. While females swerve so that their bodies move unidirectionally, in a cephalocaudal manner, away from the opponent (Figure 9.2A), males are more likely to couple this evasion with a movement of the pelvis toward the opponent (Figure 9.2B) (Pellis & Pellis, 1987; Pellis, 1989). That is, males not only move their nape away from the attacker; they also use their lower body to block the approach of the opponent.

Given that males are more likely to counterattack than are females (Pellis & Pellis, 1990), it is possible that they may be organizing their evasive maneuver so as to functionally enhance their ability to counterattack. Analysis of another context in which lateral evasive movements are performed but where counterattacks do not occur does not support this hypothesis. Instead, this analysis supports an alternative hypothesis, that the differences in movements used are intrinsic to sex differences in the motor system and are not functionally tied to the contingencies of the task.

Figure 9.2
A Consequence of the Sex-Typical Dodges for Female and Male Rats

A . FEMALE   B . MALE

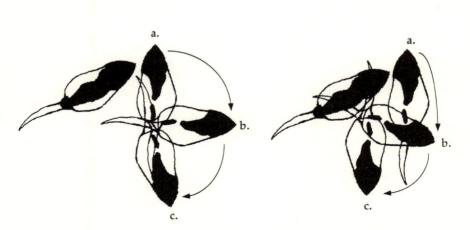

Source: Reprinted from *Neuroscience & Biobehavioral Reviews* 21, by S. M. Pellis, E. F. Field, L. K. Smith, and V. C. Pellis. Multiple differences in the play fighting of male and female rats: Implications for the causes and functions of play, pp. 105–120. Copyright 1997, with kind permission from Elsevier Science Ltd, The Boulevard, Langford Lane, Kidlington OX5 1GB, UK.

A consequence of the sex-typical dodges is that the female (A), by pivoting on her pelvis and moving forward, increases her distance from the opponent (left). In contrast, the male (B), by pivoting around the midbody and moving backward, closes the gap with his opponent, often making contact with his rump (right). The lowercase letters represent three successive stages of movement during dodges, so that (a) represents the initial position and (c) represents the final position. The intermediate position is represented by the gray drawing (b).

DODGING WHEN PROTECTING A FOOD ITEM

When eating a food item, a rat will typically hold the food in both forepaws and lean backwards onto its hindpaws. If another rat approaches from the side and attempts to grab the food pellet, the rat that is feeding will dodge laterally away in a manner similar to the evasion present in play fighting. This defensive dodging can be filmed from underneath, through plexiglass. This permits a detailed analysis of the body movements and stepping patterns performed (Pinel, Jones, & Whishaw, 1992; Whishaw & Tomie, 1987, 1988; Whishaw, 1988). In this test paradigm, pairs of rats which are partially food deprived are placed in a circular test enclosure. One pairmate is then given a food pellet which it keeps from the other partner by dodging away horizontally (Whishaw, 1988). Comparison of such dodges by males and females has revealed that they differ in their organization (Field, Whishaw, & Pellis, 1994; Field, Whishaw, & Pellis, 1996).

Females typically pivot away from the robber by moving around a point located near the pelvis, whereas males typically pivot away from the robber by moving around a point located near the midbody. Both sexes thus produce a large trajectory with the snout. However, while the excursion travelled by the female's pelvis is small, that traced by the male's pelvis is large (Figure 9.3). By pivoting around the midbody, the male moves its head away from the robber, simultaneously moving the pelvis toward and potentially blocking the movement of the robber.

These two types of lateral dodges, while superficially similar and functionally designed to move the head away from the robber, arise from a different combination of stepping patterns and shifts of body weight (Field, Whishaw, & Pellis, 1994; 1996). This dodging appears at around weaning (Bolles & Woods, 1964), with the sex-based preference for a pivot pattern detectable shortly thereafter.

Given that both male and female robbers stop moving toward the defender shortly after the dodge has commenced, the difference in the type of dodge pattern used cannot be accounted for by differences in the behavior of male and female robbers (Field, Whishaw, & Pellis, 1996). Rats, however, can modulate the magnitude of the dodge based on the properties of the food pellet. With increasing size or hardness of a food item the eating time is increased; this leads to a dodge of a larger magnitude (Whishaw & Gorny, 1994). These findings suggest that rats are capable of modifying their dodges in a manner sensitive to subtle contextual features beyond the immediate movements of the partner. For example, when play fighting, males and females alter their defensive responses depending on the sex of the attacking play partner, even though the form of the attack does not appear to differ (Pellis & Pellis, 1990). Therefore, the sex-specific dodging patterns may be a byproduct of the fact that we had used isosexual pairs in our first experiments (Field, Whishaw, & Pellis, 1996). Subsequent data, however, have shown that the composition of the dodge performed by males and females is not determined by the sex of the robber

Figure 9.3
The Trajectories of the Snout and Pelvis for an Unconstrained Female and Male Dodge

A . FEMALE   B . MALE

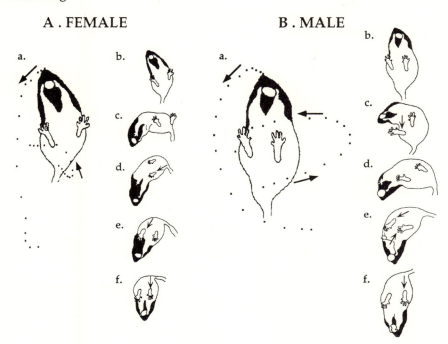

Source: Reprinted from *Journal of Comparative Psychology* 110, by E. F. Field, I. Q. Whishaw, and S. M. Pellis. A kinematic analysis of evasive dodging movements used during food protection in the rat: Evidence for sex differences in movement, pp. 298–306. Copyright © 1996 by the American Psychological Association. Reprinted with permission.

Each solid round dot represents two video frames, with the arrows with closed heads indicating the direction of the movement. Note that, unlike the female, the male makes a large outward swing of the pelvis. The number and direction of steps taken by the hindpaws are also indicated by the open-headed arrows. After turning laterally (Ab–c), the female makes an initial step with the paw ipsilateral to the direction of the dodge (Ad). This step is followed by a forward step of the paw contralateral to the direction of the dodge (Ae), and a final step forward by the hindpaw ipsilateral to the direction of the dodge (Af). In contrast, the male has less lateral movement of the upper body (Bb) before taking a step backward by the hindpaw ipsilateral to the direction of the dodge (Bc). This is followed by a second backward step with the ipsilateral hindpaw, with a forward step of the contralateral hindpaw shortly thereafter (Be). The ipsilateral hindpaw then makes a final forward step (Bf). The animals represented in this figure are scaled to represent the actual size of female and male adult rats.

(Pellis, Field, Smith, & Pellis, 1997; Field, Whishaw, & Pellis, 1997b); males perform midbody pivots irrespective of the sex of the robber.

The defensive lateral evasive maneuvers used during both play and dodging to protect a food item occur in a socially competitive situation, where subtle contextual factors may trigger a more formidable defensive tactic by males. Given that males engage in more combat (Blanchard, Flannelly, & Blanchard, 1988), they may have a lower threshold for the use of the midbody pivot, which maximizes defense of the head by interposing the rump between the opponent and the defender's head (Pellis & Pellis, 1992; Pellis, MacDonald, & Michener, 1996). During exploratory locomotion, an animal's movements, unlike those in dodging, are unconstrained by a partner. Therefore, sex differences during exploratory locomotion would support the possibility that males and females differ in their motor organization.

SPONTANEOUS TURNING IN AN OPEN FIELD

Turning in an open field by adult animals can be defined as a transitional act occurring between bouts of forward locomotion (Eilam, 1994). Turning is one of the first behaviors exhibited by neonate rats (Eilam & Golani, 1988; Golani, Bronchti, Moualem, & Teitelbaum, 1981), and continues to be exhibited through development and into adulthood. Previous work has shown that the motor composition of turning can be influenced by body morphology (Eilam, 1994), and central neural systems (Cools, Scheenen, Eilam, & Golani, 1989; Miklyaeva, Martens, & Whishaw, 1995).

Sex differences in turning behavior are usually documented in terms of the frequency of rotations in the horizontal plane (Carlson & Glick, 1996). These studies, however, have not looked at whether the composition of the behavior exhibited is different between males and females. We conducted a study to examine whether males and females use different movement patterns when turning laterally in an open field (Pellis, Pellis, & Field, 1995). Turning was defined as a cessation of forward movement and a change in the horizontal position of the head and upper body by ninety degrees or greater (Eilam, 1994). Turns that were immediately preceded by another behavior, such as rearing or grooming, or turns that were constrained by the plexiglass cylinder and involved vertical movements were not included. For each example chosen, the fore- and hindpaw stepping patterns were noted in their order of occurrence.

There were three sequences of hindpaw stepping patterns exhibited during spontaneous turns; in all cases hindpaw stepping was preceded by forepaw stepping. In Figure 9.4A, the hindpaw that is contralateral to the direction of the turn steps first, moving the pelvis into alignment with the forequarters, which have already turned. This first step is then followed by a forward step of the ipsilateral hindpaw. In Figure 9.4B, the hindpaw ipsilateral to the turn makes an initial step backward toward the midline of the body. This step is followed by a forward step of the contralateral hindpaw. A third forward step is then made by the ipsilateral hindpaw. Finally, in Figure 9.4C, the initial hindpaw step is made in a forward direction by the ipsilateral hindpaw. This is followed by a forward step of the contralateral hindpaw.

Figure 9.4
Stepping Patterns for the Three Types of Ninety-Degree Turns Commonly Used by Adult Rats

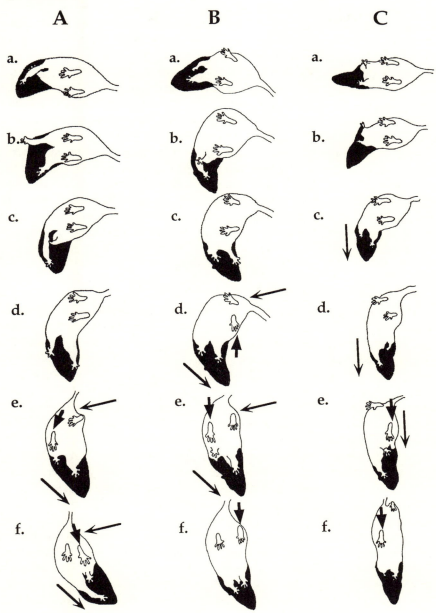

The male-typical patterns (A & B) result in movement by the pelvis in the direction opposite to that of the turn (d–f open arrows). In contrast, the female-typical pattern (C) shows unidirectional movement as indicated by the open arrows (d–f). In conjunction with the differences in pelvic movement there are differences in the stepping patterns that accompany the three types of turns. All three types of hindfeet stepping patterns are preceded by forelimb stepping. The closed arrows show the hindpaw that is stepping and the direction of the step. The direction of movement of the body is depicted by the larger arrow.

When turning, males appear to move their pelvis more, producing a different pattern of stepping than that seen in females. In about 70 percent of cases, females turn their forequarters toward the direction of the turn and follow this with the sequence of steps as described in Figure 9.4C; this produces a small amount of horizontal displacement of the pelvis. In contrast, males are significantly different from females in that they use hindlimb stepping patterns which produce a greater amount of pelvic movement. Therefore, after the initial movement of the forequarters in the direction of the turn, males are more likely to step in the manner described in Figure 9.4A and 9.4B in about 89 percent of cases.

Preliminary findings suggest that these sex differences in spontaneous turning are present shortly after birth (Field, 1996). It is likely, therefore, that the sex differences in dodging patterns are not simply differences in the selection of sex-typical behavior patterns, but rather reflect underlying differences in how the movements are generated. This possibility is further supported by the presence of sex differences in stepping and pelvic movements during forward locomotion.

FORWARD LOCOMOTION

The term locomotion has been defined as any forward movement that involves rhythmic limb movements. In this experiment (Pellis, Field, & Pellis, 1995), only slow walking, where at least three paws are in contact with the plexiglass surface at all times, was analyzed (Gambaryan, 1974, p. 20–21). Whereas sex differences in general locomotor activity and open field behavior have been documented (Stewart & Cygan, 1980; Beatty, 1992), differences in the pattern of movements during rhythmic forward locomotion have not been described in detail. Parker and Clarke (1990) showed that there is a difference in stride width for male and female Wistar rats. Even though this measure increased with increased body size, the sex difference remained present at all body sizes. Therefore, the difference in step parameters cannot be accounted for by the size differences between males and females.

We have further characterized the sex differences in locomotion. The amount of sway by the pelvis during a hindpaw step was calculated, and each step was chosen from within a sequence of steps so that they were not involved in the initiation or cessation of walking. In replicating the results of Parker and Clarke (1990), it was found that males had significantly more displacement of the pelvis than females (Pellis, Field, Smith, & Pellis, 1997). In part, the increased "swagger" of the male's pelvis was produced by the way in which the hind paws were placed. To measure this, in ten steps for each rat the angle of the long axis of the placed hind paw was scored relative to the direction of movement. On average, in the initial step placed, the males turned their hindpaws inward in reference to the midline of the body, whereas the females placed their hindpaws outward in reference to the midline of the body (Pellis,

Field, Smith, & Pellis, 1997). Thus, even simple forward locomotion involves kinematic differences between the sexes (Pellis, Field, & Pellis, 1995). These findings further support the hypothesis that there are major sex differences in the organization of motor patterns.

SEX DIFFERENCES IN MOVEMENT AND POSTURE

We have provided evidence for sex differences in the composition of four movement patterns having the same endpoint: evasion during play, dodging to protect a food item, spontaneous turning, and forward locomotion. In all cases it appears that the underlying difference between males and females is in their ability to coordinate fore- and hindquarter movements. Females use patterns of movement where the hindquarters generally follow the direction of the forequarters. This results in minimal hindquarter movement. In contrast, males use simultaneous movements of the fore- and hindquarters, often with the hindquarters moving in the direction opposite to the forequarters (Figure 9.5).

Figure 9.5
Lateral Turning Movements in Female and Male Rats

A . FEMALE   B . MALE

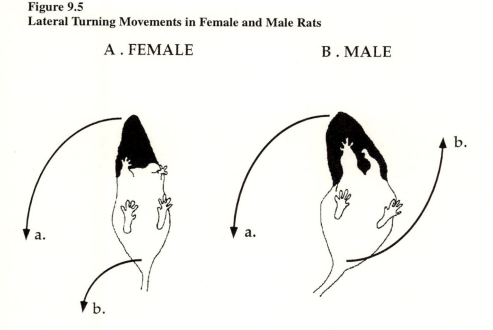

When turning laterally, whatever the behavioral context, females (A) generally move in a unidirectional manner, where the hindquarters (Ab) follow the movement of the forequarters (Aa). In contrast, males generally move their hindquarters (Bb) in the direction opposite that of the forequarters (Ba).

That the underlying factor generating the sex differences in movement patterns around the horizontal plane is a difference in the coordination of movement of the fore- and hindquarters is supported by sex differences in other planes of movement. For example, in rats the ability to turn from a supine position on the ground to prone is present from birth. At first, the rats use varying combinations of limb and body movements to rotate the longitudinal axis of the body to prone. Eventually, by about three weeks of age, they use the adult-typical pattern of cephalocaudal axial rotation to right to prone (Pellis, Pellis, & Teitelbaum, 1991). Males and females appear to use a different combination of limb and body movements to achieve the prone position, and these differences become evident within the first few days after birth. At two days after birth, males right the hindquarters following rotation of the forequarters to prone in about half the time that it takes females. This appears to be due to a difference in the coordination of the movements of the forequarters with those of the hindquarters (Martens, Field, Pellis, & Pellis, 1996). Therefore, we suggest that, in part, the differences in the composition of the behavior patterns of righting arise from a sex difference in the coordination of the anterior and posterior parts of the body. Some evidence suggests that a separate postural difference may also be involved.

Male and female rats shift their body weights differently when rearing onto their hindpaws. Whereas males tend to rear away from the walls of a testing container, females tend to rear by placing their forepaws against the vertical surface of the enclosure. Following the method devised by Clarke and Williams (1994) to determine where an animal is placing its weight on its paws, it was found that when rearing males place most of their weight on the posterior part of the hindpaw. In contrast, females appear to maintain most of their weight on the anterior part of the hindpaw (Field & Pellis, unpublished observations). This differential weight placement on the hindpaws is likely to be a contributing factor in determining the differences between males and females when rearing.

This conclusion has been supported by similar sex differences in another behavioral context. When facing downward on an inclined plane, rats respond to the resultant downward force by turning around to face upward (Crozier & Pincus, 1926). The eliciting stimulus for this response appears to be the pressure exerted on the limbs, which brace against the incline by pushing backward (Morrissey, Pellis, Pellis, & Teitelbaum, 1989). Preliminary observations have shown that females turn at a lower angle than do males (Field, Whishaw, & Pellis, 1997c). This is consistent with the hypothesis that females, by differentially placing their body weight on the anterior portions of their paws, are more likely to overbalance in response to the downward force. An alternative explanation, however, is that females may have a lower threshold to initiate a locomotor response to the incline of the board. That is, the difference may be locomotor, not postural.

To test this alternative possibility, another approach was used. Rats that are made cataleptic by the blockade or depletion of ascending dopamine systems no longer initiate movement (Mason, 1984). However, these rats have intact postural support reflexes and are able to maintain and regain stable static equilibrium (Teitelbaum, Schallert, DeRyck, Whishaw, & Golani, 1980). Therefore, cataleptic postural mechanisms can be studied in isolation from movement (Teitelbaum, 1982). For example, when pushed, cataleptic rats will brace against the applied force, but once stability has been regained the rats resume an immobile state (Schallert, DeRyck, Whishaw, Ramirez, & Teitelbaum, 1979; Pellis, Chen, & Teitelbaum, 1985).

When placed on a sloping board, rats treated with a cataleptogenic agent such as haloperidol will initially brace against the downward force. However, when the angle of the board is increased and the downward force becomes greater, the rats begin to slip and subsequently leap forward (Morrissey, Pellis, Pellis, & Teitelbaum, 1989); upon landing, they will once again resume an immobile state. Female rats treated with 5 mg/kg of haloperidol jumped off a sloping board at a lower angle than did males. Frame-by-frame inspection of these jumps revealed that the females, even when bracing, continued to place more of their weight on the anterior portion of their paws. This resulted in the females sliding downward on the inclined board sooner than did the males (Field, Whishaw, & Pellis, 1997c). Therefore, this experiment shows that when posture is tested independently from locomotion, females differ from males in their relative distribution of body weight.

We hypothesize that the sex differences present in the composition of movements during various experimental paradigms arise from a combination of differences in both the anterior–posterior coordination of the body and in the postural support mechanisms. How sex differences in these two factors interact will likely depend on the task performed and will require detailed analyses of movements by males and females in a variety of behavioral tasks. However, two major questions arise from this difference between males and females: How are these sex differences in motor organization developed, and why are they there?

SEX DIFFERENCES AND THE ROLE
OF PERIPHERAL ANATOMY

Sex differences in movement and posture may arise from peripheral differences in musculoskeletal morphology, especially of the pelvic area, given the functional requirements of gestation and parturition of female mammals. Sex differences in the composition of the pelvis have been reported for humans (Coleman, 1969), rats (Bernstein & Crelin, 1967), mice (Shimizu & Awata, 1984), and rabbits (Lowrance, 1968). While it is obvious that differences in peripheral anatomy are likely to be involved in differential patterns of movement, there are several reasons to believe that this does not explain all the differences in movement. Preliminary observations have shown that the differences in lateral movements between male and female rats are similar to the sex differences present in mice, hamsters, and domestic cats. Even though male and female rats are more similar in body morphology than rats are to hamsters, in terms of the organization of lateral movements male rats are more like male hamsters than like female rats. Furthermore, sex differences in movement patterns of rats are present in infancy, and thus before the onset of changes in body form (Bernstein & Crelin, 1967). That is, the differences in movement appear when physical differences in the morphology of the bony pelvis are minimal. Indeed, given the wider pelvis of female rats, one might expect that females should move the pelvis more than males. This is opposite to what was found in the behavioral contexts we analyzed.

Some human pathologies also suggest that movement differences are not solely due to sex differences in body morphology. For example, it has been suggested that girls with congenital adrenal hyperplasia (CAH) who are prenatally androgenized appear to exhibit more masculine behavior (Collaer & Hines, 1995). Indeed, based on a questionnaire study of afflicted subjects, their unafflicted sisters, and their mothers, Dittman (1992) reported that the CAH variant with the most strongly masculinized body morphology (i.e., the simple-virilizing variant) was reported to be the least male-like in movement, whereas the variant that was reported to be the most female-like in body morphology was the most masculine in movement. Also consistent with these data are some experimental findings. Vega Matuszczyk and Larsson (1995) have shown that treatment of male rats prenatally with an antiandrogen did not significantly alter their sexual behavior, even though further analysis showed that anatomically they had a poorly developed penis and a blind-ending vagina. These results demonstrate that even with incomplete development of male genitalia male sexual behavior is still present, suggesting that the behavior is independent of peripheral anatomical development. These findings support the idea that sex differences in movement are not solely due to differences in musculoskeletal morphology.

Again, given that many of the movement differences emerge before the differences in skeletal anatomy, we think that it is unlikely that this is an adequate explanation for sex differences in the organization of movement. In fact, it has been shown that neural sex differences may precede peripheral anatomical ones. Kelley and Dennison (1990) have shown that a sex difference exists in the number of motoneurons that innervate the larynx of male clawed frogs (*Xenopus laevis*) prior to the development of sex differences within the larynx. Indeed, Reisert and Pilgrim (1991) discuss findings where they show structural differences in midbrain dopaminergic neurons taken from male and female embryos that exist prior to hormonal influences. Therefore, it is possible that small, neurally based differences between males and females generate different patterns of movement, and these, in turn, may influence the development of a differential peripheral anatomy. An alternative possibility, however, is that differences in peripheral anatomy generate neural differences (Balaban, 1994). This process has been described for the differential size of muscles and innervating motoneuron nuclei of the bulbocavernosus (BC) and levator ani (LA) muscles that control penile reflexes, which atrophy in females shortly after birth (Cihak, Gutmann, & Hanzilikova, 1970). This difference is determined by the direct effect of testosterone on the muscles (BC/LA) to prevent their atrophy, and this in turn spares the motoneurons innervating them (Breedlove, 1992). The challenge for future research will be to trace the developmental pathways by which these interactive processes emerge to create the differences in movement that are generated by sexually dimorphic behavioral phenotypes.

SEX DIFFERENCES IN MOVEMENT AND THE ROLE OF GONADAL HORMONES

Whether small neural differences magnify peripheral differences or small peripheral differences magnify neural differences, our studies have shown that functionally similar behavior patterns performed by male and female rats involve different combinations of movements and postural adjustments. For the various reasons outlined, it is unlikely that peripheral anatomical differences can account for these motor differences, at least not completely. We further investigated the motor differences between the sexes by examining the role of gonadal hormones in the genesis of these differences. For each of the behaviors described, forward locomotion, spontaneous lateral turns, evasive movements during play, and dodging to protect a food item, we have examined the role of testicular hormones by either gonadectomizing male pups on the day of birth or injecting females with 200 l testosterone propionate on the day of birth and the next day (Field, Whishaw, & Pellis, 1995; 1997a; Pellis, Pellis, & Field, 1995; Pellis, Field, & Pellis, 1995; Pellis, Field, Smith, & Pellis, 1997). Males castrated at birth are more like females in their movements, and females administered testosterone propionate at birth are more like males in their movements. These findings support the conclusion that gonadal hormones have an organizational role in the development of sex differences in movement composition. Data on males gonadectomized after weaning and prior to puberty show that sex differences in these movements are not dependent on the presence of circulating hormones (Field, Whishaw, & Pellis, 1997a). How and when gonadal hormones exert their organizational effects in the perinatal period is yet to be determined.

CONCLUSION

Studies on nonreproductive sex differences have indicated that "These differences are typically small in magnitude, and tend to vary with the genotype and prior behavioral history of the individual" (Beatty, 1992, p. 115). However, most studies have not investigated the organization of the movements performed. As shown here, even behavior patterns that appear to be the same in both sexes can differ markedly in motoric organization. This suggests that the measurement of the frequency of occurrence of a behavior at its endpoint may not adequately describe the behavioral differences between males and females. To understand how sex differences develop and their relationship to anatomical differences, we need also consider the structure of a particular behavior and whether this structure is sexually dimorphic. In this way, we may gain a greater understanding of the relationship between anatomy and behavior. Furthermore, it is clear that the differences in movement organization between males and females is not task-specific, but rather is a sex-typical difference in the composition of similar movements that occur in such diverse contexts as play (Pellis et al., 1994; Pellis & Pellis, 1990), aggression (Blanchard, Blanchard, Takahashi, & Kelly, 1977; Pellis & Pellis, 1987), sex (Whishaw & Kolb, 1985), and spontaneous turning (Eilam & Golani, 1988).

That similar nonreproductive behavior patterns differ in form, and not only in the likelihood of occurrence, suggests there are some fundamental differences in the environmental milieu faced by each sex. What these functional contingencies may be is uncertain, but the existence of robust sex differences in the organization of movement provides an opportunity for further analysis. Clues may be sought from the development of these motoric differences and the comparative analysis of the distribution of such differences in a diversity of mammals and other vertebrates that vary in body morphology and ecological niche. In conjunction with this, the possible role of hormones, neural maturation, and behavioral experience during development need to be addressed in future research to determine how sex differences in movement composition arise and why they exist.

ACKNOWLEDGMENTS

We thank Vivien C. Pellis and Ian Q. Whishaw for their valuable collaboration on some of the research, and Vivien C. Pellis for her helpful comments on earlier versions of this manuscript. This work was in part supported by a grant to Sergio M. Pellis from the Natural Sciences and Engineering Council of Canada.

NEURO-COGNITIVE ASPECTS OF MALE/ FEMALE DIFFERENCES IN BEHAVIOR

Chapter 10

Cerebral Asymmetry and Cognitive Performance Show Complementary Fluctuations across the Menstrual Cycle

Geoff Sanders and Deborah Wenmoth

Over the last decade, interest in possible biological influences on neuropsychological development and performance has focused on the possible role of hormones, specifically the gonadal steroids for which two distinct effects have been identified (for reviews, see Becker, Breedlove, & Crews, 1992; Nelson, 1995). During critical prenatal or perinatal periods, gonadal steroids exert permanent organizational effects on brain and behavior (Collaer & Hines, 1995). In adulthood, these same hormones exert phasic activational effects (Kimura & Hampson, 1994). One approach to the study of activational effects in humans is to look for potential changes in performance across the menstrual cycle. Such changes have been reported for cognitive performance and functional cerebral asymmetry and it is this relationship that we explore here.

In the review that follows, we shall show that reports of significant changes in functional cerebral asymmetry across the menstrual cycle reveal an inconsistent relationship between maximum asymmetry and point in cycle. However, we shall argue that this inconsistency disappears when direction of hemispheric advantage is considered. Right hemisphere tasks reveal greater asymmetry when estrogen is low, whereas left hemisphere tasks reveal greater asymmetry when estrogen is high. To support this position we describe data obtained from a dichotic listening study in which women performed two tasks at two points in their menstrual cycle. Our left hemisphere verbal task showed greater asymmetry during the midluteal phase, when estrogen is high, while our right hemisphere music task showed greater asymmetry at menses, when estrogen is low. From menses to the midluteal phase hemispheric performance showed the same changes for both tasks: right hemisphere performance decreased while left hemisphere performance showed a nonsignificant increase. Drawing on the literature, we shall argue that these changes correlate with estrogen rather than progesterone levels and we shall draw attention to recent evidence for a causal relationship between estrogen and task performance. Finally, having noted reports that testosterone levels correlate with spatial ability, we conclude that differential hemispheric effects of gonadal steroids during adult life may explain the often elusive nature of sex differences in the literature on cerebral asymmetry and cognitive abilities.

SEX DIFFERENCES IN COGNITIVE ABILITIES
AND CEREBRAL ASYMMETRY

Exposure to gonadal steroids differs markedly between the sexes and there are many reports of sex differences in both cognitive performance and functional cerebral asymmetry (Halpern, 1992). On average, women score higher than men on verbal tasks, whereas men score higher than women on spatial and mathematical reasoning tasks (Maccoby & Jacklin, 1974). In terms of cerebral asymmetry, men are said to be more lateralized than women (McGlone, 1980). However, the existence of sex differences in both cognitive abilities (Caplan, MacPherson, & Tobin, 1985; Fausto-Sterling, 1992; Hyde & Linn, 1988) and cerebral asymmetry (Fairweather, 1982; Fausto-Sterling, 1992; Hahn, 1987) has been questioned, largely on the grounds that a high proportion of studies have failed to find significant effects. Studies may fail to find a sex difference because the tasks employed are insensitive or the sample size too small. The critical question concerns reports of significant sex differences. If these are chance occurrences, then the significant effects should split 50–50 in favor of women and men. When Halpern (pp. 84–85) reviewed the Hyde and Linn meta-analysis of sex differences in verbal abilities, she found that forty-four of the fifty-six studies reporting significant effects found that women scored higher than men. A similar picture emerges from Hahn's review of forty-one studies which used auditory, visual, and tactual procedures to measure cerebral asymmetry in children. Though 142 of 178 same-age comparisons failed to find significant sex differences, 30 of the 36 that did found males to be more lateralized than females. It appears that sex differences in cognitive abilities and cerebral asymmetry are somewhat elusive but nonetheless real phenomena. The findings described in this chapter indicate that failure to control for potential changes in performance across the menstrual cycle is one reason for the lack of consistency in the adult sex-difference literature.

When the performance of sexually dimorphic tasks was investigated at different points in the menstrual cycle, reciprocal changes were revealed (Hampson, 1990; Hampson & Kimura, 1988). The Rod and Frame test, at which men excel, was performed more accurately at menses than during the midluteal phase, whereas tests of speeded motor coordination, at which women excel, were performed faster during the midluteal phase than at menses (Hampson & Kimura, 1988). That study did not differentiate between the possible effects of estrogen and progesterone, because both of these ovarian steroids are low at menses and high during the midluteal phase. To address this question, Hampson compared performance at menses with that at the preovulatory phase when only estrogen is high. She found that female tasks were performed better and male tasks worse during the preovulatory phase than at menses, thus implicating estrogen rather than progesterone. Hence, both studies show that tasks involving verbal ability and fine motor skill, which favor women, are performed better when estrogen is high, while spatial tasks that favor men are performed better when estrogen is low.

Sex differences in cerebral asymmetry have been used to explain sex differences in cognitive abilities. Levy (1969; 1971) proposed that male superiority in spatial ability is the product of the marked lateralization of verbal abilities to the left and spatial abilities to the right hemisphere of the male brain. In women, the presence of some verbal ability in the right hemisphere is said to account for both their superior verbal ability (a result of the additional verbal capacity in the right hemisphere) and their inferior spatial ability (a result of reduced spatial processing capacity in the right hemisphere). For this hypothesis to be supported, we would expect menstrual cycle studies to reveal changes in cerebral asymmetry that complemented those recorded for cognitive abilities. Specifically, we would expect asymmetry to be greater at menses when the performance of male (spatial) tasks is enhanced and for asymmetry to be reduced at high estrogen phases of the cycle when the performance of female (verbal) tasks is enhanced.

CHANGES IN CEREBRAL ASYMMETRY ACROSS THE MENSTRUAL CYCLE

Six studies, which together employed ten separate measures of functional cerebral asymmetry, have investigated potential changes across the cycle. Five of the measures showed no significant changes in asymmetry (Bibawi, Cherry, & Hellige, 1995; Chiarello, McMahon, & Schaefer, 1989; Heister, Landis, Regard, & Schroeder-Heister, 1989). One study (Altemus, Wexler, & Boulis, 1989) found greater asymmetry in the follicular phase compared with the late luteal phase. Unfortunately, tests conducted at these points in the cycle do not differentiate clearly between estrogen levels. During the follicular phase, six to twelve days following the onset of menses, estrogen is rising to its highest levels, while during the late luteal phase, one to seven days preceding the onset of menses, estrogen is falling to its lowest levels. Thus, high and low estrogen could be encountered within each of the sampling periods. Fortunately, the remaining four measures were administered at times which clearly

differentiate between high and low estrogen levels. In each case, performance
was compared between menses, when estrogen is low, and either the preovulatory or midluteal phases, when estrogen is high. Two of those measures
revealed greater asymmetry at menses when estrogen is low (Heister et al.,
1989; Rode, Wagner, & Gunturkun, 1995), and two found greater asymmetry
later in the cycle, when estrogen is high (Bibawi et al., 1995; Hampson, 1990).
Clearly, these findings do not support the prediction from Levy's (1969; 1971)
hypothesis that asymmetry would be greater at menses, when the performance
of spatial tasks is better, than later in the cycle, when the performance of
verbal tasks is enhanced. Given that greater asymmetry was found at both
low and high estrogen phases of the cycle, we looked at the nature of the
paradigms and tasks that generated these conflicting findings.

Table 10.1 shows that the six menstrual cycle studies employed either the
divided visual field or dichotic listening paradigm with verbal and nonverbal
tasks. The two measures that revealed greater asymmetry at menses when
estrogen is low used nonverbal tasks which generated a right hemisphere advantage (bold script in Table 10.1). Heister and colleagues (1989) used a
face/nonface discrimination and Rode, Wagner, and Gunturkun (1995) used
irregular polygon matching. The other three measures that revealed significant changes in asymmetry across the cycle used tasks, which generated a
left hemisphere advantage (bold italic script in Table 10.1). These findings
require closer attention. As noted, the phases of the cycle at which testing
was conducted by Altemus and colleagues (1989) do not differentiate between high and low estrogen levels. Of the two others, Hampson (1990) used
a verbal dichotic listening task and found greater asymmetry at the preovulatory phase when estrogen is high, and Bibawi and colleagues (1995) used a
"neutral" chair identification task and found greater asymmetry during the
high-estrogen midluteal phase.

Taken together, these observations suggest that asymmetry is greater when
estrogen is low for tasks which typically generate a right hemisphere advantage, whereas for tasks that typically reveal a left hemisphere advantage asymmetry may be greater when estrogen is high. If these findings are replicable,
it should be possible to record concurrent but reciprocal changes in functional cerebral asymmetry across the cycle. However, none of the studies that
employed both verbal and nonverbal tasks (Table 10.1) were able to demonstrate concurrent shifts in asymmetry for the two tasks. We investigated this
possibility using dichotic verbal and music tasks for which marked left and
right hemisphere advantages have been recorded.

A STUDY OF DICHOTIC VERBAL AND MUSIC TASK
PERFORMANCE ACROSS THE MENSTRUAL CYCLE

Our chosen left hemisphere verbal task was a consonant–vowel identification task, which typically generates a right ear advantage in our laboratory.
For the right hemisphere task we chose a musical chord recognition task for

Table 10.1
Changes in Functional Cerebral Asymmetry across the Menstrual Cycle

Study	Paradigm	Task	Hemispheric Advantage [a]	Greater asymmetry [b]
Altemus et al., 1989 [c]	dichotic	*verbal*	*Left*	*follicular*
				(?) estrogen [c]
Chiarello et al., 1989	visual	verbal	Left	Ns
		nonverbal	*ns*	Ns
Heister et al., 1989	visual	verbal	Left	Ns
		nonverbal	**Right**	menses
				low estrogen
Hampson, 1990	dichotic	*verbal*	*Left*	*preovulatory*
				high estrogen
Bibawi et al., 1995 [d]	visual	*neutral* [d]	*(left)* [d]	*midluteal*
				high estrogen
		nonverbal	Right	Ns
Rode et al., 1995	visual	verbal	Left	Ns
		nonverbal	**Right**	menses
				low estrogen

[a]The hemispheric advantage shown is that recorded for the task in the study cited.

[b]Entries show the phase of cycle and estrogen level at which greater asymmetry was recorded, with Ns indicating no significant change in asymmetry.

[c]This study does not differentiate clearly between high and low estrogen because testing was conducted during the follicular phase when estrogen is rising to its highest level and during the late luteal phase when estrogen is falling to its lowest level.

[d]The neutral task used by Bibawi et al. was so called because it generated no hemispheric advantage in men nor in women at menses; however, it produced a marked left hemisphere advantage in women during the midluteal phase.

which a marked left ear advantage has been reported (Gordon, 1980). Thirty-two right-handed women aged eighteen to thirty-seven years (mean 24), who were not taking oral contraceptives nor other steroid medication, participated in the study. They had no known hormonal dysfunction and all reported regular menstrual cycles of between twenty-six and thirty days. The verbal and music tasks were administered at menses and at the midluteal phase in a counterbalanced repeated measures design. We chose to test at these points because facilities for hormone assays were not available and these phases provide large windows for high and low estrogen levels. The high estrogen midluteal testing was conducted between two and eleven (mean 7.7) days prior to the start of menstruation with all but five of the subjects tested between five and ten days. For low estrogen we tested three to five (mean 4.3) days following the start of menstruation in order to avoid any discomfort that may have been associated with Days 1 and 2. For each task we recorded the total number of sounds correctly identified at each ear.

The verbal task (Figure 10.1) shows the predicted right ear (left hemisphere) advantage, which was greater during the midluteal phase than at menses. In contrast, the music task (Figure 10.2) shows the expected left ear (right hemisphere) advantage, which was greater during menses than during the midluteal phase. These reciprocal changes in asymmetry across the menstrual cycle were the result of consistent changes in ear performance. For both tasks, from menses to the midluteal phase, left ear (right hemisphere) performance fell significantly while right ear (left hemisphere) performance showed a small but nonsignificant increase. It is important that these task-dependent reciprocal changes in functional cerebral asymmetry were recorded concurrently from the same subjects using two measures of asymmetry presented sequentially at two phases of the cycle in a counterbalanced repeated measures design. Previous studies have reported greater asymmetry at only one point in the cycle, but when the outcomes of those studies are taken together and analyzed by task (Table 10.1), the findings are concordant with those described here. Two points emerge clearly from these findings: First, the degree of cerebral asymmetry recorded is dependent on the phase of the menstrual cycle at which testing occurs; second, the phase at which greater asymmetry is recorded is dependent on the type of task employed.

ARE THE CHANGES IN PERFORMANCE ACROSS THE CYCLE RESTRICTED TO THE RIGHT HEMISPHERE?

From the present findings it is also clear that for each of the two tasks the change in asymmetry, albeit reciprocal, arises from a reduction in left ear (right hemisphere) performance from menses, when estrogen is low, to the midluteal phase, when estrogen is high. Given that this change was recorded for verbal and music tasks, the data suggest that the underlying effect is a general decrement in right hemisphere performance. Similar findings have

Figure 10.1
Verbal Task: Total Correct Identifications (Mean and Standard Error)
Recorded for Items Presented to the Left and Right Ears at Menses and the
Midluteal Phase of the Cycle

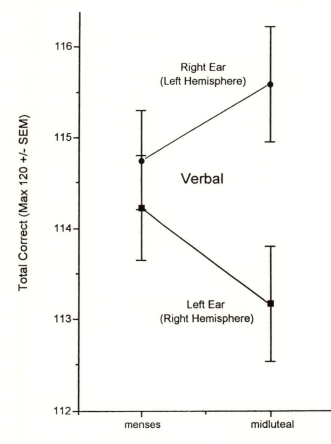

There is a right ear (left hemisphere) advantage ($F_{1,31} = 10.23$, $p < 0.005$) and a significant interaction between ears and phase of cycle ($F_{1,31} = 12.31$, $p = 0.005$). From menses to the midluteal phase, left ear (right hemisphere) performance falls significantly (Tukey HSD test $p < 0.05$), whereas right ear (left hemisphere) performance shows a small but nonsignificant increase (Tukey HSD test $p > 0.05$). As a result, the right ear advantage, and hence the degree of functional asymmetry, is greater during the midluteal phase than at menses.

been reported recently by Mead and Hampson (1995), in a study which used the divided visual field paradigm. They found that left visual field performance was better at menses than during the midluteal phase for both a verbal left hemisphere rhyming task and a nonverbal right hemisphere face recognition task. Thus, both studies have recorded a decrease in right hemisphere

Figure 10.2
Music Task: Total Correct Recognitions (Mean and Standard Error) Recorded for Chords Presented to the Left and Right Ears at Menses and the Midluteal Phase of the Cycle

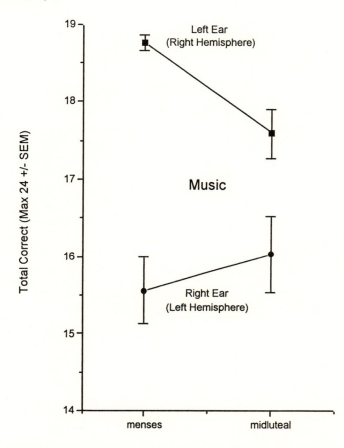

There is a left ear (right hemisphere) advantage ($F_{1,31} = 40.69$, $p < 0.001$) with a significant interaction between ears and phase of cycle ($F_{1,31} = 11.12$, $p < 0.005$). From menses to the midluteal phase, left ear (right hemisphere) performance falls significantly (Tukey HSD test $p < 0.05$), whereas right ear (left hemisphere) performance shows a small but nonsignificant increase (Tukey HSD test $p > 0.05$). As a result, the left ear advantage, and hence the degree of functional asymmetry, is greater at menses than during the midluteal phase.

performance from menses to the midluteal phase. The parallel increase in left hemisphere performance noted in our study with both tasks was small and not statistically significant (Figures 10.1 and 10.2). However, before concluding that hemispheric changes across the menstrual cycle are restricted to the right hemisphere, we should consider other studies that have found significant left hemisphere effects.

The verbal dichotic listening data reported by Hampson (1990) showed statistically significant changes in both ears, with a left ear (right hemisphere) decrease and a right ear (left hemisphere) increase in performance from menses to the high-estrogen preovulatory phase. Bibawi and colleagues (1995) used a neutral nonlateralized chair identification task in a specific attempt to chart hemispheric activation across the cycle. Though this task produced no significant asymmetry in men or women at menses, during the midluteal phase it generated a marked right visual field advantage arising from a significant improvement in left hemisphere performance and a nonsignificant decrease in right hemisphere performance. Together, these findings suggest that changes from low to high estrogen phases of the cycle have opposing effects, suppressing the activity of the right hemisphere while simultaneously enhancing the activity of the left. Such reciprocal changes in hemispheric activity provide an explanation for the parallel changes in the performance of sexually dimorphic tasks, which shows a deterioration in right hemisphere spatial ability and an improvement in left hemisphere verbal ability from low to high estrogen phases of the cycle (Hampson, 1990; Hampson & Kimura, 1988). Phase of cycle is not normally controlled in studies of sex differences in cognitive abilities and cerebral asymmetry; therefore, it is not surprising that reviews have found such differences to be somewhat elusive.

ACTIVATIONAL EFFECTS OF HORMONES ON ASYMMETRY AND COGNITION

We turn now to the question of possible hormonal influences on cerebral asymmetry and cognitive ability across the menstrual cycle. Rode and colleagues (1995) were unable to find significant correlations between either estrogen or progesterone levels and the change in cerebral asymmetry that they recorded. Despite this failure to find a significant correlation, no other mechanism for the menstrual-related changes in asymmetry was proposed and gonadal steroids remain the most likely mediating agents. Levels of both estrogen and progesterone are higher at the midluteal than the menstrual phase; however, Hampson (1990) differentiated between these two ovarian steroids by testing during the preovulatory phase when progesterone remains low though estrogen is rising to its preovulatory peak. Using a verbal dichotic listening task, she found greater asymmetry at the higher estrogen phase, supporting the view that changes in estrogen rather than progesterone levels correlate with the changes in asymmetry. In the same study, Hampson showed that changes in the performance of sexually dimorphic tasks also appear to be dependent on estrogen rather than progesterone levels.

Preliminary evidence for a causal effect of both estrogen and testosterone on pattern of cognitive ability has been obtained from studies of transsexuals selected for hormone therapy. Van Goozen, Cohen-Kettenis, Gooren, Frijda, and van de Poll (1994) have described a rapid shift from the female to the male pattern of cognitive abilities in female-to-male transsexuals treated with testosterone. Compared with their performance just before treatment began, they showed deterioration in verbal and improvement in spatial abilities. In a subsequent study (Van Goozen, Cohen-Kettenis, Gooren, Frijda, & van de Poll, 1995), they found that male-to-female transsexuals treated with antiandrogens and estrogen showed the reverse changes, with an improvement in verbal and a deterioration in spatial abilities. These findings support a causal effect of gonadal steroids on the brain functions that underlie sexually dimorphic cognitive abilities and indicate that, whatever organizational changes result from prenatal effects, the human brain remains susceptible to the activational effects of gonadal steroids in adult life. In this context it is interesting to note reports that fluctuations in spatial ability correlate with seasonal (Kimura & Hampson, 1994) and diurnal (Moffat & Hampson, 1996) variations in testosterone level.

SUMMARY AND CONCLUSIONS

In this chapter we have examined the relationships among gonadal steroids, cerebral asymmetry, and cognition. In doing so we have demonstrated that the belief exemplified by the Cognitive Crowding Hypothesis, first proposed by Levy (1969; 1971), is untenable. Levy suggested an association between sex differences in cerebral asymmetry and those reported for cognitive abilities. The hypothesis contrasted the reduced asymmetry and better verbal ability seen in women with marked asymmetry and better spatial ability seen in men. Our argument against this hypothesis begins with reports that sexual dimorphic cognitive abilities change reciprocally across the menstrual cycle. Female-favoring verbal tasks are performed better during the preovulatory and midluteal phases when estrogen is high, while male-favoring spatial tasks are performed better at menses when estrogen is low. From the Cognitive Crowding Hypothesis we would predict that cerebral asymmetry should be greater during menses when spatial ability is better and that asymmetry would be reduced later in the cycle when verbal ability is greater. Contrary to this prediction, in reviewing the literature on changes in functional cerebral asymmetry across the menstrual cycle we saw that greater asymmetry is not restricted to menses but has been reported for the preovulatory and midluteal phases as well. This apparent inconsistency may be understood in light of the data from our dichotic listening study, which show that patterns of functional cerebral asymmetry across the menstrual cycle are not only phase but also task dependent.

Our left hemisphere verbal task showed greater asymmetry during the midluteal phase, whereas the right hemisphere music task showed greater asymmetry at menses. The concurrent reciprocal changes recorded in this study are in agreement with the changes in asymmetry obtained with the left or right hemisphere tasks reported from other studies (Table 10.1). Our findings are also concordant with the concurrent changes obtained with divided visual field tasks by Mead and Hampson (1995). The reciprocal changes in asymmetry for left and right hemisphere tasks are dependent on consistent reciprocal changes in hemispheric activity. Right hemisphere performance deteriorates and left hemisphere performance improves from menses to the preovulatory and midluteal phases. We have seen that similar performances during the preovulatory and midluteal phases, which contrast with those at menses, indicate that the changes in cerebral asymmetry and cognitive performance correlate with estrogen rather than progesterone levels. In addition, we noted that there is preliminary evidence from studies of the cross-sex hormone treatment of transsexuals for a causal effect of both estrogen and testosterone on cognitive performance.

Two points clearly emerge from the menstrual cycle studies: First, the degree of cerebral asymmetry recorded is dependent on the phase of the cycle at which testing occurs; second, the phase at which greater asymmetry is recorded is dependent on the type of task employed. As estrogen levels rise, activity in the right hemisphere is suppressed while that in the left is enhanced. These lateralized changes in hemispheric activity underlie reciprocal changes in functional cerebral asymmetry and cognitive ability that have been recorded across the menstrual cycle. Cerebral asymmetry is greater for nonverbal right hemisphere tasks at low estrogen levels when the male-typical pattern of better spatial ability is observed. In contrast, asymmetry is greater for verbal tasks at high estrogen levels when the female-typical pattern of better verbal is found. It is possible that testosterone exerts similar but reverse effects by suppressing left hemisphere activity and promoting right hemisphere spatial ability. The finding that performance on cognitive tasks during the preovulatory phase is similar to that recorded at the midluteal phase implicates estrogen rather than progesterone. In addition, the transsexual studies imply a causal relationship. Overall, it appears that estrogen exerts phasic effects on the functional organization of the adult human brain and thereby on the performance of sexually dimorphic cognitive tasks. The presence of such dynamic hormone-dependent changes in hemispheric functioning provides one explanation for the often elusive nature of sex differences in cerebral asymmetry and cognitive abilities.

Chapter 11

Gender-Related Individual Differences and National Merit Test Performance: Girls Who Are "Masculine" and Boys Who Are "Feminine" Tend to Do Better

Richard Lippa

In a classic monograph on sex differences in cognitive abilities, Eleanor Maccoby (1966) summarized evidence suggesting that "analytic thinking, creativity, and high general intelligence are associated with cross-sex-typing, in that the men and boys who score high are more feminine, and the women and girls more masculine, than their low-scoring same-sex counterparts" (p. 35). Maccoby noted that, though the evidence for this proposition was stronger and more consistent for girls and women than for boys and men, there were still "few exceptions in the literature to this generalization."

Signorella and Jamison (1986) conducted a meta-analysis of seventy-three studies investigating links between the masculinity and femininity of individuals' self-concept and their cognitive abilities. They found evidence for a number of significant links between masculinity and femininity and specific cognitive abilities. For example, girls and women who were more masculine in self-concept performed better on spatial perception tests than those who were less masculine. Though the findings were weaker for boys, there was a tendency for boys with feminine self-concepts to perform better on spatial perception tests than boys with more masculine self-concepts. Similarly, among adolescents, mathematical ability was associated with more masculine self-concepts for girls and with more feminine self-concepts for boys. In general, Signorella and Jamison found that cognitive abilities tended to show stronger relationships with bipolar masculinity–femininity than with unidimensional masculinity (i.e., masculine instrumentality) or femininity (i.e., feminine expressiveness). Various operationalizations of masculinity, femininity, and masculinity–femininity will be discussed later in this chapter.

More recently, Lubinski and Humphreys (1990) analyzed the correlates of mathematical giftedness in tenth-grade boys and girls and found that mathematically precocious adolescents were less sex-typed in their interests and behaviors than nongifted adolescents were. Lubinski and Humphreys investigated other kinds of giftedness as well; for example, exceptional spatial ability and verbal skills. Their findings were invariant across the domains of giftedness, leading Lubinski and Humphreys to conclude, "Intellectually precocious males *and* females are less [gender] stereotyped regardless of whether they are verbally gifted or intellectually gifted in spatial visualization. Less [gender] stereotypic behavior appears to be 'simply' a corollary of intellectual giftedness in general" (p. 343).

Why should sex-typing (or the lack thereof) be linked to cognitive abilities and giftedness? Maccoby (1966, p. 47) offered one hypothesis: Stereotypic masculinity and femininity might be linked to an inhibition–impulsiveness dimension. Compared with boys, girls might tend to be inhibited, and feminine girls might be so inhibited as to interfere with their intellectual and creative accomplishments. According to Maccoby, extremely feminine girls might be overly passive, controlled, and unassertive when working in academic settings and on creative projects. On the other hand, boys might tend to be impulsive, and masculine boys might be so impulsive as to interfere with their intellectual and creative accomplishments. Extremely masculine boys might be overly aggressive and "act out" too much. Maccoby suggested that, if her hypothesis were true, "Most girls need to become less passive and inhibited, while most boys need to become less impulsive" to display optimal scholastic performance.

Lubinski and Humphreys (1990) offered a "masculine identification hypothesis" as another possible explanation for links between sex-typing and cognitive abilities (see also Signorella & Jamison, 1986; Nash, 1979). According to this perspective, children develop a self-concept of masculinity or femininity and internalize accompanying sex-role standards. Boys who develop a masculine self-concept attempt to behave in ways consistent with this self-concept (see Kohlberg, 1966, for a classic cognitive account of sex-typing). In the realm of cognitive abilities and academic performance, masculine boys might then tend to gravitate to and excel in areas that are stereotypically masculine (e.g., science, math, mechanical work) and avoid and perform relatively poorly in areas that are stereotypically feminine (the arts, humanities, literature). Feminine girls might show just the reverse pattern, gravitating to academic domains that are stereotypically feminine.

As noted earlier, Lubinski and Humphreys's (1990) empirical work found that the linkage between giftedness and sex-typing did not depend on the particular cognitive domain studied. For example, they found that boys gifted in math were not particularly masculine in their interests. Rather, they found that, for both boys and girls, giftedness in all cognitive domains was associated with nongender-stereotypic interests. Thus, their data argued against the masculine identification hypothesis (and the corresponding, if unstated, feminine identification hypothesis for girls).

Simonton (1994) has offered yet another explanation for why gender-related individual differences (including minority sexual orientations) might be related to creativity and intellectual accomplishment. Individuals who are not sex-typed are cultural nonconformists according to Simonton, and many kinds of creativity and intellectual innovation require freedom of thought and freedom from cultural conventions. In Simonton's words,

To attain the highest success, a certain amount of personal independence is essential. To conform to all the dictates of one's culture is to condemn oneself to creative mediocrity. In fact, empirical studies show that creativity is linked with autonomy, or even a radical anticonformity. This is what makes ethnic marginality such a useful developmental force. A person standing at the intersection of two separate cultures can grab more freedom from the norms of either. Orphanhood and other kinds of childhood and adolescent trauma may fulfill a similar function, by disrupting the inculcation of traditional mores. The upshot of these and functionally equivalent experiences is to generate a personality who refuses to accept received opinions. This enables the person to embark on new, even grandiose schemes of achievement. The same process also creates an individual less willing to abide by societal prescriptions about acceptable sexual activities. An alternative life style can even advertise one's autonomous genius. (1994, pp. 169–170)

Simonton lists a number of ways in which creative geniuses may be gender nonconformists. They are more likely to have unconventional sexual orientations and lifestyles. They are more likely to remain unmarried. (Among the great bachelor philosophers, Simonton lists Hobbes, Descartes, Pascal, Spinoza, Locke, Leibniz, Voltaire, Kant, Schopenhauer, Kierkegaard, Santayana, and Wittgenstein.) Simonton notes that the "Eminent are . . . more inclined to be androgynous. The males entertain more feminine traits, the females more masculine attributes. Socialization into stereotyped gender roles often betrays a broader acceptance of societal customs and prejudices" (p. 170).

The explanations of observed links between sex-typing and intellectual achievement that have just been summarized focus on the differing temperaments of boys and girls (Maccoby's impulsiveness–inhibition explanation), gender-related self-concepts (the masculine and feminine identification hypotheses), and gender nonconformity as a route to more general cultural nonconformity (Simonton's speculation). These explanations need not be mutually exclusive. Furthermore, it is important to note that biological as well as cultural and intrapsychic factors may help explain observed links between sex-typing and cognitive abilities. For example, hormone levels and sex-linked brain structures may influence both gender-related behavioral traits and cognitive abilities (see Nyborg, 1994a; 1994b for a model proposing that individuals levels of testosterone and estrogen influence cognitive abilities, temperaments, occupational choices, and even body types). Finally, it should be noted that the cultural, psychological, and biological processes that serve to link sex-typing and intellectual achievement may not be the same for boys and girls or for men and women.

The current research provides new empirical data relevant to the relationship between sex-typing and intellectual ability. It focuses on three main questions: (1) Are there links between within-sex gender-related individual differences (i.e., "masculinity" and "femininity") and cognitive abilities among adolescents? (2) If there are such links, are they the same for boys and girls? and (3) what accounts for such links?

To provide new empirical perspectives on these questions, I conducted analyses of data from a classic twin study (Loehlin & Nichols, 1976). These analyses provide fresh evidence on relationships among masculinity, femininity, and cognitive abilities. The original data were collected from a large nationwide sample of students who took the National Merit Scholarship Qualifying Test in 1962. This test comprised five subtests (English Usage, Math Usage, Natural Science Reading, Social Science Reading, and Vocabulary [Word Usage]) that provide measures of cognitive abilities varying in their degree of stereotypic masculinity and femininity. Thus, the data provide evidence on whether the stereotypic masculinity–femininity of an intellectual domain moderated the relationship between subjects' test performance and their assessed masculinity and femininity.

The current research moves beyond previous studies in that it employs a new methodology for assessing within-sex gender-related individual differences—namely, the method of gender diagnosticity (a technique to be described in more detail in the next section; see Lippa & Connelly, 1990; Lippa, 1991; 1995a; 1995b). The current research also assesses subjects on measures of masculine instrumentality and feminine expressiveness. Thus, in the context of the same study and subject population, the current research operationalizes within-sex gender-related individual differences in several different ways, thus permitting a more complete and comprehensive analysis of possible links between gender-related individual differences and cognitive abilities in a given population of subjects.

MEASURING GENDER-RELATED
INDIVIDUAL DIFFERENCES

To understand the formal measures of gender-related individual differences used in the current research, it helps to briefly review the history of empirical attempts to assess masculinity and femininity. Modern research on this topic began with the 1936 publication of Terman and Miles's *Sex and Personality*, which presented a bipolar conception of masculinity–femininity (M–F). In essence, this approach held that M–F is a single dimension and that masculinity and femininity are polar opposites. Terman and Miles and their many successors included in their M–F scales items that showed reliable and strong sex differences in normative populations. The bipolar approach to M–F that began in the 1930s waned by the early 1970s in the face of conceptual and empirical critiques (e.g., Block, 1973; Constantinople, 1973), which argued in part that supposedly unidimensional M–F scales were in fact multidimensional measures that did not tap consistent and coherent domains of gender-related behavior.

The 1970s witnessed the demise of the bipolar unidimensional approach to M–F and the concurrent rise of two-dimensional conceptions of masculinity and femininity. The two-dimensional approach, which has been dominant for the past twenty years, holds that masculinity and femininity are separate dimensions, with masculinity (M) defined in terms of instrumental personality traits (e.g., self-confident, dominant, independent) and femininity (F) defined in terms of expressive traits (warm, sensitive, nurturant).[1] During the 1970s a number of self-report inventories were developed to assess M and F as two separate dimensions. The best known of these are the Bem Sex-Role Inventory (BSRI) (Bem, 1974; 1981a) and the Personal Attributes Questionnaire (PAQ) (Spence, Helmreich, & Stapp, 1974; Spence & Helmreich, 1978). A huge empirical literature now exists on the psychometric properties and correlates of M and F as assessed by these scales (see Ashmore, 1990; Cook, 1985; Lenney, 1991).

The PAQ and BSRI continue to be widely used in research on gender-related individual differences. However, like earlier M–F scales, M and F scales have been subject to telling critiques. Indeed, the authors of the best-known M and F scales have themselves modified their original conceptions of their constructs, sometimes even arguing that their scales do not really measure masculinity and femininity at all. For example, PAQ authors Janet Spence and Bob Helmreich (1980) have written that M and F scales are in fact instrumentality and expressiveness scales and, as such, show at best weak and inconsistent relationships to other kinds of gender-related behaviors and attitudes (see Spence and Buckner, 1995 for a recent theoretical discussion of M and F).

Sandra Bem (1974; 1975; 1976) proposed in her early work on M and F that "sex-typed" individuals (men high on M and low on F, and women low on M and high on F) show trait-like consistencies in their gender-related behaviors, whereas androgynous individuals (men and women who are high on both M and F) display more variable and inconsistent gender-related behaviors. By the early 1980s, however, Bem had abandoned her early conceptions of M and F in favor of gender schema theory (Bem, 1981b; 1985), which holds that masculinity and femininity are cognitive constructs rather than psychological realities. In the context of gender schema theory and research, M and F scales serve to assess whether people are gender schematic or aschematic—that is, whether they strongly perceive themselves and others in terms of gender categories—not necessarily the degree to which they possess trait-like masculinity or femininity.

I have argued elsewhere (Lippa & Connelly, 1990; Lippa, 1991; 1995a; 1995b) that M and F scales and their associated constructs suffer from a number of additional problems. As Bem properly noted, M and F scales reify gender-related individual differences; they transform social stereotypes and lay conceptions of masculinity and femininity into "real" traits. I have further noted that this reification may restrict masculinity and femininity to broad but overly limited domains of behavior. Because M and F scales define masculinity and femininity in terms of gender-stereotypic instrumental and expressive personality traits, they fail to embrace a host of other characteristics that are highly relevant to everyday conceptions of masculinity and femininity, characteristics such as gender-related appearances, nonverbal behaviors, hobbies, interests, ways of relating to friends, spouses, and lovers, and so on. And because of their fixed and limited item content, M and F scales fail to acknowledge that masculinity and femininity are fluid concepts that are culturally and historically relative.

To address some of these problems, I proposed a new approach to assessing within-sex gender-related individual difference, an approach termed *gender diagnosticity* (GD) (Lippa, 1991; 1995a; 1995b; Lippa & Connelly, 1990). In brief, gender diagnosticity refers to the probability that an individual is predicted to be male or female based on some set of gender-related indicators (such as occupational preference ratings). According to the GD perspective, a masculine person is an individual who shows "male-like" behaviors in comparison to a normative group of males and females, and a feminine person is an individual who shows "female-like" behaviors. That is, gender-related individual differences—within as well as across the sexes—are defined by behaviors that distinguish males and females in a given population at a given time. Indeed, such gender-related individual differences can be defined and measured only in relation to particular populations of males and females at particular points in time.

One virtue of the GD approach is that it acknowledges that a given indicator of masculinity or femininity may vary over time and over different populations of men and women. For example, American college students' interest in becoming lawyers was probably more gender diagnostic fifty years ago than it is today, whereas students' interest in becoming mechanical engineers was strongly gender diagnostic fifty years ago and continues to be so today. By implication, a college woman's interest in becoming a lawyer is probably not viewed as particularly masculine in contemporary America, but it may have been so viewed fifty years ago in America.

GD is formally computed from sets of indicators (such as occupational preference ratings) through the application of discriminant analyses (see Lippa, 1991; 1995b; Lippa & Connelly, 1990). Prior research on GD shows that it can be measured reliably within the sexes from self-report data, such as occupational preference ratings, and that GD measures are factorially distinct from M and F as assessed by the PAQ and BSRI (Lippa, 1991; 1995b; Lippa & Connelly, 1990). Furthermore GD measures are largely independent of the Big Five personality superfactors, whereas M and F are not. Indeed, M and F correlate substantially with Big Five dimensions, with M loading highly on Extraversion and Neuroticism and F on Agreeableness (Lippa, 1991; 1995b). Finally, and perhaps most importantly in the context of the current research, GD measures often predict varied gender-related behaviors and attitudes within the sexes (e.g., math SAT performance, visual–spatial ability, nonverbal masculinity–femininity, masculinity–femininity of chosen college major, self-ascribed masculinity–femininity, attitudes toward women's roles, and attitudes toward gay people) better than M and F do (Lippa & Connelly, 1990; Lippa, 1991; 1995b).

The research to be described here assessed subjects on three of the measures of gender-related individual differences just reviewed—M, F, and GD measures—and then examined their links with subjects' cognitive abilities as measured by the National Merit Scholarship Qualifying Test.

Method

The data analyzed here are a subset of the data described by Loehlin and Nichols (1976) in their classic book, *Heredity, Environment, and Personality*. In this study, over 800 pairs of twins who took the National Merit Qualifying Test in 1962 were assessed on a variety of self-report scales and inventories, including measures of their degree of participation in everyday activities, their occupational interests, and personality. More specifically, self-report measures included self-rated frequency of engaging in 324 everyday activities (e.g., "played checkers," "made minor repairs around the house," "said grace before meals," "rode a motorcycle," "drove a car over 80 M.P.H."), self-rated interest in 160 occupations (e.g., "aviator," "private investigator," "YMCA secretary," "nursery school teacher," "lawyer"), and completion of 480 items of the California Psychological Inventory (CPI) (Gough, 1957) and a 159-item version of the Adjective Check List.

As noted earlier, subjects had completed the National Merit Scholarship Qualifying Test, which yielded their subtest scores in English Usage, Mathematics Usage, Social Science Reading, Natural Science Reading, and Word Usage (Vocabulary), as well as a total score. Personality questionnaires and self-report inventories were mailed out to subjects in 1963, more than a year after they had completed the National Merit Test. At the time of this assessment, subjects were approaching the end of the senior year in high school.

In soliciting their sample, Loehlin and Nichols (1976) contacted all same-sex twins (1,507 pairs) identified from the almost 600 thousand U.S. high school juniors who took the National Merit test in 1962. Because of the conscientiousness of their research effort, Loehlin and Nichols obtained an impressive response rate of 79 percent. The final sample included 216 pairs of male identical twins, 135 pairs of male fraternal twins, 293 pairs of female identical twins, and 195 pairs of female fraternal twins, yielding a grand total of 839 twin pairs comprising 1,678 individuals.

As Loehlin and Nichols (1976) noted, students who take the National Merit Test tend to be above average in their academic and intellectual ability, and this was so for the twins in their sample, who on average ranked at the seventy-ninth percentile in their high school classes (which is similar to the mean rankings of National Merit Test takers in general). Loehlin and Nichols reported that their twins' mean scores on California Psychological Inventory scales were quite close to high school and college norms presented in the CPI manual. Thus, though the subjects in the twin sample were relatively able academically, they seemed quite typical and representative of their peers in terms of assessed personality.

Results

Because subjects were members of 839 twins pairs, the data from the two members of each twin pair were clearly not statistically independent (members of each twin pair shared both genes and family upbringing). Therefore, in all the analyses that follow, results will be presented for two separate groups of subjects, one consisting of all the first members of twin pairs (Twins A) and the other consisting of all the second members of twin pairs (Twins B). The first member of a pair was simply the twin whose data were first listed in Loehlin and Nichols's data file, and the second member was the twin whose data were listed second. In most analyses that follow, results are also presented separately for males and for females.

Separating twin pairs achieved the statistical goal of creating two groups of subjects with the property that, within groups, subjects' data were statistically independent. Presenting analyses for the two groups (Twins A and Twins B) permits the possibility for a crude kind of "cross-validation" of results. While it is important to again note that members of twin pairs are very definitely not statistically independent of one another, it is still possible, by examining corresponding results for Twins A and for Twins B, to gain some idea of which findings tended to be robust and replicable (across members of twin pairs) and which findings tended not to be.

MEASURES OF GENDER-RELATED
INDIVIDUAL DIFFERENCES COMPUTED
IN THE CURRENT RESEARCH

Subjects' gender diagnosticity scores were computed from three kinds of self-report data: ratings of participation in everyday activities, ratings of occupational preferences, and self-ratings on items of the California Psychological Inventory (see Lippa & Connelly, 1990; Lippa, 1991; 1995b for additional details about the computation and psychometrics of gender diagnosticity measures).

To compute gender diagnostic probabilities (GD scores) from subjects' occupational preference ratings, sixteen discriminant analyses were conducted on discrete sets of ten occupations each. Thus, the sixteen discriminant analyses included all 160 occupational preference items. Each discriminant analysis yielded the probability, computed from each subject's discriminant function score, that a given subject was male (or, by subtracting this probability from 1, female). Thus, on the basis of their occupational preference ratings, each subject had sixteen separate gender diagnostic probabilities, each computed from a distinct subset of rated occupations. A subject's overall GD score was simply the average of the sixteen probabilities.

The reason multiple gender diagnostic probabilities were computed for each subject was to provide a means to assess their reliability (see Lippa & Connelly, 1990; Lippa, 1991). The reliability of GD based on occupational preferences was high for all subjects (alpha = 0.93 for Twins A and 0.92 for Twins B) as well as for men only (alpha = 0.85 for Twins A and 0.87 for Twins B) and women only (alpha = 0.82 for Twins A and 0.77 for Twins B).

Similarly, to compute GD scores from subjects' everyday activity ratings, fifteen discriminant analyses were conducted on discrete sets of twenty-one or twenty-two activities each. Thus, the fifteen discriminant analyses included all 324 everyday activity items. The reliability of GD based on everyday activity items was acceptably high for all subjects (alpha = 0.95 for Twins A and 0.95 for Twins B). However, within-sex reliabilities were somewhat lower than for GD computed from occupational preferences (for men, alpha = 0.56 for Twins A and 0.65 for Twins B, and for women, alpha = 0.61 for Twins A and 0.58 for Twins B).

Finally, to compute GD scores from subjects' California Psychological Inventory items, fifteen discriminant analyses were conducted on discrete sets of thirty-two items each. Thus, the fifteen discriminant analyses included all 480 personality items. The reliability of GD based on CPI items was acceptably high for all subjects (alpha = 0.85 for Twins A and 0.90 for Twins B). Within-sex reliabilities were somewhat lower for GD based on CPI items than for GD computed from occupational preferences (for men, alpha = 0.47 for Twins A and 0.68 for Twins B, and for women, alpha = 0.57 for Twins A and 0.67 for Twins B).

Subjects' scores on masculine instrumentality and feminine expressiveness were computed from their Adjective Check List responses. (Because Loehlin and Nichols's [1976] data were collected before the development of inventories such as the Personal Attributes Questionnaire and the Bem Sex-Role Inventory, it was necessary to compute proxy measures of M and F.) The following eight Adjective Check List items provided a relatively pure measure of M: Aggressive, Assertive, Confident, Dominant, Forceful, Outspoken, Self-confident, and Independent. It should be noted that many of these items are quite similar to and even identical to items that appear on the PAQ and BSRI M scales. The following seven Adjective Check List items provided a relatively pure measure of F: Cooperative, Helpful, Kind, Sensitive, Tactful, Thoughtful, and Warm. Again, many of these items are quite similar to and even identical to items that appear on the PAQ and BSRI F scales.

A subject's M score was simply the total number of M items he or she endorsed as self-descriptive, normalized (divided) by the total number of Adjective Check List items endorsed. Similarly, a subject's F score was simply the total number of F items endorsed as self-descriptive, normalized by the total number of Adjective Check List items endorsed. M and F scores were normalized to control for subjects' overall response set to endorse many or few Adjective Check List items in general. The reliabilities of M and F measures were acceptably high. For example, for Twins A the reliability of raw M was 0.69 and the reliability of raw F was 0.68. Reliabilities for normalized M and F were, respectively, 0.99 and 0.95.

CORRELATIONS BETWEEN MEASURES OF GENDER-RELATED INDIVIDUAL DIFFERENCES AND NATIONAL MERIT TEST SCORES

Were there significant links between subjects' masculinity and femininity and their performance on the National Merit Scholarship Qualifying Test? To answer this question, I correlated subjects' GD, M, and F scores with their National Merit Test scores. These correlations were computed separately for males (Table 11.1), females (Table 11.2), and Twins A and Twins B.

Table 11.1 shows a number of significant correlations between gender diagnosticity measures and National Merit Test scores among boys. In general, correlations were negative, indicating that boys who were more male-typical in their occupational preferences, everyday activities, and CPI personality item responses tended to score lower on the National Merit Test. For boys, GD computed from occupational preferences proved to correlate especially strongly with National Merit Test scores.

Examination of the correlations in Table 11.1 indicates that the negative correlations between GD and test scores were significant, particularly for three subtest domains: English Usage, Vocabulary, and Social Science Reading. On the other hand, GD tended to be uncorrelated with scores on the Mathematics and Natural Science Reading subtests for boys.

Finally, Table 11.1 shows that, for boys, there were few consistent relationships between M, F, and National Merit Test performance. Among Twins A there was a hint that feminine expressiveness was negatively related with test performance, but this finding did not replicate for Twins B.

Correlations between F and test scores were stronger for girls. As Table 11.2 shows, feminine expressiveness showed a fairly consistent pattern of negative correlations with National Merit Test scores among girls, and this was true for both Twins A and Twins B. Thus, girls who were high on feminine expressiveness tended to perform lower on the National Merit Test, and these findings were fairly consistent across National Merit subtests. M tended to display weaker and more inconsistent correlations with test scores for girls than F did.

Among girls, GD measures also showed a fairly robust and consistent pattern of correlations with National Merit Test scores. In general, girls who were more male-typical in their occupational preferences, everyday activities, and CPI personality item responses tended to score better on the National Merit Test (five of the six correlations between GD scores and total National Merit Test scores are statistically significant in Table 11.2), and these findings were fairly consistent across National Merit subtests. In general, correlations between GD measures and test scores were stronger for girls than for boys. In other words, having interests and behaviors that were not sex-typed provided more of an intellectual advantage to girls than to boys.

DISCUSSION

The current data replicate the findings of previous reviews and empirical studies, suggesting that there are within-sex links between gender-related individual differences and cognitive abilities. As Maccoby (1966) suggested in her classic monograph, and as others have found in more recent empirical investigations, cognitive aptitude tends to be negatively correlated with sex-typed patterns of interests and activities, and this is true for both boys and girls. In the current study, girls who were more male-like on gender diagnosticity measures and who were lower on feminine expressiveness tended to perform better on the National Merit Scholarship Qualifying Test. Boys who were more female-like on GD measures tended to perform better on the National Merit Test, particularly on the English Usage, Vocabulary, and Social Science Reading subtests. The significant findings reported here are particularly impressive given that assessed cognitive abilities had a somewhat restricted range in the current sample (as noted earlier, subjects tended to be above average in their scholastic performance) and, if anything, this would likely reduce the magnitude of correlations.

The generally weak findings for masculine instrumentality argue against Maccoby's (1966, p. 47) early hypothesis that inhibition and passivity account for the link between sex-typing and reduced cognitive performance in girls. Recall that in the current analyses girls who were high on M reported being aggressive, assertive, confident, dominant, forceful, and independent. However, girls who possessed these decidedly nonpassive traits did not display enhanced performance on the National Merit Test.

The current findings are not fully consistent with the masculine identification or feminine identification hypotheses. Masculine self-concepts and in-

Table 11.1
Correlations between Gender Diagnosticity Scores, Masculinity, Femininity, and National Merit Test Scores for Boys

TWINS A

National Merit Subtest

	English	Vocab	Soc. Sci.	Math	Natural Sci.	Total
GD-Occup (N=346)	-.11*	-.21***	-.16**	.01	-.05	-.12*
GD-Activ (N=350)	-.09*	-.10*	-.10*	.02	-.01	-.06
GD-CPI (N=326)	-.11*	-.13*	-.09	-.05	-.07	-.10*
Masc (N=351)	.07	.04	.08	.11*	.08	.09*
Fem (N=351)	-.08	-.03	-.08	-.11*	-.13*	-.10*

188

TWINS B

National Merit Subtest

	English	Vocab	Soc. Sci.	Math	Natural Sci.	Total
GD-Occup (N=344)	-.18***	-.15**	-.12*	.01	-.01	-.10*
GD-Activ (N=351)	-.10*	-.10*	-.11*	.00	-.03	-.07
GD-CPI (N=326)	-.08	-.09	-.07	-.01	-.04	-.07
Masc (N=351)	.01	.09	.07	.09*	.04	.07
Fem (N=351)	.03	-.07	-.01	-.04	-.04	-.03

Note: * p < 0.05, 1-tailed; ** p < 0.01, 1-tailed; *** p < 0.001, 1-tailed.

Table 11.2
Correlations between Gender Diagnosticity Scores, Masculinity, Femininity, and National Merit Test Scores for Girls

TWINS A

National Merit Subtest

	English	Vocab	Soc. Sci.	Math	Natural Sci.	Total
GD–Occup (N=488)	.13**	.16***	.15***	.23***	.18*	.21***
GD–Activ (N=488)	06	.16***	.12*	.15***	.10*	.14**
GD–CPI (N=481)	.09*	.22***	.17***	.21***	.20***	.21***
Masc (N=488)	.04	.08*	.04	.08*	.03	.07
Fem (N=488)	-.12**	-.18***	-.17***	-.17***	-.17***	-.19***

190

terests in boys were not associated with high performance on National Merit subtests that tapped masculine intellectual domains (e.g., natural science and math). Similarly, feminine self-concepts and interests among girls were not correlated with high performance in feminine intellectual domains (e.g., English). Rather, for girls feminine expressiveness and female-typical occupational preferences, activities, and personality test responses were related to poorer overall National Merit test performance and poorer subtest performance regardless of the subject area. Thus, consistent with Simonton's (1994, pp. 169–170) "cultural conformity" hypothesis, girls who adhered to traditional and conventional sex roles (that is, girls high on F and who were female-typical in their interests and activities) tended to show lower intellectual achievement. Of course, traditional feminine roles may not be simply an indicator of cultural conformity and conventionality in girls. Such roles may also more actively impede intellectual achievement in girls insofar as they prescribe that women's roles lie in the home rather than in the world of academic and creative achievement. (It is worth recalling that the adolescent subjects in Loehlin and Nichols's [1976] study were assessed in the early 1960s, a time when traditional sex roles were more extreme and rigid than today.)

While the current results for girls provide little support for the feminine identification hypothesis (that a feminine self-concept and interests lead girls to perform better in stereotypically feminine academic domains), the corresponding results for boys provide partial support for the masculine identification hypothesis. For boys, more female-like patterns of activities, occupational preferences, and personality item response correlated with better National Merit Test scores, particularly in the feminine domains of English Usage, Vocabulary, and Social Science Reading. However, male-typical patterns of activities, occupational preferences, and personality item responses were not associated with better performance on the masculine domains of Math and Natural Science Reading. In other words, for boys nonmasculine interests and behaviors were sometimes an asset for test performance, but sex-typed interests and behaviors were not an asset, even in the stereotypically masculine domains of math and natural science. Thus the current results provide at best a kind of half support for the masculine identification hypothesis.

The current findings add to existing evidence that gender nonconformity is associated with intellectual and academic excellence. Furthermore, the findings suggest that the association between gender nonconformity and cognitive ability may be more domain specific for boys and more domain general for girls. As Maccoby's (1966, pp. 25–55) review suggested, the current results seems a bit more robust and consistent for girls than for boys. Finally, of the three measures of within-sex gender-related individual differences employed in the current research, GD and F were more likely than M to show links to cognitive ability and academic excellence in adolescents. Further research is clearly warranted to identify the factors that cause these observed links between gender-related individual differences and cognitive abilities.

ACKNOWLEDGMENT

I wish to express great appreciation to John Loehlin for giving me permission to analyze the raw data from the Loehlin and Nichols (1976) study and for electronically transmitting his data file to me.

NOTE

1. In reviewing this chapter, the Editor noted that not all theorists who view masculinity and femininity as different dimensions equate these dimensions with instrumentality and expressiveness. For example, see Ellis and Ames (1987) for a discussion of "masculine" and "feminine" sexual behaviors. Though biological and comparative psychologists have sometimes considered masculinity and femininity to comprise more than just instrumental and expressive behaviors, personality and social psychologists have tended to define masculinity primarily as instrumentality and femininity primarily as expressiveness.

Chapter 12

Gender Differences in Bereavement Response and Longevity: Findings from the California State University Twin Loss Study

Nancy L. Segal

Factors underlying individual differences in bereavement response have attracted considerable research interest (Stroebe & Stroebe, 1987; Sanders, 1989; McCrae & Costa, 1993; Rynearson & McCreery, 1993; Hofer, 1994). Such factors include but are not limited to nature of death (expected vs. unexpected), socioeconomic status, availability of social support, gender, age of survivor, age of deceased, and degree of genetic relatedness. A primary focus of this chapter is an analysis of gender-related differences in bereavement response among male and female identical or monozygotic (MZ) twins and fraternal or dizygotic (DZ) twins. These twins were participants in the California State University Twin Loss Study. This unique sample has been used in the past to examine evolutionary-based hypotheses concerning the contributions of genetic relatedness to bereavement processes and outcomes (Segal & Bouchard, 1993; Segal, Wilson, Bouchard, & Gitlin, 1995), as well as genetic and environmental influences on suicidal behavior (Segal & Roy, 1996; Roy, Segal, Sarchiapone, & Lavin, 1994). The present analysis thus extends this ongoing research program by (1) examining gender-related differences in measures of bereavement and (2) directing needed attention to the significance of twin and sibling loss. Opportunities to contribute to research concerned with sex differences in longevity and cause of death were also provided. Selected findings are considered with reference to an evolutionary perspective on bereavement.

GENDER-RELATED DIFFERENCES IN
BEREAVEMENT AND GRIEVING

Females typically express higher levels of grief-related mental and physical symptoms than males (Gallagher-Thompson, Futterman, Farberow, Thompson, & Peterson, 1993; Shucter & Zisook, 1993; also see Stroebe & Stroebe, 1987). Interestingly, some other studies have reported an increased risk of mortality among bereaved males than females following the loss of a close relative, especially a spouse (Osterweis, Solomon, & Green, 1984; Gallagher-Thompson et al., 1993). It is possible that while males may express less death anxiety than females, this difference may reflect the cultural expectation that males display fortitude during times of stress (Lonnetto & Templer, 1986), rather than genuine gender-related differences in bereavement response. Consistent with this view, Sanders (1989) observed that bereaved males seem better able to regain emotional control and may do so by channeling behavior in the direction of aggressive actions. In contrast, she found that females direct efforts more toward control of their environments, leading to "safe, but nonadaptive modes of behavior" (p. 90).

Stroebe and Stroebe (1985; 1993, pp. 212–213) found that widows who refused to participate in a study designed to evaluate coping behaviors, grief symptoms, and health consequences of bereavement were less depressed than those who agreed to participate; the opposite was found for widowers. They suggested that, due to societal norms which grant greater acceptability to the expression of grief among females than males, highly depressed males may have avoided participation for fear of emotional upset. It is also the case that widowers tend to remarry with greater frequency than widows, leaving a higher proportion of widows in long-term studies (see Sanders, 1989, p. 137). Interestingly, Stroebe and Stroebe (1987; 1993) have argued that widowers may experience greater adjustment difficulties than widows, owing in part to the unavailability of support systems. Finally, several studies have failed to find evidence of gender differences on selected bereavement measures, such as emotional and health adjustment (Lund, Caserta, & Dimond, 1993). Difficulties in the selection of appropriate samples are recognized in bereavement research (Sanders, 1989, pp. 115–116), and may explain, in part, some observed inconsistencies across studies.

A recent study by Sprang, McNeil, and Wright (1992–1993) underlines the complexity of gender differences in bereavement. Grief among family members following a death by homicide was examined. Gender was significantly associated with grief, as measured by the Texas Inventory of Grief (TRIG), with females obtaining higher scores than males. More interesting, perhaps, was that sociodemographic and other variables differentially contributed to the prediction of grief when analyses were performed separately by gender. For example, extent of mourning (as assessed by an eight-item summative index derived from Part 2 of the TRIG; see Sprang et al., 1992–1993, pp. 149, 159–160) proved a more powerful predictor of grief among males than females. Extent of mourning was a function of the use of available social supports and time since loss for males, while it was a function of religiosity, age, income, and time since loss for females. In addition, sociodemographic measures directly and indirectly affected level of grief for females, while they functioned only as intervening variables for males. Support systems had an important affect on the grief experience of females, but were of less direct significance for males.

In summary, the psychological and medical literature is generally consistent in reporting higher levels of bereavement-related behaviors among females than males. There is less consensus as to explanations for these differences and their significance for intervention.

AGE AT LOSS

A second focus of this chapter concerns sex-related differences in age at loss. The greater susceptibility of males than females to relatively reduced longevity has been documented by researchers representing numerous behavioral and medical science disciplines. The earlier age at death among males has been variously associated with their increased risk for infection and fatal conditions such as coronary heart disease, and for their more strenuous and dangerous lifestyles (Wingard, 1984, p. 453; Trivers, 1985, p. 306; Sigelman & Shaffer, 1991, p. 540). Trivers has suggested that traits associated with earlier male mortality may be those associated with their higher reproductive success in the past (p. 301). As such, selection would have been for traits associated with reproductive success at the expense of survival. Specifically, characteristics associated with male–male conflict over females may expose males to more life-threatening situations and events. The higher rate of death by murder, accidents, and suicide among males is most likely explained, in part, by lifestyle and behavioral differences.

Only a few twin studies of longevity are available. Wyshak (1978), using genealogical records from a Mormon population, found that male twins were disadvantaged relative to their nontwin male siblings. In contrast, longevity differences were not observed among female sibships. A recent Swedish study by McGue, Vaupel, Holm, and Harvald (1993) reported an underrepresentation of male twins among a sample in which both co-twins survived until at least age fifteen years. They suggested that this finding reflected the greater susceptibility of males than females to early mortality. The absence of a significant sex difference in age at loss among twins in their adult sample was thought to reflect early life selection for vitality.

CAUSE OF DEATH AND NATURE OF LOSS

A final area of interest concerns associations between grief response and cause and nature of loss. The increased rate of accidents among males, a sex difference which tends to increase with age, has been well documented (Matheny,

1988). Increased scores by males on inventories assessing sensation-seeking and risk-taking tendencies (see Resnick, Gottesman, & McGue, 1993) are consistent with these findings concerning sex differences in frequency of injuries. Sex differences in hormone levels (e.g., testosterone) may partly explain observed sex differences in risk-taking behaviors (Zuckerman, 1995). It was thus anticipated that a higher proportion of deaths among male than female twins would be associated with accidents, rather than illnesses, as a reflection of their more high-risk lifestyles.

Accidents tend to occur suddenly. In contrast, most illnesses tend to be prolonged so that the eventuality of death is not unexpected. Not surprisingly, nature of loss (sudden or anticipated) has been associated with differences in bereavement response among survivors. Specifically, sudden loss has been associated with more persistent emotional stress and physiological change than expected loss (Martin & Dean, 1993; Epstein, 1993). Results are, however, not consistent across studies and may be most applicable to younger populations (Stroebe & Stroebe, 1993). In contrast, expected loss may afford opportunities for family and friends to prepare psychologically and emotionally for the death.

THEORETICAL APPROACHES TO BEREAVEMENT

Psychological correlates and sociocultural influences relevant to bereavement have been of considerable interest to bereavement researchers (see Sanders, 1989; Stroebe, Stroebe, & Hansson, 1993). Most recently, there has been increased attention to biological aspects of grieving and the use of animal models in bereavement research. A psychobiological approach examines disruption in biological regulatory processes following traumatic events and the significance of these events for physical and psychological functioning (Hofer, 1994); much of this work is traceable to that of Bowlby (1980). Sanders's (1989) intergrative theory acknowledges that the psychological effects of bereavement have a "biological anlage" that affects physical health. Bereavement has, for example, been associated with changes in neuroendocrine (Kim & Jacobs, 1993) and immune functioning (Irwin & Pike, 1993). Elaboration of these various approaches is beyond the scope of this chapter. In contrast, evolutionary theory has (with a few exceptions) rarely been referenced in explanations of individual differences in grief response, despite recognition that responses to separation have evolutionary roots (Osterweis et al., 1984). An evolutionary perspective on bereavement is presented in the next section.

Evolutionary Perspective on Bereavement

The evolutionary perspective in social science is concerned with the origins, functions and adaptive significance of behavior (Segal, 1993; Buss, 1995a). Hamilton (1964a; 1964b) developed a theory of kin selection which has profoundly influenced thinking and research on the nature and bases of human social behavior. Central to the theory is that natural selection favors alleles predisposing individuals to act in ways that promote transmission of those alleles. Alleles that influence individuals to favor others likely to carry replicas of those alleles is an indirect process by which these alleles can achieve future representation. Altruistic behaviors directed toward a close relative may reduce the reproductive fitness of the donor, yet may be selected for if those behaviors increase the fitness of the benefactor. This process can facilitate continued representation of shared genes, a concept termed *inclusive fitness*.

Evolutionary reasoning has yielded novel interpretations of behavior in numerous domains. For example, with respect to mate selection, Buss (1995a, p. 8) notes that males and females differ in the qualities they value in a mate, and these differences are associated with adaptive problems specific to males and females. Daly and Wilson (1987) dispel the notion that all children in a given family may be equally susceptible to parental abuse (pp. 295–305). They demonstrate that, within families, certain child characteristics (e.g., young age, poor health, and lack of genetic relatedness to parents) may be associated with increased risk for abuse. There have, however, been fewer evolutionary-based inquiries into bereavement-related behaviors, though available studies have yielded compelling findings. Loss of a close relative, such as a child with whom one shares 50 percent of his or her genes, reduces opportunities to enhance inclusive fitness. Such reasoning suggests that grief response might vary as a function of genetic relatedness as well as age of the deceased (individuals beyond the reproductive years might be grieved for less intensely than those who are reproductively active). A number of reports in the bereavement literature are consistent with this view (see, e.g., Littlefield & Rushton, 1986; Crawford, Salter, & Jang, 1989; Sanders, 1989; Rubin, 1989–1990). Twin research has also found increased grief intensity and bereavement-related symptoms among genetically identical than genetically nonidentical twin survivors (Woodward, 1988; Segal & Bouchard, 1993; Segal, Wilson, Bouchard, & Gitlin, 1995). In addition, twins (MZ and DZ combined) expressed greater grief intensity for deceased co-twins than for deceased nontwin relatives (Segal, 1997).

Not all researchers would agree that grief represents an adaptive behavioral response, given the accompanying physical and emotional stress. Archer (1992) has suggested that grief may represent a byproduct of a characteristic that does enhance fitness; for example, investment in a close personal relationship (p. 124). Extended discussion of this issue is presented by Segal, Wilson, Bouchard, & Gitlin (1995).

An evolutionary perspective on gender-related differences in bereavement response has never been applied using a twin or sibling sample. A brief description of the unique relationships generated by the members of MZ twin families, which suggest some interesting evolutionary-based predictions (Segal, 1993), is a necessary prelude to understanding how twin methods can be applied for testing evolutionary-based hypotheses. The children of MZ twins (while first cousins) are genetically equivalent to half-siblings since they share a genetically identical parent (twin mother or twin father). From the twin's perspective, nieces and nephews are genetically equivalent to children because the true parent is genetically identical to the self. These relationships do not characterize DZ twin families, because DZ twins share the same genetic relationship as ordinary siblings (i.e., 50% shared genes, on average). Having nieces and nephews is one means by which future genetic representation may be achieved. It is conceivable that the greater relatedness of MZ than DZ twin parents to nieces and nephews might be associated with their increased level of social closeness to twins and to nieces and nephews, as well as increased bereavement-related behaviors in response to their loss (Segal, 1993; Segal, Wilson, Bouchard, & Gitlin, 1995). Behavioral geneticists have recognized the value of this naturally occurring design for disentangling genetic and environmental influences underlying human behavioral variation (Gottesman & Bertelsen, 1989), yet this family constellation has been overlooked by evolutionary psychologists.

Paternal uncertainty refers to the reduced certainty among males that they are the true fathers of their children. In contrast, females can be certain of their relationship to their children. This gender difference has been associated with parental differences in rearing practices and investment (see Barash, 1982, p. 318; Daly & Wilson, 1987, p. 304). It is possible that uncertain paternity may raise different expectations for grief response in surviving male and female same-sex twins. Specifically, same-sex male twins may grieve relatively less for deceased twin siblings than same-sex female twins because of uncertainty surrounding their true relatedness to nieces and nephews (i.e., their co-twins' children). Female twins, in contrast, should be more certain of their relatedness to nieces and nephews. Consistent with this reasoning, Littlefield and Rushton (1986) reported lower grief intensity ratings for deceased children by fathers than mothers, by maternal grandfathers and paternal grandmothers (combined) than maternal grandmothers, and by fathers' siblings than mothers' siblings.

A possible association between paternity uncertainty and grief response becomes especially interesting in the case of surviving opposite-sex twins. Thornhill and Thornhill (1989) note that if "reliability of paternity is low in general, a man's brothers are also likely to have reduced paternity reliability and therefore represent less appropriate recipients of potentially reproductive benefits than a man's sisters" (p. 282). This reasoning suggests that surviving males from opposite-sex pairs should indicate greater bereavement response for their deceased twin sisters than for deceased nontwin brothers (because of the loss of potential offspring), and possibly greater bereavement response for the twin than surviving female twins from opposite-sex pairs. Males may be certain that they share a genetic relationship with nieces and nephews (their twin sister's children), while female twins may be less certain of their relationship to their twin brother's children. However, the generally increased expressivity and emotionality of females (Hoyenga & Hoyenga, 1993a), their greater tendency to seek professional assistance for illness and stress (Wingard, 1984), or the greater significance of kin for females than for males (Salmon & Daly, 1996) could yield disconfirming evidence. In the present study, comparison of male and female opposite-sex twins was precluded by the availability of only two males from these pairs.

The extent to which cause of death and nature of loss might be associated with individual differences in grieving was of interest. Evolutionary theory suggests that the unexpected loss of a young healthy individual should prove especially devastating, as it would eliminate a potential source of inclusive fitness. In contrast, less severe bereavement response should be associated with illness as a cause of death. This is because unhealthy individuals are less likely to reproduce, thus reducing opportunities for improving inclusive fitness among relatives. This reasoning is not inconsistent with the psychological explanations of differences in grief associated with cause and nature of loss that have been presented. Littlefield and Rushton (1986) found that healthy children were grieved for more than unhealthy children. However, if accidents are associated with increased grief and occur more frequently among males than females, then this might affect bereavement response.

CALIFORNIA STATE UNIVERSITY TWIN LOSS STUDY

The California State University Twin Loss Study (formerly the Minnesota Twin Loss Project) was launched in 1983. The study is designed to provide knowledge about response to death, bereavement, and grieving among members of multiple births, and to generate guidelines for assisting survivors of twin loss. A comprehensive Twin Loss Survey (TLS) developed by the investigators (see Segal & Bouchard, 1993) is completed by twins who have lost their co-twin. The three major components of the TLS are (1) a Grief Intensity Scale (GIS) (adapted from Littlefield & Rushton, 1986), (2) the Grief Experience Inventory (GEI) (Sanders, Mauger, & Strong, 1985), and (3) a Coping Scale (Littlefield, unpublished); details about these questionnaires is provided in the following sections. Additional items concern the circumstances surrounding the twin's death, age at death, the nature of the twin relationship, reactions to the loss of nontwin relatives and acquaintances, and other measures of interest.

Participants

Participants are identified through twins' associations, twin loss support groups, personal referrals, the media, and attorneys working with wrongful death cases. Participants are located in the United States, Canada, Great Britain, and Australia. Approximately 50 percent of the twins were recruited through mailings sent to the memberships of twin loss support groups. Recent collaboration with investigators associated with the Australian National Health and Medical Research Council Twin Registry, in Carlton, Victoria, has identified additional participants whose enrollment in the registry occurred prior to the loss. These individuals will be included in future papers from this ongoing study.

The present analyses are limited to gender-related differences in bereavement response among the first 280 bereaved twins. Analyses were restricted to twins whose age at loss was fifteen years or later; these individuals would have shared the majority of their early developmental years and would be able to recall the loss experience. Organizing the twin survivors by sex yielded 80 males and 200 females. The majority of twins for whom information on cause of death was available (n = 271) died due to illness (57.6%) or accident (27.7%). Mean age in years at the time of participation was 46.05 (SD = 16.20) and did not differ between male and female twins. Mean number of years since loss (time between the loss of the twin and participation in the study) was 6.93 (SD = 8.97). This interval was higher for males than for females, a difference that approached statistical significance (t [118.68] = 1.90, p < 0.06). The age variance was also higher for males, a difference that was highly significant (F = 1.57, p < 0.01). Age data are summarized in Table 12.1.

Twins were classified as MZ or DZ based upon responses to the Nichols and Bilbro (1966) physical resemblance questionnaire completed by the surviving co-twin. Scoring rules were slightly modified, given that information was obtained from only one pair member. On occasion, the accuracy of these assignments was improved by evaluation of photographs of the twins by individuals specializing in twin research. Serological analysis, or blood-typing, of some twins had been completed prior to the death, enabling classification with a high degree of accuracy. The present sample included 188 MZ twins and 87 DZ twins; 45 DZ twins (43 of whom were female) were from opposite-sex pairs. Zygosity classifications were not possible for 5 twins due to incomplete or unclear information.

The considerable excess of females (71%) and MZ twins (68%) deserves comment. The higher female than male representation is typical among other twin studies (Finkel, Whitfield, & McGue, 1995), as well as the general population (Sigelman & Shaffer, 1991). Females comprise the majority of participants in most published studies of loss and bereavement, with the proportion reaching as high as 78 percent in some cases. Several explanations are possible. As indicated, males typically express less death anxiety than females, so would be less likely to seek or volunteer for research participation. An earlier average age at loss for males than females would also be associated with reduced male participation.

MZ twins, which are generally believed to represent one-third of twin populations (Bulmer, 1970), were more highly represented than DZ twins. These data are consistent with the "Rule of Two-Thirds" (Lykken, Bouchard, McGue,

Table 12.1
Age at Participation, Age at Loss, and Years since Loss for Participating Male and Female Twins

	N	Age at Participation	Age at Loss	Years Since[a,b] Loss
Sex		M SD	M SD	M SD
Males	80	45.24 (16.87) [17 - 94]	36.52 (17.40) [15 - 85]	8.72 (10.56) [0 - 44]
Females	200	46.37 (15.95) [16 - 90]	40.15 (16.13) [15 - 87]	6.22 (8.18) [0 - 52]
Combined	280	46.05 (16.20) [16 - 94]	39.11 (16.55) [15 - 87]	6.93 (8.97) [0 - 52]
Same-Sex				
Males	78	45.54 (16.96) [17 - 94]	36.81 (17.52) [15 - 85]	8.72 (10.61) [0 - 44]
Females	157	46.50 (16.21) [16 - 90]	40.76 (16.33) [15 - 87]	5.73 (6.74) [0 - 28]
Combined	235	46.18 (16.43) [16 - 94]	39.45 (16.80) [15 - 87]	6.73 (8.33) [0 - 44]

Note: Number in brackets is range.
[a]Male variance > female variance, $p < 0.01$; [b]male mean > female mean, $p < 0.06$, male variance > female variance, $p < 0.001$.

& Tellegen, 1990), or the observation that females and MZ twins often comprise two-thirds of volunteer twin samples. A consequent concern of behavioral geneticists is that DZ twin volunteers may be more phenotypically similar than nonvolunteers, thus reducing estimates of genetic influence. This concern appears most serious when twins volunteer in the absence of solicitation. However, new data suggest that the distribution of MZ and DZ twins in volunteer samples may be a more genuine reflection of the relative population frequencies of the two twin types than has been previously believed. Hur, McGue, and Iacono (1995), in a review of twin births from Minnesota occurring between 1971 and 1984, found rates of 4.09 and 2.60 out 1,000 for MZ and DZ same-sex twins, respectively. Possible explanations for the relatively lower DZ twinning rate included stress associated with industrialization and environmental pesticides which might reduce sperm count. These data are consistent with other recent studies reviewed in that report.

The present study was concerned with gender differences in bereavement-related behaviors and symptoms, not in estimates of genetic influence, so the imbalance of MZ and DZ twin was not a concern. (The relative proportions of MZ and DZ twins among male and female survivors from same-sex pairs were similar.) However, the decreased proportion of male respondents raises the possibility that males who did participate may be especially grieved, thus reducing anticipated gender differences in the dependent measures.

Procedures

Participants completed a comprehensive Twin Loss Survey, mostly by mail. Components of the survey included a Grief Intensity Scale, the Grief Experience Inventory, and a Coping Scale. Gender-related differences in the GIS and GEI findings are the focus of this report. Additional analyses concern sex-related differences in age at loss and cause and nature of death.

The GIS is a seven-point scale (1 = No Grief to 7 = Total Devastation, Suicide Point) along which participants indicated the magnitude of grief experienced one to two months following the loss of the co-twin. This scale was adapted from one used by Littlefield & Rushton (1986). Twins were also asked to indicate the magnitude of grief experienced in response to the loss of other relatives and acquaintances, though these data will be reported elsewhere. The validity of this instrument is evidenced by significant correlations between the grief intensity rating and total score on the GEI ($r = 0.52$, $p < 0.001$) (Littlefield & Rushton, 1986). In that study, reliability was indicated by correlations between own grief intensity rating and spouses' rating of grief intensity ($r = 0.50$, $p < 0.01$), and between spouses' ratings of grief intensity of child's maternal grandfather ($r = 0.72$, $p < 0.01$), child's maternal grandmother ($r = 0.66$, $p < 0.01$) and child's paternal grandfather ($r = 0.61$, $p < 0.01$); spouses' ratings of grief intensity of child's maternal grandfather showed a lower correlation ($r = 0.32$, $p < 0.05$). An earlier analysis of the present twin data further supported the validity of the GIS, given a significant correlation between ratings of grief intensity and life in general as experienced one to two months following the loss of the twin ($r = -0.56$, $p < 0.001$, $n = 62$ [Segal & Bouchard, 1993]). The negative correlation reflects the assignment of values to these scales; life in general is rated on a five-point scale: 1 = extremely poor to 5 = extremely well. This finding was confirmed by the present data ($r = -0.46$, $p < 0.01$, $n = 261$).

The GEI is a self-report inventory designed "to assess experiences, feelings, symptoms, and behaviors of individuals during the grief process" (Sanders, 1979–1980, p. 308). It includes 135 true/false questions reflecting the subject's current experience of grief. The multidimensional nature of the GEI is demonstrated by nine bereavement scales (Despair, Anger/Hostility, Guilt,

Social Isolation, Loss of Control, Rumination, Depersonalization, Somatization, and Death Anxiety), six research scales (Sleep Disturbance, Appetite, Loss of Vigor, Physical Symptoms, Optimism/Despair, and Dependency), and three validity scales (Denial, Atypical Responses, and Social Desirability). The research scales were recently developed and further analyses are needed to assess their clinical utility.

In the present study, items were reworded to refer to the twin and to the one to two month period following the loss. For example, the item, "I am strongly preoccupied with the image of the deceased," was rewritten to read, "I was strongly preoccupied with the image of my deceased twin." Data were available for eight of the nine bereavement scales and for three validity scales; additional details about the items as administered in the present study are available in Segal, Wilson, Bouchard, & Gitlin (1995). Present versions of the TLS include the original (present tense) GEI items, though they are reworded to refer to the twin.

Nine-week test–retest reliabilities using twenty-two college students (for whom loss had occurred within the previous five years), range from 0.71 to 0.84 for the bereavement scales, 0.53 to 0.61 for the validity scales, and 0.52 to 0.87 for the research scales. Lower test–retest reliabilities were obtained using seventy-nine individuals for whom loss occurred within three months of test administration and an interval of eighteen months. Sanders, Mauger, and Strong (1985) suggested that these lower reliabilities may reflect genuine change in grief processes over time. Additional psychometric characteristics of the GEI are provided in the inventory manual (Sanders et al., 1985).

Participants' age at the loss of the co-twin was obtained to assess relationships between this measure and scores on the various bereavement scales. Information on age at loss also enabled assessment of sex-related differences in longevity. (Sex of survivors from opposite-sex pairs was recoded for this analysis, yielding 159 deceased females and 121 deceased males.) It was anticipated that age at death would occur earlier for males than for females. A significant sex difference in this measure would render the excess representation of females in the sample more comprehensible.

Participants were requested to describe the circumstances surrounding the death of the twin. Responses were classified as illness, accident, suicide, murder, aging (unspecified causes associated with death among the elderly), and other. Again, the sex of twins from opposite-sex pairs was recoded for these analyses.

Nature of death was classified as anticipated or sudden. Anticipated death included cases in which there was a prognosis of death, and death occurred. Sudden death included cases in which loss occurred prior to the expected time, or cases initally diagnosed as possibly terminal but diagnosed as nonterminal at the time of loss (Rando, 1987). Cases in which death was due to a terminal illness and occurred within seven days from the time that the survivor learned of the death prognosis were also classified as sudden (Sand-

ers, 1979–1980). In some cases, classification was assisted by other information provided by the respondent. Finally, there is controversy among bereavement researchers as to whether suicide represents an anticipated or sudden
event (Sanders, 1989; Reed & Greenwald, 1991). In the present study, cases
of suicide were classified as sudden. In the present chapter, analyses of cause
of death and nature of loss include only those cases in which cause of death
was due to accident or illness, given the relative infrequency of the other
classifications.

RESULTS

Correlations between Gender and Time-Related Measures

Age at loss of the co-twin showed a negligible relationship with gender
among the participant sample. A significant negative (albeit modest) relationship was found between gender of participants and years since loss ($r = -0.13$,
$p < 0.05$). As indicated, the time interval between the loss of the twin and
participation in the study was somewhat longer for males than for females.

Grief Intensity Scale

Age at loss showed a significant negative (but modest) correlation with the
grief intensity rating by participants ($r = -0.19$, $p < 0.01$), demonstrating that
younger age at loss is associated with higher grief intensity ratings. Years since
loss showed a negative but nonsignificant relationship with grief ($r = -0.10$,
ns). Analysis of covariance (using sex as an independent variable and age at
loss as a covariate) indicated significantly higher grief intensity ratings by
surviving female twins ($M = 5.92$, $SD = 1.20$, $n = 199$) than by surviving
male twins ($M = 5.62$, $SD = 1.24$, $n = 78$) ($F [1, 274] = 4.99$, $p < 0.05$). The
proportion of explained variance was, however, modest. The same pattern of
findings emerged using the sample of surviving same-sex twins only (males,
$M = 5.62$, $SD = 1.25$, $n = 76$; females, $M = 5.95$, $SD = 1.20$, $n = 156$) ($F [1, 229]$
$= 5.70$, $p < 0.05$).

This analysis was repeated using sex of deceased as the independent variable.
Mean grief intensity scores were significantly higher when the decedent was
female, confirming that deceased female twins are grieved for more highly than
deceased male twins (deceased males, $M = 5.69$, $SD = 1.23$, $n = 119$; deceased
females, $M = 5.94$, $SD = 1.19$, $n = 158$) ($F [1, 274] = 4.36$, $p < 0.05$).

Grief Experience Inventory

Age at loss showed significant negative correlations with the eight GEI
scales and single validity scale (Atypical Response) for which data were available, with *r*s ranging from -0.23 to -0.37. Younger age at loss was, therefore,

associated with higher levels of bereavement symptoms, as was true for the GIS. Years since loss showed significant negative correlations with some but not all of the scales, with rs ranging from –0.18 to –0.26. Thus, age at loss was more closely related to bereavement response than was the interval since the loss. Additional discussion of these data is available in Segal et al. (1995).

Mean bereavement scale scores of females significantly exceeded those of males on six of the eight bereavement scales (Despair, Anger/Hostility, Social Isolation, Loss of Control, Depersonalization, and Somatic) and on the single validity scale (Atypical Response) for which data were available. Female scores also exceeded male scores on the remaining two scales (Rumination and Guilt), though the difference was nonsignificant. Restricting analyses to same-sex twins only yielded the same pattern of findings, with the exception that the gender difference for Guilt became statistically significant. Means, standard deviations, and correlations of each variable with gender of survivor are provided in Tables 12.2 and 12.3.

Table 12.2
GEI Scale Scores Obtained by Male and Female Twin Survivors, and Correlations with Sex

Scale	Males	Females	r (sex, scale)
	M SD	M SD	
Despair***	9.73 (5.23)	11.99 (4.47)	.22**
Anger/Host**	4.60 (2.96)	5.67 (2.59)	.18**
Guilt	2.78 (1.96)	3.10 (1.82)	.08
Social Isolation**	3.73 (2.29)	4.47 (1.96)	.16**
Loss of Control**	5.32 (2.18)	6.33 (2.29)	.20**
Rumination	7.41 (3.17)	7.58 (2.87)	.03
Depersonalization*	5.52 (2.43)	6.20 (1.94)	.15*
Somatic***	7.15 (4.92)	9.25 (4.33)	.21**
Atypical Response*	9.34 (3.86)	10.55 (3.82)	.14*

Note: n (males) = 62–77; n (females) = 151–194; * p < 0.05; ** p < 0.01; *** p < 0.001.

Table 12.3
GEI Scale Scores Obtained by Male and Female Survivors from Same-Sex Twin Pairs, and Correlations with Sex

Scale	Males		Females		r (sex, scale)
	M	SD	M	SD	
Despair***	9.58 (5.22)		12.05 (4.51)		.24**
Anger/Host**	4.51 (2.95)		5.71 (2.49)		.21**
Guilt*	2.74 (1.97)		3.32 (1.83)		.14**
Social Isolation**	3.65 (2.28)		4.52 (1.92)		.20**
Loss of Control**	5.33 (2.15)		6.19 (2.31)		.18**
Rumination	7.40 (3.20)		7.66 (2.93)		.04
Depersonalization*	5.47 (2.44)		6.24 (1.88)		.17**
Somatic**	7.06 (4.88)		8.96 (4.46)		.19**
Atypical Response**	9.34 (3.86)		10.91 (3.69)		.20**

Note: n (males) = 62–75; n (females) = 115–148; * p < 0.05; ** p < 0.01; *** p < 0.001.

Age at Loss

Mean age at loss for the combined sample of male and female twins was 39.11 years (SD = 16.55). Age at loss, while younger for deceased males (M = 37.20 years, SD = 16.73, n = 121) than for deceased females (M = 40.57 years, SD = 16.32, n = 159), did not show a significant sex difference. Repeating this analysis using only same-sex twins yielded a similar pattern of findings. Age at loss, while lower for deceased same-sex males (M = 36.81 years, SD = 17.52, n = 78), did not differ significantly from that of deceased same-sex females (M = 40.76 years, SD = 16.32, n = 157).

Cause of Death and Nature of Loss

It was anticipated that the proportion of males whose death was associated with an accident would exceed that of females. An analysis restricted to males (n = 95) and females (n = 136) whose death was due to an accident or illness was undertaken. The gender difference in this proportion was in the expected direction (males, 38%; females, 29%), though the magnitude of the difference was not statistically significant. Death occurred suddenly among 59 percent of the males and among 50 percent of the females, a difference that was in the expected direction but was nonsignificant.

The grief intensity rating showed a very modest but significant correlation with cause of death ($r = 0.14$, $p < 0.05$) and nature of loss ($r = 0.18$, $p < 0.01$). Specifically, grief intensity ratings were higher when death was due to an accident rather than to an illness, and were higher when loss was sudden rather than expected. This same pattern of findings emerged when analyses were restricted to same-sex twin survivors.

DISCUSSION

Gender Differences in Bereavement

The finding of higher grief intensity ratings and higher grief experience scores among surviving female twins than male twins is consistent with previous reports in the bereavement literature. The same pattern of findings emerged when analyses were restricted to same-sex twin survivors and when sex of deceased was used as the independent variable in the analysis of grief intensity ratings. However, the observed gender differences were not large, perhaps for two reasons. First, it is possible that differences might have been greater if a more representative sample had been available. Given that 50 percent of the twins were identified through twin loss support groups, the males in particular may have been especially bereaved, possibly narrowing male–female differences in response. Second, full understanding of the nature and complexity of gender differences in bereavement may be assisted by longitudinal follow-up and more comprehensive assessment instruments. Finally, it is important to emphasize that loss of a twin is a very painful experience for both male and female survivors. Framing future research questions and hypotheses in terms of gender differences in quality or content of response, rather than magnitude, may be most appropriate.

Most bereavement studies have offered psychosocial and cultural explanations of individual differences in bereavement behaviors. For example, more intense grieving by mothers than by fathers has been associated with differences in parental attachment. It is suspected that mothers feel more isolated than fathers following child loss because fathers turn to occupations for comfort, leaving mothers at a loss during much of the time (Sanders, 1989, p. 138). As indicated, male–female differences in bereavement have also been associated with cultural expectations of greater fortitude among males than females during times of stress. An evolutionary perspective is compatible with these explanations, yet lends an additional level of interpretation, as discussed in the next section.

The present pattern of findings concerning same-sex male and female twins is consistent with evolutionary reasoning, which suggests that uncertainty of relatedness to nieces and nephews by males may be associated with lower grief intensity ratings and lower GEI scale scores relative to females. However, it is not implied that individuals consciously consider the genetic relatedness of present or potential kin when responding in social situations or conferring benefits. Dawkins (1989) has proposed that individuals may be influenced by their genes to react in ways that are consistent with such considerations. Evolutionary psychology thus offers novel hypotheses and explanations of human behavior; indeed, many psychologists seem unaware of the evolutionary implications of their research (Scarr, 1995). However, the need for additional multidisciplinary efforts remains. Bereavement and grieving are highly complex responses, associated with a broad array of physiological and psychological factors that function at many levels.

Time between loss and participation in the study was somewhat longer for males than for females, a factor that may have mitigated grief somewhat. Years since loss did show significant but very modest correlations with some but not all GEI scales, with the largest correlation reaching $r = -0.26$. Years since loss was unrelated to the magnitude of the grief intensity ratings. It would therefore seem that these factors did not substantially contribute to the observed gender differences.

Age at Loss

The smaller proportion of participating males than females and their somewhat younger age at loss suggests, in part, greater susceptibility to early mortality among males. This is consistent with the greater male mortality which begins *in utero* and continues across the lifespan (see Trivers, 1985, p. 306). The sex difference in age at loss was, however, nonsignificant. A similar result was reported by McGue and colleagues (1993) in their Swedish twin study, suggesting early life selection for vitality.

Cause of Death and Nature of Loss

A higher proportion of males than females died due to accidents than illnesses, though the difference was slight. The deaths of a higher proportion of males than females occurred suddenly, though this difference was also nonsignificant. (The correlation between cause and nature of loss was high; $r = 0.74$, $p < 0.01$).

The absence of a significant sex difference in cause of death in the present sample may partly reflect the relatively smaller male sample size. In addition, analyses did not include suicides and murders, due to their relative infrequency. Future analyses using larger age-specific samples may uncover meaningful interactions between sex and cause and nature of death. There is evidence that sex-specific causes of death are related to age. For example, accidents occur more frequently among all males, with the exception of individuals past eighty-five years of age (Trivers, 1985).

Future Research Directions

Gender-related differences in bereavement response have been well documented by psychological and psychiatric investigators, yet the bases of the observed differences are not yet resolved. Critical tasks for the future are the procurement of representative samples of bereaved males and females and the application of fresh theoretical approaches. An evolutionary perspective may be valuable for generating novel hypotheses and for reappraising existing findings.

There is a need to identify the mechanisms underlying gender differences in bereavement response. Mechanisms responsible for recognition and discrimination among relatives have been of continued interest, as well as controversy, among evolutionary psychologists (Dawkins, 1989). Phenotypic matching (using the degree of similarity between one's own phenotype and that of another organism for assessing relatedness) has been proposed as a means for discriminating between and among kin (Sherman & Holmes, 1985). Interestingly, males and females in diploid outbreeding species, such as humans, vary in degrees of relatedness as a function of the location of the gene. For example, male siblings have a 50 percent chance of sharing a gene on the X chromosome, while female siblings have a 75 percent chance (Trivers, 1985, p. 137). Genomic imprinting (the process by which allelic expression is affected by whether the gene was transmitted by the mother or the father) has recently challenged traditional beliefs concerning laws of inheritance (Barlow, 1995). If and how these processes may underlie variations in social relatedness within and between male and female sibships is intriguing.

The psychological correlates specific to twin and sibling loss have been less well studied by bereavement researchers than those associated with parental, child, and spousal loss. Some recent analyses have, however, underlined the impact of twin and sibling loss as significant and enduring (Bank & Kahn, 1982; Segal, Wilson, Bouchard, & Gitlin, 1995). Increased focus on opposite-sex twins and siblings promises to yield informative findings of both theoretical and practical significance with respect to gender differences in grief, as well as differences in age at loss and cause of death. Greater attention to personality characteristics, the previous sibling relationship, and life crises that may have preceeded the death is also needed. The growing availability of specialized twin registries should facilitate efforts along these lines.

SUMMARY

Gender-related differences in bereavement response among surviving male and female twins, as measured by a Grief Intensity Scale and Grief Experience Inventory, were presented. Females obtained consistently higher scores on these measures, the majority of them significant. This pattern of findings is consistent with previous studies in the bereavement literature. While most studies have assigned psychosocial or cultural explanations to male–female differences in grieving, this study examined the findings with reference to an evolutionary perspective. Some novel interpretations of the data, as well as new directions for future research activity, were suggested.

Age at loss was younger for males than females, as expected, though the difference was not significant. A sex difference in the frequency of accidents as a cause of death was higher among males than females, but the difference was slight. This finding may reflect the relatively smaller number of male participants.

ACKNOWLEDGMENTS

This research was supported, in part, by a Hughes Faculty Research Award and a National Science Foundation Career Advancement Award to Dr. Nancy L. Segal (BNS-8709207), the Minnesota Center for Twin and Adoption Research at the University of Minnesota, and the Twin Studies Center at California State University, Fullerton. Research staff at the Australian National Health and Medical Research Council Twin Registry in Carlton, Victoria, contributed greatly to this project. Dr. Raymond W. Brandt, Director of the Twinless Twins Support Group International, and Dr. Catherine M. Sanders, Director of the Center for the Study of Separation and Loss, are acknowledged for invaluable assistance and support. Colette M. Lay, M.A.; Karen M. Nelson, M.A.; Shelly A. Blozis, M.A.; Jennifer Giordano, B.A.; Carrie Ortega, B.A.; Elena Alvarez, B.A.; and Steven M. Wilson, M.A. provided research services.

Chapter 13

Applying the Interpersonal Circle and Evolutionary Theory to Gender Differences in Psychopathological Traits

Katharine Blick Hoyenga, Kermit T. Hoyenga, Kenneth Walters, and James A. Schmidt

As Buss (1995a) pointed out, psychology is currently in disarray due to its many unrelated and often conflicting branches, each with its own disparate minitheories accompanied by vast arrays of underorganized data. The solution is to try to organize past data and gather new data using theories that can predict and explain a variety of phenomena in many different areas. Two such theories are evolutionary theory and the Big Five theory of personality. Following the lead of other theorists (e.g., Buss, 1991; 1995a; 1995b; MacDonald, 1995), we will explicitly relate those two theories to each other, pointing out how individual differences in personality-trait dimensions could have evolved and remained a stable aspect of human lives for generations. By collecting data guided by evolutionary theory, and by using well-validated and theoretically coherent measures of personality, the data and models employed by one investigator can be meaningfully related to and combined with the data and models used by another, even in a different area.

Two other considerations have guided our research. First, we have concluded that, as we will describe, one of the most frequently replicated findings in biopsychology is that a low level of brain serotonin can lead to problems with impulse control. Second, understanding any given sex difference demands a context.[1] The relevant context includes but is not limited to patterns of sexual dimorphisms in all traits possibly related to that specific sex difference. The context of the sexually dimorphic traits described in this chapter includes biopsychological traits, evolutionary theories of sex differences, and personality theory. We have used these three context areas to test two sets of hypotheses regarding sex differences in depression and sociopathy, one set tested with rat subjects and another set tested with human subjects.

BACKGROUND: THEORY AND DATA

The Big Five Personality Traits

The Five Factor model of personality was developed through extensive factor analytic studies of dozens of existing personality measures (see the literature cited by Buss, 1991; MacDonald, 1995). The resulting five independent factors were then extensively validated, including behaviorally. These factors or trait dimensions are usually described as being extroversion (or surgency), nurturance, openness to experience (or intellect), neuroticism, and conscientiousness (or will to achieve). An individual's scores on each of these five basic or elemental personality traits captures his or her basic aspects of personality. Developmental environments and genetic predispositions together determine an individual's trait levels on each of these dimensions.

Sex differences are found on all of the five personality-trait dimensions. Females get significantly higher scores on all five, with the largest sex differences seen in neuroticism and nurturance scores, and only a small sex difference found for extroversion scores (Corbitt & Widiger, 1995; Feingold, 1994). Furthermore, each major factor has several subfactors or facets, and sex differences can vary among the individual facets. For example, among the facets of extroversion, men get higher scores on excitement seeking and assertiveness, but women get higher scores on warmth (Corbitt & Widiger, 1995).

These sex differences can be understood from an evolutionary point of view (Buss, 1995b; Corbitt & Widiger, 1995). In general, any type of individual differences on trait scores remain in the population because the relevant genes show frequency-dependent selection: The value of having a particular trait varies inversely according to how many other people in a given social group are also high in that trait (Buss, 1991; 1995a; 1995b; MacDonald, 1995). In addition, since the inheritance of these traits depends on multiple genes as well as on individually unique developmental environments, offspring also differ somewhat in personality from either parent, which is of advantage in a changing environment. Sex differences in these personality traits can be related to sex differences in evolutionary adaptive problems, such as the sex differences in obligate parental investments: Males have been under somewhat more selection pressure to seek multiple mates, while females have been under more pressure to select a single, committed, resource-investing mate (Ellis, 1989, p. 68; Buss, 1995b).

The Two Interpersonal Personality-Trait Dimensions

Two other personality-trait dimensions, dominance and warmth, are closely related to the Big Five traits of extroversion and nurturance. These interpersonal types of personality dimensions are the ones most relevant to predicting and explaining social interactions, including mating and parental interactions. The dominance dimension varies from dominant to submissive, and the warmth dimension varies from sociable and agreeable at one end to cold and withdrawn at the other. These same two personality-trait dimensions of dominance and warmth can be identified in the interpersonal styles of socially living primates other than humans (Clarke & Boinski, 1995; de Waal, 1989; Hoyenga & Hoyenga, 1993a, pp. 339–351; 1993b, pp. 149–170).

These interpersonal types of traits are central to the sex differences in the reproductive roles just described (MacDonald, 1995; Wiggins, 1991). Males, in competition with other males, might have been under greater evolutionary pressure for dominance-related traits (Buss, 1995a; 1995b; Ellis, 1995), probably including the interpersonal dominance trait. This would have led to some of the relevant-trait genes becoming sex limited, or to the trait appearing only in the presence of a sufficient level of the right kind of sex hormone.[2] Females, because of greater obligatory parental investment, might have been under greater evolutionary pressure to become warmer and more nurturant in personality predispositions. These two dimensions are the basis of the Interpersonal Circle.

The Interpersonal Circle

The Interpersonal Circle was originally developed by the Kaiser Permanente group for clinical research (Freedman, Leary, Ossario, & Coffey, 1951; Laforge, Leary, Naboisek, Coffey, & Freedman, 1954), and has seen occasional revision and refinement (e.g., Kiesler, 1983; Wiggins, 1979). As a structural model of personality, the Circle has the two basic orthogonal dimensions just described: dominance (or control) and agreeableness or warmth (sometimes also called affiliation; Freedman et al., 1951; Kiesler, 1983; Wiggins, 1979; 1982). Numerous schemes have been devised to measure this two-dimensional and circular space. For the current discussion, we will concern ourselves with research done with the trait adjectives scale developed by Wiggins and his colleagues, the Interpersonal Adjectives Scales (IAS-R) (Wiggins, 1979; 1982; Wiggins & Broughton, 1985; Wiggins & Pincus, 1989a; 1989b; 1994; Wiggins, Trapnell, & Phillips, 1988).

The two basic interpersonal trait dimensions are illustrated in Figure 13.1A. Since they are independent of each other, they are represented as two orthogonal (vertical and horizontal) axes. The two other axes of the Circle, the oblique axes, represent "blends" of the basic two dimensions just described. Thus, extroversion is a "blend" of dominance and warmth; a person becomes extroverted by being both dominant and warm. A person becomes arrogant and calculating by being both cold and dominant.

Individual's scores on the Interpersonal Adjectives Scales form distinctive patterns. First, any individual's personality-trait patterns are measured by self-report scores on eight sets of eight adjectives, one set of adjectives measuring

Figure 13.1
Several Views of How the Interpersonal Circle Can Be Measured and Visualized

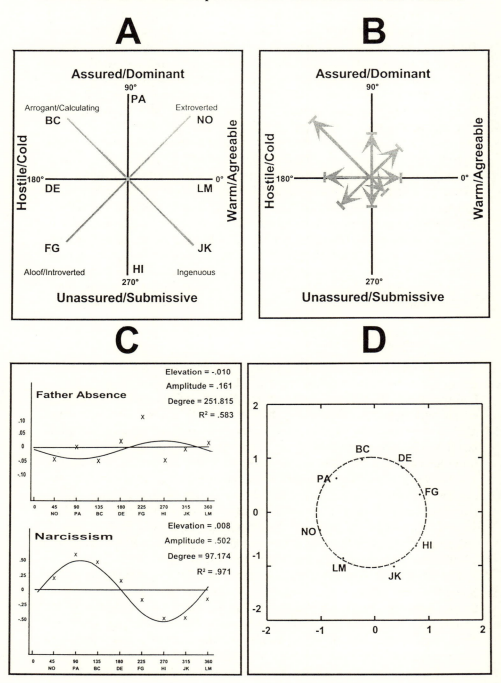

A shows the letter names for the traits on all four dimensions; **B** is a vector length, Cartesian analysis; **C** contains two cosine analyses; **D** represents the results from a multidimensional scaling analysis. The vector analysis depicted in **B** is usually represented by connecting the ends of the vectors; for the sake of clarity, we omitted this step.

the trait found at each of the eight ends of the four dimensions. When correlation coefficients are calculated between pairs of scores from the eight traits for a group of subjects, the coefficients form a specific pattern. Adjacent dimensions, separated by a 45° angle, are positively related to each other (expected correlation = 0.707). The ends of any two dimensions separated by a 90° angle are expected to be independent of each other (correlation = 0). One end of any dimension is expected to be strongly negatively correlated with the other end of that dimension; for example, dominance is negatively correlated with submission. Thus, as you move around the dimensions (Figure 13.1A) clockwise the expected correlations among trait scores will form a sine-shaped wave, which appears as a circle when plotted in two-dimensional space (see Figure 13.1D). For example, the expected correlations of the seven other trait scores with individuals' scores on the dominance trait would be, in clockwise order, +0.707, 0, –0.707, –1.0, –0.707, 0, +0.707. These numbers will look like a cosine wave when plotted (see Figure 13.1C, bottom).

Measuring Individuals, Traits, or Groups of Individuals

The Interpersonal Circle can be used to plot individuals or to plot traits; in addition, groups of individuals who all have a similar personality can also be plotted. You plot an individual to measure the dominant personality trait of that individual. If a personality trait such as narcissism is plotted, you are measuring the degree to which narcissism can be seen to have an interpersonal component, or the degree to which narcissism can be explained by the traits found on the Interpersonal Circle. Similarly, when you plot a group of individuals who have been found to have a similar personality, such as having a similar diagnosis of narcissistic personality disorder, you are measuring the degree to which that diagnosis has interpersonal components. You can plot individuals or traits in two-dimensional or Cartesian space; you can plot traits or groups of individuals with a similar trait either in Cartesian space or with a cosine analysis.

Cartesian Space Analysis Cartesian space is used to analyze vector lengths as a way of finding out what an individual's strongest or most important trait might be. In this case, a vector length is the sum of the scores on the specific adjectives associated with each one of the eight trait clusters, which is taken to indicate the degree to which that individual possesses each particular trait. A longer vector (larger sum) means that the person will score further from the origin or center of the axis on that particular dimension when the sums of scores for all eight traits are plotted in Cartesian space. For an individual, the longest vector (the largest sum or score) indicates his or her preeminent trait orientation. A person with scores on dominance higher than his or her scores on any of the other seven adjective sets would have a dominant type of personality. A vector plot is illustrated in Figure 13.1B (this individual has higher scores on "arrogant, calculating" than on any of the other seven trait dimensions).

An extreme vector length for an individual—one vector being much longer than any of the others—implies a lack of flexibility. An individual with one extremely long vector, one trait which was much stronger than any of the seven others, would tend to act a certain way regardless of the situation and thus the appropriateness of that type of behavior. A person with an extreme vector length for dominance would, for example, tend to display dominant actions even when interacting with his or her boss, which may not be a very effective course of action in those circumstances.

The interpersonalness of any trait or characteristic can be measured by analyzing the pattern of correlations of that trait with the eight interpersonal traits, or by analyzing the interpersonal profile (vector lengths) of a group of people, all of whom possess high levels of that particular trait. In the first case, which is what we did and which will be described in more detail, you would give a group of subjects some instrument measuring the eight interpersonal traits and also give that group one or more measures of one or more other personality traits that you think might have interpersonal components. In the second case, the interpersonal traits of a group of people that all had exactly the same diagnosis would be measured; all the people might have been clinically diagnosed as sociopathic, for example. For a group of people with a similar diagnosis, the average score of that group on each of the eight interpersonal traits would be plotted, just as in Figure 13.1B. The degree to which one vector was longer than any other for a group of people sharing a given diagnosis measures the degree to which that particular form of psychopathology reflects, and so can be understood by, interpersonal traits. If all the vectors are of equal length, the diagnosis does not have any important interpersonal components.

Cosine Analyses   A cosine analysis can be used to measure the degree to which scores on any given trait measure might have an interpersonal component, following the procedures of Gurtman (1991; 1992). A cosine analysis examines the pattern formed by the correlations of the scores on the trait measure with each the eight interpersonal traits, taken in order (see Figure 13.1C). A cosine analysis measures the degree to which the sizes of the correlation coefficients vary in a cosine-shaped wave. A cosine analysis of the set of correlations with the eight interpersonal trait cluster scores can be carried out for scores on any measure of psychopathy that you think might be related to interpersonal traits on theoretical or experimental grounds.

Two different traits are analyzed in Figure 13.1C. Note that the waves are sinusoidal in shape (shaped like a sine or cosine wave) and simply represent the plots of the correlations of scores on the trait in question (father absence and narcissism, respectively) with each of the eight interpersonal trait scores. The order of traits on the abscissa simply comes from moving clockwise around the circle. The scores are derived from the best fitting cosine wave. Two numbers, amplitude and goodness of fit, measure the degree to which the trait in question has an interpersonal component. The amplitude of the wave corresponds to the degree to which the trait in question has an interpersonal component; in Cartesian space (Figure 13.1B), this corresponds to the degree to which one vector is longer than any other. Goodness of fit, as measured by R^2, indicates the degree to which the correlations can be made to fit the cosine pattern.

Two other numbers, elevation and displacement, indicate something about the nature of the traits involved. The elevation measures some often unknown general factor orthogonal to the Circle but which uniformly affects all the correlation coefficients, such as activity level or distress. Elevation appears when the cosine wave of correlation coefficients is moved up or down instead of centering around zero. Displacement is the angular location of the vector in interpersonal space, measured in degrees from the Warm/Agreeable pole of the affiliation axis, which historically has been designated as 0°. In interpersonal terms, displacement represents the interpersonal trait cluster that is most highly correlated to the trait in question. Displacement thus indicates which interpersonal trait style is most strongly related to the trait in question.

Looking at the two traits plotting in Figure 13.1C, one is clearly interpersonal and the other, just as clearly, is not. The trait on the top, reflecting the degree to which the father was absent during development as measured in the current study, is clearly not an interpersonal trait: Its amplitude is small (0.161), and it has a poor fit to a cosine curve ($R^2 = 0.583$). Narcissism, which was also measured in the current study, just as clearly is an interpersonal trait. It has a much larger amplitude (0.502, which leads to a much more clearly discernable sinusoidal shape to the correlation coefficients) and a much higher R^2.

The Interpersonal Circle Is Useful in Understanding Some Gender-Related Differences

This Interpersonal Circle provides a theory useful to understanding some gender-related differences in personality, for several reasons. First, since the two basic dimensions are related to the two interpersonal traits from the Big Five personality traits, prior research done with the Big Five model is also relevant to the Interpersonal Circle. Scores from the Big Five traits, as measured by Costa and McCrae's (1985) NEO personality inventory, were factor analyzed along with scores from the two basic interpersonal dimensions (Briggs, 1992; McCrae & Costa, 1989; Trapnell & Wiggins, 1990). The dominance and warmth dimensions of the Circle turned out to be simply 40° rotations of the extroversion and agreeableness dimensions of the Big Five traits.

Second, the model is both theoretically and behaviorally coherent. As illustrated in Figure 13.1C, self-report scores on the eight sets of adjectives do form a circle when plotted in a two-dimensional, multidimensional scaling analysis solution. In fact, the data in that figure are based on scores from the subjects in the present experiment.

Third, interpersonal traits are sexually dimorphic. According to Feingold (1994), based on his meta-analytic reviews of normative samples given various personality tests, the effect size of the sex difference is 0.49 for assertiveness (favoring males) and −1.07 for tendermindedness (favoring females). These effect sizes have remained relatively constant across ages, years, education levels, and nations. The Bem Sex Role Inventory (BSRI) and Spence's Personal Attributes Questionnaire (PAQ) are very good measures of interpersonal traits, the masculine items on both measuring dominance and the feminine items measuring warmth and agreeableness, respectively (Wiggins & Holzmuller, 1978; 1981; Wiggins & Broughton, 1985). The most sexually dimorphic dimension is the one running from the upper left to the lower right, the arrogant/calculating to ingenuous dimension shown in Figure 13.1A. This dimension is also sometimes labeled as hostile dominance to friendly submission.

The basic axes of the Circle are sexually dimorphic, at least partially because of sex differences in sex hormones. Our own surveys of the literature (Hoyenga & Hoyenga, 1993a, pp. 339–351; 1993b, pp. 149–170) have summarized the degree to which both warmth and dominance may be sensitive to both perinatal and postpubertal manipulations and measurements of hormone levels.[3] More recently, research done by Hampson, Rovet, and Altmann (1995) and Collaer and Hines's review (1995) have suggested that sex differences in aggressiveness (cold plus dominant, in interpersonal terms) are sensitive to prenatal hormones in humans. Other researchers (Van Goozen, Cohen-Kettenis, Gooren, Frijda, & van de Poll, 1995; Van Goozen, Frijda, & van de Poll, 1994) and reviews (e.g., Archer, 1991; Ellis & Coontz, 1990) have discussed how aggression tends to vary directly with individual differences in testosterone levels and with changes in the individual's adult levels of testosterone. Finally, Udry (1991), who used BSRI and PAQ scores as part of a "gendered" trait measure, found that scores on the trait were directly related to adult levels of androstenedione, prenatal testosterone, and their interaction.

However, this association of trait scores with hormone levels does not rule out a large role for socialization. Thus, sex differences in developmental experiences and in adult environments are also relevant to sex differences in interpersonal trait scores. Father absence is the socialization factor in our research, one which might differentially impact males and females.

Some sex differences in psychopathology can be explained by the sex differences in interpersonal traits (Corbitt & Widiger, 1995). An exaggerated vector length, as illustrated in Figure 13.1B, demonstrates not only a lack of flexibility, but also an increased vulnerability to psychopathology specific to that trait. Take depression, for example. In past research, females have been found to be about twice as likely as males to suffer from clinical depression (Dawkins, 1995; Heller, 1993; Hoyenga & Hoyenga, 1993a, pp. 360–368; 1993b, pp. 153–170; Nolen-Hoeksema, 1987). A dependent personality may be one vulnerability factor for clinical depression (Bagby et al., 1994; Bornstein, 1994; Nietzel & Harris, 1990). Dependent personality has been located in the lower right quadrant of the Circle (Figure 13.1A), reflecting an exaggerated ingenuous or agreeable submission trait (Pincus & Wiggins, 1990; Trapnell & Wiggins, 1990; Wiggins, 1982; Wiggins & Pincus, 1989a; 1989b; 1994; Wiggins, Phillips, & Trapnell, 1989).

Sex differences in sociopathy and narcissism can also be explained by Circle traits. Though we use the terms "sociopathy," "psychopathy," and "antisocial personality disorder" interchangeably, we are well aware that there are differences in diagnostic criteria. We are most interested in the trait found in many psychopaths, impulsive aggression, which, in its most extreme form, leads to impulsive homicide. At the peak age for violent crimes (22 to 23), the rate for males is nearly ten times the rate for females (Cairns, 1986). From four to eight times as many males as females are diagnosed with sociopathy (Corbitt & Widiger, 1995; Regier et al., 1993; Robins & Regier, 1991). In past research, scales measuring psychopathy and narcissism have been found to be located in the upper left quadrant of the Circle, where the arrogant/calculating trait is found (Hare, Hart, & Harpur, 1991; Harpur, Hare, & Hakstian, 1989; Pincus & Wiggins, 1990; Trapnell & Wiggins, 1990; Wiggins, 1982; Wiggins & Pincus, 1989a; 1989b; 1994; Wiggins et al., 1989). Though narcissism is positively correlated with psychopathy, narcissism would reflect a less pathologically exaggerated vector length than would sociopathy.

Is Brain Serotonergic Activity Inversely Related to Vector Length in the Circle?

Lowered brain levels of serotonergic activity have been consistently related to depression.[4] Past research has found that low levels of serotonin in an individual's brain may be a risk factor for depression (Ellis & Salmond, 1994; Maes & Meltzer, 1995). As those reviews point out, currently the most commonly used antidepressants tend to increase brain serotonin. Most convincingly, experimentally induced decreases in brain serotonin cause depressive moods in men with a family history of depression (Benkelfat, Ellenbogen, Dean, Palmour, & Young, 1994). Furthermore, depressed people may have anatomical deficits in the brain's major source of serotonergic neurons (Becker et al., 1995).

In other research, a trait called impulsive irritability (and subsequent assaults and murders), as well as antisocial disorder itself, have been found to be strongly associated with having lower brain serotonergic activities. For example, in Raine's meta-analytic review (1993, pp. 86–89), the average estimated effect size was –0.468 (moderate). Studies published since 1989 have continued finding the link between low serotonin and impulsive aggression (Coccaro, 1992; Coccaro, Kavoussi, & Hauger, 1995; Coccaro, Kavoussi, & Lesser, 1992; Coccaro, Silverman, Klar, Horvath, & Siever, 1994; Moeller et al., 1994). Experimentally induced decreases in brain serotonin increase aggression in human males, especially when combined with alcohol (Pihl et al., 1995). A similar link between serotonergic activities and impaired impulse control or heightened aggression has also been found in other species, including other primates (Kyes, Botchin, Kaplan, Manuck, & Mann, 1995; Mehlman et al., 1994; Shively, Fontenot, & Kaplan, 1995). In fact, lowered serotonin seems to decrease impulse control in general, predisposing toward violent suicide (Cremniter et al., 1994), impulsiveness in schizophrenia (Serres, Daissa, Azorin, & Jeanningros, 1995), and anger attacks, binging, and depression in eating-disorder patients (Fava, Rappe, West, & Herzog, 1995).

Thus, perhaps lowered serotonin can be thought of as increasing vector length in the Circle, decreasing flexibility and increasing the likelihood of developing psychopathology. The type of pathology that would develop would depend on the person's dominant interpersonal style or vector location. Thus, lowered serotonin could lead to impulsive aggressive or to depression, depending on whether the person's dominant trait vector were arrogance or ingenuousness.

Sex Differences in Brain Serotonergic Activities

Sex differences have been consistently found in brain serotonergic activities in many different species. Females tend to have higher levels of serotonergic activities, possibly because of the sex difference in sex hormones, since sex hormones regulate serotonin levels both perinatally and after puberty (Hoyenga & Hoyenga, 1993a, pp. 368–369; 1993b, pp. 153–156; Spigset & Mjörndal, 1997; Young, Gauthier, Anderson, & Purdy, 1980). A recent report of greater rates of serotonin synthesis being found in human male brains than in female brains (Nishizawa et al., 1997) might be explained by sex differences in stress responses. In the rat, the male's brain responds to stress with a greater increase in serotonin synthesis than is true of the female's brain (Curzon, Kennett, Sarna, & Whitton, 1992). So in the human research, the stress associated with the measurement technology might have triggered the greater male serotonin synthesis. Most relevant to our hypotheses, female humans also have more serotonin reuptake sites in the right orbital frontal cortex than males do (Arató, Frecska, Tekes, & MacCrimmon, 1991). This is of interest, since murderers show a bilateral deficit in prefrontal metabolism (Raine et al., 1994), and depressives have a left dorsolateral deficit (Henrique & Davidson, 1990).

In addition to hormones, sex differences in serotonin may reflect sex differences in current and developmental environments or sex differences in response to those environments. For example, stress activates serotonergic neurons—often in a sexually dimorphic fashion—and eventually depletes the serotonin in the brain (Haleem, Kennett, & Curzon, 1988; Heinsbroek et al., 1990; Jacobs & Fornal, 1995; Kennett, Chaouloff, Marcou, & Curzon, 1986). Also, being raised in a father-absent environment may decrease brain serotonergic activity (Gerra et al., 1993). Since developmental paternal absence seems to be a major factor in human impulsive aggression (Draper & Belsky, 1990; Draper & Harpending, 1982; Hoyenga & Hoyenga, 1993a, pp. 222–

223, 356), decreased serotonin may link father absence to increased aggression, especially in males.

OUR MODEL AND HYPOTHESES

In our model of sex differences, we view both depression and sociopathy as representing exaggerations of traits at the opposite ends of the dimension running from arrogant to ingenuous (Figure 13.1A). The exaggeration of vector length might be inversely related to brain serotonergic activities. Thus, males' personalities are more likely to be found in the upper left quadrant, where lowered serotonergic activity would lead to impulsive aggression or to psychopathy. Females' personalities are more likely to be found in the lower right quadrant, where exaggerated dependency could lead to depression, especially when combined with the risk factors of genes and stress (Hoyenga & Hoyenga, 1993a, pp. 360–367).

In our model, there are two reasons why the sex difference favoring men for psychopathy is larger than the sex difference favoring women for depression. One is that females tend to have more serotonin than males do, decreasing the likelihood of developing a psychopathologically exaggerated vector length. Second, there are several types of depression (Fava et al., 1993; Mann, McBride, Malone, DeMeo, & Keilp, 1995; Nordström, Schalling, & Åsberg, 1995; von Zerssen, Tauscher, & Pössl, 1994). One may be the dependency type, characterized by agreeableness or agreeable submissiveness, cooperativeness, and stable emotional bonds. The other types would include the depression associated with disagreeable submissiveness (exaggerated introversion) and the depression associated with narcissistic and antisocial traits (exaggerated arrogance). The latter types would not be expected to show the typical female preponderance.

Given these data and our model, we generated the following hypotheses to be tested, using human subjects for some and rats subjects for others:

1. Scores on a set of questions that have been found to be inversely associated to brain serotonergic activity in humans (Coccaro, Bergman, & McClearn, 1993) will be directly related to the vector length of the arrogance trait and to measures of sociopathy.

2. A behavioral measure of impulse control (ability to withhold dominant or prepotent actions) will be inversely related to sociopathy but will be unrelated to Circle traits.

3. Manipulations of brain serotonin will change rats' reactions to stress in a rotational/confinement model for human sex differences in depression (Beatty, Hoyenga, & Hoyenga, 1992).

4. Because of sex differences in evolution, the interpersonalness of various traits will appear as sex differences in the amplitude and location of traits in the cosine analysis, including antisocial traits, dependent traits, and narcissistic traits.

RAT RESEARCH

Subjects

Male and female rats from 75 to 150 days of age had their brain serotonin levels manipulated prior to stress exposure. There were four different drug groups, with an equal number of males and females assigned to each drug condition. There were from five to six rats per group, with matching according to littermates. In addition, some of the drug conditions were repeated on younger males. Thus, there were 104 rats tested.

Drugs

All drugs were given via subcutaneous injections. Ritanserin, a serotonin antagonist (a $5\text{-}HT_2$ and $5\text{-}HT_{1a}$ antagonist), was mixed with saline and antifreeze and given at 5 mg/kg the day prior to and the first day of stress to block the stress-induced surge of serotonin activity.[5] BMY, a $5\text{-}HT_{1a}$ agonist, was mixed with saline and given at 3 mg/kg. DOI, a $5\text{-}HT_{1c}$ and $5\text{-}HT_2$ agonist, was also mixed with saline and given at 0.25 mg/kg. Both BMY and DOI injections were given once a day for the week prior to stress, as well as on every day of stress at least two hours prior to the onset of stress; such a procedure can block stress effects (Beck & Fibiger, 1995). An equal volume of normal saline was used as the control injection. All drugs were given to an equal number of males and females at 150 days of age. In addition, a separate group of younger males was given Ritanserin and saline for reasons that will be described in the next section.

Procedure

A rat stress model for human sex differences in depression was used, the only stress model in which the normal human sex difference (more impact on females than on males) is reproduced. This model was based on research done earlier by Curzon and his colleagues (Curzon, Kennett, Sarna, & Whitton, 1992; Haleem et al., 1988; Kennett et al., 1986). However, we were unable to replicate this research, which used restraint stress, so we used a rotational and restraint stress model and replicated the same pattern of sex differences (Beatty, Hoyenga, & Hoyenga, 1992). In our procedure, rats were confined to plastic water bottles and rotated around a vertical shaft, at 5 mm per minute, for two hours. When five days of stress are used, males adapt to the stress: By the fifth day, their body weights, food intakes, activity levels, and emotionality are back to normal. Females tend to be less affected than males by the first day of stress, but females do not adapt: With each day of stress, they lose successively more weight.

In the present study, we gave all the older rats five days of stress and measured food intake and body weight for several days before, as well as during, the stress. In addition, we measured activity levels and emotionality in an open field after the first day of stress and again after the fifth day of stress.

However, as will be described, these males, which were older than the ones tested in the earlier study (Beatty, Hoyenga, & Hoyenga, 1992), showed no evidence of adaptation to stress. Because of this, we added a second study, using younger males. The younger males were tested in a 2 × 2 factorial design, the factors being stress (present or absent) and drug (Ritanserin or saline).

Analyses and Data

The data from the rat subjects were analyzed with ANOVAs and ANCOVAs (using body weight or food intake prior to stress as the covariate) (*Systat for Windows*, 1995). The ANOVAs and ANCOVAs led to the following conclusions, all supported by significant ($p < 0.05$) effects. Only the young males showed any evidence of adaptation to stress. Neither the old females (as expected) nor the old males (which was unexpected) showed any evidence of adaptation: These animals continued losing weight on each day throughout the series of five stressors. Since age changes biochemical responses to stress (Mabry, Gold, & McCarty, 1995), and since the biochemical stress responses are directly related to the sex differences in adaptation (Haleem et al., 1988), this effect of age is probably related to the biochemistry of aging.

The drugs did significantly affect the stress responses, as predicted. DOI slowed the onset of stress effects, though only in males: Males given DOI showed loss of appetite and loss of body weight only beginning with the third day of stress. BMY prevented stress effects, but only in females: Females given BMY did not gain weight, but neither did they lose weight over the five days of stress. Most interesting of all, Ritanserin, the antagonist, prevented the effects of trials in both sexes and both ages. That is, young males normally adapt to stress, but in the presence of Ritanserin on the day before and the day of the first stress, there was no adaptation. Older males and females normally show increasingly negative effects with each day of stress, but in the presence of Ritanserin there was no change in weight or food intake over trials. Thus, there were sexually dimorphic effects of serotonergic manipulations on rats' responses to repeated stress.

HUMAN RESEARCH

Subjects

The subjects were 129 students in advanced psychology classes participating for extra credit, including 54 males and 75 females. The testing was done in two periods, the first occurring within a classroom and the second, approximately a week later, occurring at individually scheduled times. During the second sessions, 46 males and 57 females were tested.

Measures

Circle Traits   The Interpersonal Adjectives Scales was used to measure Circle traits (Wiggins et al., 1988). Subjects were given one score for each of the eight different adjective clusters, each cluster being used to measure the traits found on both ends of each of the four dimensions. The reliability and validity data can be found in Wiggins and colleagues (1988).

Antisocial Traits   Two measures of antisocial traits were used. The validity and reliability information for each scale can be found in the original references. One was the Psychopathic States Inventory (PSI) developed by Haertzen, Martin, Ross, and Neidert (1980), which has six subscales. Two of them (increased needs and hypophoria), as well as the total scale score, have been found to be inversely related to a measure of brain serotonergic activity (Moss, Yao, & Panzak, 1990). This scale was given to our subjects during the second testing session. The Minnesota Multiphasic Personality Inventory (MMPI) Antisocial Scale, developed by Morey, Waugh, and Blashfield (1985), was given during the first testing period. This scale has been used with both normal and clinical populations and has been found to have a weak interpersonal component, being located in the upper left quadrant (BC in Figure 13.1A) (Pincus & Wiggins, 1990; Wiggins & Pincus, 1989a; 1989b; 1994).

Dependency   Since dependent personality is a risk factor for depression, subjects were also given the MMPI Dependency Scale, also developed by Morey and colleagues (1985). This subscale has also been found to be interpersonal, located in the lower right quadrant (Pincus & Wiggins, 1990; Wiggins & Pincus, 1989a; 1989b; 1994).

Narcissism   The Narcissistic Personality Inventory (NPI) developed by Raskin and Hall (1981) has five subscales. The interpersonal properties of this scale have been previously explored by Gurtman (1992), and the location of the narcissism trait was also found to be in the upper left quadrant. Similarly, Buss and Chiodo (1991) found that NPI scores were most strongly positively correlated with arrogance, and the strongest negative correlation occurred with ingenuousness. Gurtman (1992) found that some items on the NPI scale were associated with higher distress or higher elevations: The higher distress items were also located (as measured by degree; see Figure 13.1C) more toward arrogance, whereas the lower distress items were located closer to dominance. Therefore, we also looked at distress (negative) items and nondistress (positive) items.

Serotonin Items   Questions that may be inversely related to brain serotonergic activities (Coccaro et al., 1993) were also given to the subjects. Coccaro and his colleagues felt, based on their extensive past research with serotonin and impulsive aggression, that the impulsive irritability subscale of their questionnaire contained the types of items most likely to be inversely related to brain serotonin levels. They also found these questions to have some genetic basis.

Father Absence   Because of the evidence cited that father absence may be related to aggression, we gave subjects a single question to measure degree of father absence. A Likert-type response format was used, and subjects were to rate the degree to which their father was involved in their childhood, with "not present during any of my childhood" on the high end and "extensively involved in my day-to-day activities throughout my childhood" on the low end.

Modified Stroop Test The Stroop test has proven to be sensitive to antisocial predispositions (Kosson & Newman, 1986; 1989) as well as to prefrontal brain damage (Vendrell et al., 1995). We gave subjects two versions of a modified Stroop test, based on some earlier work with other forms of psychopathology (Giles & Cairns, 1989; Mattia, Heimberg, & Hope, 1993). On each of sixteen slides, eight words were presented, each word printed in a randomly selected color. Each slide was presented for five seconds. Eight of the slides had control words, which were common nouns. The other eight slides contained the adjectives from the Interpersonal Adjectives Scales. The two types of slides were alternated, starting with a control slide. The subject's task was to write down, on a specially prepared answer sheet, the colors in which each of the eight words on each slide were printed, in order. Both number of correct identifications of color and number of errors were recorded. For the second series, the same slides were presented again, but this time an auditory interference task was added. However, since the interference task was so difficult, few subjects were able to carry it out and these data were not analyzed. The very first slide was a practice slide containing control nouns for which subjects had all the time they needed.

Analysis

A variety of analyses were performed on the human data (*Systat for Windows*, 1995). To analyze the interpersonalness of the various trait measures, a cosine analysis was carried out on each trait and a multidimensional scaling procedure was also employed. Sex differences on trait scores were examined with t tests. Several multiple regression analyses were carried out, to see how well scores on the trait measures of psychopathology and scores on the modified Stroop could be predicted from normal personality, serotonin scores, and father absence. Correlations among trait scores were also examined for each gender separately, in order to explicate some of the results. Finally, a canonical correlation analysis was carried out to examine the degree to which normal personality traits and psychopathological traits could be found to share dimensions in common.

Results

Cosine Analyses As can be seen in Table 13.1, some of the traits related to interpersonal traits in earlier research were clearly interpersonal (e.g., high amplitude and R^2) in our research as well, and some just as clearly showed sex differences in either location or amplitude or both. Though these analyses

Table 13.1
Sex Differences in the Circle: Gender Affects the Interpersonalness of Traits

Measure	Elevation	Amplitude	Degree	R^2
NPI Total score				
Male	.008	.502	97.17°	.971
Female	.038	.570	114.59°	.975
NPI nondistress items				
Male	-.005	.381	122.33°	.961
Female	-.002	.335	122.73°	.967
NPI distress items				
Male	.013	.438	96.31°	.986
Female	.058	.449	132.01°	.977
MMPI antisocial scale				
Male	-.007	.384	134.47°	.980
Female	.013	.367	125.03°	.908

are not presented in any of the tables, the superiority subscale of the Narcissism Personality Inventory was located at 88° for males but at 102° for females; similarly, the NPI exploitativeness subscale was at 87° for males and 110° for females. These locations are similar to what Gurtman found (1991) (see Figure 13.1C, bottom).

Table 13.1 (*continued*)

Measure	Elevation	Amplitude	Degree	R^2
MMPI dependent scale				
Male	.035	.239	164.21°	.721
Female	-.004	.487	295.24°	.845
Serotonin: Impulsive irritability				
Male	.008	.398	125.82°	.975
Female	-.004	.487	295.24°	.845
Psychopathic States Scale: Hypophoria				
Male	-.005	.308	217.38°	.749
Female	-.020	.143	185.98°	.378
Psychopathic States Scale: Sociopathy				
Male	.010	.267	152.64°	.865
Female	-.052	.266	130.63°	.491

MMPI scales were also interpersonal. We found more interpersonalness for the MMPI antisocial scale than did Wiggins and Pincus (1989a; 1989b; 1994). We also found it to be more dominant (for Wiggins and Pincus, location = 135° or 180°, depending on sample; in our data, males = 134° and females = 125°). For MMPI dependency, we found a sex difference: The location for females was similar to the location that Wiggins and Pincus (1989a; 1989b) found (earlier research = 275–293°; our females = 295°; the location for our males was 251°). Also, the scale seemed to be more interpersonal for females than for males, females having a higher amplitude and larger R^2.

Other scales were less interpersonal. The Psychopathic States Inventory sociopathic subscale was both less interpersonal and also "colder" than was the MMPI antisocial scale. Furthermore, the two PSI subscales most closely related to serotonin levels were not interpersonal (the impulsive and the needs subscales). The total PSI score was most highly correlated with the arrogant interpersonal trait (males = +0.314; females = +0.377, $p < 0.005$), and with its opposite, the ingenuous trait (males = –0.339; females = –0.366, $p < 0.005$). The serotonin questionnaire items were very weakly interpersonal for both sexes, and answers to the father-absence question were clearly not interpersonal (see Figure 13.1C, top).

t Tests   Table 13.2 presents some t tests for sex differences. As expected, males scored higher on MMPI antisocial and females higher on MMPI dependency scale, similar to what Morey and colleagues (1985) had found earlier. Contrary to what we expected for the modified Stroop, males made fewer errors on either the control or the interpersonal adjective slides, and had a greater total correct on the adjective slides.

With regard to the Interpersonal Adjectives Scales traits, females scored higher on all traits to the left of the vertical, dominance axis, and males on traits to the right of that axis. Similar to what other recent research on college populations has found (BSRI, Twenge, 1995; IAS-R, Trapnell & Wiggins, 1990), the sexes showed only very small differences for dominance and submissiveness. This may be because of a recent selection bias or cultural change. Another possibility is that a greater proportion of high dominant females are attending college now rather than earlier, whereas some of the most dominant males are seeking status outside of college.

Multidimensional Scaling   Results from the multidimensional scaling (MDS) are shown in Figures 13.1 and 13.2. When MDS is carried out just on the IAS–R scores, two dimensions account for nearly 99.7 percent of the variance, and the items scale onto almost a perfect circle (Figure 13.1D). When scores from other questionnaires are included, a three-dimensional structure accounts for over 87 percent of the variance. Two of the three dimensions are from the IAS–R (Figure 13.2A). The third dimension is anchored by Stroop scores and by answers to the father-absence question (Figure 13.2B), further demonstrating that these two are not interpersonal characteristics.

Multiple Regression Analyses   In predicting scores on the MMPI antisocial scale, the multiple R was 0.588 (Table 13.3). Some of the best predictors were father absence, serotonin, and the arrogant/ingenuous dimension of the Interpersonal Adjectives Scales (subtracting arrogant scores from ingenuous scores to give a single dimension score). In addition, the interaction of serotonin with father absence also added to the multiple R (+0.016). In this case,

Table 13.2
Sex Differences in Trait Scores

Scale	Male Mean (SD)	Female Mean (SD)	Probability
NPI nondistress items	2.46 (1.2)	1.92 (1.2)	.020
IAS-R: PA	43.41 (6.6)	41.35 (7.9)	.122
IAS-R: BC	39.02 (8.2)	31.65 (7.5)	.000
IAS-R: DE	12.24 (8.7)	18.00 (7.0)	.021
IAS-R: FG	26.28 (10.1)	22.16 (7.7)	.010
IAS-R: HI	30.46 (7.9)	30.35 (8.2)	.936
IAS-R: JK	29.02 (7.2)	34.02 (7.3)	.000
IAS-R: LM	47.63 (7.2)	52.01 (6.0)	.000
IAS-R: NO	44.09 (8.1)	48.64 (6.2)	.000
MMPI Antisocial Scale	10.46 (3.6)	8.65 (4.2)	.011
MMPI Dependency Scale	4.91 (3.0)	6.43 (3.6)	.013
Stroop Control Slides: Errors	23.233 (8.6)	26.95 (7.7)	.026
IAS-R: Stroop Correct	9.20 (9.8)	4.68 (5.1)	.003
IAS-R: Stroop Errors	24.01 (8.6)	28.53 (8.0)	.008

Note: Though all the IAS-R scores are included, only significant differences on other scales are presented.

Figure 13.2
A Three-Dimensional, Multidimensional Scaling Solution to the Circle Traits and Various Measures of Psychopathology Used in the Current Study

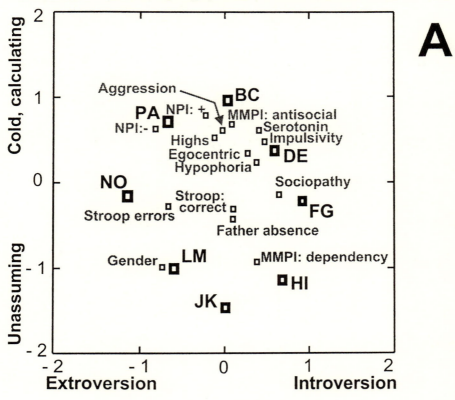

serotonin items (high scores indicate low serotonin activities) were related to antisocial scores only when the father was present during development. Similarly, in correlational analyses among the IAS-R adjective clusters, the arrogant items were the ones that were most strongly correlated with MMPI antisocial scores ($r = 0.479$).

The multiple R for predicting the MMPI dependency scale scores was 0.380. Gender, father absence, the arrogance/ingenuous dimension, the hypophoria subscale from the Psychopathic States Inventory, and serotonin questions all contributed. Father absence increased risk of dependency, as did low serotonin and high hypophoria scores. In addition, two interactions also contributed. Father absence magnified the effect of serotonin on dependency (R increment +0.036) and also magnified the effect of hypophoria (R increment +0.035).

For the multiple regression predicting the number correct on the modified Stroop, gender, number of errors, and scores on the control slides were always left in the equations to get at the factors that uniquely contributed to

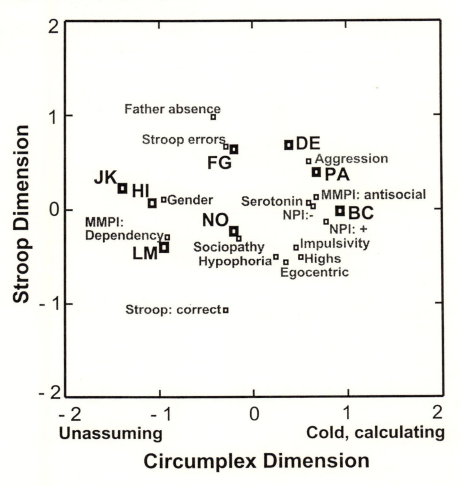

B

scores on the slides containing the interpersonal adjectives. As can be seen in Table 13.3, the impulsive serotonin items were negatively related to number correct. Introversion (FG) also contributed negatively, but MMPI antisocial scores and the sociopathy subscale (as well as other subscales) of the Psychopathic States Inventory contributed positively. In other words, the more antisocial the person, the higher that person's Stroop correct scores. Similarly, Voss and Norman (1995) found that antisocials showed higher scores on a different measure, one involving conflict between identifying a picture versus identifying a word superimposed on top of the picture. Thus, tendencies toward psychopathy may, in some cases, lead to a lack of distractibility.

Some Correlations   Some correlations are presented in Table 13.4. The probability level for significance was set at 0.01 to control alpha. Moss and colleagues (1990) earlier found Psychopathic States Inventory total scores to be correlated

Table 13.3
Multiple Regression Analyses of Psychopathology and IAS-R Stroop Correct

Predictor	Standardized Coefficient	T
Predicting MMPI Antisocial Scores Multiple R = .588, F = 16.42		
Father Absence Item	.786	1.98
BC Dimension	.301	3.77
Serotonin: Impulsive irritability	.720	3.28
Serotonin x Father Absence	-.750	-1.76
Predicting MMPI Dependency Scores Multiple R = .380, F = 2.72		
Serotonin: Impulsive irritability	.320	1.52
Psychopathic States: Hypophoria	1.174	2.05
Father Absence Item	.353	1.55
BC Dimension	-.279	-2.72
Serotonin x Hypophoria	-.641	-1.10
Father Absence x Hypophoria	-.576	-1.73

–0.34 with a biological measure of brain serotonergic sensitivity, and we found that PSI total scores to be similarly correlated with serotonin item scores (reflecting low serotonin) for both males (r = 0.40) and females (r = 0.41). The MMPI antisocial scale scores were only weakly correlated with PSI total for males (r = 0.171, ns), but the correlation was stronger for females (r = 0.54). Note that

Table 13.3 (continued)

Predictor	Standardized Coefficient	T
Predicting Total Correct on the Stroop IAS-R Slides Multiple R = .687, F = .7.29		
Stroop Control Slides, # Correct	-.013	-0.17
Stroop Control Slides, Errors	-.428	-3.21
Stroop IAS-R Slides, Errors	-.197	-1.46
Gender (Male = 1, Female = 2)	-.221	-2.42
IAS-R: BC	-.133	-1.30
IAS-R: DE	.217	2.134
IAS-R: FG	-.270	-2.60
MMPI Antisocial Scale	.208	2.06
Psychopathic States: Highs	-.205	-2.14
Psychopathic States: Sociopathy	.236	2.68
Serotonin: Impulsive irritability	-.103	-1.01

for both males and females, narcissism nondistress (positive) items were positively correlated with MMPI antisocial scores, but the distress (negative) items were negatively correlated with MMPI dependent scores. This suggests that the nondistress items were the ones mostly closely associated with sociopathy, though this was more true of males than of females (see Table 13.1).

Table 13.4
Some Correlations among the Variables

	1	2	3	4	5	6	7	8	9	10	11	12
1 NPI: pos.		51**	53**		46**	54**	47**	44**				41**
2 NPI: neg.	34*			-41**								
3 Antisocial	47**					40**						
4 Dependent		-38**										
5 Aggression	46**		56**	-38**		43**						
6 Serotonin			52**					48**				40*
7 Highs			44**						46**	46**		53**
8 Impulsivity			48**				40**		51**	48**	44**	76**
9 Egocentric	44**		40**			40**	49**	52**		72**		81**
10 Hypophoria			54**				55**	55**	62**			82**
11 Sociopathy				42**			40**	59**	42**	56**		63**
12 PSI Total			54**				61**	80**	78**	83**	80**	

Note: Significant correlations for males are above the diagonal, females are below; the decimal point was omitted in the interest of brevity; 3 and 4 are the subscales taken from the Minnesota Multiphasic Personality Inventory; 7–12 are from the Psychopathic States Inventory scale; * = $p < 0.01$; ** $p = < 0.005$.

Some correlations not included in the table are also of interest. Since father absence was related to few other scores, it is not included in the table. Nonetheless, it was positively related to Psychopathic States Inventory aggression scores for females ($r = 0.40$, $p < 0.002$). Though interpersonal trait measures are not presented in the table, father absence was somewhat negatively related to arrogance scores, but only for males ($r = -0.301$, $p < 0.05$). The serotonin item score was positively correlated with arrogance scores for males ($r = 0.562$, $p < 0.001$) but not for females ($r = 0.249$, ns).

Canonical Correlation Analysis In a canonical correlation analysis, successive pairs of weighted linear combinations of variables (called canonical variates) are derived from two sets of variables (psychopathology and personality in the current analysis) so as to maximize the canonical correlation between each pair. Within each set of variables, the canonical variates are uncorrelated with each other; there is a zero correlation between each variate and all variates in the opposite variable set. Each significant correlation reflects a dimension shared by the two sets of variables. In other words, this analysis combines the techniques of factor analysis and multiple regression to find the degree to which two sets of variables can be found to share a common set of factors.

The results of the canonical analysis are presented in Table 13.5. Three canonical variates were found to be important (ps = 0.000, 0.000, and 0.032), and Wilks multivariate test of significance revealed a significant F of 3.52 (p < 0.000). The first canonical variate is dominated by serotonin and by the two interpersonal dimensions of arrogance to ingenuous and dominance to submission (e.g., BC minus JK scores, and PA minus HI scores to measure the dimensions; see Figure 13.1A). On the psychopathology side, the first canonical variate is dominated by narcissism, MMPI Antisocial, and several factors from the Psychopathic States Inventory. Thus, being cold and dominant predicted being narcissistic and antisocial.

The other two variates were most strongly related to dependency and to subscales from the PSI. The second canonical variate was determined largely by the dominance and extroversion dimensions, and (negatively) by low serotonin items. The correlations with the psychopathology variables suggest that being dominant and extroverted and having high serotonin decreased dependency, hypophoria, and PSI sociopathy. The third variate was determined by extroversion and by having a father actively involved in development; this predicted PSI highs (e.g., searching for emotional highs).

IMPLICATIONS

Five implications seem to be most important. First, and most important, the Interpersonal Circle can be a fruitful source of hypotheses and a theory-generating structure for understanding sex differences in various kinds of interpersonal traits, both psychopathological and normal. This includes research done with nonhuman subjects, albeit a socially living species. In other words, nonhuman socially living animals also have interpersonal-like traits, and using interpersonal and evolutionary theories can lead to testable hypotheses. In the case of humans, an extreme vector length of an interpersonal trait does seem to reliably predict at least some forms of psychopathology.

Second, the interpersonalness of psychopathological traits may be sexually dimorphic, a possibility that has not been explored before in the literature. For example, antisocial traits seem to be more cold for males and more dominant for females. The interpersonal theory does not yet have a context for explaining why the sexes may differ in the meanings of interpersonal traits, especially since the structure of the interpersonal traits has been found

Table 13.5
Results of the Canonical Analysis Showing Correlations of the Canonical Variates with the Psychopathology and Predictor (Personality) Variables

Variable	Canonical Variates		
	I	II	III
Psychopathology Variables			
NPI: nondistress items	-.659		
NPI: distress items	-.566	.391	.339
MMPI Antisocial	-.779		
MMPI Dependent	.321	-.888	
PSI Highs	-.548		.558
PSI Impulsivity	-.602	-.415	
PSI Egocentric	-.304		
PSI Hypophoria	-.326	-.446	
PSI Sociopathy	-.244	-.693	-.306
Prediction of Psychopathology Variates			
% Variance: predicted by personality variables	14.3%	8.8%	1.4%
% Variance: predicted by psychopathology variables	26.5%	21.4%	7.1%
Personality Variables			
BC Dimension	-.894		
PA Dimension	-.666	.663	-.800
LM Dimension	.381		
NO Dimension		.320	.745
Father Absence			-.373
Serotonin	-.690	-.446	
Prediction of Personality Variates			
% Variance: predicted by personality variables	31.1%	12.9%	12.3%
% Variance: predicted by psychopathology variables	16.8%	5.4%	2.5%

Note: Only correlations 0.30 are shown.

to apply equally well to both sexes, both in the present research (results not presented), as well as in prior research (Wiggins & Holzmuller, 1978; 1981; Wiggins & Broughton, 1985). Does the trait of dominance have a different nature (anatomical and biochemical structure) in males as opposed to females? Or is it just that, because of socialization and, possibly, sex differences in sex hormone levels, males and females tend to express dominance in somewhat different ways?

Third, serotonin was related to psychopathology. In the rat research, in a stress model of human depression, manipulations of the brain's serotonergic activities systematically changed rats' responses to stress. Even more important, the serotonergic manipulations exerted sexually dimorphic effects, presumably because of the sex differences that normally exist in brain serotonergic activity. In particular, blocking the effects of serotonin on the first day of stress with the serotonin antagonist Ritanserin seemed to prevent the effects of trials: The adaptation of young males and the sensitization of older males and of females were blocked. Thus, if the increase in the activity of serotonergic neurons that normally occurs under stress is blocked, even on only the first day of stress, then there will be no changes over future trials of stress; neither adaptation (a decrease in the response to repeated stress) nor sensitization (an increase in the response to repeated stress). Thus, preventing serotonergic effects on the first day of stress (and the day prior to stress) affects the future responses to four other days of stress. This means that serotonergic activity on the first day of stress, either indirectly or directly, is required for any effects of the repetition of stress to be seen, whether the effect is sensitization (older males and all females) or adaptation (young males).

This effect of Ritanserin makes sense in light of its ability to successfully treat the symptoms of dysthmia in humans (Bakish et al., 1993). It might be effective because it blocks the effects of the stress-induced surge in serotonin activity. Rats with a greater increase in basal levels of serotonin are, at least initially, more adversely affected by the stress (Petty, Kramer, Wilson, & Jordan, 1994), and other serotonin antagonists, given on the day of stress, can block the effects of that stress in the Curzon model of stress-induced depression in rats (Curzon et al., 1992).

In humans as well, serotonin was related to psychopathology. For the human subjects, scores on the serotonin items were directly related to the vector length of the arrogance/ingenious interpersonal trait, at least in males, just as predicted. Serotonin items were also related to dependency scores and so having low serotonin may contribute to the vulnerability to depression. In light of the results from the rat research, this vulnerability factor may have some sexually dimorphic effects and implications.

Fourth, the Stroop as modified here may be measuring empathy rather than impulse control. For example, introversion leads to worse performance, males perform better than females do, and people who score high on antisocial traits do better than people who score low on antisocial traits. Thus, having higher levels of empathy may cause people to pay more attention to the interpersonal adjective words, distracting them from the color in which those words are printed and thereby impairing their performances.

Finally, psychopathological traits may be inherently interactive. For example, in the current model, which was supported by the results of this research, serotonin would be related to impulsive aggression only when that person is also relatively high on the arrogance personality dimension. In other words, only if the person was high on the trait of hostile aggression would serotonergic activity levels reliably affect, predict, and be related to impulsive aggression: Coccaro, Kavoussi, and Hauger (1995) found a strong relationship in men with a personality disorder, for example. Other instances of interactions also appear in our data, such as father absence being related to antisocial traits only when the other risk factor, low serotonin, was not present, and father absence magnifying the risks of low serotonin and hypophoria for depression. Thus, some of the failures to replicate biopsychological findings that have been reported in the literature may be related to variations in the developmental histories and genetics, and therefore in the resultant personality types that appear in the populations being tested. Thus, measuring personality traits can be used to predict and explain individual differences in the effects and implications of having lower than normal serotonin levels, for example, as well as variations in results across studies.

In conclusion, using well-validated and theoretically coherent models, such as interpersonal theory and evolutionary theory, along with well-validated measures of traits relevant to those models, is a very useful way of doing research.

NOTES

1. Because we wish to avoid any implications of an artificial dichotomy between biological and social/developmental/cultural factors, we use gender, sex, and gender-related differences interchangeably, with no connotation of differential meanings among these terms.

2. Since most of the effects of sex hormones are genomic—operating at the level of genes by turning genes on or off—this implies that the sex hormones are either controlling the same brain physiology and/or anatomy that the products of the personality trait genes are, or that the trait genes have come under the direct control of sex hormones. Either possibility would make the personality trait sex limited (Hoyenga & Hoyenga, 1993a, pp. 133–136).

3. Perinatal means prenatal and neonatal; in both periods of development, the sexes are exposed to sexually dimorphic levels of sex hormones, with males being exposed to more testosterone and to all of its metabolites, including estradiol.

4. Serotonin is one of the major transmitter substances in the limbic (emotional) areas of the brain. Serotonin levels have been related to many different types of behavior, from food intake to compulsive behaviors. However, in the context of the present model, the most relevant effect of serotonin is its link to the ability of the organism to inhibit or delay prepotent actions (i.e., impulse control).

5. Ritanserin was provided courtesy of Janssen Pharmaceutica, Beerse, Belgium.

References

Abbott, D. H. (1984). Differentiation of sexual behavior in female marmoset monkeys: Effects of neonatal testosterone or a male co-twin. *Progress in Brain Research, 61,* 349–358.

Abercrombie, E. D., Levin, E. S., & Jacobs, B. L. (1988). Microinjected morphine suppresses the activity of moving cats. *Neuroscience Letters, 86,* 334–339.

Adami, S., Fossaluzza, V., Rossini, M., Bertoldo, F., Gatti, G., Zamberlan, M., & Lo-Cascio, D. (1991). The prevention of corticosteroid induced osteoporosis with nandrolone decanoate. *Bone & Mineralization, 15,* 73–81.

Adkins-Regan, E. (1981). Early organizational effects of hormones: An evolutionary perspective. In N. Alder (Ed.), *Neuroendocrinology of reproduction* (pp. 159–221). New York: Plenum.

Adkins-Regan, E. (1988). Sex hormones and sexual orientation in animals. *Psychobiology, 16,* 335–347.

Agarwal, H. C, Glisson, S. N., & Himwich, W. A. (1966). Changes in monoamines of rat brain during postnatal ontogeny. *Biochimica Biophysica Acta, 130,* 511–513.

Ahnert-Hilger, G., Engele, J., Reisert, I., & Pilgrim, C. (1986). Different developmental schedules of dopaminergic and noradrenergic neurons in dissociated culture of fetal rat midbrain and hindbrain. *Neuroscience, 17*(1), 157–165.

Aiello-Zaldivar, M., Luine, V., & Frankfurt, M. (1992). 5,7-DHT facilitated lordosis: Effects of 5HT agonist. *Neuro Report, 3,* 542–544.

Albonetti, E., Gonzalez, M. I., Farabollini, F., & Wilson, C. A. (1994). Effect of neonatal treatment with DOI and ritanserin on agonistic behaviour in adult male and female rats. *Aggressive Behaviour, 20,* 235–242.

Albonetti, E., Gonzalez, M. I., Siddiqui, A., Wilson, C. A., & Farabollini, F. (1996). Involvement of the 5HT1A sub-type receptor in the neonatal organization of agonistic behaviour in the rat. *Pharmacology, Biochemistry & Behaviour.*

Allen, L. S., & Gorski, R. A. (1992). Sexual orientation and the size of the anterior commissure in the human brain. *Proceedings of the National Academy of Sciences, U.S.A., 89,* 7199–7202.

Allen, L. S., Hines, M., Shryne, J. E., & Gorski, R. A. (1989). Two sexually dimorphic cell groups in the human brain. *Journal of Neuroscience, 9,* 497–506.

Allgeier, E. R., & Wiederman, M. W. (1994). How useful is evolutionary psychology for understanding contemporary human sexual behavior? *Annual Review of Sex Research, 5,* 218–256.

Altemus, M., Wexler, B. E., & Boulis, N. (1989). Changes in perceptual asymmetry with the menstrual cycle. *Neuropsychologia, 27,* 233–240.

American Academy of Pediatrics (1996). Timing of elective surgery on the genitalia of male children with particular reference to the risks, benefits, and psychological effects of surgery and anesthesia. *Pediatrics, 97,* 590–594.

American Psychiatric Association. (1987). *Diagnostic and statistical manual of mental disorders* (3rd ed.). Washington, DC: Author.

American Psychiatric Association. (1994). *Diagnostic and statistical manual of mental disorders* (4th ed.). Washington, DC: Author.

Amir, S. M., Sullivan, R. C., & Ingbar, S. H. (1978). Binding of bovine thyrotropin to receptor in rat testis and its interaction with gonadotropin. *Endocrinology, 103,* 101–111.

Andrew, R. D., Taylor, C. P., Snow, R. W., & Dudek, F. E. (1982). Coupling in rat hippocampal slices: Dye transfer between CA1 pyramidal cells. *Brain Research Bulletin, 8,* 211–222.

Antelman, S. M., & Caggiula, A. R. (1977). Norepinephrine–dopamine interaction and behavior. *Science, 195,* 646–653.

Arakawa, K., De Jong, W., Mulder, A. H., & Versteed, D. H. (1991). The electrically stimulated release of [^{3}H]noradrenaline from nucleus tractus solitarii slices in vitro is modulated via mu-opioid receptors. *European Journal of Pharmacology, 192,* 311–316.

Arató, M., Frecska, E., Tekes, K., & MacCrimmon, D. J. (1991). Serotonergic interhemispheric asymmetry: Gender differences in the orbital cortex. *Acta Psychiatrica Scandinavica, 84,* 110–111.

Archer, J. (1975). Rodent sex differences in emotional and related behaviour. *Behavioral Biology, 14,* 451–479.

Archer, J. (1991). The influence of testosterone on human aggression. *British Journal of Psychology, 82,* 1–28.

Archer, J. (1992). *Ethology and human development.* Exeter: Harvester Wheatsheaf.

Armitage, P. (1955). Test for linear trend in proportions and frequencies. *Biometrics, 11,* 375–386.

Arnold, A., & Gorski, R. A. (1984). Gonadal steroid induction of structural sex differences in the central nervous system. *Annual Review of Neuroscience, 7,* 413–442.

Aron, C., Chateau, D., Schaeffer, C., & Roos, J. (1991). Heterotypical sexual behavior in male mammals: The rat as an experimental model. In M. Haug, P. C. Brain, & C. Aron (Eds.), *Heterotypical behavior in man and animals* (pp. 98–126). London: Chapman & Hall.

Arriaza, C. A., Mena, M. A., & Tchernitchin, A. N. (1989). Prenatal androgenisation selectively modifies some responses to oestrogen in the prepubertal rat uterus. *Journal of Endocrinology, 120,* 379–384.

Ashmore, R. D. (1990). Sex, gender, and the individual. In L. A. Pervin (Ed.), *Handbook of personality: Theory and research* (pp. 486–526). New York: Guilford Press.

Azizi, F., & Apostolos, G. (1974). Decreased serum testosterone concentration in male heroin and methadone addicts. *Steroids, 22,* 467–472.

Azukizawa, M., Kutzman, G., Pekary, A. E., & Herschman, J. K. (1977). Comparison of the binding characteristics of bovine thyrotropin and human chorionic gonadotropin to thyroid plasma membrane. *Endocrinology, 101,* 1880–1889.

Baas, P. W., Dietch, J. S., Black, M. M., & Banker, G. S. (1988). Polarity orientation of microtubules in hippocampal neurons: uniformity in the axon and nonuniformity in the dendrite. *Proceedings of the National Academy of Sciences, U.S.A., 85,* 8335–8339.

Babine, A. M., & Smotherman, W. P. (1984). Uterine position and conditioned taste aversion. *Behavioral Neuroscience, 98,* 461–466.

Bagby, R. M., Schuller, D. R., Parker, J. D. A., Levitt, A., Joffe, R. T., & Shafir, M. S. (1994). Major depression and the self-criticism and dependency personality dimensions. *American Journal of Psychiatry, 151,* 597–599.

Bagley, D. M., & Hayes, J. R. (1980). Xenobiotic imprinting of the hepatic monooxygenase system. *Biochemical Pharmacology, 34,* 1087–1094.

Bailey, J. M., & Pillard, R. C. (1991). A genetic study of male sexual orientation. *Archives of General Psychiatry, 48,* 1089–1096.

Bailey, J. M., Pillard, R. C., Neale, M. C., & Agyei, Y. (1993). Heritable factors influence sexual orientation in women. *Archives of General Psychiatry, 50,* 217–223.

Bakish, D., Lapierre, Y. D., Weinstein, R., Klein, J., Wiens, A., Jones, B., Horn, E., Browne, M., Bourget, D., Blanchard, A., Thibaudeau, C., Waddell, C., & Raine, D. (1993). Ritanserin, imipramine, and placebo in the treatment of dysthymic disorder. *Journal of Clinical Psychopharmacology, 13,* 409–414.

Balaban, E. (1994). Sex differences in sounds and their causes. In R. V. Short & E. Balaban (Eds.), *The differences between the sexes* (pp. 243–273). Cambridge: Cambridge University Press.

Balthazart, J. (Ed.). (1990). *Hormones, brain and behavior in vertebrates: Vol. 1. Sexual differentiation, neuroanatomical aspects, neurotransmitters and neuropeptides.* New York: Karger-Basel.

Bank, S. P., & Kahn, M. D. (1982). *The sibling bond.* New York: Basic Books.

Barash, D. P. (1982). *Sociobiology and behavior* (2nd ed.). New York: Elsevier.

Barbeau, A. (1969). L-DOPA therapy in Parkinson's disease: A critical review of nine years' experience. *Canadian Medical Association Journal, 101,* 791–800.

Barlow, D. (1995). Genetic imprinting in mammals. *Science, 270,* 1610–1613.

Barraclough, C. (1967). Modification in reproductive function after exposure to hormones during the prenatal and early postnatal period. In L. Martini & W. Ganong (Eds.), *Neuroendocrinology.* New York and London: Academic Press.

Barry, H., III, Bacon, M. K., & Child, I. L. (1957). A cross-cultural survey of some sex differences in socialization. *The Journal of Abnormal and Social Psychology, 55,* 327–332.

Bartlett, W. P., & Banker, G. A. (1984a). An electron microscopic study of the development of axons and dendrites by hippocampal neurons in culture. I. Cells which develop without intercellular contacts. *Journal of Neuroscience, 4,* 1944–1953.

Bartlett, W. P., & Banker, G. A. (1984b). An electron microscopic study of the development of axons and dendrites by hippocampal neurons in culture. II. Synaptic relationships. *Journal of Neuroscience, 4,* 1954–1965.

Baum, M. J. (1979). Differentiation of coital behavior in mammals: A comparative analysis. *Neuroscience & Biobehavioral Reviews, 3,* 265–284.

Baum, M. J., Carroll, R. S., Cherry, J. A., & Tobet, S. A. (1990). Steroidal control of behavioral, neuroendocrine and brain sexual differentiation: Studies in a carnivore, the ferret. *Journal of Neuroendocrinology, 2,* 401–418.

Bazzett, T. J., Eaton, R. C., Thompson, J. T., Markowski, V. P., Lumley, L. A., & Hull, E. M. (1991). Dose dependent D2 effects on genital reflexes after MPOA injections of quinelorane and apomorphine. *Life Sciences, 48,* 2309–2315.

Beach, F. A. (1974). Effects of gonadal hormones on urinary behavior in dogs. *Physiology & Behavior, 12,* 1005–1013.

Beatty, L., Hoyenga, K. B., & Hoyenga, K. T. (1992). A sex difference in adaptation to stress: Utility and validity issues in the development of an animal model of depression. Unpublished master's thesis, Western Illinois University.

Beatty, L., Hoyenga, K. B., & Hoyenga, K. T. (1993, April). Sex differences in an animal model of depression. Paper presented at the Midwestern Psychological Association, Chicago.

Beatty, W. W. (1979). Gonadal hormones and sex differences in nonreproductive behaviors in rodents: Organizational and activational influences. *Hormones & Behavior, 12,* 112–163.

Beatty, W. W. (1992). Gonadal hormones and sex differences in nonreproductive behaviors. In A. Gerall, H. Moltz, & I. L. Ward (Eds.), *Handbook of behavioral neurobiology: Vol. 11. Sexual differentiation* (pp. 85–128). New York: Plenum Press.

Beck, C. H. M., & Fibiger, H. C. (1995). Chronic desipramine alters stress-induced behaviors and regional expression of the immediate early gene, *c-fos*. *Pharmacology, Biochemistry and Behaviour, 51,* 331–338.

Becker, G., Becker, T., Struck, M., Lindner, A., Burzer, K., Retz, W., Bogdahn, U., & Beckman, H. (1995). Reduced echogenicity of brainstem raphe specific to unipolar depression: A transcranial color-coded real-time sonography study. *Biological Psychiatry, 38,* 180–184.

Becker, J. B., Breedlove, S. M., & Crews, D. (Eds.). (1992). *Behavioral Endocrinology*. Cambridge: MIT Press.

Belisle, S., & Tulchinsky, D. (1980). Amniotic fluid hormones. In D. Tulchinsky & K. J. Ryan (Eds.). *Maternal-fetal endocrinology* (pp. 169–195). Philadelphia: W. B. Saunders.

Bem, S. L. (1974). The measurement of psychological androgyny. *Journal of Consulting and Clinical Psychology, 42,* 165–172.

Bem, S. L. (1975). Sex role adaptability: One consequence of psychological androgyny. *Journal of Personality and Social Psychology, 31,* 634–643.

Bem, S. L. (1976). Probing the promise of androgyny. In A. G. Kaplan & J. P. Bean (Eds). *Beyond sex-role stereotypes: Readings toward a psychology of androgyny*. Boston: Little, Brown.

Bem, S. L. (1981a). *Bem Sex-Role Inventory professional manual.* Palo Alto, CA: Consulting Psychologists Press.

Bem, S. L. (1981b). Gender schema theory: A cognitive account of sex typing. *Psychological Review, 88,* 354–364.

Bem, S. L. (1985). Androgyny and gender schema theory: A conceptual and empirical integration. In T. B. Sonderegger (Ed.), *Psychology and gender: Nebraska Symposium on Motivation, 1984* (pp. 179–226). Lincoln: University of Nebraska Press.

Bem, S. L. (1995). Dismantling gender polarization and compulsory heterosexuality: Should we turn the volume down or up? *Journal of Sex Research, 32,* 329–334.

Benbow, C. P., & Lubinski, D. (1993). Consequences of gender differences in mathematical reasoning ability and some biological linkages. In M. Haug, R. E. Whalen, C. Aron, & K. L. Olsen (Eds.), *The development of sex differences and similarities in behavior, NATO ASI Series.* Dordrecht: Kluwer Academic Publishers.

Benbow, C. P., & Stanley, J. C. (1983). Sex differences in mathematical ability: More facts. *Science, 222,* 1029–1031.

Benirschke, K., Anderson, J. M., & Brownhill, L. E. (1962). Marrow chimerism in marmosets. *Science, 138,* 513–515.

Benkelfat, C., Ellenbogen, M. A., Dean, P., Palmour, R. M., & Young, S. N. (1994). Mood-lowering effect of tryptophan depletion: Enhanced susceptibility in young men at genetic risk for major affective disorders. *Archives of General Psychiatry, 51,* 687–697.

Bern, H. A., Gorski, R. A., & Kawashima, S. (1973). Long-term effects of perinatal hormone administration. *Science, 18,* 189–190.

Bern, H. A., Jones, L. A., Mori, T., & Young, P. W. (1975). Exposure of neonatal mice to steroids: Long term effect on the mammary gland and other reproductive structures. *Journal of Steroid Biochemistry, 6,* 673–676.

Bernstein, P., & Crelin, E. S. (1967). Bony pelvis sexual dimorphism in the rat. *Anatomical Records, 157,* 517–526.

Bettini, E., Pollio, G., Santagati, S., & Maggi, A. (1992). Estrogen receptor in rat brain: Presence in the hippocampal formation. *Neuroendocrinology, 56,* 502–508.

Beyer, C., & Feder, H. H. (1987). Sex steroids and afferent input: Their role in brain sexual differentiation. *Annual Reviews in Physiology, 49,* 349–364.

Beyer, C., Wozniak, A., & Hutchison, J. B. (1993). Sex-specific aromatisation of testosterone in mouse hypothalamic neurones. *Neuroendocrinology, 58,* 673–681.

Bibawi, D., Cherry, B., & Hellige, J. B. (1995.) Fluctuation of perceptual asymmetry across time in women and men: Effects related to the menstrual cycle. *Neuropsychologia, 33,* 131–138.

Biegon, A., & McEwen, B. S. (1982). Modulation by estradiol of serotonin receptors in brain. *Journal of Neuroscience, 2,* 199–205.

Big and Smelly. (1992). *Discover, 13,* 13.

Bitran, D., & Hull, E. M. (1987). Pharmacological analysis of male rat sexual behavior. *Neuroscience & Biobehavioral Reviews, 11,* 365–389.

Blanchard, D. C., Shepherd, J. K., Carobrez, A. D. P., & Blanchard, R. J. (1991). Sex effects in defensive behavior: Baseline differences and drug interactions. *Neuroscience & Biobehavioral Reviews, 15,* 461–468.

Blanchard, R. J., Blanchard, D. C., Takahashi, T., & Kelly, M. J. (1977). Attack and defensive behavior in the albino rat. *Animal Behaviour, 12,* 622–634.

Blanchard, R. J., Flannelly, K. J., & Blanchard, D. C. (1988). Life-span studies of dominance and aggression in established colonies of laboratory rats. *Physiology & Behavior, 43,* 1–7.

Blazquez, E. B., Rubalcava, B., Montesano, R., Orci, L., & Unger, R. H. (1976). Development of insulin and glucagon binding and the adenylate cyclase response in liver membranes of the prenatal, postnatal and adult rat: Evidence of glucagon "resistance." *Endocrinology, 98,* 1014–1023.

Blizard, D. A., Lippman, H. R., & Chen, J. J. (1975). Sex differences in open-field behaviour in the rat: the inductive and activational role of gonadal hormones. *Physiology & Behavior, 14,* 601–608.

Block, J. H. (1973). Conceptions of sex roles: Some cross-cultural and longitudinal perspectives. *American Psychologist, 28,* 512–526.

Blum, K., Noble, E. P., Sheridan, P. J., Montgomery, A., Ritchie, T., Jadadeeswaran, P., Nogami, H., Briggs, A. H., & Cohn, J. B. (1990). Allelic association of human dopamine D2 receptor gene in alcoholism. *Journal of the American Medical Association, 263,* 2055–2059.

Blyne, W., & Parsons, B. (1993). Human sexual orientation: The biologic theories reappraised. *Archives of General Psychiatry, 50,* 228–239.

Boklage, C. E. (1985). Interactions between same-sex-dizygotic fetuses and the assumption of Weinberg difference method epidemiology. *American Journal of Human Genetics, 37,* 591–605.

Boklage, C. E. (1987). Race, zygosity, and mortality among twins: Interactions of myth and method. *Acta Geneticae Medicae et Gemellologiae, 32,* 275–288.

Bolles, R. C., & Woods, P. J. (1964). The ontogeny of behavior in the albino rat. *Animal Behaviour, 12,* 427–441.

Bonson, K. R., Johnson, R. G., Fiorella, D., Rabin, R. A., & Winter, J. C. (1994). Serotonergic control of androgen-induced dominance. *Pharmacology, Biochemistry & Behaviour, 49,* 313–322.

Bonson, K. R., & Winter, J. C. (1992). Reversal of testosterone-induced dominance by the serotonergic agonist quipazine. *Pharmacology, Biochemistry & Behaviour, 42,* 809–813.

Bornstein, R. F. (1994). Adaptive and maladaptive aspects of dependency: An integrative review. *American Journal of Orthopsychiatry, 64,* 622–635.

Bowers, M. B., van Woert, M., & Davis, L. (1971). Sexual behavior during l-DOPA treatment for Parkinsonism. *American Journal of Psychiatry, 127,* 1691.

Bowlby, J. (1980). *Loss: Sadness and depression.* New York: Basic Books.

Breedlove, S. M. (1992). Sexual dimorphism in the vertebrate nervous system. *The Journal of Neuroscience, 12,* 4133–4142.

Breedlove, S. M. (1994). Sexual differentiation of the human nervous system. *Annual Reviews in Psychology, 45,* 389–418.

Breedlove, S. M., Jacobson, C. D., Gorski, R. A., & Arnold, A. P. (1982). Masculinization of the female rat spinal cord following a single neonatal injection of testosterone propionate but not estradiol benzoate. *Brain Research, 237,* 173–181.

Briggs, S. R. (1992). Assessing the five-factor model of personality description. *Journal of Personality, 60,* 253–293.

Buhrich, N. (1977). A case of familial heterosexual transvestism. *Acta Psychiatrica Scandinavica, 55,* 199–201.

Bulmer, M. G. (1970). *The biology of twinning in man.* Oxford: Oxford University Press.

Buss, D. M. (1991). Evolutionary personality psychology. *Annual Review of Psychology, 42,* 459–491.

Buss, D. M. (1994). *The evolution of desire.* New York: Basic Books.

Buss, D. M. (1995a). Evolutionary psychology: A new paradigm for psychological science. *Psychological Inquiry, 6,* 1–30.

Buss, D. M. (1995b). Psychological sex differences: Origins through sexual selection. *American Psychologist, 50,* 164–168.

Buss, D. M., & Chiodo, L. M. (1991). Narcissistic acts in everyday life. *Journal of Personality, 59,* 179–215.

Butcher, K. F., & Case, A. (1994). The effect of sibling sex composition on women's education and earnings. *Quarterly Journal of Economics, 109,* 531–563.

Cairns, R. B. (1986). An evolutionary and developmental perspective on aggressive patterns. In M. C. Zahn-Waxler, E. M. Cummings, & R. Tonnotti (Eds.), *Altruism and aggression.* Cambridge: Cambridge University Press.

Campbell, P. S. (1983). An early effect of testosterone propionate upon hypothalamic function in the neonatal rat. *Experientia, 39,* 108–109.

Caplan, P. J., MacPherson, G. M., & Tobin, P. (1985). Do sex-related differences in spatial abilities exist? *American Psychologist, 40,* 786–799.

Carlson, J. N., & Glick, S. D. (1996). Circling behavior in rodents. In P. R. Sanberg, K.-P. Ossenkopp, & M. Kavaliers (Eds.), *Motor activity and movement disorders: Recent issues and applications* (pp. 269–300). Totowa, NJ: Humana Press.

Carrer, H. F., & Aoki, A. (1982). Ultrastructural changes in the hypothalamic ventromedial nucleus of ovariectomized rats after estrogen treatment. *Brain Research, 240,* 221–233.

Carson, D. J., Okuno, A., Lee, P. A., Stetten, G., Didolkar, S. M., & Migeon, C. J. (1982). Amniotic fluid steroid levels. *American Journal of Diseases of Children, 136,* 218–222.

Carter, H. D. (1932). Twin similarities in occupational interests. *The Journal of Education Psychology, 23,* 641–655.

Carter, H. D., & Strong, E. K. (1933). Sex differences in occupational interests of high school students. *The Personnel Journal, 12,* 166–175.

Chase, T. N., Geoffrey, V., Gillespie, M., & Burrows, G. H. (1986). Structural and functional studies of Gilles de la Tourette syndrome. *Revue Neurology (Paris), 142,* 851–855.

Cherry, J. A., Tobet, S. A., DeVoogd, T. J., & Baum, M. J. (1992). Effects of sex and androgen treatment on dendritic dimensions of neurons in the sexually dimorphic preoptic/anterior hypothalamic area of male and female ferrets. *Journal of Comparative Neurology, 323,* 577–585.

Chevalier, G., & Deniau, J. M. (1990). Disinhibition as a basic process in the expression of striatal functions. *Trends in Neurosciences, 13,* 277–280.

Chiarello, C., McMahon, M. A., & Schaefer, K. (1989). Visual cerebral lateralization over phases of the menstrual cycle: A preliminary investigation. *Brain Cognition, 11,* 18–36.

Chodorow, N. J. (1978). *The reproduction of mothering: Psychoanalysis and the sociology of gender.* Berkeley and Los Angeles: University of California Press.

Chung, S. K., McVary, K. T., & McKenna, K. E. (1988). Sexual reflex in male and female rats. *Neuroscience Letters, 94,* 343–348.

Chung, S., Pfaff, D., & Cohen, R. (1988). Estrogen-induced alterations in synaptic morphology in the midbrain central gray. *Experimental Brain Research, 69,* 522–530.

Cicero, T. J., Meyer, E. R., Bell, R. D., & Koch, G. A. (1976). Effects of morphine and methadone on serum testosterone and luteinizing hormone levels and on the secondary sex organs of the male rat. *Endocrinology, 98*(2), 367–372.

Cicero, T. J., O'Connor, L. H., & Bell, R. D. (1976). Acute reduction in serum testosterone levels by narcotics in the male rat: Stereospecificity, blockade by naloxone, and tolerance. *Journal of Pharmacology and Experimental Therapeutics, 198,* 340–346.

Cihak, R., Gutmann, E., & Hanzilikova, V. (1970). Involution and hormone-induced persistence of the muscle sphincter (levator) ani in female rats. *Journal of Anatomy, 106,* 93–110.

Civelli, O., Bunzow, J. R., & Grandy, D. K. (1993). Molecular diversity of the dopamine receptors. *Annual Review of Pharmacology and Toxicology, 33,* 281–307.

Civelli, O., Bunzow, J. R., Grandy, D. K., Zhou, Q. Y., & Vantol, H. H. M. (1991). Molecular biology of the dopamine receptors. *European Journal of Pharmacology—Molecular Pharmacology, 207,* 277–286.

Clark, M. M., Bone, S., & Galef, B. G. (1988). Uterine positions and schedules of urination: Correlates of differential maternal anogenital stimulation. *Developmental Psychobiology, 22,* 389–400.

Clark, M. M., & Galef, B. G. (1988). Effects of uterine position on rate of sexual development in female Mongolian gerbils. *Physiology & Behavior, 42,* 15–18.

Clark, M. M., & Galef, B. G. (1989). Sexual segregation in the left and right horns of the gerbil uterus: The male embryo is usually on the right, the female on the left (Hippocrates). *Developmental Psychobiology, 23,* 29–37.

Clark, M. M., Malenfant, S. A., Winter, D. A., & Galef, B. G. (1990). Fetal uterine position affects copulation and scent markings by adult male gerbils. *Physiology & Behavior, 47,* 301–305.

Clark, M. M., Tucker, L., & Galef, B. G. (1992). Stud males and dud males: Intrauterine position effects on the reproductive success of male gerbils. *Animal Behaviour, 43,* 215–221.

Clark, M. M., vom Saal, F. S., & Galef, B. G. (1992). Intrauterine positions and testosterone levels of adult male gerbils are correlated. *Physiology & Behavior, 51,* 957–960.

Clarke, A. S., & Boinski, S. (1995). Temperament in nonhuman primates. *American Journal of Primatology, 37,* 103–125.

Clarke, K. A., & Williams, E. (1994). Development of locomotion in the rat—spatiotemporal footfall patterns. *Physiology & Behavior, 55,* 151–155.

Clemens, L. G. (1974). Neurohormonal control of male sexual behavior. In W. Montagna & W. A. Sadler (Eds.), *Reproductive behavior.* New York: Plenum Press.

Clendenin, N., Petriats, M., & Simon, E. J. (1976). Ontological development of opiate receptors in rodent brain. *Brain Research, 118,* 157–160.

Clough, R. W., & Rodriguez-Sierra, J. F. (1983). Synaptic changes in the hypothalamus of the prepubertal female rat administered estrogen. *American Journal of Anatomy, 167,* 205–214.

Coccaro, E. F. (1992). Impulsive aggression and central serotonergic system function in humans: An example of a dimensional brain-behavior relationship. *International Clinical Psychopharmacology, 7,* 3012.

Coccaro, E. F., Bergman, C. S., & McClearn, G. E. (1993). Heritability of irritable impulsiveness: A study of twins reared together and apart. *Psychiatry Research, 48,* 229–242.

Coccaro, E. F., Kavoussi, R. J., & Hauger, R. L. (1995). Physiological responses to *d*-fenfluramine and ipsapirone challenge correlate with indices of aggression in males with personality disorder. *International Clinical Psychopharmacology, 10,* 177–179.

Coccaro, E. F., Kavoussi, R. J., & Lesser, J. C. (1992). Self- and other-directed human aggression: The role of the central serotonergic system. *International Clinical Psychopharmacology, 6*(Suppl. 6), 70–83.

Coccaro, E. F., Silverman, J. M., Klar, H. M., Horvath, T. B., & Siever, L. J. (1994). Familial correlates of reduced serotonergic system function in patients with personality disorders. *Archives of General Psychiatry, 51,* 318–324.

Cochran, W. G. (1954). Some methods for strengthening the common X^2 tests. *Biometrics, 10,* 417–454.

Cole-Harding, S., Morstad, A. L., & Wilson, J. R. (1988). Spatial ability in members of opposite-sex twin pairs. *Behavior Genetics, 18,* 710.

Coleman, W. H. (1969). Sex differences in the growth of the human bony pelvis. *American Journal of Physical Anthropology, 31,* 125–152.

Collaer, M. L., & Hines, M. (1995). Human behavioral sex differences: A role for gonadal hormones during early development? *Psychological Bulletin, 118,* 55–107.

Comings, D. E. (1987). A controlled study of Tourette syndrome. VII. Summary a common genetic disorder causing disinhibition of the limbic system. *American Journal of Human Genetics, 41,* 839–866.

Comings, D. E. (1989). The genetics of human behavior: Lessons for two societies. *American Journal of Human Genetics, 44,* 452–460.

Comings, D. E. (1990). *Tourette Syndrome and Human Behavior.* Duarte, CA: Hope Press.

Comings, D. E. (1992). The D2 dopamine receptor and Tourette's syndrome. *Journal of the American Medical Association, 267,* 652.

Comings, D. E. (1994a). Genetic factors in substance abuse based on studies of Tourette syndrome and ADHD probands and relatives. II. Alcohol abuse. *Drug and Alcohol Dependence, 35,* 17–24.

Comings, D. E. (1994b). The role of genetic factors in human sexual behavior based on studies of Tourette syndrome and ADHD probands and their relatives. *American Journal of Medical Genetics (Neuropsychiatric Genetics), 54,* 227–241.

Comings, D. E. (1995). Tourette syndrome: A hereditary neuropsychiatric spectrum disorder. *Annals of Clinical Psychiatry, 6,* 235–247.

Comings, D. E. (1996). *Search for the Tourette syndrome and human behavior genes.* Duarte, CA: Hope Press.

Comings, D. E., & Comings, B. G. (1982). A case of familial exhibitionism in Tourette's syndrome successfully treated with haloperidol. *American Journal of Psychiatry, 139,* 913–915.

Comings, D. E., & Comings, B. G. (1984). Tourette's syndrome and attention deficit disorder with hyperactivity: Are they genetically related? *Journal of the American Academy of Child and Adolescent Psychiatry, 23,* 138–146.

Comings, D. E., & Comings, B. G. (1985). Tourette syndrome: Clinical and psychological aspects of 250 cases. *American Journal of Human Genetics, 37,* 435–450.

Comings, D. E., & Comings, B. G. (1987a). A controlled study of Tourette syndrome. I–VII. *American Journal of Human Genetics, 41,* 701–866.

Comings, D. E., & Comings, B. G. (1987b). A controlled study of Tourette syndrome. I. Attention-deficit disorder, learning disorders, and school problems. *American Journal of Human Genetics, 41,* 701–741.

Comings, D. E., & Comings, B. G. (1990). A controlled family history study of Tourette syndrome. II. Alcoholism, drug abuse and obesity. *Journal of Clinical Psychiatry, 51,* 281–287.

Comings, D. E., & Comings, B. G. (1993). Comorbid behavioral disorders in Tourette Syndrome and related disorders. In R. Kurlan (Ed.), *Handbook of Tourette's Syndrome and Related Tic and Behavioral Disorders* (pp. 111–147). New York: Marcel-Decker.

Comings, D. E., Comings, B. G., Muhleman, D., Dietz, G., Shahbahrami, B., Tast, D., Knell, E., Kocsis, P., Baumgarten, R., Kovacs, B. W., Levy, D. L., Smith, M., Kane, J. M., Lieberman, J. A., Klein, D. N., MacMurray, J., Tosk, J., Sverd, J., Gysin, R., & Flanagan, S. (1991). The dopamine D2 receptor locus as a modifying gene in neuropsychiatric disorders. *Journal of the American Medical Association, 266,* 1793–1800.

Comings, D. E., Wu, H., Chiu, C., Ring, R. H., Dietz, G., & Muhleman, D. (1996). Polygenic inheritance of Tourette syndrome, stuttering, ADHD, conduct and oppositional defiant disorder: The additive and subtractive effect of the three dopaminergic genes—DRD2, DbH and DAT1. *American Journal of Medical Genetics (Neuropsychiatric Genetics), 67,* 264–288.

Conney, A. H. (1986). Induction of microsomal cytochrome P450 enzymes: The first Bernard B. Brodie Lecture of Pennsylvania State University. *Life Sciences, 39,* 2493–2518.

Constantinople, A. (1973). Masculinity–femininity: An exception to a famous dictum? *Psychological Bulletin, 80,* 389–407.

Cook, E. H., Stein, M. A., Krasowski, M. D., Cox, N. J., Olkon, D. M., Kieffer, J. E., & Leventhal, B. L. (1995). Association of attention-deficit disorder and the dopamine transporter gene. *American Journal of Human Genetics, 56,* 993–998.

Cook, E. P. (1985). *Psychological androgyny.* New York: Pergamon Press.

Cools, A. R., Scheenen, W., Eilam, D., & Golani, I. (1989). Evidence that apomorphine and (+)-amphetamine produce different types of circling in rats. *Behavioural Brain Research, 34,* 111–116.

Corbier, P. (1985). Sexual differentiation of positive feedback: Effect of hour of castration at birth on estradiol-induced luteinizing hormone secretion in immature male rats. *Endocrinology, 116,* 142–147.

Corbitt, E. M., & Widiger, T. A. (1995). Sex differences among the personality disorders: An exploration of the data. *Clinical Psychology: Science and Practice, 2,* 225–238.

Costa, P. T., & McCrae, R. R. (1985). *The NEO Personality Inventory Manual.* Odessa, FL: Psychological Assessment Resources.

Costa, P. T., & McCrae, R. R. (1992). The five-factor model of personality and its relevance to personality disorders. *Journal of Personality Disorders, 6,* 343–359.

Coyle, J. T. (1973). The development of catecholaminergic neurons of the central nervous system. *Neuroscience Research,* 35–52.

Coyle, J. T., & Axelrod, J. (1971). Development of uptake and storage of L(^{3}H)norepinephrine in the rat brain. *Journal of Neurochemistry, 18,* 2061–2075.

Coyle, J. T., & Pert, C. B. (1976). Ontogenetic development of (^{3}H)-naloxone binding in the rat brain. *Neuropharmacology, 15,* 555–560.

Crapo, R. H. (1990). *Cultural Anthropolgy* (2nd ed.). Guilford, CT: Dushkin.

Crawford, C. B., Salter, B. E., & Jang, K. L. (1989). Human grief: Is its intensity related to the reproductive value of the deceased? *Ethology and Sociobiology, 10,* 293–309.

Cremniter, D., Thenault, M., Jamain, S., Meidinger, A., Delmas, C., & Gaillard, M. (1994). Serotonin and suicide: A preliminary study concerning a sample of violent suicidal patients. *Progress in Neuro-Psychopharmacology & Biological Psychiatry, 18,* 871–878.

Critchley, M. A., & Handley, S. L. (1987). Effects in the X-maze anxiety model of agents acting at 5HT1 and 5HT2 receptors. *Psychopharmacology, 93,* 502–506.

Critchley, M. A., Njunge, K., & Handley, S. L. (1992). Actions and some interactions of 5HT1A ligands in the elevated X-maze and effects of dorsal raphe lesions. *Psychopharmacology, 106,* 484–496.

Crozier, W. J., & Pincus, G. (1926). The geotropic conduct of young rats. *Journal of General Physiology, 10,* 257–269.

Csaba, G. (1980). Phylogeny and ontogeny of hormone receptors: The selection theory of receptor formation and hormonal imprinting. *Biological Reviews of Cambridge Phylosophical Society, 55,* 47–63.

Csaba, G. (1981). *Ontogeny and phylogeny of hormone receptors.* New York: Karger-Basel.

Csaba, G. (1984). The present state in the phylogeny and ontogeny of hormone receptors. *Hormone and Metabolic Research, 16,* 329–335.

Csaba, G. (1985). The unicellular Tetrahymena as a model cell for receptor research. *International Review of Cytology, 95,* 327–377.

Csaba, G. (1986). Receptor ontogeny and hormonal imprinting. *Experientia, 42,* 750–759.

Csaba, G. (1991). Interactions between the genetic programme and environmental influences in the perinatal critical period. *Zoological Science, 8,* 813–825.

Csaba, G. (1994). Phylogeny and ontogeny of chemical signaling: Origin and development of hormone receptors. *International Review of Cytology, 155,* 1–48.

Csaba, G., & Gaál, A. (1997). Effect of perinatal vitamin A or retinoic acid treatment (hormonal imprinting) on the sexual behavior of adult rats. *Human and Experimental Toxicology, 16,* 193–197.

Csaba, G., & Inczefi-Gonda, Á. (1984). Effect of benzo(a) pyrene treatment of neonatal and growing rats on steroid receptor binding capacity in adulthood. *General Pharmacology, 15,* 557–558.

Csaba, G., & Inczefi-Gonda, Á. (1990). Effect of late steroid imprinting of the thymus on the hormone binding capacity of thymocytic receptor in adulthood. *Acta Physiologica Hungarica, 75,* 195–199.

Csaba, G., & Inczefi-Gonda, Á. (1992a). Benzpyrene exposure at 15 days of prenatal life reduces the binding capacity of thymic glucocorticoid receptors in adulthood. *General Pharmacology, 23,* 123–124.

Csaba, G., & Inczefi-Gonda, Á. (1992b). Life-long effect of a single neonatal treatment with estradiol or progesterone on rat uterine estrogen receptor binding capacity. *Hormone and Metabolic Research, 24,* 167–171.

Csaba, G., & Inczefi-Gonda, Á. (1993a). Anabolic steroid (nandrolone) treatment during adolescence decreases the number of glucocorticoid and estrogen receptors in adult female rats. *Hormone and Metabolic Research, 25,* 353–355.

Csaba, G., & Inczefi-Gonda, Á. (1993b). Uterus estrogen receptors binding capacity is reduced in rat if exposed by benzpyrene neonatally. *Journal of Developmental Physiology, 19,* 217–219.

Csaba, G., & Inczefi-Gonda, Á. (1994). Breastmilk can mediate chemical imprinting: Benzpyrene exposure during lactation reduces the thymic glucocorticoid receptor density of the offspring. *General Pharmacology, 25,* 603–606.

Csaba, G., & Inczefi-Gonda, Á. (1996). Effect of perinatal triiodothyronine (T3) treatment on adult thymus glucocorticoid and estrogen receptors and uterus estrogen receptors: Receptor selectivity during hormonal imprinting. *Acta Physiologica Hungarica, 84,* 19–24.

Csaba, G., & Inczefi-Gonda, Á. (1997). Effect of combined neonatal imprinting by vitamin A, vitamin D3, benzpyrene and allylestrenol on adult rat thymus glucocorticoid and uterine estrogen receptors. *General Pharmacology, 29,* 779–781.

Csaba, G., Inczefi-Gonda, Á., & Dobozy, O. (1986). Imprinting by steroids: A single neonatal treatment with diethylstilbestrol (DES) or allylestrenol (AE) gives rise to a lasting decrease in the number of rat uterine receptors. *Acta Physiologica Hungarica, 17,* 207–212.

Csaba, G., Inczefi-Gonda, Á., & Dobozy, O. (1989). Hormonal imprinting in adults: Insulin exposure during regeneration alters the later binding capacity of the hepatic insulin receptor. *Acta Physiologica Hungarica, 73,* 461–464.

Csaba, G., Inczefi-Gonda, Á., Karabélyos, Cs., & Pap, E. (1995). The peroxisome proliferator clofibrate moderately influences the glucocorticoid and estrogen receptors, the sexual-hormone level and the sexual behaviour after neonatal treatment (hormonal imprinting) of the rat. *Physiology & Behavior, 58,* 1203–1207.

Csaba, G., Inczefi-Gonda, Á., & Szeberényi, Sz. (1991). Lasting impact of a single benzpyrene treatment in prenatal and growing age on the thymic glucocorticoid receptors of rat. *General Pharmacology, 22,* 815–818.

Csaba, G., & Karabélyos, Cs. (1995). Pubertal benzpyrene exposition decreases durably the sexual activity of the adult male and female rats. *Hormone and Metabolic Research, 27,* 279–282.

Csaba, G., Karabélyos, Cs., & Dalló, J. (1993). Fetal and neonatal action of a polycyclic hydrocarbon (benzpyrene) or a synthetic steroid hormone (allylestrenol) as requested by the sexual behaviour of adult rats. *Journal of Developmental Physiology, 19,* 67–70.

Csaba, G., Mag, O., Inczefi-Gonda, Á., & Szeberényi, Sz. (1991). Persistent influence of neonatal 2,3,7,8-tetrachloro-dibenzo-p-dioxin (TCDD) treatment on glucocorticoid receptors and on the microsomal enzyme sytem. *Journal of Developmental Physiology, 15,* 337–340.

Csaba, G., & Nagy, S. U. (1976). Plasticity of hormone receptors and possibility of their deformation in neonatal age. *Experientia, 32,* 651–652.

Csaba, G., & Nagy, S. U. (1978). The binding of 125I-TSH to thyroid cell receptor previously deformed (in neonatal age) by gonadotropin treatment. *Biology of Neonate, 34,* 275–277.

Csaba, G., & Nagy, S. U. (1985). Influence of the neonatal suppression of TSH production (neonatal hyperthyroidism) on response to TSH in adulthood. *Journal of Endocrinological Investigation, 8,* 557–561.

Csaba, G., Szeberényi, Sz., & Dobozy, O. (1986). Influence of a single neonatal treatment with allylestrenol or diethylstilbestrol (DES) on microsomal enzyme activity in adulthood. *Medical Biology, 64,* 197–200.

Curzon, G., Kennett, G. A., Sarna, G. S., & Whitton, P. S. (1992). The effects of tianeptine and other antidepressants on a rat model of depression. *British Journal of Psychiatry, 160*(Suppl. 15), 51–55.

Dahlberg, G. (1926). *Twin births and twins from a heredity point of view*. Stockholm: Bokforlags-A.-B. Tidens Tryckeri.

Daly, M., & Wilson, M. (1987). Evolutionary psychology and family violence. In C. Crawford, M. Smith, & D. Krebs (Eds.), *Sociobiology and psychology: Ideas, issues and applications* (pp. 293–309). Hillsdale, NJ: Lawrence Erlbaum.

d'Amato, T., Leboyer, M., Malafosse, A., Samolyk, D., Lamouroux, A., Junien, C., Mallet, J. (1989). Two Taq I dimorphic sites at the human b-hydroxylase locus. *Nucleic Acids Research, 17,* 5871.

Darwin, C. R. (1871). *The descent of man, and selection in relation to sex*. New York: D. Appleton & Co.

Datla, K. P., Mitra, S. K., & Bhattacharya, S. K. (1991). Serotonergic modulation of footshock induced aggression in paired rats. *Indian Journal of Experimental Biology, 29,* 631–635.

Dawkins, K. (1995). Gender differences in psychiatry: Epidemiology and drug response. *CNS Drugs, 5,* 393–407.

Dawkins, R. (1989). *The extended phenotype*. Oxford: Oxford University Press.

Deaux, K. (1985). Sex and gender. *Annual Review of Psychology, 36,* 49–81.

De Jonge, F. H., Muntje Werff, J.-W., Loumerse, A. L., & van de Poll, N. E. (1988). Sexual behaviour and sexual orientation of the female rat after hormonal treatment during various stages of development. *Hormones & Behavior, 22,* 100–115.

Devinsky, O. (1983). Neuroanatomy of Gilles de la Tourette's syndrome: Possible midbrain involvement. *Archives of Neurology, 40,* 508–514.

Devor, E. J. (1992). D2-dopamine receptor and neuropsychiatric illness [letter]. *Journal of the American Medical Association, 267,* 651.

De Vries, G. J. (1990). Sex differences in neuro-transmitter systems. *Journal of Neuroendocrinology, 2,* 1–14.

DeVries, G. J., De Bruin, J. P. C., Uylings, H. B. M., & Corner, M. A. (Eds.). (1984). Sex differences in the brain: The relation between structure and function. *Progress in Brain Research, 61.*

de Waal, F. B. M. (1989). Commentary on "Gender and political cognition: Integrating evolutionary biology and political science": Commitments and grudges. *Politics and the Life Sciences, 8,* 27–33.

Diamond, M. (1965). A critical evaluation of the ontogeny of human sexual behavior. *Quarterly Review of Biology, 40,* 147–175.

Diamond, M. (1984). Age, sex, and environmental influences. In N. Geschwind & A. M. Galaburda (Eds.), *Cerebral dominance: The biological foundations* (pp. 134–146). Cambridge: Harvard University Press.

Diamond, M. (1997). Sexual identity and sexual orientation in children with traumatized or ambiguous genitalia. *Journal of Sex Research, 34,* 199–122.

Diamond, M., Binstock, T., & Kohl, J. V. (1996). From fertilization to adult sexual behavior. *Hormones & Behavior, 30,* 333–353.

Diamond, M., Dowling, G. A., & Johnson, R. E. (1981). Morphological cerebral cortical asymmetry in male and female rats. *Experimental Neurology, 71,* 261–268.

Diamond, M., & Sigmundson, H. K. (1997). Sex reassignment at birth: A long term review and clinical implications. *Archives of Pediatric and Adolescent Medicine, 150,* 298–304.

Diaz, H., Lorenzo, A., Carrer, H. F., & Caceres, A. (1992). Time-lapse study of neurite growth in hypothalamic dissociated neurons in culture: Sex differences and estrogen effects. *Journal of Neuroscience Research, 33,* 266–281.

Diez-Guerra, F. J., Augood, S., Emson, P. C., & Duer, R. G. (1987). Opioid peptides inhibit the release of noradrenalin from slices of rat median preoptic area. *Experimental Brain Research, 66,* 378–384.

Dittman, R. W. (1992). Body positions and movement patterns in female patients with congenital adrenal hyperplasia. *Hormones & Behavior, 26,* 441–456.

Dittman, R. W., Kappes, M. H., Kappes, M. E., Borger, D., Stegner, H., Willig, R. H., & Wallis, H. (1990). Congenital adrenal hyperplasia: 1. Gender-related behavior and attitudes in female patients and sisters. *Psychoneuroendocrinology, 15,* 401–420.

Dixson, A. F. (1986). Plasma testosterone concentrations during postnatal development in the male common marmoset. *Folia Primatologica, 47,* 166–170.

Dixson, A. F. (1993a). Effects of testosterone propionate upon the sexual and aggressive behavior of adult marmosets (*Callithrix jacchus*) castrated as neonates. *Hormones & Behavior, 27,* 216–230.

Dixson, A. F. (1993b). Sexual and aggressive behavior of adult male marmosets (*Callithrix jacchus*) castrated neonatally, prepubertally or in adulthood. *Physiology & Behavior, 54*(2), 301–307.

Döhler, K. D. (1978). Is female sexual differentiation hormone-mediated? *Trends in Neurosciences, 1,* 138–140.

Donis, J. A., Ventosa-Michelman, M., & Neve, R. L. (1993). Comparison of expression of a series of mammalian vector promoters in the neuronal cell lines PC12 and HT4. *Biotechniques, 15,* 786–787.

Dörner, G., Poppe, I., Stahl, F., Kolzsch, J., & Uebelhack, R. (1991). Gene- and environment-dependent neuroendocrine etiogenesis of homosexuality and transsexualism. *Experimental and Clinical Endocrinology, 98,* 141–150.

Draper, P., & Belsky, J. (1990). Personality development in evolutionary perspective. *Journal of Personality, 58,* 141–161.

Draper, P., & Harpending, H. (1982). Father absence and reproductive strategy. *Journal of Anthropological Research, 38,* 255–272.

Eagly, A. H. (1987). *Sex differences in social behavior: A social-role interpretation.* Hillsdale, NJ: Lawrence Erlbaum.

Eagly, A. H., & Johnson, B. T. (1990). Gender and leadership styles: A meta-analysis. *Psychological Bulletin, 198,* 233–256.

Eaves, L. J., Eysenck, H. J., & Martin, N. G. (1989). *Genes, culture, and personality.* London: Academic Press.

Eilam, D. (1994). Influence of body morphology on turning behavior in carnivores. *Journal of Motor Behavior, 26,* 3–12.

Eilam, D., & Golani, I. (1988). The ontogeny of exploratory behavior in the house rat (*Rattus rattus*): The mobility gradient. *Developmental Psychobiology, 21,* 679–710.

Eisler, J. A., Tannenbaum, P. L., Mann, D. R., & Wallen, K. (1993). Neonatal testicular suppression with a GnRH agonist in rhesus monkeys: Effects on adult endocrine function and behavior. *Hormones & Behavior, 27,* 551–567.

Ekbom, A., Trichopoulos, D., Adami, H., Hsieh, C., & Lan, S. (1992). Evidence of prenatal influences on breast cancer risk. *Lancet, 340,* 1015–1018.

Eldridge, R., Sweet, R., Lake, R., Ziegler, M., & Shapiro, A. K. (1977). Gilles de la Tourette's syndrome: Clinical, genetic, psychologic, and biochemical aspects in 21 selected families. *Neurology, 27,* 115–124.

Ellis, L. (1989). *Theories of rape: Inquiries into the causes of sexual aggression.* New York: Hemisphere.

Ellis, L. (1995). Dominance and reproductive success among nonhuman animals: A cross-species comparison. *Ethology and Sociobiology, 16,* 257–333.

Ellis, L. (1996a). A discipline in peril: Sociology's future hinges on curing its biophobia. *American Sociologist, 27,* 21–41.

Ellis, L. (1996b). The role of perinatal factors in determining sexual orientation. In R. C. Savin-Williams & K. M. Cohen (Eds.), *The lives of lesbians, gays, and bisexuals: Children to Adults* (pp. 35–70). Fort Worth, TX: Harcourt Brace.

Ellis, L., & Ames, M. A. (1987). Neurohormonal functioning and sexual orientation: A theory of homosexuality–heterosexuality. *Psychological Bulletin, 101,* 233–258.

Ellis, L., Ames, M. A., Peckham, W., & Burke, D. (1988). Sexual orientation of human offspring may be altered by severe maternal stress during pregnancy. *The Journal of Sex Research, 25,* 152–157.

Ellis, L., & Coontz, P. D. (1990). Androgens, brain functioning, and criminality: The neurohormonal foundations of antisociality. In L. Ellis & H. Hoffman (Eds.), *Crime in biological, social, and moral contexts* (pp. 162–193). New York: Praeger.

Ellis, L., & Peckham, W. (1991). Prenatal stress and handedness. *Pre- and Peri-Natal Psychology Journal, 6,* 135–144.

Ellis, P. M., & Salmond, C. (1994). Is platelet imipramine binding reduced in depression? A meta-analysis. *Biological Psychiatry, 36,* 262–299.

Engel, W., Pfafflin, F., & Wiedeking, C. H.-Y. (1980). Antigen in transsexuality, and how to explain testis differentiation in H-Y antigen-negative males and ovary differentiation in H-Y antigen-positive females. *Human Genetics, 55,* 315–319.

Engele, J., & Pilgrim, C. (1987). Nigrostriatal dopaminergic neurons in culture are sexually dimorphic. *Neuroscience, 22,* S235.

Engele, J., & Pilgrim, C. (1989). Early sexual differentiation of diencephalic dopaminergic neurons of the rat in vitro. *Cell Tissue Research, 255,* 411–417.

Engele, J., Pilgrim, C., Kirsch, M., & Reisert, I. (1989). Different developmental potentials of diencephalic and mesencephalic dopaminergic neurons in vitro. *Brain Research, 483,* 98–109.

Engele, J., Pilgrim, C., & Reisert, I. (1989). Sexual differentiation of mesencephalic neurons in vitro: Effects of sex and gonadal hormones. *International Journal of Developmental Neuroscience, 7,* 603–611.

Epple, G., Alveario, M. C., & Belcher, A. M. (1990). Copulatory behavior of adult tamarins (*Saguinas fuscicollis*) castrated as neonates or juveniles: Effects of testosterone treatment. *Hormones & Behavior, 24,* 470–483.

Epple, G., Alveario, M. C., & St. André, E. (1978). Sexual and social behavior of saddle-back tamarins (*Saguinas fuscicollis*) castrated as neonates or juveniles. *American Journal of Primatology, 13,* 37–49.

Epple, G., Belcher, A. M., Kuderling, I., Zeller, U., Scolnick, L., Greenfield, K. L., & Smith, A. B. (1993). Making sense out of scents: Species differences in scent glands, scent-marking behaviour, and scent-mark composition in the Callitrichidae. In A. B. Rylands (Ed.), *Marmosets and Tamarins: Systematics, Behaviour, and Ecology* (pp. 123–151). Oxford: Oxford University Press.

Epstein, S. (1993). Bereavement from the perspective of cognitive-experiential self-theory. In M. S. Stroebe, W. Stroebe, & R. O. Hansson (Eds.), *Handbook of bereavement: Theory, research, and intervention* (pp. 112–125). Cambridge: Cambridge University Press.

Erlenmeyer-Kimling, L., & Jarvik, L. R. (1963). Genetics and intelligence: A review. *Science, 142,* 1477–1479.

Ernst, C., & Angst, J. (1983). *Birth order: Its influence on personality.* New York: Springer-Verlag.

Erskine, M. S. (1989). Solicitation behavior in the estrous female rat: A review. *Hormones & Behavior, 23,* 473–502.

Eusterschulte, B., Reisert, I., & Pilgrim, C. (1991). Sex differences in the development of the Wolffian duct: A parameter for early gonadal testosterone secretion. *Verhandlungen der Anatomischen Gesellschaft (Jena), 86,* 76.

Evans, R. M. (1988). The steroid and thyroid hormone receptor superfamily. *Science, 240,* 889–89.

Eysenck, H. J., & Wilson, G. (1979). *The psychology of sex.* London: J. M. Dent & Sons.

Fagen, R. (1981). *Animal play behavior.* New York: Oxford University Press.

Fairweather, H. (1982). Sex differences: Little reason for females to play midfield. In J. G. Beaumont (Ed.), *Divided visual field studies of cerebral organisation* (pp. 147–194). London: Academic Press.

Fajer, A. B., Hoffman, D., & Shillito, E. (1970). Inhibitory effect of p-chlorophenylalanine on the sexual maturation of female rats. *Journal of Reproduction and Fertility, 22,* 379–380.

Farabollini, F., Hole, D. R., & Wilson, C. A. (1988). Behavioral effects in adulthood of serotonin depletion by p-chlorophenylalanine given neonatally to male rats. *International Journal of Developmental Neuroscience, 41,* 187–199.

Fausto-Sterling, A. (1985). *Myths of gender: Biological theories about women and men.* New York: Basic Books.

Fausto-Sterling, A. (1992). *Myths of gender: Biological theories about women and men* (2nd ed.). New York: Basic Books.

Fava, M., Rappe, S. M., West, J., & Herzog, D. B. (1995). Anger attacks in eating disorders. *Psychiatry Research, 56,* 205–212.

Fava, M., Rosenbaum, J. R., Pava, J. A., McCarthy, M. K., Steingard, R. J., & Bouffides, E. (1993). Anger attacks in unipolar depression: 1. Clinical correlates and responses to fluoxetine treatment. *American Journal of Psychiatry, 8,* 1158–1163.

Feingold, A. (1994). Gender differences in personality: A meta-analysis. *Psychological Bulletin, 116,* 429–456.

Fels, E., & Bosch, L. R. (1971). Effect of prenatal administration of testosterone on ovarian function in rats. *American Journal of Obstetrics and Gynecology, 111,* 964–969.

Ferreira, A., & Caceres, A. (1991). Estrogen-enhanced neurite outgrowth: Evidence for a selective induction of Tau and stable microtubules. *Journal of Neuroscience, 11,* 392–400.

Field, E. F. (1996). Sex differences in movement organization. M. Sc. thesis, University of Lethbridge, Lethbridge, Alberta.

Field, E. F., Whishaw, I. Q., & Pellis, S. M. (1994, June). *An analysis of sex differences in the movement patterns used during the food wrenching and dodging paradigm.* Poster presented at the annual meeting of the Brain, Behaviour, and Cognitive Science Society, Vancouver, British Columbia, Canada.

Field, E. F., Whishaw, I. Q., & Pellis, S. M. (1995, November). *The relationship between sex, neonatal hormone exposure and movement patterns in a competitive feeding paradigm using adult rats.* Poster presented at the annual meeting for the Society for Neuroscience, San Diego, CA.

Field, E. F., Whishaw, I. Q., & Pellis, S. M. (1996). A kinematic analysis of evasive dodging movements used during food protection in the rat: Evidence for sex differences in movement. *Journal of Comparative Psychology, 110,* 298–306.

Field, E. F., Whishaw, I. Q., & Pellis, S. M. (1997a). A kinematic analysis of sex-typical movement patterns used during evasive dodging to protect a food item: The role of testicular hormones. *Behavioral Neuroscience, 111,* 808–815.

Field, E. F., Whishaw, I. Q., & Pellis, S. M. (1997b). Organization of sex-typical patterns of defense during food protection in the rat: The role of the opponent's sex. *Aggressive Behaviour, 23,* 197–214.

Field, E. F., Whishaw, I. Q., & Pellis, S. M. (1997c, May). *Seemingly paradoxical jumping in cataleptic haloperidol-treated rats is sexually dimorphic: The organizational and activational influences of gonadal steroid hormones on postural support.* Poster presented at the inaugural meeting of the Society for Behavioral Neuroendocrinology and the 29th meeting of the Conference on Reproductive Behavior, Baltimore, MD.

File, S. E. (1992). Behavioral detection of anxiolytic action. In J. M. Elliott, D. J. Heal, & C. A. Marsden (Eds.), *Experimental approaches to anxiety and depression* (pp. 25–44). New York: John Wiley & Sons.

Finkel, D., Whitfield, K., & McGue, M. (1995). Genetic and environmental influences on functional age: A twin study. *Journal of Gerontology, 50B,* 104–113.

Fischbein, S. (1978). School achievement and test results for twins and singletons in relation to social background. In W. E. Nance (Ed.), *Twin research: Part A. Psychology and methodology.* New York: Liss.

Fischbein, S., Frank, O., & Cenner, S. (1991). Popularity ratings of twins and non-twins at age 11 and 13. *Scandinavian Journal of Educational Research, 35,* 227–238.

Fischette, C. T., Bigeon, A., & McEwen, B. S. (1983). Sex differences in serotonin$_1$ receptor binding. *Science, 222,* 333–335.

Fitch, R. H., Cowell, P. E., Schrott, L. M., & Denenberg, V. H. (1991). Corpus callosum: Ovarian hormones and feminization. *Brain Research, 542,* 313–317.

Forest, H. G., Deperetti, E., & Bertrand, J. (1976). Hypothalamic–pituitary–gonadal relationships from birth to puberty. *Clinical Endocrinology, 5,* 551–569.

Forest, M. G. (1990). Pituitary gonadotropin and sex steroid secretion during the first two years of life. In M. M. Grumbach, P. C. Sizonenko, & M. L. Auberrt (Eds.), *Control of the onset of puberty* (pp. 451–477). Baltimore: William and Wilkins.

Frankfurt, M., Gould, E., Woolley, C. S., & McEwen, B. S. (1990). Gonadal steroids modify dendritic spine density in ventromedial hypothalamic neurons: A Golgi study in the adult rat. *Neuroendocrinology, 51,* 530–535.

Freedman, M. B., Leary, T. F., Ossario, A. G., & Coffey, H. S. (1951). The interpersonal dimensions of personality. *Journal of Personality, 20,* 143–161.

Freud, S. (1925). Some psychical consequences of the anatomical distinction between the sexes. In J. Strachey (Ed.), *Collected papers by Sigmund Freud* (Vol. 5). London: Hogarth Press.

Freud, S. (1953). *Three essays on the theory of sexuality.* Standard edition 7. London: Hogarth Press. (Original work published in 1905.)

Gaál, A., & Csaba, G. (1997). The effect of neonatal treatment (imprinting) with retinoids (vitamin A or retinoic acid) on the binding capacity of thymic gluco-corticoid receptor and uterine estrogen receptor in adult rats. *Endocrinology and Metabolism, 4,* 115–119.

Gaffney, G. R., Lurie, S. F., & Berlin, F. S. (1984). Is there familial transmission of pedophilia? *Journal of Nervous and Mental Disease, 172,* 546–548.

Gagnon, J. (1977). Introduction. In J. Gagnon (Ed.), *Human sexuality in today's world* (pp. 11–14). Boston: Little, Brown.

Galaburda, A. M. (1992). Neurology of developmental dyslexia. *Current Opinion in Neurology and Neurosurgery, 5,* 71–76.

Gallagher-Thompson, D., Futterman, A., Farberow, N., Thompson, L. W., & Peterson, J. (1993). The impact of spousal bereavement on older widows and widowers. In M. S. Stroebe, W. Stroebe, & R. O. Hansson (Eds.), *Handbook of bereavement: Theory, research, and intervention* (pp. 227–239). Cambridge: Cambridge University Press.

Gambaryan, P. P. (1974). *How mammals run: Anatomical adaptations.* New York: John Wiley & Sons.

Gandelman, R. (1986). Uterine position and the activation of male sexual activity in testosterone propionate-treated female guinea pigs. *Hormones & Behavior, 20,* 287–293.

Gandelman, R. (1992). *Psychobiology of behavioral development.* Oxford: Oxford University Press.

Gandelman, R., vom Saal, F. S., & Reinisch, J. M. (1977). Contiguity to male fetuses affects morphology and behavior of female mice. *Nature, 266,* 722–724.

Gaulin, S. J. C., & FitzGerald, R. W. (1986). Sex differences in spatial ability: An evolutionary hypothesis and test. *American Naturalist, 127,* 74–88.

Gelernter, J., Pauls, D. L., Leckman, J., Kidd, K. K., & Kurlan, R. (1994). D2 dopam-ine receptor alleles do not influence severity of Tourette's syndrome. *Archives of Neurology, 51,* 397–400.

Gelernter, J., Pauls, D. L., Leckman, J., & Kurlan, R. (1992). Evidence that D2 dopam-ine receptor alleles do not influence severity of Tourette's syndrome. *American Journal of Psychiatry APA Meeting Abstracts,* A127–A128.

Gerra, G., Caccavari, R., Delsignore, R., Passeri, M., Fertonani, A. G., Maestri, D., Monica, C., & Brambilla, F. (1993). Parental divorce and neuroendocrine changes in adolescents. *Acta Psychiatrica Scandinavica, 87,* 350–354.

Geschwind, N., & Galburda, A. M. (1987). *Cerebral lateralization.* Cambridge: MIT Press.

Gesell, A., Thompson, A., Ilg, F., Castner, B., Ames, L., & Amatruda, C. S. (1940). *The first five years of life.* New York: Harper.

Gesell, A., Thompson, H., & Amatruda, C. S. (1938). *The psychology of early growth, including norms of infant behavior and a method of genetic analysis.* New York: Macmillan.

Gibson, D. F. C., Roberts, S. A., & Evans, G. S. (1991). Changes in the hormone dependency of epithelial cell proliferation in the genital tract of mice follow-ing neonatal oestrogen treatment. *European Journal of Cancer, 27,* 1295–1301.

Gibson, M., & Tulchinsky, D. (1980). The maternal adrenal. In D. Tulchinsky & K. J. Ryan (Eds.), *Maternal-fetal endocrinology.* Philadelphia: W. B. Saunders.

Giles, M., & Cairns, E. (1989). Colour naming of violence-related words in Northern Ireland. *British Journal of Clinical Psychology, 28,* 87–88.

Gilligan, C. (1982). *In a different voice*. Cambridge: Harvard University Press.

Giulian, D., Pohorecky, L. A., & McEwen, B. S. (1973). Effects of gonadal seroids upon brain 5-hydroxytryptamine levels in the neonatal rat. *Endocrinology, 93,* 1329–1335.

Gladue, B. A., Humphreys, R. R., De Bold, J. F., & Clemens, L. G. (1977). Ontogeny of biogenic amine systems andmodification of indole levels upon adult sexual behaviour in the rat. *Pharmacology, Biochemistry & Behaviour, 7,* 253–258.

Glass, C. K., Holloway, J. M., Devary, O. V., & Rosenfeld, M. G. (1988). The thyroid hormone receptor bind with opposite transcriptional effects to a common sequence motit in thyroid hormone and estrogen response elements. *Cell, 54,* 313–323.

Glick, S. D., & Shapiro, R. M. (1988). Functional and neurochemical asymmetries. In N. Geshwind & A. M. Galaburda (Eds.), *Cerebral dominance: The biological foundations* (pp. 147–167). Cambridge: Harvard University Press.

Golani, I., Bronchti, G., Moualem, D., & Teitelbaum, P. (1981). "Warm-up" along dimensions of movement in the ontogeny of explorations in rats and other infant mammals. *Proceedings of the National Academy of Sciences U.S.A., 78,* 7226–7229.

Goldstein, L. A., Kurz, E. M., & Sengelaub, D. R. (1990). Androgen regulation of dendritic growth and retraction in the development of a sexually dimorphic spinal nucleus. *Journal of Neuroscience, 10,* 935–946.

Gonon, F. G., Suaud-Chagny, M. F., Mermet, C. C., & Buda, M. (1991). Relation between impulse flow and extracellular catecholamine levels as studied by in vivo electrochemistry in CNS. In K. Fuxe and L. F. Agnati (Eds.), *Transmission in the brain* (pp. 337–350). New York: Raven Press.

Gonzalez, M. I., Albonetti, J. E., Siddiqui, A., Farabollini, F., & Wilson, C. A. (1996). Neonatal organizational effects of the 5HT2 and 5HT1A subsystems on adult behaviour in the rat. *Pharmacology, Biochemistry and Behaviour, 54,* 195–203.

Gonzalez, M. I., Farabollini, F., Albonetti, E., & Wilson, C.A. (1994). Interactions between 5-hydroxytryptamine (5HT) and testosterone in the control of sexual and non-sexual behaviour in male and female rats. *Pharmacology, Biochemistry & Behaviour, 47,* 591–601.

Gonzalez, M. I., & Leret, M. L. (1992). Neonatal catecholaminergic influence on behavior and sexual hormones. *Physiology & Behavior, 51,* 527–531.

Gordon, H. W. (1980). Degree of ear asymmetries for perception of dichotic chords and for illusory chord localization in musicians of different levels of competence. *Journal of Experimental Psychology: Human Perception and Performance, 6,* 516–527.

Gorski, R. A. (1984). Criticial role for the medial preoptic area in the sexual differentiation of the brain. *Progress in Brain Research, 61,* 129–146.

Gorski, R. A. (1985). Gonadal hormones as putative neurotrophic substances. In C. W. Cotman (Ed.), *Synaptic plasticity* (pp. 287–310). New York: Guilford.

Gorski, R. A., Harlan, R. E., Jacobson, C. D., Shryne, J. E., & Southam, A. M. (1980). Evidence for the existence of a sexually dimorphic nucleus in the preoptic area in the rat. *Journal of Comparative Neurology, 193,* 529–539.

Gorzalka, B. B., Mendelson, B. D., & Watson, N. V. (1990). Serotonin receptor subtypes and sexual behaviour. *Annals of New York Academy of Sciences, 600,* 435–444.

Gottesman, I. I., & Bertelsen, A. (1989). Confirming unexpressed genotypes for schizophrenia. *Archives of General Psychiatry, 46,* 867–872.

Gough, H. B. (1957). *CPI Manual.* Palo Alto, CA: Consulting Psychologists Press.

Gould, E., Woolley, C. S., Frankfurt, M., & McEwen, B. S. (1990). Gonadal steroids regulate dendritic spine density in hippocampal pyramidal cells in adulthood. *Journal of Neuroscience, 10,* 1286–1291.

Goy, R. W., Bercovitch, F. B., & McBrair, M. (1988). Behavioral masculinization is independent of genital masculinization in prenatally androgenized female rhesus macaques. *Hormones & Behavior, 22,* 552–571.

Goy, R. W., & McEwen, B. S. (1980). *Sexual differentiation of the brain.* Cambridge: MIT Press.

Goy, R. W., & Resko, J. A. (1972). Gonadal hormones and behavior of normal and pseudohermaphroditic nonhuman female primates. In E. B. Eastwood (Ed.), *Recent progress in hormone research* (pp. 707–735). New York: Academic Press.

Goy, R. W., & Roy, M. (1991). Heterotypical sexual behavior in female mammals. In M. Haug, P. C. Brain, & C. Aron (Eds.), *Heterotypical behavior in man and animals* (pp. 71–97). London: Chapman & Hall.

Goy, R. W., Wolf, J. E., & Eisele, S. G. (1978). Experimental female hermaphroditism in female rhesus monkeys: Anatomical and psychological characteristics. In J. Money & H. Mustaph (Eds.), *Handbook of Sexology* (Vol. 2, pp. 141–156). New York: Elsevier.

Graves, J. A. M. (1995). The origin and function of the mammalian Y chromosome and Y-borne genes: An evolving understanding. *BioEssays, 17,* 311–320.

Gray, J. A. (1979). Sex differences in the emotional behaviour of laboratory rodents: Comment. *British Journal of Psychology, 70,* 35–36.

Gray Nelson, K., Sakai, Y., Eitmann, B., Steed, T., & McLahlan, J. (1994). Exposure to dyethylstilbestrol during a critical developmental period of mouse reproductive tract leads to a persistent induction of two androgen-regulated genes. *Cell Growth and Differentiation, 5,* 595–606.

Green, S. (1992). Receptor-mediated mechanism of peroxisome proliferators. *Biochemical Pharmacology, 43,* 393–401.

Greene, L. A., Aletta, J. M., Rukenstein, A., & Green, S. H. (1987). PC12 pheochromocytoma cells: Culture, nerve growth factor treatment, and experimental exploitation. *Methods in Enzymology, 147,* 207–216.

Gubbay, J., Collignon, J., Koopman, P., Capel, B., Economou, A., Munsterbert, A., Vivian, N., Goodfellow, P., & Lovell-Badge, R. (1990). A gene mapping to the sex-determining region of the mouse Y chromosome is a member of a novel family of embryonically expressed genes. *Nature, 346,* 245–250.

Gurtman, M. B. (1991). Evaluating the interpersonalness of personality scales. *Personality and Social Psychology Bulletin, 17,* 670–677.

Gurtman, M. B. (1992). Construct validity of interpersonal personality measures: The interpersonal circle as a nomological net. *Journal of Personality and Social Psychology, 63,* 105–118.

Gustafsson, J.-A., Carlstedt-Duke, J., & Poellinger, L. (1987). Biochemistry, molecular biology and physiology of the glucocorticoid receptor. *Endocrinological Reviews, 8,* 185–234.

Haertzen, C. A., Martin, W. R., Ross, F. E., & Neidert, G. L. (1980). Psychopathic State Inventory (PSI): Development of a short test for measuring psychopathic states. *International Journal of the Addictions, 15,* 137–146.

Hahn, W. K. (1987). Cerebral lateralization of function: From infancy through childhood. *Psychological Bulletin, 101,* 376–392.

Haleem, D. J., Kennett, G., & Curzon, G. (1988). Adaptation of female rats to stress: Shift to male pattern by inhibition of corticosterone synthesis. *Brain Research, 458*, 339–347.

Halpern, D. F. (1992). *Sex differences in cognitive abilities* (2nd ed.). Hillsdale, NJ: Lawrence Erlbaum.

Hamdi, G. E. L., Boutroy, M. J., & Nehlig, A. (1991). Microdioenzymatic determination of regional levels of dopamine and norepinephrine in the developing rat brain. *Biogenic Amines, 8*, 115–125.

Hamer, D. H., Hu, S., Magnuson, V. L., Hu, N., & Pattatucci, A. M. L. (1993). A linkage between DNA markers on the X chromosome and male sexual orientation. *Science, 261*, 321–327.

Hamilton, W. D. (1964a). The genetical evolution of social behaviour: I. *Journal of Theoretical Biology, 7*, 1–16.

Hamilton, W. D. (1964b). The genetical evolution of social behaviour: II. *Journal of Theoretical Biology, 7*, 17–52.

Hammer, R. P., Jr. (1993). Effects of opioids on the developing brain. In R. P. Hammer, Jr. (Ed.), *The neurobiology of opiates* (pp. 1–21). Boca Raton, FL: CRC Press.

Hammer, R. P., Jr., & Jacobson, C. D. (1984). Sex difference in dendritic development of the sexually dimorphic nucleus of the preoptic area in the rat. *International Journal of Developmental Neuroscience, 2*, 77–82.

Hampson, E. (1990). Estrogen-related variations in human spatial and articulatory motor skills. *Psychoneuroendocrinology, 15*, 97–111.

Hampson, E., & Kimura, D. (1988). Reciprocal effects of hormonal fluctuations on human motor and perceptual-spatial skills. *Behavioral Neuroscience, 102*, 456–459.

Hampson, E., Rovet, J. F., & Altmann, D. (1995, May). *Sports participation and physical aggressiveness in children and young adults with congenital adrenal hyperplasia*. Poster session presented at the International Behavioral Development Symposium: Biological Basis of Sexual Orientation and Sex-typical Behavior, Minot, ND.

Handley, S. L., & Mithani, S. (1984). Effect of alpha-adrenoceptor agonists and antagonists in a maze-exploration model of "fear" motivated behavior. *Naunyn Schniedebergs Arch. Pharmacology, 327*, 1–5.

Hankinson, O. (1994). The role of the aryl hydrocarbon receptor nuclear translocator protein in aryl hydrocarbon receptor action. *Trends in Endocrinology and Metabolism, 5*, 240–244.

Haqq, C. M., King, C. Y., Donahoe, P. K., & Weiss, M. A. (1993). SRY recognizes conserved DNA sites in sex-specific promoters. *Proceedings of the National Academy of Sciences, U.S.A., 90*, 1097–1101.

Hare, R. D., Hart, S. D., & Harpur, T. J. (1994). Psychopathy and the *DSM-IV* criteria for antisocial personality disorder. *Journal of Abnormal Psychology, 100*, 391–398.

Harlow, H. (1965). Sexual behavior in the rhesus monkey. In F. A. Beach (Ed.), *Sex and behavior* (pp. 234–259, 265). New York: John Wiley & Sons.

Harpur, T. J., Hare, R. D., & Hakstian, A. R. (1989). Two-factor conceptualization of psychopathy: Construct validity and assessment implications. *Psychological Assessment: A Journal of Consulting and Clinical Psychology, 1*, 6–17.

Hart, B. L. (1967). Testosterone regulation of sexual reflexes in spinal male rats. *Science, 155*, 1283–1284.

Heinsbroek, R. P. W., van Haaren, F., Feenstra, G. P., van Galen, H., Boer, G., & van de Poll, N. E. (1990). Sex differences in the effects of inescapable footshock on central catecholaminergic and serotonergic activity. *Pharmacology, Biochemistry & Behaviour, 37,* 539–550.

Heister, G., Landis, T., Regard, M., & Schroeder-Heister, P. (1989). Shifts of functional cerebral asymmetry during the menstrual cycle. *Neuropsychologia, 27,* 871–880.

Heller, W. (1993). Gender differences in depression: Perspectives from neuropsychology. *Journal of Affective Disorders, 29,* 129–143.

Hendricks, S. E. (1992). Role of estrogens and progestins in the development of female sexual behavior potential. In A. A. Gerall, H. Moltz, & I. L. Ward (Eds.), *Handbook of behavioral neurobiology, Vol. 11. Sexual differentiation* (pp. 129–149). New York: Plenum.

Henrique, J. B., & Davidson, R. J. (1990). Regional brain electrical asymmetries discriminate between previously depressed and healthy control subjects. *Journal of Abnormal Psychology, 99,* 22–31.

Herbst, A. L., Postkanzer, D. C., Robboy, S. J., Fridlander, L., & Scully, R. E. (1975). Prenatal exposure to stilbestrol. *New England Journal of Medicine, 284,* 878–884.

Herbst, A. L., Uhlfelder, H., & Postkanzer, D. C. (1971). Adenocarcinoma of the vagina: Association of maternal stilbestrol therapy with tumor appearance in young women. *New England Journal of Medicine, 284,* 878–884.

Hier, D. B., & Crowley, W. F. (1982). Spatial ability in androgen-deficient men. *New England Journal of Medicine, 306,* 1202–1205.

Hines, M. (1982). Prenatal gonadal hormones and sex differences in human behavior. *Psychological Bulletin, 92,* 56–80.

Hines, M., & Kaufman, F. R. (1994). Androgen and the development of human sex-typical behavior: Rough and tumble play and sex of preferred playmates in children with congenital adrenal hyperplasia (CAH). *Child Development, 65,* 1042–1053.

Hofer, M. A. (1994). Hidden regulators in attachment, separation, and loss. In N. A. Fox (Ed.), *The development of emotion regulation: Biological and behavioral considerations. Monographs of the Society for Research in Child Development, 59,* 192–207.

Holm, N. V. (1988). Studies of cancer etiology in the Danish twin population: I. Breast cancer. In L. Gedda, P. Parisi, & W. Nance (Eds.), *Twin research 1: Part A. Twin biology and multiple pregnancy* (pp. 211–216). New York: Alan R. Liss

Horney, K. (1926). The flight from womanhood: The masculinity-complex in women as viewed by men and by women. *International Journal of Psychoanalysis, 7,* 324–329.

Hoyenga, K. B., & Hoyenga, K. T. (1993a). *Gender-related differences: Origins and outcomes.* Boston: Allyn & Bacon.

Hoyenga, K. B., & Hoyenga, K. T. (1993b). *Instructor's manual for gender-related differences: Origins and outcomes.* Boston: Allyn & Bacon.

Hruska, R. E., & Silbergeld, E. K. (1980). Estrogen treatment enhances dopamine receptor sensitivity in the rat striatum. *European Journal of Pharmacology, 61,* 397–401.

Hsieh, C., Lan, S., Ekbom, A., Adami, H., Petridou, E., & Trichopoulos, D., (1992). Twin membership and breast cancer risk. *American Journal of Epidemiology, 136,* 1321–1326.

Hubbert, W. T., & Miller, W. J. (1974). Immunogenetic ontogeny of cellular membrane function. *Journal of Cellular Physiology, 84,* 429–444.

Huhtaniemi I., Dunkel, L., & Perheentupa, J. (1986). Transient increase in postnatal testicular activity is not revealed by longitudinal measurements of plasma testosterone. *Paediatric Research, 20,* 1324–1327.

Hull, E. M. (1995). Dopaminergic influences on male rat sexual behavior. In P. Micevych & R. P. Hammer (Eds.), *Neurobiological effects of sex steroid hormones* (pp. 234–253). Cambridge: Cambridge University Press.

Hull, E. M., Bazzett, T. J., Warner, R. K., Eaton, R. C., & Thompson, J. T. (1990). Dopamine receptors in the ventral tegmental area modulate male sexual behavior in rats. *Brain Research, 512,* 1–6.

Hull, E. M., Bitran, D., Pehek, E. A., Warner, R. K., Band, L. C., & Holmes, G. M. (1986). Dopaminergic control of male sex behavior in rats: Effects of an intracerebrally infused agonist. *Brain Research, 370,* 73–81.

Hull, E. M., Du, J., Lorrain, D. S., & Matuszewich, L. (1995). Extracellular dopamine in the medial preoptic area: Implications for sexual motivation and hormonal control of copulation. *Journal of Neuroscience, 15,* 7465–7471.

Hull, E. M., Eaton, R. C., Markowski, V. P., Moses, J., Lumley, L. A., & Loucks J. A. (1992). Opposite influence of medial preoptic D1 and D2 receptors on genital reflexes: Implications for copulation. *Life Sciences, 51,* 1705–1713.

Hull, E. M., Nishita, J. K., Bitran, D., & Dalterio, S. (1984). Perinatal dopamine-related drugs demasculinize rats. *Science, 224,* 1011–1013.

Hull, E. M., Warner, R. K., Bazzett, T. J., Eaton, R. C., Thompson, J. T., & Scaletta, L. L. (1989). D2/D1 ratio in the medial preoptic area affects copulation of male rats. *Journal of Pharmacology and Experimental Therapeutics, 251,* 422–427.

Hull, E. M., Weber, M. S., Eaton, R. C., Dua, R., Markowski, V. P., Lumley L. A., & Moses, J. (1991). Dopamine receptors in the ventral tegmental area affect motor, but not motivational or reflexive, components of copulation in male rats. *Brain Research, 554,* 72–76.

Hunter, W. T., & Miller, W. J. (1974). Immunogenetic ontogeny of cellular membrane function: A review. *Journal of Cell Physiology, 84,* 429–444.

Hur, Y. M., McGue, M., & Iacono, W. G. (1995). Unequal rate of monozygotic and like-sex dizygotic twin births: Evidence from the Minnesota Twin Family Study. *Behavior Genetics, 25,* 337–340.

Husen, T. (1959). *Psychological twin research.* Stockholm: Almqvist & Wiksell.

Hutchings, D. E. (1993). A contemporary overview of behavioral teratology: A perspective from the field of substance abuse. In H. Kalter (Ed.), *Issues and reviews in Teratology* (pp.125–167). New York: Plenum Press.

Hutchings, D. E., Zmitrovich, A. C., Brake, S. C., Church, S. H., & Malowany, D. (1993). Prenatal administration of methadone in the rat increases offspring acoustic startle amplitude at three weeks of age. *Neurotoxicology and Teratology, 15,* 65–69.

Hutchings, D. E., Zmitrovitch, A. C., Brake, S. C., Malowany, D., Church, S. H., & Nero, T. J. (1992). Prenatal administration of methadone using osmotic minipump: Effects on maternal and offspring toxicity, growth, and behavior in the rat. *Neurotoxicology and teratology, 14,* 65–71.

Hyde, C., & Kenna, J. C. (1977). A male MZ twin pair, concordant for transsexualism, discordant for schizophrenia. *Acta Psychiatrica Scandinavica, 56,* 265–275.

Hyde, J., Fennema, S. E., & Lamon, S. J. (1990). Gender differences in mathematics performance: A meta-analysis. *Psychology Bulletin, 107,* 139–155.

Hyde, J. S., & Linn, M. C. (1988). Gender differences in verbal ability: A meta-analysis. *Psychological Bulletin, 104,* 53–69.

Hyyppa, M., Lampiren, P., & Lehtinin, P. (1972). Alterations in the sexual behaviour of male and female rats after neonatal administration of p-chlorophenylalanine. *Psychopharmacology, 25,* 125–161.

Iguchi, T. (1992). Cellular effects of early exposure to sex hormones and antihormones. *International Review of Cytology, 139,* 1–57.

Inczefi-Gonda, Á., & Csaba, G. (1985). Prolonged influence of a single neonatal steroid (dexamethasone) treatment on thymocytic steroid binding. *Experimental and Clinical Endocrinology, 85,* 358–360.

Inczefi-Gonda, Á., Csaba, G., & Dobozy, O. (1986). Reduced thymic glucocorticoid reception in adult male rats prenatally treated with allylestrenol. *Acta Physiologica Hungarica, 67,* 27–29.

Inoue, T. (1993). Effect of conditioned fear stress on immunoaminergic systems in the rat brain. *Hokkaido Journal of Medical Science, 68,* 377–390.

Irwin, M., & Pike, J. (1993). Bereavement, depressive symptoms, and immune function. In M. S. Stroebe, W. Stroebe, & R. O. Hansson (Eds.), *Handbook of bereavement: Theory, research, and intervention* (pp. 160–171). Cambridge: Cambridge University Press.

Issemann, I., & Green, S. (1990). Activation of a member of the steroid hormone receptor superfamily by peroxisome proliferators. *Nature, 347,* 645–649.

Jackisch, R., Gepper, M., & Illes, P. (1986). Characterization of opioid receptors modulating noradrenaline release in the hippocampus of the rabbit. *Journal of Neurochemistry, 46,* 1802–1810.

Jacklin, C. N., Maccoby, E., & Doering, C. H. (1983). Neonatal sex-steroid hormones and timidity in 6–18-month-old boys and girls. *Developmental Psychobiology, 16*(3), 163–168.

Jacobs, B. L., & Azmitia, E. C. (1992). Structure and function of the brain serotonin system. *Physiological Reviews, 72,* 165–229.

Jacobs, B. L., & Fornal, C. A. (1995). Serotonin and behavior: A general hypothesis. In F. E. Bloom & D. J. Kupfer (Eds.), *Psychopharmacology: The fourth generation of progress.* New York: Raven Press.

Jacobs, J. R., & Stevens, J. K. (1986). Changes in the organization of the neuritic cytoskeleton during nerve growth factor-activated differentiation of PC12 cells: A serial electron microscopic study of the development and control of neurite shape. *Journal of Cell Biology, 103,* 895–906.

Jacobson, C. D., Csernus, V. J., Shryne, J. E., & Gorski, R. A. (1981). The influence of gonadectomy, androgen exposure, or a gonadal graft in the neonatal rat on the volume of the sexually dimorphic nucleus of the preoptic area. *Journal of Neuroscience, 1,* 1142–1147.

James, S., Orwin, A., & Davies, D. W. (1972). Sex chromosome abnormality in a patient with transsexualism. *British Medical Journal, 3,* 29.

Jiang, S. Y., & Jordan, V. C. (1992). Growth regulation of estrogen receptor-negative breast cancer cells transfected with complementary DNA's for estrogen receptor. *Journal of the National Cancer Institute, 84,* 580–591.

Johansson-Wallsten, C. E., Berg, M., & Meyerson, B. J. (1993). The effects of long-term treatment with the 5HTIA receptor agonist 8-OH-DPAT and the 5HT$_{2/1C}$ receptor agonist DOI in the neonatal rat. *European Journal of Pharmacology, 243,* 149–154.

Johnson, M .D., & Crowley, W. R. (1982). 5HT turnover in individual brain nuclei: Evaluation of three methods using liquid chromotography with electrochemical detection. *Life Science, 31,* 589–595.

Johnston, H. M., Payne, A. P., & Gillmore, D. P. (1992). Perinatal exposure to morphine affects the adult sexual behavior of the male golden hamster. *Pharmacology, Biochemistry & Behaviour, 42,* 41–44.

Johnston, H. M., Payne, A. P., & Gillmore, D. P. (1994). Effects of exposure to morphine throughout gestation on feminine and masculine adult sexual behavior in golden hamster. *Journal of Reproduction & Fertility, 100,* 173–176.

Joyce, P. R., & Ding, L. (1985). Transsexual sisters. *Australian and New Zealand Journal of Psychiatry, 19,* 188–189.

Juraska, J. M. (1990). The structure of the rat cerebral cortex: Effects of gender and the environment. In B. Kolb & R. C. Tees (Eds.), *The cerebral cortex of the rat* (pp. 483–505). Cambridge: MIT Press.

Kalra, S. P. (1981). Neural loci involved in naloxone-induced luteinizing hormone release: Effects of a norepinephrine synthesis inhibitor. *Endocrinology, 109,* 1805–1810.

Kalra, S. P., & Kalra, P. S. (1984). Opioid-adrenergic connection in regulation of luteinizing hormone secretion in rat. *Neuroendocrinology, 38,* 418–426.

Kaprio, J., Koskenvuo, M., & Rose, R. J. (1990). Population-based twin registries: illustrative applications from genetic epidemiology and behavioral genetics from the Finnish twin cohort study. *Acta Geneticae Medicae et Gemellologiae, 39,* 427–439.

Karabélyos, Cs., Csaba, G., & Dalló, J. (1994). Effect of treatments with contraceptive steroids on the sexual behaviour of rats pretreated with benzpyrene or allylestrenol in fetal or neonatal age. *Hormone and Metabolic Research, 26,* 371–373.

Karabélyos, Cs., Dalló, J., & Csaba, G. (1994). Effects of benzpyrene and allylestrenol administered during pregnancy on the sexual behaviour of castrated and hormone treated adult rats. *Acta Physiologica Hungarica, 82,* 175–180.

Karabélyos, Cs., Szeberényi, Sz., & Csaba, G. (1994). Effect of allylestrenol exposure during pregnancy on the activity of microsomal enzyme system (PSMO) of the rat in the F1 and F2 generations. *Acta Physiologica Hungarica, 82,* 15–22.

Kason, M. L., Ward, O. B., Grisham, W., & Ward, I. L. (1992). Prenatal-endorphin can modulate some aspects of sexual differentiation in rats. *Behavioral Neuroscience, 106*(3), 555–562.

Kelley, D. B., & Dennison, J. (1990). The vocal motor neurons of *Xenopus laevis*: Development of sex differences in axon number. *Journal of Neurobiology, 21,* 869–882.

Kellogg, C. K., & Rettel, T. M. (1986). Release of ^{3}H norepinephrine: Alterations by early developmental exposure to diazepam. *Brain Research, 366,* 137–144.

Kemper, T. D. (1992). *Social structure and testosterone.* New Brunswick: Rutgers University Press.

Kennett, G. A., Chaouloff, F., Marcou, M., & Curzon, G. (1986). Female rats are more vulnerable than males in an animal model of depression: The possible role of serotonin. *Brain Research, 382,* 416–421.

Kerr, J. E., Allore, R. J., Beck, S. G., & Handa, R. J. (1995). Distribution and hormonal regulation of androgen receptor (AR) and AR messenger ribonucleic acid in the rat hippocampus. *Endocrinology, 136,* 3213–3221.

Khachaturian, H., & Watson, S. J. (1982). Some perspectives on monoamine-opioid peptide interaction in rat central nervous system. *Brain Research, 9,* 441–462.

Kiesler, D. J. (1983). The 1982 interpersonal circle: A taxonomy for complementarity in human transactions. *Psychological Review, 90,* 185–214.

Kim, K., & Jacobs, S. (1993). Neuroendocrine changes following bereavement. In M. S. Stroebe, W. Stroebe, & R. O. Hansson (Eds.), *Handbook of bereavement: Theory, research, and intervention* (pp. 143–159). Cambridge: Cambridge University Press.

Kimball, M. M. (1995). *Feminist visions of gender similarities and differences.* New York: Haworth Press.

Kimura, D., & Hampson, E. (1994). Cognitive pattern in men and women is influenced by fluctuations in sex hormones. *Current Directions in Psychological Science, 3,* 57–61.

Kinsley, C., Konen, C., Miele, J., Ghiraldi, L., & Svare, B. (1986). Intrauterine position modulates maternal behavior in female mice. *Physiology & Behavior, 36,* 793–799.

Kinsley, C., Miele, J., Konen, C., Ghiraldi, L., Broida, J., & Svare, B. (1986). Intrauterine contiguity influences regulatory activity in adult male and female mice. *Hormones & Behavior, 20,* 7–12.

Kinsley, C., Miele, J., Wagner, C. K., Ghiraldi, L., Broida, J., & Svare, B. (1986). Prior intrauterine position influences body weight in male and female mice. *Hormones & Behavior, 20,* 201–211.

Kiyatkin, E. A. (1995). Functional significance of mesolimbic dopamine. *Neuroscience and Biobehavioral Reviews, 19,* 573–598.

Kleiman, R., Banker, G., & Steward, O. (1990). Differential subcellular localization of particular mRNAs in hippocampal neurons in culture. *Neuron, 5,* 821–830.

Klein, M. (1975). Early stages of the Oedipus conflict. In *Love, guilt and reparation and other works, 1921–1945: The writings of Melanie Klein* (Vol. 1). New York: Delacorte Press/Seymour Lawrence. (Original work published in 1928.)

Koch, H. L. (1955). Some personality correlates of sex, sibling position, and sex of sibling among five- and six-year-old children. *Genetic Psychology Monographs, 52,* 3–50.

Koch, H. L. (1966). *Twins and twin relations.* Chicago: University of Chicago Press.

Kohlberg, L. (1966). A cognitive developmental analysis of children's sex-role concepts and attitudes. In E. E. Maccoby (Ed.), *The development of sex differences* (pp. 82–173). Stanford, CA: Stanford University Press.

Kolb, B., & Stewart, J. (1991). Sex-related differences in dendritic branching of cells in the prefrontal cortex of rats. *Journal of Neuroendocrinology, 3,* 95–99.

Kosaka, T., & Hama, K. (1985). Gap junctions between non-pyramidal cell dendrites in the rat hippocampus (CA1 and CA3 regions): A combined Golgi-electron microscopy study. *Journal of Comparative Neurology, 231,* 150–161.

Kosson, D. S., & Newman, J. P. (1986). Psychopathy and the allocation of attentional capacity in a divided-attention situation. *Journal of Abnormal Psychology, 95,* 257–263.

Kosson, D. S., & Newman, J. P. (1989). Socialization and attentional deficits under focusing and divided attention conditions. *Journal of Personality and Social Psychology, 57,* 87–99.

Kuipers, H., Wijnen, J. A., Hartgens, F., & Willems, S. M. (1991). Influence of anabolic steroids on body composition, blood pressure, lipid profile and liver functions in body builders. *International Journal of Sports and Medicine, 12,* 413–418.

Kujawa, K. A., & Jones, K. J. (1990). Testosterone-induced acceleration of recovery from facial paralysis in male hamsters: Temporal requirements of hormone exposure. *Physiology & Behavior, 48,* 765–768.

Kyes, R. C., Botchin, M. B., Kaplan, J. R., Manuck, S. B., & Mann, J. J. (1995). Aggression and brain serotonergic responsivity: Response to slides in male macaques. *Physiology & Behavior, 57,* 205–208.

Ladosky, W., & Gaziri, L. C. (1970). Brain serotonin and sexual differentiation of the nervous system. *Neuroendocrinology, 6,* 168–174.

Laforge, R., Leary, T. F., Naboisek, H., Coffey, H. S., & Freedman, M. B. (1954). The interpersonal dimensions of personality: II. An objective study of repression. *Journal of Personality, 21,* 129–153.

Lal, S. (1988). Apomorphine in the evaluation of dopaminergic function in man. *Progress in Neuro-Psychopharmacology and Biological Psychiatry, 12,* 117–164.

Landers, D. M. (1970). Sibling-sex-status and ordinal position effects on female sport participation and interests. *The Journal of Social Psychology, 80,* 247–248.

Landis, S. C. (1983). Neuronal growth cones. *Annual Review of Physiology, 45,* 567–580.

Langer, S. Z. (1977). Presynaptic receptors and their role in the regulation of transmitter release. *British Journal of Pharmacology, 60,* 481–497.

Langley, J. N. (1906). On nerve-endings and on special excitable substances in cells. *Proceeding of the Royal Society of London, 78* (Series B), 170–194.

Lankford, K. L., DeMello, F. G., & Klein, W. L. (1988). D1-type dopamine receptors inhibit growth cone motility in cultured retina neurons: Evidence that neurotransmitters act as morphogenic growth regulators in the developing central nervous system. *Proceedings of the National Academy of Sciences, U.S.A., 85,* 2839–2843.

Larsson, K., Sodersten, P., Beyer, C., Morali, G., & Perez-Palacios, G. (1976). Effects of estrone, estradiol, and estriol combined with dihydrotestosterone on mounting and lordosis behavior in castrated male rats. *Hormones & Behavior, 7,* 379–390.

Lauder, J. M. (1990). Ontogeny of the serotonergic system in the rat: Serotonin as a developmental signal. In P. M. Whitaker-Azmitia & S. J. Peroutka (Eds.), *The neuropharmacology of serotonin* (pp. 297–314). New York: New York Academy of Sciences.

Lauder, J. M. (1993). Neurotransmitters as growth regulatory signals: Role of receptors and second messengers. *Trends in Neurosciences, 16,* 223–240.

Lee, P. C. (1976). Anthropology and sex differences. In P. C. Lee & R. S. Stewart (Eds.), *Sex differences: Cultural and developmental dimensions* (pp. 153–159). New York: Urizen Books.

Lee, P. C., & Stewart, R. S. (1976). *Sex differences: Cultural & developmental dimensions*. New York: Urizen Books.

Leers, J., Steiner, C., Rankowitz, R., & Muller, M. (1994). A thyroid hormone receptor dependent glucocorticoid induction. *Molecular Endocrinology, 8,* 440–447.

Lenney, E. (1991). Sex roles in the measurement of masculinity, femininity, and androgyny. In J. P. Robinson, P. R. Shaver, & L. S. Wrightsman (Eds.), *Measures of personality and social psychological attitudes: Vol. 1. Measures of psychological attitudes* (pp. 573–660). San Diego: Academic Press.

Lephart, E. D., Fleming, D. E., & Rhees, W. (1989). Fetal male masculinization in control and prenatally stressed rats. *Developmental Psychobiology, 22,* 707–716.

Leret, M., Gonzalez, M. I., Tranque, P., & Fraile, A. (1987). Influence of sexual differentiation on striatal and limbic catecholamines. *Comparative Biochemistry and Physiology, 86C,* 299–303.

LeVay, S. (1991). A difference in hypothalamic structure between heterosexual and homosexual men. *Science, 253,* 1034–1037.

Leventhal, G. S. (1970). Influence of brothers and sisters on sex-role behavior. *Journal of Personality and Social Psychology, 16,* 452–465.

Levin, M. (1987). *Feminism & freedom*. New Brunswick: Transaction Books.

Levy, J. (1969). Possible basis for the evolution of lateral specialization of the human brain. *Nature, 224,* 612–615.

Levy, J. (1971). Lateral specialization of the human brain: Behavioral manifestations and possible evolutionary basis. In J. A. Kiger, Jr. (Ed.), *The biology of behavior* (pp. 159–180). Corvallis: Oregon State University Press.

Liakos, A. (1967). Familial transvestism. *British Journal of Psychiatry, 113,* 49–51.

Lippa, R. (1991). Some psychometric characteristics of gender diagnosticity measures: Reliability, validity, consistency across domains and relationship to the Big Five. *Journal of Personality and Social Psychology, 61,* 1000–1011.

Lippa, R. (1995a). Do sex differences define gender-related individual differences within the sexes? Evidence from three studies. *Personality and Social Psychology Bulletin, 21,* 349–355.

Lippa, R. (1995b). Gender-related individual differences and psychological adjustment in terms of the Big Five and circumplex models. *Journal of Personality and Social Psychology, 69,* 1184–1202.

Lippa, R., & Connelly, S. C. (1990). Gender diagnosticity: A new Bayesian approach to gender-related individual differences. *Journal of Personality and Social Psychology, 59,* 1051–1065.

Littlefield, C. H., & Rushton, J. P. (1986). When a child dies: The sociobiology of bereavement. *Journal of Personality and Social Psychology, 51,* 797–802.

Liu, F.-C., Takahashi, H., McKay, R. D. G., & Graybiel, A. M. (1995). Dopaminergic regulation of transcription factor expression in organotypic cultures of developing striatum. *Journal of Neuroscience, 15,* 2367–2384.

Loehlin, J. C., & Nichols, R. C. (1976). *Heredity, environment, and personality: A study of 850 sets of twins*. Austin: University of Texas Press.

Loizou, L. A. (1972). The postnatal ontogeny of monoamine containing neurons in the central nervous system of the albino rat. *Brain Research, 40,* 395–418.

Lonnetto, R., & Templer, D. I. (1986). *Death anxiety*. Washington, DC: Hemisphere.

Lorenz, K. (1965). *Evolution and modification of behavior*. Chicago: University of Chicago Press.

Lorenzo, A., Diaz, H., Carrer, H. F., & Caceres, A. (1992). Amygdala neurons in vitro: Neurite growth and effects of estradiol. *Journal of Neuroscience Research, 33,* 418–435.

Lowrance, E. W. (1968). Linear growth and appearance of sex difference in the rabbit pelvis. *Anatomical Records, 161,* 413–418.

Loy, R., & Milner, T. A. (1980). Sexual dimorphism in extent of axonal sprouting in rat hippocampus. *Science, 208,* 1282–1284.

Lubinski, D., & Humphreys, L. G. (1990). A broadly based analysis of mathematical giftedness. *Intelligence, 14,* 327–355.

Lucot, J. B., & Seiden, L. S. (1986). Effects of serotonergic agonists and antagonists on the locomotor activity of neonatal rats. *Pharmacology, Biochemistry and Behaviour, 24,* 537–541.

Luine, V. N., & McEwen, B. S. (1983). Sex differences in cholinergic enzymes of diagonal band nuclei in rat preoptic area. *Neuroendocrinology, 36,* 475–482.

Lund, D. A., Caserta, M. S., & Dimond, M. F. (1993). The course of spousal bereavement in late life. In M. S. Stroebe, W. Stroebe, & R. O. Hansson (Eds.), *Handbook of bereavement: Theory, research, and intervention* (pp. 240–254). Cambridge: Cambridge University Press.

Lunn, S. F., Recio, R., Morris, K., & Fraser, H. M. (1994). Blockade of the neonatal rise in testosterone by a gonadotrophin-releasing hormone antagonist: Effects on timing of puberty and sexual behavior in the male marmoset monkey. *Journal of Endocrinology, 141,* 439–447.

Lustig, R. H., Hua, P., Smith, L. S., Wang, C., & Chang, C. (1994). An *in vitro* model for the effects of androgen on neurons using androgen receptor-transfected PC12 cells. *Molecular and Cellular Neurosciences, 5,* 587–596.

Lustig, R. H., Hua, P., Yu, W., Ahmad, F., & Baas, P. W. (1994). An *in vitro* model for the effects of estrogen on neurons using estrogen receptor-transfected PC12 cells. *Journal of Neuroscience, 14,* 3945–3957.

Lustig, R. H., Sharp, D. J., & Baas, P. W. (1995, June). *Androgen stimulates axonal outgrowth at the expense of dendritic outgrowth in primary hippocampal neurons in culture*. Poster presentation at the 77th annual meeting of the Endocrine Society, Washington, DC.

Luttge, W. G., & Whalen, R. E. (1970). Dihydrotestosterone, androstenedione, testosterone: Comparative effectiveness in masculinizing and defeminizing reproductive systems in male and female rats. *Hormones & Behavior, 1,* 265–281.

Lykken, D. T., Bouchard, T. J., McGue, M., & Tellegen, A. (1990). The Minnesota twin family registry: Some initial findings. *Acta Geneticae Medicae et Gemellologiae, 39,* 35–70.

Mabry, P. D., & Campbell, B. A. (1974). Ontogeny of serotonergic inhibition of behavioral arousal in the rat. *Journal of Comparative Physiology and Psychology, 86,* 193–201.

Mabry, T. R., Gold, P. E., & McCarty, R. (1995). Age-related changes in plasma catecholamine responses to chronic intermittent stress. *Physiology & Behavior, 58,* 49–56.

Maccoby, E. E. (1966). Sex difference in intellectual functioning. In E. E. Maccoby (Ed.), *The development of sex differences* (pp. 25–55). Stanford, CA: Stanford University Press.

Maccoby, E. E., Doering, C. H., Jacklin, C. N., & Kraemer, H. (1979). Concentrations of sex hormones in umbilical cord blood: Their relation to sex and birth order in infants. *Child Development, 50,* 632–642.

Maccoby, E. E., & Jacklin, C. N. (1974). *The psychology of sex differences.* Stanford, CA: Stanford University Press.

MacDonald, K. (1995). Evolution, the five-factor model, and levels of personality. *Journal of Personality, 63,* 525–567.

MacLusky, N. J., Clark, A. S., Naftolin, F., & Goldman-Rakic, P. S. (1987). Estrogen formation in the mammalian brain: Possible role of aromatase in sexual differentiation of the hippocampus and neocortex. *Steroids, 50,* 459–474.

MacLusky, N. J., & Naftolin, F. (1981). Sexual differentiation of the central nervous system. *Science, 211,* 1294–1303.

MacMurray, J., Saucier, G., Muhleman, D., Gade, R., Ferry, L., Miller, W., Wu, S., Blake, H., Johnson, J., Verde, R., & Comings, D. (1996). Polygenic prediction of parity: $GABA_A$-B3 and dopamine DRD4 gene markers. *Psychiatric Genetics, 6,* 161.

Maes, M., & Meltzer, H. Y. (1995). The serotonin hypothesis of major depression. In F. E. Bloom & D. J. Kupfer (Eds.), *Psychopharmacology: The fourth generation of progress.* New York: Raven Press.

Maggi, A., Susanna, L., Bettini, E., Mantero, G., & Zucchi, I. (1989). Hippocampus: A target for estrogen action in mammalian brain. *Molecular Endocrinology, 3,* 1165–1170.

Malmnas, C. O. (1973). Monoaminergic influence on testosterone-activated copulatory behavior in the castrated male rat. *Acta Physiologica Scandinavica, Supplementum, 395,* 1–128.

Malmnas, C. O. (1977). Dopaminergic reversal of the decline after castration of rat copulatory behavior. *Endocrinology, 73,* 187–188.

Mankes, R. F., Glick, S. D., Van der Hoeven, F., & LeFevre, R. (1991). Alcohol preference and hepatic alcohol dehydrogenase activity in adult long-evans rats is affected by intrauterine sibling contiguity. *Alcohol: Clinical and Experimental Research, 15,* 80–85.

Mann, D. R., & Fraser, H. M. (1996). The neonatal period: A critical interval in primate development. *Journal of Endocrinology.*

Mann, D. R., Gould, K. G., Collins, D. C., & Wallen, K. (1989). Blockade of neonatal activation of the pituitary-testicular axis: Effect on peripubertal lutenizing hormone and testosterone secretion and on testicular development in male monkeys. *Journal of Clinical Endochronology and Metabolism, 68,* 600–607.

Mann, J. J., McBride, P. A., Malone, K. M., DeMeo, M., & Keilp, J. (1995). Blunted serotonergic responsivity in depressed inpatients. *Neuropsychopharmacology, 13,* 53–64.

Margolis, R., Tanner, K., Seminara, D., & Taylor, S. I. (1990). Insulin receptors in developing rat liver. *Biology of Neonate, 58,* 227–235.

Markowski, V. P., Eaton, R. C., Lumley, L. A., Moses, J., & Hull, E. M. (1994). A D1 agonist in the MPOA facilitates copulation in male rats. *Pharmacology, Biochemistry, & Behaviour, 47,* 483–486.

Marson, L., List, M. S., & McKenna, K. E. (1992). Lesions of the nucleus paragigantocellularis alter ex copula penile reflexes. *Brain Research, 592,* 187–192.

Marson, L., & McKenna, K. E. (1990). The identification of a brainstem site controlling spinal sexual reflexes in male rats. *Brain Research, 515,* 303–308.

Marson, L., & McKenna, K. E. (1992). A role for 5-hydroxytryptamine in descending inhibition of spinal sexual reflexes. *Experimental Brain Research, 88,* 313–320.

Marson, L., & McKenna, K. E. (1994). Serotonergic neurotoxic lesions facilitate male sexual reflexes. *Pharmacology, Biochemistry & Behaviour, 47,* 883–888.

Martens, D. J., Field, E. F., Pellis, V. C., & Pellis, S. M. (1996, November). *The development of rotatory movements around the longitudinal axis during contact fighting: Sex differences in the organization of rotatory movements.* Poster presented at the Society for Neuroscience, Washington, DC.

Martin, J. L., & Dean, L. (1993). Bereavement following death from AIDS: Unique problems, reactions, and special needs. In M. S. Stroebe, W. Stroebe, & R. O. Hansson (Eds.), *Handbook of bereavement: Theory, research, and intervention* (pp. 317–330). Cambridge: Cambridge University Press.

Martin, N. G., Eaves, L. J., Heath, A. C., Jardine, R., Lynn, R., Feingold, M., & Eysenck, H. J. (1986). Transmission of social attitudes. *Proceedings of the National Academy of Sciences, U.S.A., 838.*

Mason, S. T. (1984). *Catecholamines and behavior.* Cambridge: Cambridge University Press.

Matheny, A. P. (1988). Accidental injuries. In D. K. Routh (Ed.), *Handbook of pediatric psychology* (pp. 108–134). New York: Guilford Press.

Matsumoto, A. (1991). Synaptogenic action of sex steroids in developing and adult neuroendocrine brain. *Psychoneuroendocrinology, 16,* 25–40.

Matsumoto, A. (1992). Sex steroid induction of synaptic reorganization in adult neuroendocrine brain. *Reviews in the Neurosciences, 3,* 287–306.

Matsumoto, A., & Arai, Y. (1979). Synaptogenic effect of estrogen on the hypothalamic arcuate nucleus of the adult female rat. *Cell and Tissue Research, 198,* 427–433.

Matsumoto, A., & Arai, Y. (1980). Sexual dimorphism in "wiring pattern" in the hypothalamic arcuate nucleus and its modification by neonatal hormonal environment. *Brain Research, 190,* 238–242.

Matsumoto, A., & Arai, Y. (1986). Development of sexual dimorphism in synaptic organization in the ventromedial nucleus of the hypothalamus in rats. *Neuroscience Letters, 68,* 165–168.

Matsumoto, A., Arnold, A. P., Zampighi, G. A., & Micevych, P. E. (1988). Androgenic regulation of gap junctions between motoneurons in the rat spinal cord. *Journal of Neuroscience, 8,* 4177–4183.

Matsumoto, A., Micevych, P. E., & Arnold, A. P. (1988). Androgen regulates synaptic input to motoneurons of the adult rat spinal cord. *Journal of Neuroscience, 8,* 4168–4176.

Mattia, J. I., Heimberg, R. G., & Hope, D. A. (1993). The revised Stroop color-naming task in social phobics. *Behavioral Research and Therapy, 31,* 305–313.

McCrae, R. R., & Costa, P. T. (1989). The structure of interpersonal traits: Wiggins's Circle and the five-factor model. *Journal of Personality and Social Psychology, 56,* 586–595.

McCrae, R. R., & Costa, P. T. (1993). Psychological resilience among widowed men and women: A longitudinal follow-up of a national sample. In M. S. Stroebe, W. Stroebe, & R. O. Hansson (Eds.), *Handbook of bereavement: Theory, research, and intervention* (pp. 196–207). Cambridge: Cambridge University Press.

McDermott, N. J., Gandleman, R., & Reinisch, J. M. (1978). Contiguity to male fetuses influences ano-genital distance and time of vaginal opening in mice. *Psychology & Behavior, 20,* 661–663.

McEwen, B. S. (1978). Sexual maturation and differentiation: The role of the gonadal steroids. *Progress in Brain Research, 48,* 281–307.

McEwen, B. S. (1983). Gonadal steroid influences on brain development and sexual differentiation. In *Reproductive physiology IV* (pp. 99–123). Baltimore: University Park Press.

McEwen, B. S., Bigeon, A., Fischette, C. T., Luine, V. N., Parsons, B., & Rainbow, T. C. (1984). Sex differences in programming of responses to estradiol in the brain. In M. Serio (Ed.), *Sexual differentiation: Basic and clinical aspects* (pp. 93–98). New York: Raven Press.

McEwen, B. S., Lieberburg, I., Chaptal, C., & Krey, L. C. (1977). Aromatization: Important for sexual differentiation of the neonatal rat brain. *Hormones & Behavior, 9,* 249–263.

McEwen, B. S., Pfaff, D. W., & Zigmond, R. E. (1970). Factors influencing sex hormone uptake by rat brain regions: III. Effects of competing steroids on testosterone uptake. *Brain Research, 21,* 29–38.

McFadden, D. (1993a). A masculinizing effect on the auditory systems of human females having male co-twins. *Proceedings of the National Academy of Sciences, U.S.A., 90,* 11900–11904.

McFadden, D. (1993b). A speculation about the paralleled ear asymmetries and sex differences in hearing sensitivity and otoacoustic emissions. *Hearing Research, 68,* 143–151.

McGlone, J. (1980). Sex differences in human brain asymmetry: A critical survey. *The Behavioral and Brain Sciences, 3,* 215–263.

McGue, M., Vaupel, J. W., Holm, N., & Harvald, B. (1993). Longevity is moderately heritable in a sample of Danish twins born 1870–1880. *Journal of Gerontology, 48,* B237–B244.

McKee, E. A., Roback, H. B., & Hollender, M. H. (1976). Transsexualism in two male triplets. *American Journal of Psychiatry, 133,* 334–340.

McKenna, K. E., Chung, S. K., & McVary, K. T. (1991). A model for the study of sexual function in anesthetized male and female rats. *American Journal of Physiology, 261,* R1276–R1285.

Mead, L. A., & Hampson, E. (1995). A selective effect of ovarian hormones on left visual field performance in verbal and nonverbal tachistoscopic tasks. *Journal of the International Neuropsychological Society, 1,* 176.

Mead, L. A., Hargreaves, E. L., & Galea, L. A. M. (1996). Sex differences in rodent spontaneous activity levels. In P. R. Sanberg, K.-P. Ossenkopp, & M. Kavaliers (Eds.), *Motor activity and movement disorders: Recent issues and applications* (pp. 111–139). Totowa, NJ: Humana Press.

Mead, M. (1935). *Sex and temperament in three primitive societies.* New York: Wm. Morrow.

Meaney, M. (1988). The sexual differentiation of social play. *Trends in Neuroscience, 11,* 54–58.

Meaney, M. (1989). The sexual differentiation of social play. *Psychiatric Developments, 3,* 347–361.

Meaney, M. J., & Stewart, J. (1981). A descriptive study of social development in the rat (*Rattus norvegicus*). *Animal Behaviour, 29,* 34–45.

Meaney, M. J., Stewart, J., & Beatty, W. W. (1985). Sex differences in social play: The socialization of sex roles. *Advances in the Study of Behavior, 15,* 1–58.

Mehlman, P. T., Higley, J. D., Faucher, I., Lilly, A. A., Taub, D. M., Vickers, J., Suomi, S. J., & Linnoila, M. (1994). Low CSF 5-HIAA concentrations and severe aggression and impaired impulse control in nonhuman primates. *American Journal of Psychiatry, 151,* 1485–1491.

Meisel, R. L., & Sachs, B. D. (1994). The physiology of male sexual behavior. In E. Knobil and J. D. Neill (Eds.), *Physiology of reproduction* (2nd ed., pp. 3–106). New York: Raven Press.

Meisel, R. L., & Ward, I. L. (1981). Fetal female rats are masculinized by male litter mates located causally in the uterus. *Science, 213,* 239–241.

Melis, M. R., & Argiolas, A. (1993). Nitric oxide synthase inhibitors prevent apomorphine- and oxytocin-induced penile erection and yawning in male rats. *Brain Research Bulletin, 32,* 71–74.

Melis, M. R., & Argiolas, A. (1995). Dopamine and sexual behavior. *Neuroscience and Biobehavioral Reviews, 19,* 19–38.

Mendelson, S. D., & Gorzalka, B. B. (1986). 5HT1A receptors: Differential involvement in female and male sexual behaviour in the rat. *Physiology & Behavior, 37,* 345–351.

Meulenberg, P. M. M., & Hofman, J. A. (1990). Maternal testosterone and fetal sex. *Journal of Steroid Biochemistry and Molecular Biology, 39,* 51–54.

Meyer-Bahlburg, H. F. L. (1997). The role of prenatal estrogens in sexual orientation. In L. Ellis & L. Ebertz (Eds.), *Sexual orientation: Toward biological understanding.* Westport, CT: Praeger.

Meyerson, B., & Malmnas, C. (1978). Brain monoamines and sexual behaviour. In J. Hutchinson (Ed.), *Biological determinants of sexual behavior* (pp.165–191). New York: John Wiley & Sons.

Meyerson, B. J., & Terenius, T. N. (1977). Beta-endorphin and male sexual behavior. *European Journal of Pharmacology, 42,* 191–192.

Miklyaeva, E. I., Martens, D. J., & Whishaw, I. Q. (1995). Impairments and compensatory adjustments in spontaneous movements after unilateral dopamine-depletion in rats. *Brain Research, 681,* 23–40.

Miller, E. M. (1992). On the correlation of myopia and intelligence. *Genetic, Social, and General Psychology Monographs, 118,* 363–383.

Miller, E. M. (1994a). Prenatal sex hormone transfer: A reason to study opposite-sex twins. *Personality and Individual Differences, 17,* 511–529.

Miller, E. M. (1994b). The relevance of group membership for personnel selection: A demonstration using Bayes theorem. *Journal of Social, Political, and Economic Studies, 19,* 323–359.

Miller, E. M. (1995). Reported myopia in opposite sex twins: A hormonal hypothesis. *Optometry and Vision Sciences, 72,* 34–36.

Miller, E. M., & Martin, N. G. (1995) Analysis of the effects of hormones on opposite-sex twin attitudes. *Acta Geneticae Medicae et Gemellologiae, 44,* 41–52.

Miller, W. B., MacMurray, J., Chiu, C., Wu, S., Pasta, D. J., & Comings, D. E. (1996). *Dopamine receptor genes are associated with age at first intercourse.* Manuscript submitted for publication.

Mirzahosseini, S., Karabélyos, Cs., Dobozy, O., & Csaba, G. (1996). Changes in sexual behaviour of adult male and female rat neonatally treated with vitamin D$_3$. *Human & Experimental Toxicology, 15,* 573–576.

Mitchel, J. E., Baker, L. A., & Jacklin, C. N. (1989). Masculinity and femininity in twin children: Genetic and environmental factors. *Child Development, 60,* 1475–1485.

Mitchell, V., Beauvillian, J. C., Poulain, P., & Mazzuca, M. (1977). Catecholamine and male sexual behaviour. *European Journal of Pharmacology, 42,* 191–192.

Mitchell, V., Beauvillian, J. C., Poulain, P., & Mazzuka, M. (1988). Catecholamine innervation of enkephalinergic neurons in guinea pig hypothalamus: Demonstration by an in vivo autoradiographic technique combined with a post-embedding immunogold method. *Journal of Histochemistry and Cytochemistry, 36,* 611–617.

Moeller, F. G., Steinberg, J. L., Petty, F., Fulton, M., Cherek, D. R., Kramer, G., & Garver, D. L. (1994). Serotonin and impulsive/aggressive behavior in cocaine dependent subjects. *Progress in Neuro-Psychopharmacology & Biological Psychiatry, 18,* 1027–1035.

Moffat, S. D., & Hampson, E. (1996). A curvilinear relationship between testosterone and spatial cognition in humans: Possible influence of hand preference. *Psychoneuroendocrinology, 21,* 323–337.

Moir, A., & Jessel, D. (1992). *Brain sex.* New York: Dell.

Money, J. (1988). *Gay, straight and in-between: The sexology of erotic orientation.* New York: Oxford University Press.

Money, J., & Ehrhardt, A. A. (1972). *Man and woman, boy and girl.* Baltimore: Johns Hopkins University Press.

Moore, K. E., & Johnston, C. A. (1982). The median eminence aminergic control mechanisms. In J. E. Mullerand & J. R. MacLeod (Eds.), *Neuroendocrine Perspectives* (Vol. 1, pp. 23–68). Amsterdam: Elsevier.

Moore, K. E., & Lookingland, K. J. (1995). Dopaminergic systems in the hypothalamus. In F. E. Bloom & D. J. Kupfer (Eds.), *Psychopharmacology: The fourth generation of progress* (pp. 245–256). New York: Raven Press.

Morey, L. C., Waugh, M. H., & Blashfield, R. K. (1985). MMPI scales for DSM-III personality disorders: Their derivation and correlates. *Journal of Personality Assessment, 49,* 245–251.

Morilak, D. A., Somogyi, P., Lujan-Miras, R., & Ciaranello, R. D. (1994). Nervous expressing 5HT$_2$ receptors in the rat brain: Neurochemical identification of cell types by immunocytochemistry. *Neuropsychopharmacology, 11,* 157–166.

Morissetti, M., & di Paolo, T. (1993). Sex and estrous cycle variations of rat striatal dopamine uptake sites. *Neuroendocrinology, 58,* 16–22.

Morrissey, T. K., Pellis, S. M., Pellis, V. C., & Teitelbaum, P. (1989). Seemingly paradoxical jumping in cataleptic haloperidol-treated rats is triggered by postural instability. *Behavioural Brain Research, 35,* 195–207.

Mos, J., Olivier, B., Potts, M., & van Aben, H. (1992). The effects of intraventricular administration of eltoprazine, 1-(3-trifluoromethylphenyl)-piperazine hydrochloride and 8-hydroxy-2-(di-n-propylamino) tetralin on resident-intruder aggression in the rat. *European Journal of Pharmacology, 212,* 295–298.

Moses, J., Loucks, J. A., Watson, H. L., Matuszewich, L., & Hull, E. M. (1995). Dopaminergic drugs in the medial preoptic area and nucleus accumbens: Effects on motor activity, sexual motivation and sexual performance. *Pharmacology, Biochemistry, & Behaviour, 51,* 681–686.

Moss, H. B., Yao, J. K., & Panzak, G. L. (1990). Serotonergic responsivity and behavioral dimensions in antisocial personality disorder with substance abuse. *Biological Psychiatry, 28,* 325–338.

Mowrer, E. (1954). Some factors in the affectional adjustment of twins. *American Sociological Review, 19,* 468–471.

Mowszowicz, I., Lee, H. J., Chen, H. T., Mestayer, C., Portois, M. C., Cabrol, S., Mauvais-Jarvis, P., & Chang, C. (1993). A point mutation in the second zinc finger of the DNA-binding domain of the androgen receptor gene causes complete androgen insensitivity in two siblings with receptor-positive androgen resistance. *Molecular Endocrinology, 7,* 861–869.

Mulder, A. H., Burger, D. M., Wardeh, G., Hogenboom, F., & Frankhuyzen, A. L. (1991). Pharmacological profile of various κ-agonist at κ-, μ- and δ-opioid receptors mediating presynaptic inhibition of neurotransmitter release in the rat brain. *British Journal of Pharmacology, 102,* 518–522.

Mulder, A. H., Hogenboom, F., Wardeh, G., & Schoffelmer, A. N. (1987). Morphine and enkephalins potently inhibit [³H]noradrenaline release from rat brain cortex synaptosomes: Further evidence for presynaptic localization of μ-opioid receptors. *Journal of Neurochemistry, 48,* 1043–1047.

Mulder, A. H., Wardeh, G., Hogenboom, F., & Frankhuyzen, A. L. (1989). Selectivity of various opioid peptides toward δ-, κ- and μ-opioid receptors mediating presynaptic inhibition of neurotransmitter release in the brain. *Neuropeptides, 14,* 99–104.

Muller, J., & Skakkeback, N. E. (1984). Fluctuations in the number of germ cells during the late foetal and early postnatal periods in boys. *Acta Endocrinologica, 105,* 271.

Myoga, H., Nonaka, S., Matsuyama, K., & Mori, S. (1995). Postnatal development of locomotor movements in normal and para-chlorophenylalanine-treated newborn rats. *Neuroscience Research, 21,* 211–221.

Nash, S. C. (1979). Sex role as a mediator of intellectual functioning. In M. A. Wittig & A. C. Petersen (Eds.), *Sex-related differences in cognitive functioning: Developmental issues* (pp. 303–332). New York: Academic Press.

Nass, R., & Baker, S. (1991). Androgen effects on cognition: Congenital adrenal hyperplasia. *Psychoneuroendocrinology, 16,* 189–202.

Nass, R., Baker, S., Speiser, P., Virdis, R., Balsamo, A., Cacciari, E., Loche, A., Dumic, M., & New, M. (1987). Hormones and handedness: Left-hand bias in female congenital adrenal hyperplasia patients. *Neurology, 37,* 711–715.

Nee, L. E., Caine, E. D., Polinsky, R. J., Eldridge, R., & Ebert, M. H. (1980). Gilles de la Tourette syndrome: Clinical and family study of 50 cases. *Annuals of Neurology, 7,* 41–49.

Nelson, R. J. (1995). *An introduction to behavioral endocrinology.* Sunderland, MA: Sinauer Associates.

Nichols, R. C., & Bilbro, W. C. (1966). The diagnosis of twin zygosity. *Acta Geneticae et Statistica Medicae, 16,* 265–275.

Nielson, J. M. (1990). *Sex and gender in society* (2ⁿᵈ ed.). Prospect Heights, IL: Waveland.

Nietzel, M. T., & Harris, M. J. (1990). Relationship of dependency and achievement/ autonomy to depression. *Clinical Psychology Review, 10,* 279–297.

Nishizawa, S., Benkelfat, C., Young, S. N., Leyton, M., Mzengeza, S., De Montigny, C., Blier, P., & Diksic, M. (1997). Differences between males and females in rates of serotonin synthesis in human brain. *Proceedings of the National Academy of Sciences, U.S.A., 94,* 5308–5313.

Nishizuka, M., & Arai, Y. (1981a). Organizational action of estrogen on synaptic pattern in the amygdala: Implications for sexual differentiation of the brain. *Brain Research, 213,* 422–426.

Nishizuka, M., & Arai, Y. (1981b). Sexual dimorphism in synaptic organization in the amygdala and its dependence on neonatal hormone environment. *Brain Research, 212,* 31–38.

Nolen-Hoeksema, S. (1987). Sex differences in unipolar depression: Evidence and theory. *Psychological Bulletin, 101,* 259–282.

Nordström, P., Schalling, D., & Åsberg, M. (1995). Temperamental vulnerability in attempted suicide. *Acta Psychiatrica Scandinavica, 92,* 155–160.

Nöthen, M. M., Hebebrand, J., Knapp, M., Hebebrand, K., Camps, A., von Gontard, A., Wettke-Schäfer, R., Cichon, S., Poustka, F., Schmidt, M., Lehmkuhl, G., Remschmidt, H., & Propping, P. (1994). Association analysis of the dopamine D2 receptor gene in Tourette's syndrome using the haplotype relative risk method. *American Journal of Medical Genetics (Neuropsychiatric Genetics), 54,* 249–252.

Nyborg, H. (1994a). *Hormones, sex and society: The science of physicology.* Westport, CT: Praeger.

Nyborg, H. (1994b). The neuropsychology of sex-related differences in brain and specific abilities: Hormones, developmental dynamics, and new paradigm. In P. A. Vernon (Ed.), *The neuropsychology of individual differences* (pp. 59–113). San Diego: Academic Press.

O'Keefe, J. A., & Handa, R. J. (1990). Transient elevation of estrogen receptors in the neonatal rat hippocampus. *Developmental Brain Research, 57,* 119–127.

O'Kelly, C. G., & Carney, L. S. (1986). *Women and men in society: Crosscultural perspectives on gender stratification* (2nd ed.). Belmont, CA: Wadesworth.

Oldfield, R. C. (1971). The assessment and analysis of handedness: The Edinburgh inventory. *Neuropsychologia, 9,* 97–101.

Osterweis, M., Solomon, F., & Green, M. (1984). *Bereavement: Reactions, consequences, and care.* Washington, DC: National Academy Press.

Ounsted, C., & Taylor, D. (1972). *Gender differences: Their ontogeny and significance.* Baltimore: Williams & Wilkins.

Pap, E., & Csaba, G. (1994). Benzpyrene treatment in adulthood increases the testosterone level in neonatally steroid (allylestrenol) treated male rats. *General Pharmacology, 25,* 1699–1701.

Pap, E., & Csaba, G. (1995a). Effect of neonatal allylestrenol treatment (hormonal imprinting) on the serum testosterone and progesterone level in adult rat. *Reproduction, Fertility and Development, 7,* 1249–1251.

Pap, E., & Csaba, G. (1995b). Effect of prenatal allylestrenol treatment (hormonal imprinting) on the serum testosterone and progesterone level in adult rats. *General Pharmacology, 26,* 365–367.

Parker, A. J., & Clarke, K. A. (1990). Gait topography in rat locomotion. *Physiology & Behavior, 48,* 41–47.

Pehek, E. A., Thompson, J. T., & Hull, E. M. (1989). The effects of intracranial administration of the dopamine agonist apomorphine on penile reflexes and seminal emission in the rat. *Brain Research, 500,* 325–332.

Pehek, E. A., Warner, R. K., Bazzett, T. J., Bitran, D., Band, L. C., Eaton, R. C., & Hull, E. M. (1988). Microinjections of cis-flupenthixol, a dopamine antagonist, into the medial preoptic area impairs sexual behavior of male rats. *Brain Research, 443,* 70–76.

Pellis, S. M. (1989). Fighting: The problem of selecting appropriate behavior patterns. In R. J. Blanchard, P. F. Brain, D. C. Blanchard, & S. Parmigiani (Eds.), *Ethoexperimental approaches to the study of behavior* (pp. 361–374). The Netherlands: Dordrecht.

Pellis, S. M., Chen, Y.-C., & Teitelbaum, P. (1985). Fractionation of the cataleptic bracing response in rats. *Physiology & Behavior, 34,* 815–823.

Pellis, S. M., Field, E. F., Smith, L. K., & Pellis, V. C. (1997). Multiple differences in the play fighting of male and female rats: Implications for the causes and functions of play. *Neuroscience & Biobehavioral Reviews, 21,* 105–120.

Pellis, S. M., McDonald, N., & Michener, G. (1996). Lateral display as a combat tactic in Richardson's ground squirrel *Spermophilus richardsonii. Aggressive Behavior, 22,* 119–134.

Pellis, S. M., McKenna, M. M., Field, E. F., Pellis, V. C., Prusky, G. T., & Whishaw, I. Q. (1996). The uses of vision by rats in play fighting and other close-quarter interactions. *Physiology & Behavior, 59,* 905–913.

Pellis, S. M., & Pellis, V. C. (1987). Play-fighting differs from serious attack in both target of attack and tactics of fighting in the laboratory rat *Rattus norvegicus. Aggressive Behavior, 13,* 227–242.

Pellis, S. M., & Pellis, V. C. (1990). Differential rates of attack, defense and counterattack during the developmental decrease in play fighting by male and female rats. *Developmental Psychobiology, 23,* 215–231.

Pellis, S. M., & Pellis, V. C. (1992). An analysis of the targets and tactics of conspecific attack and predatory attack in northern grasshopper mice *Onychomys leucogaster. Aggressive Behavior, 18,* 301–316.

Pellis, S. M., Pellis, V. C., & Field, E. F. (1995, November). *Spontaneous turning behavior in male and female adult rats: The effects of neonatal castration and testosterone treatment on sex typical patterns of turning.* Poster presented at the annual meeting for the Society for Neuroscience, San Diego, CA.

Pellis, S. M., Pellis, V. C., & McKenna, M. M. (1993). Some subordinates are more equal than others: Play fighting amongst adult subordinate male rats. *Aggressive Behavior, 19,* 385–393.

Pellis, S. M., Pellis, V. C., & McKenna, M. M. (1994). Feminine dimension in the play fighting of rats (*Rattus norvegicus*) and its defeminization neonatally by androgens. *Journal of Comparative Psychology, 108,* 68–73.

Pellis, S. M., Pellis, V. C., & Whishaw, I. Q. (1992). The role of the cortex in play-fighting by rats: Developmental and evolutionary implications. *Brain, Evolution & Behavior, 39,* 270–284.

Pellis, V. C., Field, E. F., & Pellis, S. M. (1995, November). *The influence of sex and neonatal hormone exposure on locomotion in adult rats.* Poster presented at the anual meeting of the Society for Neuroscience, San Diego, CA.

Pellis, V. C., Pellis, S. M., & Teitelbaum, P. (1991). A descriptive analysis of the postnatal development of contact-fighting in rats. *Developmental Psychobiology, 24,* 237–263.

Pellow, S., Johnston, A., & File, S. E. (1987). Selective agonists and antagonists for 5-hydroxytryptamine receptor subtypes and interactions with yohimbine and FG 7142 using the elevated plus-maze in the rat. *Journal of Pharmacy & Pharmacology, 39,* 917–928.

Perez, J., Naftolin, F., & Garcia Segura, L. M. (1990). Sexual differentiation of synaptic connectivity and neural plasma membrane in the arcuate nucleus of the hypothalamus. *Brain Research, 527,* 116–122.

Petty, F., Kramer, G., Wilson, L., & Jordan, S. (1994). In vivo serotonin release and learned helplessness. *Psychiatry Research, 52,* 285–293.

Pfaff, D. W., & Zigmond, R. E. (1971). Neonatal androgen effects on sexual and nonsexual behaviour of adult rats tested under various hormone regimes. *Neuroendocrinology, 7,* 129–145.

Pfaus, J. G., & Gorzalka, B. B. (1987). Opioids and sexual behavior. *Neuroscience and Biobehavioral Reviews, 11,* 1–34.

Pfaus, J. G., & Phillips, A. G. (1991). Role of dopamine in anticipatory and consummatory aspects of sexual behavior in the male rat. *Behavioral Neuroscience, 105,* 727–743.

Phoenix, C. H. (1974). Prenatal testosterone in the non-human primate and its consequences for behavior. In R. C. Friedman, R. M. Richart, & R. L. Vande Wiele (Eds.), *Sex differences in behavior* (pp. 19–32). New York: John Wiley & Sons.

Phoenix, C. H., Goy, R. W., Gerall, A. A., & Young, W. C. (1959). Organizing action of prenatally administered testosterone propionate on the tissues mediating mating behavior in the female guinea pig. *Endocrinology, 65,* 369–382.

Phoenix, C. H., Goy, R. W., & Resko, J. A. (1968). Psychosexual differentiation as a function of androgenic stimulation. In M. Diamond (Ed.), *Perspectives in reproduction and sexual behavior* (pp. 33–49). Bloomington: Indiana University Press.

Piaget, J. (1952). *The origins of intelligence in children.* New York: International Universities Press.

Piaget, J. (1972). Intellectual development from adolescence to adulthood. *Human Development, 15,* 1–12.

Pierini, A. A., & Nusimovich, B. (1981). Male diabetic impotence: Effects of dopaminergic agents. *Archives of Andrology, 6,* 347–350.

Pihl, R. O., Young, S. N., Harden, P., Plotnick. S., Chamberlain, B., & Ervin, F. R. (1995). Acute effects of altered tryptophan levels and alcohol on aggression in normal human males. *Psychopharmacology, 119,* 353–360.

Pilgrim, C., & Hutchison, J. B. (1994). Developmental regulation of sex differences in the brain: Can the role of gonadal steroids be redefined? *Neuroscience, 60,* 843–855.

Pincus, A. L., & Wiggins, J. S. (1990). *Interpersonal traits, interpersonal problems, and personality disorders: Dual Circle analyses.* Paper presented at the annual American Psychological Association Conference, Boston.

Pinel, J. P. J., Jones, C. H., & Whishaw, I. Q. (1992). Behavior from the ground up: Rat behavior from the ventral perspective. *Psychobiology, 20,* 185–188.

Poellinger L., Gottlicher, M., & Gustafsson J.-A. (1992). The dioxin and peroxisome activated receptors: Nuclear receptors in search of endogeneous ligands. *Trends in Pharmacological Science, 13,* 241–245.

Pomerantz, S. M., Goy, R. W., & Roy, M. M. (1986). Expression of male-typical behavior in adult female pseudohermaphrodite rhesus: Comparison with normal males and with neonatally gonadectomized males and females. *Hormones & Behavior, 20,* 483–500.

Pozzo Miller, L. D., & Aoki, A. (1991). Stereological analysis of the hypothalamic ventromedial nucleus: II. Hormone-induced changes in the synaptogenic pattern. *Developmental Brain Research, 61,* 189–196.

Pranzatelli, M. R. (1992). Serotonin receptor ontogeny: Effects of agonists in 1-day-old rats. *Pharmacology, Biochemistry & Behavior, 43,* 1273–1277.

Pranzatelli, M. R. (1994). Dissociation of the plasticity of $5HT_{1A}$ sites & 5HT transporter sites. *Neurochemical Research, 19,* 311–315.

Quinn, G. E., Dobson, V., Repaka, M. X., Reynolds J., Kivlin J., Davis B., Buckley, E., Flynn, J. T., & Palmer, E. A. (1992). Development of myopia in infants with birth weights less than 1251 grams. *Opthalmology (Rochester) 99,* 329–340.

Quissell, D. Q. (1993). Steroid hormone analysis in human saliva. In D. Malamud & L. Tabak (Eds.), Saliva as a diagnostic fluid. *Annals of the New York Academy of Sciences, 694,* 143–145.

Rainbow, T. C., Parsons, B., & McEwen, B. S. (1982). Sex differences in rat brain oestrogen and progestin receptors. *Nature, 300,* 648–649.

Raine, A. (1993). *The psychopathology of crime: Criminal behavior as a clinical disorder.* San Diego, CA: Academic Press.

Raine, A., Buchsbaum, M. S., Stanley, J., Lottenberg, S., Abel, L., & Stoddard, J. (1994). Selective reductions in prefrontal glucose metabolism in murderers. *Biological Psychiatry, 36,* 365–373.

Rainer, J. D. (1971). Chronological parameters, twin studies, and mental diseases. *Acta Genetica Medica Gemellologiae (Roma), 20,* 359–372.

Raisman, G., & Field, P. M. (1973). Sexual dimorphism in the neuropil of the preoptic area of the rat and its dependence on neonatal androgen. *Brain Research, 54,* 1–29.

Rando, T. A. (1987). The unrecognized impact of sudden death in terminal illness and in positively progressing convalescence. *Israel Journal of Psychiatry Related Science, 24,* 125–135.

Rao, A., & Steward, O. (1991). Evidence that protein constituents of postsynaptic membrane specialization are locally synthesized: Analysis of proteins synthesized within synaptosomes. *Journal of Neuroscience, 11,* 2881–2895.

Raskin, R. N., & Hall, C. S. (1981). The Narcissistic Personality Inventory: Alternate form reliability and further evidence of construct validity. *Journal of Personality Assessment, 45,* 159–162.

Record, R. G, McKeown, T., & Edwards, J. H. (1970). An investigation of the difference in measured intelligence between twins and single births. *Annals of Human Genetics, 34,* 11–20.

Reed, M. D., & Greenwald, J. Y. (1991). Survivor-victim status, attachment, and sudden death bereavement. *Suicide and Life-Threatening Behavior, 21,* 385–401.

Regier, D. A., Farmer, M. E., Rae, D. S., Myers, J. K., Kramer, M., Robins, L. N., George, L. K., Karno, J. M., & Locke, B. Z. (1993). One-month prevalence of mental disorders in the United States and sociodemographic characteristics: The Epidemiologic Catchment Area study. *Acta Psychiatrica Scandinavica, 88,* 35–47.

Reinisch, J. M., & Sanders, S. A. (1992). Prenatal hormonal contributions to sex differences in human cognitive and personality development. In A. A. Gerall, H. Moltz, & I. L. Ward (Eds.), *Handbook of behavioral neurobiology: Vol. 11. Sexual differentiation* (pp. 221–239). New York: Plenum.

Reinisch, J. M., Ziemba-Davis, M., & Sanders, S. A. (1991). Hormonal contributions to sexually dimorphic behavioral development in humans. *Psychoneuroendocrinology, 19,* 213–278.

Reisert, I., Engele, J., & Pilgrim, C. (1989). Early sexual differentiation of diencephalic dopaminergic neurons of the rat in vitro. *Cell Tissue Research, 255,* 411–417.

Reisert, I., & Pilgrim, C. (1991). Sexual differentiation of monoaminergic neurons: Genetic or epigenetic? *Trends in Neurosciences, 14,* 468–473.

Resnick, S. M., Gottesman, I. I., Berenbaum, S. A., & Bouchard, T. J. (1986). Early hormonal influences on cognitive functioning in congenital adrenal hyperplasia. *Developmental Psychology, 22,* 191–198.

Resnick, S. M., Gottesman, I. I., & McGue, M. (1993). Sensation seeking in opposite-sex twins: An effect of prenatal hormones? *Behavior Genetics, 23,* 323–329.

Ricalde, A. A., & Hammer, R. P., Jr. (1991). Perinatal opiate treatment delays growth of cortical dendrites. *Neuroscience Letters, 115,* 137–143.

Richmond, G., & Sachs, B. J. (1984). Further evidence or masculinization of female rats by males located caudally in utero. *Hormones & Behavior, 18,* 484–490.

Rimanóczy, A., & Vathy, I. (1995). Prenatal exposure to morphine alters brain μ opioid receptor characteristics in rats. *Brain Research, 690,* 245–248.

Robbins, T. W., & Everitt, B. J. (1992). Functions of dopamine in the dorsal and ventral striatum. *Seminars in the Neurosciences, 4,* 119–128.

Robins, L. N., Helzer, J., Croughan, J., & Ratclif, K. S. (1981). National Institute of Health diagnostic interview schedule. *Archives of General Psychiatry, 38,* 381–389.

Robins, L. N., & Regier, D. A. (1991). *Psychiatric disorders in America.* New York: Free Press.

Rode, C., Wagner, M., & Gunturkun, O. (1995). Menstrual cycle affects functional cerebral asymmetries. *Neuropsychologia, 33,* 855–865.

Rohde Parfet, K. A., Lamberson, W. R., Ricke, A. R., Cantley, T. C., Ganjam, V. K., vom Saal, F. S., & Day, B. N. (1990). Intrauterine position effects in male and female swine: Subsequent survivability, growth rate, morphology, and semen characteristics. *Journal of Animal Science, 68,* 179–185.

Romano, G. J., Mobbs, C. V., Lauber, A. H., Howells, R. D., & Pfaff, D. W. (1990). Differential regulation of proenkephalin gene expression by estrogen in the ventromedial hypothalamus of male and female rats: Implications for the molecular basis of a sexually differentiated behavior. *Brain Research, 536,* 63–68.

Rosenberg, B. G., & Sutton-Smith, B. (1968). Family interaction effects on masculinity–femininity. *Journal of Personality and Social Psychology, 8,* 117–120.

Rosengarten, H., & Friedhoff, A. J. (1979). Enduring changes in dopamine receptor cells of pups from drug administration to pregnant and nursing rats. *Science, 203,* 1133–1135.

Roy, A., Segal, N. L., Sarchiapone, M., & Lavin. M. (1994). Attempted suicide among living co-twins of twin suicide victims. *American Journal of Psychiatry, 152,* 1075–1076.

Rubin, S. S. (1989–1990). Death of the future? An outcome study of bereaved parents in Israel. *Omega, 20,* 323–339.

Russell, P. D. (1977). Sex differences in rats' stationary exploration as a function of stimulus and environmental novelty. *Animal Learning and Behaviour, 5,* 297–302.

Rynearson, E. K., & McCreery, J. M. (1993). Bereavement after suicide: A synergism of trauma and loss. *American Journal of Psychiatry, 150,* 258–261.

Sabalis, R. F., Frances, A., Appenzeller, S. N., & Moseley, W. B. (1974). The three sisters: Transsexual male siblings. *American Journal of Psychiatry, 131,* 907–909.

Saki, L. M., Baker, L. A., Jacklin, C. N., & Shulman, I. (1992). Sex steroids at birth: Genetic and environmental variation and covariation. *Developmental Psychobiology, 24,* 559–570.

Salmon, C. A., & Daly, M. (1996). On the importance of kin relations to Canadian women and men. *Ethology and Sociobiology, 17,* 289–297.

Sanders, C. M. (1979–1980). A comparison of adult bereavement in the death of a spouse child and parent. *Omega, 10,* 303–322.

Sanders, C. M. (1989). *Grief: The mourning after.* New York: John Wiley & Sons.

Sanders, C. M., Mauger, P. A., & Strong, P. N., Jr. (1985). *A manual for the Grief Experience Inventory.* Charlotte, NC: Center for the Study of Separation and Loss.

Sanderson, S. K., & Ellis, L. (1992). Theoretical and political perspectives of American sociologists in the 1990s. *American Sociologists, 23,* 26–42.

Sandson, T., Wen, P., & LeMay, M. (1992). Reversed cerebral lateralization in women with breast cancer. *Lancet, 339,* 523–524.

Sasaki, M., & Arnold, A. P. (1991). Androgenic regulation of dendritic trees of motoneurons in the spinal nucleus of the bulbocavernosus: Reconstruction after intracellular iontophoresis of horseradish peroxidase. *Journal of Comparative Neurology, 308,* 11–27.

Sato, T., Chibo, A., Hayashi, S., Okamura, H., Ohta, Y., Takasugi, N., & Iguchi, T. (1994). Induction of estrogen receptor and cell division in genital tract of male mice by neonatal exposure to diethylstilbestrol. *Reproductive Toxicology, 8,* 145–153.

Scaletta L. L., & Hull, E. M. (1990). Systemic or intracranial apomorphine increases copulation in long-term castrated male rats. *Pharmacology, Biochemistry & Behaviour, 37,* 471–475.

Scarr, S. (1995). Psychology will be truly evolutionary when behavior genetic is included. *Psychological Inquiry, 6,* 68–71.

Schallert, T., DeRyck, M., Whishaw, I. Q., Ramirez, V. D., & Teitelbaum, P. (1979). Excessive bracing reactions and their control by atropine and L-dopa in an animal analog of Parkinsonism. *Experimental Neurology, 64,* 33–43.

Schindler, A. E. (1982). Hormones in human amniotic fluid. Berlin: Springer-Verlag.

Scholtens, B. J., Sarna, G. S., Kantamaneni, D. B., Jackson, A., Hutson, P. H., & Curzon, G. (1986). C.S.F. tryptophan and transmitter amine turnover may predict social behaviour in the normal rat. *Brain Research, 399,* 162–165.

Schulster, D., Burstein, S., & Cooke, B. A. (1976). *Molecular endocrinology of the steroid hormones.* London: John Wiley & Sons.

Schwartz-Giblin, S., & Pfaff, D. W. (1990). Ipsilateral and contralateral effects on cutaneous reflexes in a back muscle of the female rat: Modulation by steroids relevant for reproductive behavior. *Journal of Neurophysiology, 64,* 835–846.

Seatriz, J. V., & Hammer, R. P., Jr. (1993). Effects of opiates on neural development in the rat cerebral cortex. *Brain Research Bulletin, 30,* 523–527.

Segal, N. L. (1993). Twin, sibling and adoption methods: Tests of evolutionary hypotheses. *American Psychologist, 48,* 943–956.

Segal, N. L. (1997). Twin research perspective on human development. In N. L. Segal, G. E. Weisfeld, & C. C. Weisfeld (Eds.), *Uniting psychology and biology: Integrative perspectives on human development.* Washington, DC: American Psychological Association Press.

Segal, N. L., & Bouchard, T. J., Jr. (1993). Grief intensity following the loss of a twin and other relatives: Test of kinship-genetic hypotheses. *Human Biology, 65,* 87–105.

Segal, N. L., & Roy, A. (1996). Suicide attempts in twins whose co-twins' deaths were non-suicides. *Personality and Individual Differences, 19,* 937–940.

Segal, N. L., Wilson, S. M., Bouchard, T. J., Jr., & Gitlin, D. G. (1995). Comparative grief experiences of bereaved twins and other bereaved relatives. *Personality and Individual Differences, 18,* 511–524.

Segarra, A. C., & McEwen, B. S. (1991). Estrogen increases spine density in ventromedial hypothalamic neurons of peripubertal rats. *Neuroendocrinology, 54,* 365–372.

Serres, F., Daissa, D., Azorin, J.-M., & Jeanningros, R. (1995). Decrease in red blood cell l-tryptophan uptake in schizophrenic patients: Possible link with loss of impulse control. *Progress in Neuro-Psychopharmacology & Biological Psychiatry, 19,* 903–913.

Shapiro, B. H., & Bitar, M. S. (1991). Developmental levels and androgen responsiveness of hepatic monooxygenases of male rats perinatally exposed to maternally administered cimetidine. *Toxicology Letters, 55,* 85–89.

Sharma, T. R., Chan, W. C., & Gintzler, A. R. (1988). Effects of chronic naltrexone administration and its withdrawal on the regional activity of neurons that contain norepinephrine, dopamine and serotonin. *Brain Research, 442,* 379–386.

Sherman, P. W., & Holmes, W. G. (1985). Kin recognition: Issues and evidence. In B. Hölldobler and M. Lindauer (Eds.), *Experimental behavioral ecology and sociobiology: In Memoriam Karl von Frisch 1886–1982* (pp. 437–460). Sutherland, MA: Sinauer.

Shimizu, H., & Awata, T. (1984). Growth of skeletal bones and their sexual differences in mice. *Jikken Dobutsu—Experimental Animals, 33,* 69–76.

Shively, C. A., Fontenot, M. B., & Kaplan, J. R. (1995). Social status, behavior, and central serotonergic responsivity in female cynomolgus monkeys. *American Journal of Primatology, 37,* 333–339.

Short, R. V. (1974). New thoughts on sex determination and differentiation. *Glaxo Volume, 39,* 5–20.

Shucter, S. R., & Zisook, S. (1993). The course of normal grief. In M. S. Stroebe, W. Stroebe, & R. O. Hansson (Eds.), *Handbook of bereavement: Theory, research, and intervention* (pp. 23–43). Cambridge: Cambridge University Press.

Shughrue, P. J., Stumpf, W. E., MacLusky, N. J., Zielinski, J. E., & Hochberg, R. B. (1990). Developmental changes in estrogen receptors in mouse cerebral cortex between birth and postweaning: Studied by autoradiography with 11b-methoxy-16a-[^{125}I]-iodoestradiol. *Endocrinology, 126,* 1112–1124.

Siddiqui, A., & Gillmore, D. P. (1988). Regional differences in the catecholamine content of the rat brain: Effects of neonatal castration and androgenization. *Acta Endocrinologica, 118,* 483–494.

Sigelman, C. K., & Shaffer, D. R. (1991). *Life-span human development.* Pacific Grove, CA: Brooks/Cole.

Signorella, M. L., & Jamison, W. (1986). Masculinity, femininity, androgyny, and cognitive performance: A meta-analysis. *Psychological Bulletin, 100,* 207–228.

Sijbesma, H., Schippa, J., de Kloet, E. R., Mos, J., van Aken, J., & Olivier, B. (1991). Post-synaptic 5HT1 receptors and offensive aggression in rats: A combined behavioral and autoradiographic study with eltoprazine. *Pharmacology, Biochemistry & Behaviour, 38,* 447–458.

Simerly, R. B., Gorski, R. A., & Swanson, L. W. (1986). Neurotransmitter specificity of cells and fibers in the medial preoptic nucleus: An immunohistochemical study in the rat. *Journal of Comparative Neurology, 246,* 343–363.

Simerly, R. B., Swanson, L. W., & Gorski, R. A. (1985). Reversal of the sexually dimorphic distribution of serotonin-immunoreactive fibres in the medial preoptic nucleus by treatment with perinatal androgen. *Brain Research, 340,* 91–98.

Simerly, R. B., Chang, C., Muramatsu, M., & Swanson, L. W. (1990). Distribution of androgen and estrogen receptor mRNA-containing cells in the rat brain: An *in situ* hybridization study. *Journal of Comparative Neurology, 294,* 76–95.

Simonton, D. K. (1994). *Greatness: Who makes history and why.* New York: Guilford.

Sinclair, A. H., Berta, P., Palmer, M. S., Hawkins, J. R., Griffiths, B. L., Smith, M. J., Foster, J. W., Frischauf, A., Lovell-Badge, R., & Goodfellow, P. N. (1990). A gene from the human sex-determining region encodes a protein with homology to a conserved DNA-binding motif. *Nature, 346,* 240–244.

Singh, H. H., Purohit, V., & Ahluwalia, B. S. (1980). Effect of methadone treatment during pregnancy on the fetal testes and hypothalamus in rats. *Biology of Reproduction, 22,* 480–485.

Slotkin, T. A., Whitmore, W. L., Salvaggio, M., & Seidler, F. J. (1979). Perinatal methadone addiction affects brain synaptic development of biogenic amine systems in the rat. *Life Sciences, 24,* 1223–1230.

Smith, L. K., Field, E. F., Forgie, M. L., & Pellis, S. M. (1996). Dominance and age-related changes in the play fighting of intact and post-weaning castrated male rats (*Rattus norvegicus*). *Aggressive Behaviour, 22,* 215–226.

Smith, L. K., Forgie, M. L., & Pellis, S. M. (1998). The postpubertal change in the playful defense of male rats depends upon neonatal exposure to gonadal hormones. *Physiology & Behavior, 63,* 151–155.

Sodersten, P., & Hansen, S. (1978). Effects of castration and testosterone, dihydrotestosterone, or estradiol replacement treatment in neonatal rats on mounting behaviour in the adult. *Journal of Endocrinology, 76,* 251–260.

Sodersten, P., & Larsson, K. (1974). Lordosis behavior in castrated male rats treated with estradiol benzoate or testosterone propionate in combination with an estrogen antagonist, MER-25, and in intact male rats. *Hormones & Behavior, 5,* 13–18.

Solomon, S. (1988). The placenta as an endocrine organ. In E. Knobil & J. D. Neil (Eds.), *The physiology of reproduction* (pp. 2085–2091). New York: Raven Press.

Spear, L. P., Enters, E. K., Aswad, M. A., & Lonzan, M. (1985). Drug and environmentally induced manipulations of the opiate and serotonergic systems alter nociception in neonatal rat pups. *Behavioral Neural Biology, 44,* 1–22.

Spence, J. T. (1985). Gender identity and its implications for the concepts of masculinity and femininity. In T. B. Sonderegger (Ed.), *Psychology and gender: Nebraska symposium on motivation, 1984* (pp. 59–95). Lincoln: University of Nebraska Press.

Spence, J. T., & Buckner, C. (1995). Masculinity and femininity: Defining the undefinable. In P. J. Kalbfleisch & M. J. Cody (Eds.), *Gender, power, and communication in human relationships* (pp. 105–138). Hillsdale, NJ: Lawrence Erlbaum.

Spence, J. T., & Helmreich, R. L. (1978). *Masculinity and femininity: The psychological dimensions, correlates, and antecedents.* Austin: University of Texas Press.

Spence, J. T., & Helmreich, R. L. (1980). Masculine instrumentality and feminine expressiveness: Their relationships with sex role attitudes and behaviors. *Psychology of Women Quarterly, 5,* 147–163.

Spence, J. T., Helmreich, R. L., & Stapp, J. (1974). The Personal Attributes Questionnaire: A measure of sex role stereotypes and masculinity–femininity. *JSAS
Catalog of Selected Documents in Psychology, 4,* 43–44 (Ms. No. 617).

Spigset, O., & Mjörndal, T. (1997). Serotonin 5-HT$_{2A}$ receptor binding in platelets
from healthy subjects as studied by [^{3}H]-lysergic acid diethylamide ([^{3}H]-LSD):
Intra- and interindividual variability. *Neuropsychopharmacology, 16,* 285–293.

Spoljar, M., Eicher, W., Eiermann, W., & Cleve, H. (1981). H-Y antigen expression in
different tissues from transsexuals. *Human Genetics, 57,* 52–57.

Sprang, M. V., McNeil, J. S., & Wright, R. (1992–1993). Grief among surviving family members of homicide victims: A causal approach. *Omega, 26,* 145–160.

Stevens, R., & Goldstein, R. (1981) Effects of neonatal testosterone and estrogen on
open-field behaviour in rats. *Physiology and Behavior, 26,* 551–553.

Steward, O. (1983). Alterations in polyribosomes associated with dendritic spines
during the reinnervation of the dentate gyrus of the adult rat. *Journal of Neuroscience, 3,* 177–188.

Steward, O., Davis, L., Dotti, C., Phillips, L. L., Rao, A., & Banker, G. (1988). Protein
synthesis and processing in cytoplasmic microdomains beneath postsynaptic
sites on CNS neurons. *Molecular Neurobiology, 2,* 227–261.

Steward, O., & Reeves, T. M. (1988). Protein-synthetic machinery beneath postsynaptic sites on CNS neurons: Association between polyribosomes and other organelles at the synaptic site. *Journal of Neuroscience, 8,* 176–184.

Stewart, J., & Cygan, D. (1980). Ovarian hormones act early in development to feminize adult open-field behavior. *Hormones & Behavior, 14,* 20–32.

Stocks, P., & Karns, M. N. (1933). A biometric investigation of twins and their brothers and sisters: II. *Annals of Eugenics, 5,* 1–55.

Stroebe, M. S., & Stroebe, W. (1985). Social support and the alleviation of loss. In I.
G. Sarason & B. R. Sarason (Eds.), *Social support: Theory, research, and applications* (pp. 439–462). Dordrecht: Martinus Nijhoff.

Stroebe, M. S., & Stroebe, W. (1993). The mortality of bereavement: A review. In M. S.
Stroebe, W. Stroebe, & R. O. Hansson (Eds.), *Handbook of bereavement: Theory,
research, and intervention* (pp. 175–195). Cambridge: Cambridge University Press.

Stroebe, M. S., Stroebe, W., & Hansson, R. O. (Eds.). (1993). *Handbook of bereavement:
Theory, research, and intervention.* Cambridge: Cambridge University Press.

Stroebe, W., & Stroebe, M. S. (1987). *Bereavement and health: The psychological and
physical consequences of partner loss.* New York: Cambridge University Press.

Sumner, B. E., & Fink, G. (1993). Effects of acute estradiol on 5-hydroxytryptamine
and dopamine receptor subtype mRNA expression in female rat brain. *Molecular & Cellular Neuroscience, 4,* 83–92.

Surani, M. A. (1991). Genomic imprinting: Developmental significance and molecular mechanism. *Current Opinion in Genetics and Development, 1,* 241–246.

Swaab, D. F., & Hofman, M. A. (1988). Sexual differentiation of the human hypothalamus: Ontogeny of the sexually dimorphic nucleus of the preoptic area.
Developmental Brain Research, 44, 314–318.

Swaab, D. F., & Hofman, M. A. (1990). An enlarged suprachiasmatic nucleus in homosexual men. *Brain Research, 537,* 141–148.

Swarzenski, B. C., Tang, L., Oh, Y. J., O'Malley, K. L., & Todd, R. D. (1994). Morphogenic potentials of D2, D3 and D4 dopamine receptors revealed in transfected neuronal cell lines. *Proceedings of the National Academy of Sciences,
U.S.A., 91,* 649–653.

Systat for Windows: Statistics, Version 5 Edition (Computer Program). (1995). Evanston, IL: SYSTAT, Inc.

TambyRaja, R. L., & Ratnam, S. S. (1981). Plasma steroid changes in twin pregnancies. In L. Gedda, P. Parisi, & W. Nance (Eds.), *Twin research 1: Part A. Twin biology and multiple pregnancy* (pp. 190–195). New York: Alan R. Liss.

Tanaka, M., Ida, Y., & Tsuda, A. (1988). Naloxone, given before but not after stress exposure, enhances stress-induced increases in regional brain noradrenaline release. *Pharmacology, Biochemistry and Behavior, 29,* 613–616.

Tanila, H., Taira, T., Piepponen, T. P., & Honkanen, A. (1994). Effect of sex and age on brain monoamines and spatial learning in rats. *Neurobiology of Aging, 15,* 733–741.

Tanner, J. M. (1989). *Foetus into man.* Cambridge: Harvard University Press.

Taylor, D. C. (1974). The influence of sexual differentiation on growth, development, and disease. In J. A. Davis & J. Dobbing (Eds.), *Scientific foundations of paediatrics* (pp. 29–44). Philadelphia: Saunders.

Teitelbaum, P. (1982). Disconnection and antagonistic interaction of movement subsystems in motivated behavior. In A. R. Morrison & P. Strick (Eds.), *Changing concepts of the nervous system: Proceedings of the first institute of neurological sciences symposium in neurobiology and learning* (pp. 467–498). New York: Academic Press.

Teitelbaum, P., Schallert, T., DeRyck, M., Whishaw, I. Q., & Golani, I. (1980). Motor subsystems in motivated behavior. In R. F. Thompson, L. H. Hicks, & V. B. Shvyrkov (Eds.), *Neural mechanisms of goal-directed behavior and learning* (pp. 127–143). New York: Academic Press.

Terman, L. M. (1946). Psychological sex differences. In L. Carmichael (Ed.), *Manual of child psychology* (pp. 954–1000). New York: John Wiley & Sons.

Terman, L. M., & Miles, C. C. (1936). *Sex and personality: Studies in masculinity and femininity.* New York: Russell & Russell.

Teyler, T. J., Vardaris, R M., Lewis, D., & Rawitch, A. B. (1980). Gonadal steroid: Effects on excitability of hippocampal pyramidal cells. *Science, 209,* 1017–1019.

Thornhill, R., & Thornhill, N. W. (1989). Human rape: The strengths of the evolutionary perspective. In C. Crawford, M. Smith, & D. Krebs (Eds.), *Sociobiology and psychology: Ideas, issues and applications* (pp. 269–291). Hillsdale, NJ: Lawrence Erlbaum.

Tinbergen, N. (1951). *The study of instinct.* Oxford: Clarendon Press.

Tissari, A. H. (1975). Pharmacological and ultrastructural maturation of serotonergic synapses during ontogeny. *Medical Biology, 53,* 1–14.

Todd, R. D. (1992). Neural development is regulated by classical neurotransmitters: Dopamine D2 receptor stimulation enhances neurite outgrowth. *Biological Psychiatry, 31,* 794–807.

Toran-Allerand, C. D. (1980). Sex steroids and the development of the newborn mouse hypothalamus and preoptic area *in vitro*: II. Morphological correlates and hormonal specificity. *Brain Research, 189,* 413–427.

Toran-Allerand, C. D. (1984). On the genesis of sexual differentiation of the central nervous system: Morphogenetic consequences of steroidal exposure and the possible role of a-fetoprotein. *Progress in Brain Research, 61,* 63–96.

Toran-Allerand, C. D., Gerlach, J. L., & McEwen, B. S. (1980). Autoradiographic localization of ³H-estradiol related to steroid responsiveness in cultures of the hypothalamus and preoptic area. *Brain Research, 184,* 517–522.

Toran-Allerand, C. D., Hashimoto, K., Greenough, W. T., & Saltarelli, M. (1983). Sex steroids and the development of the newborn mouse hypothalamus and preoptic area *in vitro*: III. Effects of estrogen on dendritic differentiation. *Developmental Brain Research, 7,* 97–101.

Toran-Allerand, C. D., Miranda, R. C., Hochberg, R. B., & MacLusky, N. J. (1992). Cellular variations in estrogen receptor mRNA translation in the developing brain: Evidence from combined [^{125}I]estrogen autoradiography and non-isotopic *in situ* hybridization histochemistry. *Brain Research, 576,* 25–41.

Trapnell, P. D., & Wiggins, J. S. (1990). Extension of the interpersonal adjective scales to include the big five dimensions of personality. *Journal of Personality and Social Psychology, 59,* 781–790.

Trapp, M., Kato, K., Bohnet, H. G., Gerhard, I., Weise, H. C., & Leidenberger, F. (1986). Human placental lactogen and unconjugated estriol concentration in twin pregnancy: Monitoring of fetal development in intrauterine growth retardation and single intrauterine fetal death. *American Journal of Obstetrics and Gynecology, 55,* 1027–1031.

Trivers, R. (1985). *Social evolution.* Menlo Park, CA: Benjamin/Cummings.

Tronto, J. C. (1987). Beyond gender differences to a theory of care. *Signs, 12,* 644–663.

Tronto, J. C. (1993). *Moral boundaries: A political argument for an ethic of care.* New York: Routledge.

Tsur, H., Borenstein, A., & Seidman, D. S. (1991). Transsexualism. *Lancet, 338,* 945–946.

Tulchinsky, D., & Ryan, K. J. (Eds.). (1980). *Maternal–fetal endocrinology.* Philadelphia: W. B. Saunders.

Twenge, J. M. (1995, May). *Changes in sex roles across generations, regions, and universities: A quantitative analysis.* Paper presented at the Midwestern Psychological Association, Chicago.

Udry, J. R. (1991). The nature of gender. *Demography, 31,* 561–573.

Unger, R. K. (1989). *Representations: Social constructions of gender.* New York: Baywood.

Unger, R. K. (1992). Will the real sex difference please stand up? *Feminism & Psychology, 2,* 231–238.

Vandenbergh, D. J., Persico, A. M, & Uhl, G. R. (1992). A human dopamine transporter cDNA predicts reduced glycosylation, displays a novel repetitive element and provides racially-dimorphic *Taq* I RFLPs. *Molecular Brain Research, 15,* 161–166.

Van Goozen, S. H. M., Cohen-Kettenis, P. T., Gooren, L. J. G., Frijda, N. H., & van de Poll, N. E. (1994). Activating effects of androgens on cognitive performance: Causal evidence in a group of female-to-male transsexuals. *Neuropsychologia, 32,* 1153–1157.

Van Goozen, S. H. M., Cohen-Kettenis, P. T., Gooren, L. J. G., Frijda, N. H., & van de Poll, N. E. (1995). Gender differences in behaviour: Activating effects of cross-sex hormones. *Psychoneuroendocrinology, 20,* 343–363.

Van Goozen, S. H. M., Frijda, N., & van de Poll, N. E. (1994). Anger and aggression in women: Influence of sports choice and testosterone administration. *Aggressive Behaviour, 20,* 213–222.

Vathy, I. (1995). Effects of prenatal morphine and cocaine on postnatal behaviors and brain neurotransmitters. *NIDA Research Monograph Series, 158,* 88–114.

Vathy, I., & Etgen, A. M. (1989). Hormonal activation of female sexual behavior is accompanied by hypothalamic norepinephrine release. *Journal of Neuroendocrinology, 1,* 383–388.

Vathy, I., & Etgen, A. M. (1996). Effects of prenatal morphine and adult estrogen administration on μ-opioid inhibition of norepinephrine release from hypothalamic slices. *Neuroendocrinology, 63,* 61–68.

Vathy, I., Etgen, A. M., & Barfield, R. J. (1985). Effects of prenatal exposure to morphine on the development of sexual behavior in rats. *Pharmacology, Biochemistry and Behavior, 22,* 227–232.

Vathy. I., Etgen, A. M., Rabii, J., & Barfield, R. J. (1983). Effects of prenatal exposure to morphine sulfate on reproductive function of female rats. *Pharmacology, Biochemistry & Behaviour, 19,* 777–780.

Vathy, I., & Kátay, L. (1992). Effects of prenatal morphine on adult sexual behavior and brain catecholamines in rats. *Developmental Brain Research, 68,* 125–131.

Vathy, I., Kátay, L., & Mini, K. N. (1993). Prenatal cocaine, sexual dimorphism in neurochemistry and behaviors. *Developmental Brain Research, 73,* 115–122.

Vathy, I., & Marson, L. (1998). Effects of prenatal morphine and cocaine exposure on spinal sexual reflexes in male and female rats. *Physiology & Behavior, 63,* 445–450.

Vathy, I., Rimanóczy, A., Eaton, R. C., & Kátay, L. (1994). Alterations in regional brain catecholamine turnover following prenatal exposure to morphine. *Brain Research, 662,* 209–215.

Vathy, I., Rimanóczy, A., Eaton, R. C., & Kátay, L. (1995). Sex dimorphic alterations in postnatal brain catecholamines after gestational morphine. *Brain Research Bulletin, 36,* 185–193.

Vathy, I., van der Plas, J., Vincent, P. A., & Etgen, A. M. (1991). Intracranial dialysis and microinfusion studies suggest that morphine may act in the ventromedial hypothalamus to inhibit female sexual behavior. *Hormones & Behavior, 25,* 354–366.

Vega Matuszczyk, J., & Larsson, K. (1995). Sexual preference and feminine and masculine behavior of male rats prenatally exposed to antiandrogen or antiestrogen. *Hormones & Behavior, 29,* 191–206.

Vendrell, P., Junqué, C., Pujol, J., Jurado, M. A., Molet, J., & Grafman, J. (1995). The role of prefrontal regions in the Stroop task. *Neuropsychologia, 33,* 341–352.

Vito, C. C., Bates, S. E., & Fox, T. O. (1979). Putative androgen and estrogen receptors in embryonic rat hypothalamus. *Society for Neuroscience, Abstract, 5,* 463.

vom Saal, F. (1983). Variation in infanticide and parental behavior in male mice due to prior intrauterine proximity to female fetuses: Elimination by prenatal stress. *Psychology & Behavior, 30,* 675–681.

vom Saal, F. (1989). Sexual differentiation in litter-bearing mammals: Influence of sex of adjacent fetuses in utero. *Journal of Animal Science, 67,* 1824–1840.

vom Saal, F., & Bronson, F. H. (1980). Sexual characteristics of adult female mice are correlated with their blood testosterone levels during prenatal development. *Science, 208,* 597–599.

vom Saal, F., Grant, W. M., McMullen, C., Kurt W., & Laves, E. (1983). High fetal estrogen concentrations: Correlation with increased adult sexual activity and decreased aggression in male mice. *Science, 220,* 1306–1308.

von Zerssen, D., Tauscher, R., & Pössl, J. (1994). The relationship of premorbid personality to subtypes of an affective illness: A replication study by means of an operationalized procedure for the diagnosis of personality structures. *Journal of Affective Disorders, 32,* 61–72.

Voss, W. D., & Norman, J. P. (1995, May). *Processing of contextual stimuli in a psychopathic and nonpsychopathic student population.* Paper presented at the Midwestern Psychological Association Convention, Chicago.

Vreeburg, J. T. M., Van Der Vaart, D. M., & Van Der Schoot, P. (1977). Prevention of central defeminization but not masculinization in male rats by inhibition neonatally of oestrogen biosynthesis. *Journal of Endocrinology, 74,* 375–382.

Wagner, B. (1974). Ein Transexueller mit XYY-Syndrom. *Nervenarzt, 45,* 548–551.

Wallen, K., Maestripieri, D., & Mann, D. R. (1995). Effects of neonatal testicular suppression with a GnHR antagonist on social behavior in group-living juvenile rhesus-monkeys. *Hormones & Behavior, 29,* 322–337.

Walsh, T. (1995). *Biosociology: An Emerging Paradigm.* Westport, CT: Praeger.

Walton, M. T., Fineman, R. M., & Walton, P. J. (1996). Why can't a woman be more like a man? A renaissance perspective on the biological basis for female inferiority. *Women & Health, 24,* 87–95.

Ward, D. M. (1974). Correlation of hormonal structure with hormonal function in mammalian tissues. In W. J. Burdette (Ed.), *Invertebrate endocrinology and hormonal heterophylly.* Berlin: Springer Verlag.

Ward, I. L. (1992). Sexual behavior: The product of perinatal hormonal and prepubertal social factors. In A. Gerall, H. Moltz, & I. L. Ward (Eds.), *Handbook of behavioral neurobiology: Vol. 11. Sexual differentiation* (pp. 157–180). New York: Plenum Press.

Ward, I. L., & Weisz, J. (1980). Maternal stress alters plasma testosterone in fetal males. *Science, 207,* 328–329.

Ward, I. L., & Weisz, J. (1984). Differential effects of maternal stress on circulating levels of corticosterone, progesterone, and testosterone in male and female rat fetuses and their mothers. *Endocrinology, 114,* 1635–1644.

Ward, O. B., Orth, J. M., & Weisz, J. (1983). A possible role of opiates in modifying sexual differentiation. In M. Schlumpf & W. Lichtensteiger (Eds.), *Monographs in neural sciences: Vol. 9. Drugs and hormones in brain development* (pp. 194–200). Basel, Switzerland: Karger.

Warner, R. K., Thompson, J. T., Markowski, V. P., Loucks, J. A., Bazzett, T. J., Eaton, R. C., & Hull, E. M. (1991). Microinjection of the dopamine antagonist cis-flupenthixol into the MPOA impairs copulation, penile reflexes and sexual motivation in male rats. *Brain Research, 540,* 177–182.

Watson, S., & Girdlestone, D. (1995). Receptor and ion channel normenclature. *Trends in Pharmacological Sciences Supplement,* 38–41.

Weiner, R. I., & Gagnong, W. F. (1978). Role of brain monoamines and histamine in regulation of anterior pituitary secretion. *Physiological Reviews, 58,* 905–976.

Weisz, J., & Ward, I. L. (1980). Plasma testosterone and progesterone titers of pregnant rats, their male and female fetuses, and neonatal offspring. *Endocrinology, 106,* 306–316.

Werling, L. L., Brown, S. R., & Cox, B. M. (1987). Opioid receptor regulation of the release of norepinephrine in brain. *Neuropharmacology, 26,* 987–996.

Whalen, C. K., & Henker, B. (1984). Hyperactivity and the attention deficit disorders: Expanding frontiers. *Pediatric Clinics of North America, 31,* 397–427.

Whalen, R. E., & Rezek, D. L. (1974). Inhibition of lordosis in female rats by subcutaneous implants of testosterone, androstenedione, or dihydrotestosterone in infancy. *Hormones & Behavior, 5,* 125–128.

Whishaw, I. Q. (1988). Food wrenching and dodging: Use of action patterns for the analysis of sensorimotor and social behavior in the rat. *Journal of Neuroscience Methods, 24,* 169–178.

Whishaw, I. Q., & Gorny, B. P. (1994). Food wrenching and dodging: Eating time estimates influence dodge probability and amplitude. *Aggressive Behaviour, 20,* 35–47.

Whishaw, I. Q., & Kolb, B. (1985). The mating movements of male decorticate rats: Evidence for subcortically generated movements by the male but regulation of approaches by the female. *Behavioural Brain Research, 17,* 171–191.

Whishaw, I. Q., & Tomie, J. (1987). Food wrenching and dodging: Strategies used by rats (*Rattus norvegicus*) for obtaining and protecting food from conspecifics. *Journal of Comparative Psychology, 101,* 202–209.

Whishaw, I. Q., & Tomie, J. (1988). Food wrenching and dodging: A neuroethological test of cortical and dopaminergic contributions to sensorimotor behavior in the rat. *Behavioral Neuroscience, 102,* 110–123.

Whitaker-Azmitia, P. M. (1992). Role of serotonin and other neurotransmitter receptors in brain development: Basis for developmental pharmacology. *Pharmacological Reviews, 43,* 553–561.

Whitaker-Azmitia, P. M., & Azmitia, E. (1986). Autoregulation of fetal serotonergic neuronal development: Role of high affinity serotonin receptors. *Neuroscience Letters, 67,* 307–312.

Whitfield, J. B., & Martin, N. G. (1992). Sex differences in alcohol, use, peak concentration, and post-alcohol test performance in humans: A test of the effects of prenatal environment. Unpublished manuscript.

Wiggins, J. S. (1979). A psychological taxonomy of trait-descriptive terms: The interpersonal domain. *Journal of Personality and Social Psychology, 37,* 395–412.

Wiggins, J. S. (1982). Circle models of interpersonal behavior in clinical psychology. In P. C. Kendall & J. N. Butcher (Eds.), *Handbook of research methods in clinical psychology* (pp. 183–221). New York: John Wiley & Sons.

Wiggins, J. S. (1991). Agency and communion as conceptual coordinates for the understanding and measurement of interpersonal behavior. In W. M. Gove & D. Cicchetti (Eds.), *Thinking clearly about psychology: Vol. 2. Personality and psychopathology* (pp. 89–113). Minneapolis: University of Minnesota Press.

Wiggins, J. S., & Broughton, R. (1985). The interpersonal circle: A structural model for the integration of personality research. In R. Hogan & W. H. Jones (Eds.), *Perspectives in personality: A research annual* (Vol. 1, pp. 1–47). London: JAI Press.

Wiggins, J. S., & Holzmuller, A. (1978). Psychological androgyny and interpersonal behavior. *Journal of Consulting and Clinical Psychology, 46,* 40–52.

Wiggins, J. S., & Holzmuller, A. (1981). Further evidence on androgyny and interpersonal flexibility. *Journal of Research in Personality, 15,* 67–80.

Wiggins, J. S., Phillips, N., & Trapnell, P. (1989). Circular reasoning about interpersonal behavior: Evidence concerning some untested assumptions underlying diagnostic classifications. *Journal of Personality and Social Psychology, 56,* 296–305.

Wiggins, J. S., & Pincus, A. L. (1989a). Conceptions of personality disorders and dimensions of personality. *Psychological Assessment: A Journal of Counseling and Clinical Psychology, 1,* 303–316.

Wiggins, J. S., & Pincus, A. L. (1989b). Personality: Structure and assessment. *Annual Review of Psychology, 43,* 473–504.

Wiggins, J. S., & Pincus, A. L. (1994). Personality structures and the structure of personality disorders. In P. T. Costa, Jr. & T. A. Widiger (Eds.), *Personality disorders and the five-factor model of personality* (pp. 73–93). Washington, DC: American Psychological Association.

Wiggins, J. S., Trapnell, P., & Phillips. N. (1988). Psychometric and geometric characteristics of the Revised Interpersonal Adjective Scales (IAS-R). *Multivariate Behavioral Research, 23,* 517–530.

Wilkinson, M., Herdon, H., Pearce, M., & Wilson, C. A. (1979). Radioligand binding studies on hypothalamic noradrenergic receptors during the oestrous cycle or after steroid injection in ovariectomised rats. *Brain Research, 168,* 652–655.

Williams, C. L., Barnett, A. M., & Meck, W. H. (1990). Organizational effects of early gonadal secretions on sexual differentiation in spatial memory. *Behavioral Neuroscience, 104,* 84–97.

Williams, C. L., & Meck, W. H. (1991). The organizational effects of gonadal steroids on sexually dimorphic spatial ability. *Psychoneuroendocrinology, 16,* 155–176.

Wilson, C. A. (1993). Pharmacological targets for the control of male and female sexual behavior. In A. J. Riley, M. Peet, & C. Wilson (Eds.), *Sexual pharmacology* (pp. 1–58). Oxford: Clarendon Press.

Wilson, C. A., Gonzalez, M. I., & Farabollini, F. (1991). Behavioral effects in adulthood of neonatal manipulation of brain serotonin levels in normal and androgenized females. *Pharmacology, Biochemistry & Behaviour, 41,* 91–98.

Wilson, C. A., & Hunter, A. J. (1985). Progesterone stimulates sexual behaviour in female rats by increasing 5HT activity in 5HT2 receptors. *Brain Research, 333,* 223–229.

Wilson, C. A., Pearson, J. R., Hunter, A. J., Tuohy, P.A., & Payne, A. P. (1986). The effect of neonatal manipulation of hypothalamic serotonin levels on sexual activity in the adult rat. *Pharmacology, Biochemistry & Behaviour, 24,* 1175–1183.

Wilson, J. D., George, F. W., & Griffin, J. E. (1981). The hormonal control of sexual development. *Science, 211,* 1278–1284.

Wingard, D. L. (1984). The sex differential in morbidity, mortality, and lifestyle. *Annual Review of Public Health, 5,* 433–458.

Wislocki, G. B. (1939). Observations on twinning in marmosets. *American Journal of Anatomy, 64,* 445–483.

Witelson, S. F. (1989). Hand and sex differences in the isthmus and genu of the human corpus callosum: A postmortem morphological study. *Brain, 112,* 799–835.

Wittig, M. A., & Petersen, A. C. (1979). *Sex-related differences in cognitive function.* New York: Academic Press.

Woodward, J. (1988). The bereaved twin. *Acta Geneticae Medicae et Gemellologiae, 37,* 173–180.

Woolley, C. S., & McEwen, B. S. (1992). Estradiol mediates fluctuation in hippocampal synapse density during the estrous cycle in the adult rat. *Journal of Neuroscience, 12,* 2549–2554.

Wyshak, G. (1978). Fertility and longevity in twins, sibs and parents of twins. *Social Biology, 25,* 315–330.

Young, S. N., Gauthier, S., Anderson, G. M., & Purdy, W. C. (1980). Tryptophan, 5-ydroxyindoleacetic acid and indoleacetic acid in human cerebrospinal fluid: Interrelations and the influence of age, sex, epilepsy and anticonvulsant drugs. *Journal of Neurology, Neurosurgery, and Psychiatry, 43,* 438–445.

Yu, W., & Baas, P. W. (1994). Changes in microtubule number and length during axon differentiation. *Journal of Neuroscience, 14,* 2818–2829.

Yu, W. H. A., & Yu, M. C. (1983). Acceleration of the regeneration of the crushed hypoglossal nerve by testosterone. *Experimental Neurology, 80,* 349–360.

Zagon, I. S., MacLaughlin, P. J., & Thompson, C. I. (1979a). Development of motor activity in young rats following perinatal methadone exposure. *Pharmacology, Biochemistry & Behaviour, 10,* 743–749.

Zagon, I. S., MacLaughlin, P. J., & Thompson, C. I. (1979b). Learning ability in adult female rats perinatally exposed to methadone. *Pharmacology, Biochemistry & Behaviour, 10,* 889–894.

Zazzo, R. (1960). *Les jumeaux: Le couple and la personne.* Paris: Press Universitaire de France.

Zhou, J. N., Hofman, M. A., Gooren, L. J., & Swaab, D. F. (1995). A sex difference in the human brain and its relation to transsexuality. *Nature, 378,* 68–70.

Zondeck, L. H., & Zondeck, T. (1979). Observations on the determination of fetal sex in early pregnancy. *Contributions to Gynecology and Obstetrics, 5,* 91–108.

Zuckerman, M. (1995). Good and bad humors: Biochemical bases of personality and its disorders. *Psychological Science, 6,* 325–332.

Zwingman, T., Erickson, R. P., Boyer, T., & Ao, A. (1993). Transcription of the sex-determining region genes Sry and Zfy in the mouse preimplantation embryo. *Proceedings of the National Academy of Sciences, 90,* 814–817.

Name Index

Subject Index

About the Editors and Contributors

M. EMMANUELLA ALBONETTI is a research fellow at the University of Siena, Italy, where she works with Professor Farabollini in the Department of Human Physiology

DANIEL BITRAN is an associate professor of psychology at the College of the Holy Cross in Worcester, Massachusetts. He earned a Ph.D. in psychology at the State University of New York at Buffalo.

GILLIAN R. BROWN works at the Sub-Department of Animal Behaviour, University of Cambridge. He has recently completed a Ph.D. on sex differences in the development of primate behavior.

DAVID E. COMINGS is a researcher in the Department of Medical Genetics at the City of Hope Medical Center in Duarte, California. His research interests primarily pertain to the genetics surrounding how dopaminergic functioning impacts behavior.

GYÖRGY CSABA graduated from Semmelweis University in Budapest, Hungary, with a medical degree. He is a professor in the Department of Biology at the Semmelweis University of Medicine, and conducts research primarily on the phylogeny and ontogeny of hormone receptors.

MILTON DIAMOND received his Ph.D. from the University of Kansas in both anatomy and psychology. He now teaches and conducts research at the John A. Burns School of Medicine of the University of Hawaii. His primary research interests are in those factors affecting the development of sexual behaviors.

ALAN F. DIXSON conducts research in the Sub-Department of Animal Behaviour at the University of Cambridge.

JIANFANG DU is in the Department of Pathology and Anatomy at Thomas Jefferson University, Philadelphia, Pennsylvania. She earned her Ph.D. at the State University of New York at Buffalo in the Department of Psychology.

LINDA EBERTZ is a recent graduate of Minot State University with a major in psychology and concentrations in chemistry and sociology. In 1995, she and Lee Ellis organized the International Behavioral Development Symposium on the Biological Basis of Sexual Orientation and Sex-Typical Behavior, the conference on which this book is based.

LEE ELLIS is a sociologist and criminologist with a longtime interest in human development, especially with reference to sexual orientation and sex-typical behavior. While in the Division of Social Science at Minot State University in North Dakota, he has conducted extensive research on how sex hormones affect brain functioning and thereby alter behavior.

FRANCESCA FARABOLLINI is a Professor of Human Physiology at the University of Siena, Italy. She has a Ph.D., and her research interests include perception of pain, emotionality, and sexual differentiation of these aspects.

EVELYN F. FIELD holds a master's degree in behavioral neuroscience and is a research associate with the Department of Psychology and Neuroscience at the University of Lethbridge in Alberta, Canada.

M. ISABEL GONZALEZ received a Ph.D. in the field of animal physiology at the University of Madrid. Her main research interests are in the neurochemical basis for behavior. She currently is at Park-Davis Research Centre, Cambridge, as a senior research officer.

KATHARINE BLICK HOYENGA and KERMIT T. HOYENGA are both retired professors of psychology from Western Illinois University. Their research interests have focused around gender differences in a wide variety of behavior patterns. The Hoyengas currently reside in Whitehall, Montana. They each received a Ph.D. in psychology from the University of Washington and the University of Nebraska, respectively.

ELAINE M. HULL is a professor of psychology and the director of the Behavioral Neuroscience Program at the State University of New York at Buffalo. She received her Ph.D. in psychology at Indiana University, and studies the neuropharmacology of sexual behavior.

RICHARD LIPPA is a professor of psychology at California State University at Fullerton. He holds a Ph.D. from Stanford University, and is primarily interested in the biological and cognitive underpinnings of masculinity–femininity and its correlates.

DANIEL S. LORRAIN received his Ph.D. from the Department of Psychology of the State University of New York at Buffalo. He is currently in the Department of Psychiatry at the University of Chicago.

ROBERT H. LUSTIG holds a M.D. degree from Cornell University Medical College. He practices at the University of Tennessee at Memphis and St. Jude Children's Research Hospital, with interests primarily in pediatric neuroendocrinology.

LESLIE MATUSZEWICH is a postdoctoral fellow in the Department of Psychiatry at Case Western Reserve University School of Medicine in Cleveland, Ohio. Her doctorate was received in psychology at the State University of New York at Buffalo.

EDWARD M. MILLER is Research Professor of Economics and Finance at the University of New Orleans. He has authored over 150 publications on a range of topics extending far beyond the conventional boundaries of economics. He holds a Ph.D. from the Massachusetts Institute of Technology.

CLAIRE M. NEVISON is a research assistant working at the Sub-Department of Animal Behaviour, University of Cambridge.

J. KEN NISHITA is Professor of Psychology at California State University at Monterey. His Ph.D. was obtained at the State University of New York at Buffalo.

SERGIO M. PELLIS is a professor in the Department of Psychology and Neuroscience at the University of Lethbridge in Alberta, Canada. He holds a Ph.D. in zoology from Monash University in Australia. His main research interests are in various areas of neuroethology.

GEOFF SANDERS received his Ph.D. from the University College of London. He currently teaches psychology at London Guildhall University and conducts research, primarily in the field of neuroendocrinology.

LAURA L. SCALETTA holds a master's degree in psychology at University of New York at Buffalo, and is an instructor at Niagara Community College in Niagara Falls, New York.

JAMES A. SCHMIDT received his Ph.D. in clinical psychology from Virginia Commonwealth University. He is currently an associate professor at Western Illinois University. His main research interests are in personality theory.

NANCY L. SEGAL obtained a Ph.D. from the University of Chicago in behavioral science. She is currently a professor of psychology and director of the Twin Studies Center at California State University at Fullerton. Her research and writings have primarily pertained to inferring genetic influences on behavior from studying twin relationships.

ILONA VATHY, a native of Hungary, received her Ph.D. from Rutgers University in behavioral neuroscience. She is currently an associate professor of Psychiatry and Neuroscience at Albert Einstein College of Medicine in New York. Her main research interests are in the effects of prenatal opiate exposure on brain and behavior development in both genders.

KENNETH WALTERS is currently a graduate student in clinical psychology at the University of Nebraska, specializing in the study of anxiety disorders.

DEBORAH WENMOTH is a recent graduate of the Department of Psychology at London Guildhall University, where she studied under Geoff Sanders. Her professional interests are primarily in the field of neuroendocrinology.

CATHERINE A. WILSON holds a Ph.D. and a D.Sc. in reproductive physiology. Her research interests are primarily in sexual differentiation of the brain. Wilson teaches and conducts research in the Department of Obstetrics and Gynecology at St. George's Hospital Medical School in London.

ISBN 0-275-95941-4

9 780275 959418

HARDCOVER BAR CODE